'The question of what psychoanalysis can be, or do, outside the clinic haunts Freud's thinking from the beginning of his discovery of the life of the unconscious mind. Responding to the potential of psychoanalysis to intervene in the world "beyond the couch", the essays collected here generate some unexpected, even counter-intuitive, readings on the cusp between psychoanalysis, history and politics. The provocation issued by a range of critical and cultural texts is vital to that encounter opening up a space, within this volume, to listen to what can very easily remain unheard. Equally, there is a sustained commitment here to take psychoanalysis outside its "comfort zones". In so doing, this collection breaks new ground, demonstrating how, by working at its limits, psychoanalysis can be used to generate new forms of thinking about the very real disturbances in our political and social worlds.'
      Vicky Lebeau, *Professor of English, University of Sussex*

'Tracing the shifting ground between psychoanalysis, history, politics, and culture, *Wild Analysis* collects together contributions from some of the most interesting established and emerging figures in the field. By working across multiple disciplines, this fascinating collection maps out the dangers, pleasures, and value of using psychoanalytic thinking to enter and understand the terrain of the wild.'
      Laura Salisbury, *Professor of Modern Literature and*
            Medical Humanities, University of Exeter

Wild Analysis

This book argues that the notion of 'wild' analysis, a term coined by Freud to denote the use of would-be psychoanalytic notions, diagnoses, and treatment by an individual who has not undergone psychoanalytic training, also provides us with a striking new way of exploring the limits of psychoanalysis.

Wild Analysis: From the Couch to Cultural and Political Life proposes to reopen the question of so-called 'wild' analysis by exploring psychoanalytic ideas at their limits, arguing from a diverse range of perspectives that the thinking produced at these limits – where psychoanalysis strays into other disciplines, and vice versa, as well as moments of impasse in its own theoretical canon – points toward new futures for both psychoanalysis and the humanities. The book's twelve essays pursue fault lines, dissonances, and new resonances in established psychoanalytic theory, often by moving its insights radically further afield. These essays take on sensitive and difficult topics in twentieth-century cultural and political life, including representations of illness, forced migration and the experiences of refugees, and questions of racial identity and identification in post-war and post-apartheid periods, as well as contemporary debates surrounding the Enlightenment and its modern invocations, the practice of critique, and 'paranoid' reading. Others explore more acute cases of 'wilding', such as models of education and research informed by the insights of psychoanalysis, or instances where psychoanalysis strays into taboo political and cultural territory, as in Freud's references to cannibalism.

This book will be of interest to researchers, practitioners, and students working across the fields of psychoanalysis, history, literature, culture, and politics, and to anyone with an interest in the political import of psychoanalytic thought today.

Shaul Bar-Haim is a Senior Lecturer at the Department of Sociology, University of Essex. He is the author of *The Maternalists: Psychoanalysis, Motherhood, and the British Welfare State*.

Elizabeth Sarah Coles is a Marie Skłodowska-Curie Postdoctoral Fellow at the Universitat Pompeu Fabra, Barcelona, where she researches post-critical writing, literary theory, and contemporary Anglophone poetry. She is currently completing a monograph on the Canadian poet and Classicist, Anne Carson.

Helen Tyson is a Lecturer in Twentieth and Twenty-First Century British Literature at the University of Sussex, where she is also a co-director of the Centre for Modernist Studies. Helen is writing a book about the scene of reading in modernist literature, psychoanalysis, and the bestseller.

THE NEW LIBRARY OF PSYCHOANALYSIS 'BEYOND THE COUCH' SERIES

General Editor: Alessandra Lemma

The New Library of Psychoanalysis was launched in 1987 in association with the Institute of Psychoanalysis, London. It aims to promote a widespread appreciation of psychoanalysis by supporting interdisciplinary dialogues with those working in the social sciences, the arts, medicine, psychology, psychotherapy, philosophy and with the general book reading public.

The *Beyond the Couch* part of the series creates a forum dedicated to demonstrating this wider application of psychoanalytic ideas. These books, written primarily by psychoanalysts, specifically address the important contribution of psychoanalysis to contemporary intellectual, social and scientific debate.

Current members of the Advisory Board include Giovanna Di Ceglie, Liz Allison, Anne Patterson, Josh Cohen and Daniel Pick.

For a full list of all the titles in the New Library of Psychoanalysis main series and also the New Library of Psychoanalysis Teaching Series, please visit the Routledge website.

TITLES IN THE 'BEYOND THE COUCH' SERIES:

Under the Skin: A Psychoanalytic Study of Body Modification Alessandra Lemma
Engaging with Climate Change: Psychoanalytic and Interdisciplinary Perspectives Edited by Sally Weintrobe
Research on the Couch: Single-Case Studies, Subjectivity, and Psychoanalytic Knowledge R.D. Hinshelwood
Psychoanalysis in the Technoculture Era Edited by Alessandra Lemma and Luigi Caparrotta
Moving Images: Psychoanalytic Reflections on Film Andrea Sabbadini
Reflections on the Aesthetic Experience: Psychoanalysis and the Uncanny Gregorio Kohon
Psychoanalysis in the Age of Totalitarianism Edited by Matt ffytche and Daniel Pick
Sublime Subjects: Aesthetic Experience and Intersubjectivity in Psychoanalysis Giuseppe Civitarese

Wild Analysis

From the Couch to Cultural and Political Life

Edited by
Shaul Bar-Haim, Elizabeth Sarah Coles,
and Helen Tyson

LONDON AND NEW YORK

First published 2022
by Routledge
2 Park Square, Milton Park, Abingdon, Oxon OX14 4RN

and by Routledge
605 Third Avenue, New York, NY 10158

Routledge is an imprint of the Taylor & Francis Group, an informa business

© 2022 selection and editorial matter, Shaul Bar-Haim, Elizabeth Sarah Coles, and Helen Tyson; individual chapters, the contributors

The right of Shaul Bar-Haim, Elizabeth Sarah Coles, and Helen Tyson to be identified as the authors of the editorial material, and of the authors for their individual chapters, has been asserted in accordance with sections 77 and 78 of the Copyright, Designs and Patents Act 1988.

All rights reserved. No part of this book may be reprinted or reproduced or utilised in any form or by any electronic, mechanical, or other means, now known or hereafter invented, including photocopying and recording, or in any information storage or retrieval system, without permission in writing from the publishers.

Trademark notice: Product or corporate names may be trademarks or registered trademarks, and are used only for identification and explanation without intent to infringe.

British Library Cataloguing-in-Publication Data
A catalogue record for this book is available from the British Library

Library of Congress Cataloging-in-Publication Data
Names: Bar-Haim, Shaul, 1979- editor. | Coles, Elizabeth Sarah, 1983- editor. | Tyson, Helen, 1987- editor.
Title: Wild analysis : from the couch to cultural and political life / edited by Shaul Bar-Haim, Elizabeth Sarah Coles, and Helen Tyson.
Description: Abingdon, Oxon ; New York, NY : Routledge, 2022. |
Identifiers: LCCN 2021014594 (print) | LCCN 2021014595 (ebook) |
ISBN 9781032061146 (paperback) | ISBN 9781032061153 (hardback) |
ISBN 9781003200765 (ebook)
Subjects: LCSH: Psychoanalysis. | Psychoanalysis and the humanities. | Psychoanalysis and culture. | Social sciences and psychoanalysis.
Classification: LCC BF173 .W54765 2022 (print) | LCC BF173 (ebook) |
DDC 150.19/5--dc23
LC record available at https://lccn.loc.gov/2021014594
LC ebook record available at https://lccn.loc.gov/2021014595

ISBN: 978-1-032-06115-3 (hbk)
ISBN: 978-1-032-06114-6 (pbk)
ISBN: 978-1-003-20076-5 (ebk)

DOI: 10.4324/9781003200765

Typeset in Times New Roman
by Taylor & Francis Books

Contents

List of figures	ix
Acknowledgements	xi
List of contributors	xii
Preface	xv
DANIEL PICK AND JACQUELINE ROSE	
Introduction: Wild analysis	xxi
SHAUL BAR-HAIM, ELIZABETH SARAH COLES, AND HELEN TYSON	

PART 1
The mystic writing pad   1

1 D. W. Winnicott and the finding of literature   3
ELIZABETH SARAH COLES

2 Project for a scientific psychology: The impossibility of a text   16
MANUEL BATSCH

3 'Where had she walked thus and whither was she going?': Freud, Ferrante and feet in Jensen's *Gradiva*   27
SHAHIDHA BARI

PART 2
Mass psychology   37

4 Psychoanalysis and Satanism: A case of moral panic in South Africa   39
NICKY FALKOF

5 Reconstructing *Pinky*   52
IAN MAGOR

6 Freud and the cannibal: Vignettes from psychoanalysis' colonial history 67
   MARITA VYRGIOTI

PART 3
The location of cultural experience 83

7 'Little Mussolini' and the 'parasite poets': Psychoanalytic pedagogy, modernism, and the illegible child 85
   HELEN TYSON

8 Exposed to the other: Responding to the refugee in Caroline Bergvall's *Drift* 105
   CATHERINE HUMBLE

9 Between the acts, or, Melanie Klein and the representation of people with AIDS 125
   THEO GORDON

PART 4
The suppressed madness of sane men 145

10 Nazism's inner demons: Psychoanalysis and the Columbus Centre (1962–1981) 147
   DANAE KARYDAKI

11 Reaching into the blind-spot: Rape, trauma and identification in *Blasted* 165
   LEAH SIDI

12 Freud, the Enlightenment and the Public Sphere 180
   D'MARIS COFFMAN

   Index 193

Figures

7.1	Virginia Woolf engagement diaries, Monk's House Papers, University of Sussex Special Collections, SxMs-18/4/41	97
7.2	Virginia Woolf engagement diaries, Monk's House Papers, University of Sussex Special Collections, SxMs-18/4/41	98
7.3	Virginia Woolf engagement diaries, Monk's House Papers, University of Sussex Special Collections, SxMs-18/4/41	99
8.1	'Lines 11', ink on paper, from '(16 Drawings)'	106
8.2	'Lines 12', ink on paper, from '(16 Drawings)'	111
8.3	'Lines 6', ink on paper, from '(16 Drawings)'	117
9.1	Vincent Chevalier and Ian Bradley-Perrin, *Your Nostalgia is Killing Me*, 2013. Digital Print	125
9.2	Reproduction of a drawing by 'Richard'	127
9.3	Reproduction of a drawing by 'Richard'	128
9.4	*Bright Eyes*, Stuart Marshall. 1984, UK, SD video, colour, sound	129
9.5	*Los Angeles Times*, 2 October 1985	130
9.6a	*Bright Eyes*, Stuart Marshall. 1984, UK, SD video, colour, sound	132
9.6b	*Bright Eyes*, Stuart Marshall. 1984, UK, SD video, colour, sound	133
9.7a	Alon Reininger, *Ken Meeks PWA*, 1986	136
9.7b	David Pollack, Tired of Losing? Ronald Reagan, 1968 Presidential Primary Campaign Poster, 1968	137
9.7c	Detail, *Los Angeles Times*, 2 October 1985	138
9.8	Zoe Leonard, *Strange Fruit*, 1992-97. Orange, banana, grapefruit, and lemon skins, thread, buttons, zippers, needles, wax, sinew, string, snaps, and hooks. 295 parts: Dimensions variable. Installation view, Whitney Museum of American Art, New York, 2018	139

9.9   Zoe Leonard, *Strange Fruit* (detail), 1992-97. Orange, banana, grapefruit, and lemon skins, thread, buttons, zippers, needles, wax, sinew, string, snaps, and hooks. 295 parts: Dimensions variable   141

Acknowledgements

While the preliminary sketches for *Wild Analysis: From the Couch to Cultural and Political Life* were made in 2016, the wider project the book brings to a head was conceived in 2001 as the Psychoanalysis, History and Political Life Forum, founded by Professors Daniel Pick and Jacqueline Rose, and held in the University of London's School of Advanced Study at Senate House, Russell Square. In a very straightforward sense, then, this book would not exist were it not for the commitment of Daniel and Jacqueline to pushing the limits of psychoanalytic thought in one of the most fraught political moments of recent decades. Especial thanks, therefore, are due to them. We would also like to express our gratitude to the Forum's many contributors over the years – there are too many to name here, but we thank you all for participating in what was a remarkable testament to the possibilities of thinking together. In particular, we thank the authors of the chapters in this book.

We are grateful to Alessandra Lemma, editor of the Beyond the Couch series at Routledge, and to the peer reviewers for their careful and considered reading of the manuscript. Thanks are due, finally, to Kate Hawes, Hannah Wright and the editorial team at Routledge for their efficiency and professionalism during the various stages of publication.

For permission to print the 'squiggle' on the cover of this book, we are grateful to the Winnicott Trust. In gratitude for permissions to print the many other images that appear in this book, we would also like to thank: The Marsh Agency Ltd., on behalf of The Winnicott Trust CIO 1174533; the Society of Authors as the Literary Representative of the Estate of Virginia Woolf; Caroline Bergvall; Vincent Chevalier and Ian Bradley-Perrin; the Melanie Klein Archive and the Wellcome Library © Melanie Klein Trust; LUX, London; *Los Angeles Times*; Getty Images; © Alon Reininger/Contact Press Images; and © Zoe Leonard. For full details, please see the 'List of Figures'.

Contributors

Shaul Bar-Haim is a Senior Lecturer in the Department of Sociology at the University of Essex. His research focuses on the intellectual and cultural history of psychoanalysis, and related 'psy' disciplines, mainly in twentieth-century Britain. He is the author of *The Maternalists: Psychoanalysis, Motherhood and the British Welfare State* (2021).

Shahidha Bari is a Professor at London College of Fashion, University of the Arts London. She works in the fields of theory, literature and visual culture. She is the author of *Keats and Philosophy* (2012), *Dressed: The Secret Life of Clothes* (2019) and she is currently working on the philosophy of beauty.

Manuel Batsch is a Lecturer in the department of Psychosocial and Psychoanalytic Studies at the University of Essex. He works as an honorary psychotherapist at Camden Psychotherapy Unit and he is a candidate at the Institute of Psychoanalysis.

D'Maris Coffman is Professor in Economics and Finance and the Head of Department and Director of at the Bartlett School of Sustainable Construction at UCL. She is the Editor-in-Chief of *Structural Change and Economic Dynamics* and is on the advisory board of *Economia Politica*. She is a Fellow of the Royal Historical Society, a Fellow of the Society of Antiquaries of London, a Senior Fellow of the Higher Education Academy and a Fellow of Goodenough College. She is also an Academic Associate of the London Institute of Psychoanalysis. Before coming to UCL in 2014, she spent six years as a fellow of Newnham College where she variously held a junior research fellowship (Mary Bateson Research Fellowship), a post as a college lecturer, and a Leverhulme Early Career Fellow. In July 2009, she started the Centre for Financial History, which she directed through December 2014. She did her undergraduate training at the Wharton School in managerial and financial economics and her PhD in history at the School of Arts & Sciences at the University of Pennsylvania.

Elizabeth Sarah Coles is a Marie Skłodowska-Curie Postdoctoral Fellow at the Universitat Pompeu Fabra, Barcelona, where she researches post-critical writing, literary theory and contemporary Anglophone poetry. She is currently completing a monograph on the Canadian poet, essayist and translator, Anne Carson.

Nicky Falkof is a media and cultural studies scholar based at Wits University in Johannesburg, South Africa. She holds a PhD in Humanities and Cultural Studies from the London Consortium, University of London (2011). Her research centres on race and anxiety in the urban global south, with a primary focus on South Africa. She is the author of *The End of Whiteness: Satanism and Family Murder in Late Apartheid South Africa* (2015), and co-editor of *Anxious Joburg: The Inner Lives of a Global South City* (2020). She has been a visiting fellow at Sussex University, the University of Dar-es-Salaam and the Universidad Nacional Autónoma de México. Her work has appeared in publications including *The Journal of Popular Culture, The International Journal of Cultural Studies, Feminist Media Studies* and *The New York Times*.

Theo Gordon is an art historian, specialising in modern and contemporary art. He has articles forthcoming in *Art History* and *Oxford Art Journal*. He is currently Sackler Research Forum Postdoctoral Fellow at The Courtauld Institute of Art.

Catherine Humble is Executive Editor of *The International Journal of Psychoanalysis*, and she teaches Literature and Psychoanalysis at UCL. She has a PhD on Raymond Carver, has published numerous articles on American fiction, poetry and psychoanalysis, and she has edited a book on psychoanalysis and the body. Catherine is a book reviewer for several publications, including the TLS, the Telegraph, and Prospect. As well as writing short fiction, Catherine has written an award-winning short film.

Danae Karydaki is a modern historian interested in psychoanalysis, psychiatry, gender, institutions, welfare, and trauma. She is a post-doctoral researcher at the University of Thessaly, Greece and a teaching fellow at the University of Athens, Greece. She has taught at Birkbeck, University of London, from which she received her PhD. Her current research focuses on the history of the Leros Psychiatric Hospital (1957–1995) in the context of 20th-century social and political history of Greece. She has published articles in several journals and edited volumes and has edited the collection *Leros in the Spotlight* and on the *Margin: History, Politics, Psychiatry* (Psifides: 2020). Her book *History and Psychoanalysis in the Columbus Centre: The Meaning of Evil* is forthcoming from Routledge.

Ian Magor's recent PhD thesis was titled: 'The Captured Mind: Race, Brainwashing, and American Film, c1941–53' He has also made a number of video essays on cinema and psychoanalysis.

Daniel Pick is a practising psychoanalyst in London, a fellow of the British Psychoanalytical Society and professor of history at Birkbeck College. His publications include *Faces of Degeneration* (1989), *Svengali's Web* (2000), *The Pursuit of the Nazi Mind* (2012), *Psychoanalysis: A Very Short Introduction* (2015), and as co-editor, *Dreams and History* (2004), and *Psychoanalysis in the Age of Totalitarianism* (2016). Daniel Pick was the senior investigator between 2014 and 2021, on the team-based 'Hidden Persuaders' project, funded by the Wellcome Trust, which explored the history of ideas about mind control during and after the Cold War (see http://www.bbk.ac.uk/hiddenpersuaders/). His next book, with Profile and Basic Books, is entitled *Brainwashed: A New History of Thought Control*.

Jacqueline Rose is Co-Director and Professor of Humanities at Birkbeck Institute for the Humanities, University of London. She was the editor (with Juliet Mitchell) and translator of *Feminine Sexuality – Jacques Lacan and the école freudienne*. Her books include (both *Sexuality in the Field of Vision*, *The Last Resistance* (both *Verso Radical Thinkers*), *The Haunting of Sylvia Plath*, *The Question of Zion*, *Women in Dark Times*, *Mothers – An Essay on Love and Cruelty*, and most recently *On Violence and On Violence Against Women*, and the novel *Albertine*. A regular writer for *The London Review of Books*, she is a co-founder of *Independent Jewish Voices* in the UK and a Fellow of the British Academy.

Leah Sidi is Lecturer in Health Humanities at University College London. Her research focuses on dramaturgical representations of mental suffering in experimental and feminist theatre in the late twentieth and early twenty-first century.

Helen Tyson is a Lecturer in Twentieth and Twenty-First Century British Literature at the University of Sussex, where she is also a co-director of the Centre for Modernist Studies. Helen has published articles on modernist literature and psychoanalysis in *Textual Practice*, *Literature Compass*, and *Feminist Modernist Studies*. She is writing a book that examines the scene of reading in modernist literature, psychoanalysis, and the bestseller.

Marita Vyrgioti is an Associate Lecturer in Psychosocial Studies at the University of East London. She has a PhD from Birkbeck College (University of London) and a long-standing interest in the theory, history and epistemology of psychoanalysis in relation to coloniality. She is a trainee psychodynamic psychotherapist at the Tavistock and Portman NHS Foundation Trust in London.

Preface

Daniel Pick and Jacqueline Rose

This collection of essays emerges out of the workshop – 'Psychoanalytic Thought, History and Political Life' – which took place at Birkbeck and Queen Mary, both of the University of London, over roughly the first decade of the new millennium. The idea was first proposed in the months after 9/11 when the world was still reeling. The war on Afghanistan had begun, cutting off the three short weeks of pause and reflection after the attack on the Twin Towers when, as film-maker Wim Wenders observed, if only America had continued down that path instead of vengefully rushing into action, it might have changed the world for the better (Wenders and Zournazi, 2013; Wenders 2004).

As we gathered together – teachers, analysts, young researchers and students of varying generations – we were all aware that for none of us was this the first historical moment, any more than it would be the last, when the world seemed to have gone mad, when public, political life overflowed the bounds of reason, and a time of mourning was replaced by a shrill call to arms. Hence our shared wish to create a space in which this painful reality, which felt so difficult to grasp, might encounter the one form of thought dedicated to the perils of the human mind – psychoanalysis.

Our very first discussion centred, appropriately enough, on the psychoanalysis of group formation, on those often bizarre, sometimes frightening, aspects of human behaviour sparked and permitted by what Freud originally, and after him key analysts like Wilfred Bion, would refer to as the pathologies of the group or mass mind. Bion would also see the therapeutic potential and creativity of groups, and pioneered a new mode of applied psychoanalytic work, during the Second World War, with soldiers – the psychiatric casualties, so-called war neurotics, or those who would once have been labelled as 'shell-shocked'.

In fact, though the English word 'mass' is closer to the German 'die Massen' of Freud's 1921 text on this topic (first translated by James Strachey as *Group Psychology and the Analysis of the Ego*), it felt imperative for all of us to draw the line between our concerns and anything that could be tarred with the brush of 'mass' or 'crowd' delusion, which so easily tips into denigration of the people it describes (Freud, 1921). At worst it implies an elite, somehow exempt from the unconscious troubles of some 'mob' down below.

That tendency was to be found in the earlier tradition of 'crowd psychology' (Gustave Le Bon et al) with which Freud insistently engaged, and from which he took his point of departure.

For us, in the context of contemporary history and political life in the 2000s, such a view of the mass would too easily act as distraction or alibi, at a time when the pathologies of collective behaviour seemed to be just as profoundly rooted in the actions of Western governments – the recurrent violence of US intervention overseas that had barely paused after the disaster of Vietnam, the cruelties and inequalities of rampant neoliberal capitalism – as they were to be found in those cultures hastily being grouped under the rubric of 'extremist' and 'terrorist', as a justification for the aggression and prejudice that were being directed against them. After all, in this period, the so-called 'mass', at least in the UK, were if anything more thoughtful, less convinced of the pragmatism or ethical justification for military 'solutions' than the leadership.

Many of us felt at the time that, whilst appalled by the 9/11 attack and the organisation behind it, the so-called 'war on terror' was a disastrous abdication of serious thought and nuanced proportionate political response. It represented a failure to learn politically from history, or, more like a return of the repressed, to recognise any western responsibility at all for the very conditions that had enabled such movements to rise. The expression 'war on terrorism' can be traced back further, but it was George Bush junior who revived and simplified it into an unending 'war on terror' and so dramatically raised the political and military stakes. It is worth recalling his joint address to Congress and the American people in which – even before the rubble in lower Manhattan had fully been cleared – he declared, 'Our war on terror begins with al Qaeda, but it does not end there. It will not end until every terrorist group of global reach has been found, stopped and defeated'.[1] Afghanistan (the principle base for Al-Qaeda) became the first major target for American-led action. 'Terror' – not a state, or even a specific ideology – had been set up as the shadowy object of a 'war' potentially without end, or geographical confines.

Gradually we learnt about the covert as well as the overt actions this justified. Vast bombing missions, invasions, mass detention, drones, secret renditions, and systematic use of torture (albeit under a thin euphemism, 'enhanced interrogation'). Over the course of our workshop, we came to discuss the significance of what occurred at places that few of us had ever heard of before, such as Guantanamo and Abu Ghraib. We also had to consider the considerable complicity of doctors and psychologists in this endeavour (Mayer 2008; for the involvement of doctors at Guantanamo, see also the documentary film Davis 2013).

There were undoubtedly differences of political viewpoint amongst us, but we were all united in our dismay at what was occurring, while being embedded enough in psychoanalytic thinking to know that no good can ever come from assigning everything that is wrong on this earth and within our own hearts to a distant enemy whom we simply need to eliminate. To that extent we all saw psychoanalysis both as a form of dissent against the Manichean political climate of the times, and as a form of accountability, since it forced us to recognise the world's worst difficulties as our own.

As the essays in this collection amply testify, the link between psychoanalysis and political questioning has a long and complex history, at times suggestive and felicitous, at others reductive and strained. Psychoanalysis has served to consider, for better and for worse, the unconscious motives of leaders, the dynamics of groups, the pathologies of institutions, the seductions of ideologies or even, most dubiously, the 'character' of entire nations. Freud lent a hand to a 'psychobiography' of the former American president Woodrow Wilson and speculated (inconclusively) with Einstein about the deep psychological determinants driving nations to war. He himself veered between supreme confidence and the deepest caution about links or parallels that might be drawn between individual psychology and the formations or deformations of collective life.

But one thing all these essays share is the conviction that if such a dialogue is to be productive, then it cannot be by setting up psychoanalysis as masterdiscourse of all it surveys, one to which political and historical understanding should – in a parody of the least helpful version of the relationship between analyst and patient – be expected to submit. There is no one settled version of 'psychoanalysis' (as theory, mode of inquiry, or form of therapy), any more than there is a consensus upon its appropriate social, cultural or political applications. Hence the variety of psychoanalytic reference points to be found in these pages, and hence too the number of essays that take as their focus the moments in psychoanalytic thought when it frays at the edges and falters, moments which should not be seen as a failing, but quite the opposite, rather as the precise point where a productive engagement between psychoanalysis and its surrounding disciplines, then and now, might begin.

In his postscript to *The Question of Lay Analysis* of 1926, Freud called for a psychoanalytic training – 'an ideal no doubt but an ideal that can and must be realised' – based on the widest possible dialogue of disciplines. It would include 'elements from the mental sciences, from psychology from the history of civilisation, from sociology, as well as from anatomy, biology and the study of evolution' (Freud 1926, 252). In harmony with that vision, these essays are testament to the reach of psychoanalysis as they range over practices and realities as diverse as literary and visual creativity, contemporary neuro-science, post-Second World War cinematic racism, early twentieth-century debates about childhood, democracy and progressive education, whiteness in crisis at the end of apartheid, cannibalism as a trope of colonialism, fear of AIDS through the prism of Melanie Klein, the place of the witness in the current refugee emergency, psychoanalytic cultural understanding in Britain after the war, sexual violence on the modern stage, and the potential interface between the Enlightenment and Freud.

But, while a tribute to the potential range of psychoanalysis, these chapters are also issuing a caution. If such encounters are to have any value, it can only be in so far as psychoanalytic thought is willing to be confronted or even transformed by these other registers as much as the reverse. The use of the term 'wild' that gives this collection its title is therefore critical. As the editors explain in their Introduction, it was first used by Freud to condemn therapeutic practices which he considered insufficiently faithful to his own paradigms, an indication of Freud's determination to steer, and control, his own movement. It also marked his insistence that psychoanalysis of individual people required the fine grain material patients provide when 'free associating' on the couch; he was worried that psychoanalysts might damage the group if they started to analyse each other.

In this volume, 'wild' subtly shifts its meaning to become a sought-after value, a way of marking the point where psychoanalysis discovers that it cannot, either as theory or practice, remain safely within its own borders. 'Rewilding' is a term for our times, in more ways than one: witness the call to turn land back into forests, to 'rewild' vast new areas, after so much devastating deforestation, one sign of hope to save the planet in the twenty-first century, from the worst ravages of the climate catastrophe in the historical time now designated the age of the Anthropocene.

Something important of the original wildness of psychoanalytic thought is glimpsed in some of the pages below. Seen in this light, Freud's warning becomes an opportunity. In his famous essay on the uncanny, he himself had noted how a word can be oddly prone to the very meanings it seems intended to hold at bay. Thus, the term 'heimlich', or homely, begins by referring to the familiar and most private components of our domestic life, but then tips into its opposite ('unheimlich') when these most fiercely guarded, hidden, spaces return to haunt us. Something similar happens to the concept of 'wild' psychoanalysis. Psychoanalysis is never more true to the work of the unconscious, than when it flouts its own limits, admits the stranger into its midst.

In analysis, patients may well feel disturbed, as well as moved, to find themselves saying the 'wildest' things, bringing forth dreams, slips, fantasies, loves, hates, or whatever else, that they did not know they had in them, or even if they did, previously felt it impossible to share. As Freud insisted, the process needs some containment – a safe space – to bring the un-safest of thoughts to light. He did many things we would now consider bizarre ('analysing' Mahler as they walked the streets of Leiden), or unethical (analysing his own daughter Anna, and thinly disguising her in a disturbing paper). The process of 'going wild' therefore requires a safe harbour. We were reminded, reading this volume, of the wonderful illustrated story, loved by many children and adults alike, *Where the Wild Things Are*, by Maurice Sendak – a journey that visits 'the monsters', but does not leave the child reader in terror. It's 'wild' bedtime reading and yet might help one sleep better, not worse, without just 'domesticating' the terrors it hints at.

'Wild' practice, or what in the profession would now be called 'boundary violations', of course are a quite different matter, from bold, exploratory or even, indeed, the most untamed or untameable experiments in thought. And yet, even as we insist on the distinction between the ethical boundaries that must guide practice, and the freedom for patient and analyst alike to 'think as they please', or to 'think as they do not please', we recognise that many developments in psychoanalytic practice have emerged too from what were often originally seen as 'wild' experiments; analysing children, experimenting with the duration of the session, setting arbitrary end points to treatment, working with couples, families, groups, or even whole institutions, or conducting psychoanalysis on the telephone or over the Internet. After all, as the editors point out in their introduction, it was by paying attention to the 'untidiness and incorrigibility' of human sexuality that psychoanalysis unleashed its critique of the ills of civilisation into a mostly unsympathetic world. In which case, how – other than through an act of oppressive normalisation – can it lay down the law, or expect to subdue the unruly elements of its own unique form of knowledge?

If we had anything as definitive as an aim when we initiated the workshop, it might be described as an attempt – or rather a wish – to encourage the recognition of the importance of psychoanalysis as a way of thought equal to the difficulties of the world that we all faced. Since its final meetings a few years ago, those difficulties have intensified: the climate catastrophe, the dramatic growth in inequality in many countries, the Janus-face of the Internet, 'surveillance capitalism' and the 'attention economy', the rise of dictatorships across the world, right-wing populism, race-based state crime, the increasingly visible reality of gender-based violence, Brexit and the presidency of Donald Trump, some of which have felt as impossible to countenance at the exact same moment as they have felt increasingly urgent to think about and conceptualise. We are delighted to welcome this collection as a contribution to that ongoing project, one which has never felt more needed than in the times we are now living.

March 2020

Note

1 George W. Bush, 'Address to a Joint Session of Congress and the American People', 20 September 2001, White House archives, online at https://georgewbush-whitehouse.archives.gov/news/releases/2001/09/20010920-8.html

Bibliography

Freud, S. (1955) The Uncanny, 1919, *The Standard Edition of the Complete Psychological Works*, 17, London: Hogarth.

Freud, S. (1955) Group Psychology and the Analysis of the Ego, 1921, *The Standard Edition of the Complete Psychological Works*, 18, London: Hogarth.

Freud, S. (1959) The Question of Lay Analysis, 1926, *Standard Edition*, 20, London: Hogarth.

Mayer, J. (2008) *The Dark Side: The Inside Story of How the War on Terror Turned into a War on American Ideals*, New York, Random House.
Wenders, W. (2004) *Land of Plenty*.
Wenders, W., & Zournazi, M. (2013) *Inventing Peace – A Dialogue on Perception*, London: Tauris.

Introduction: Wild analysis

Shaul Bar-Haim, Elizabeth Sarah Coles and Helen Tyson

Minimal scientific rigour, reductiveness, lingering doubts surrounding its clinical efficacy: these are just a handful of the criticisms aimed at psychoanalysis in the age of the quick therapeutic fix. As neatly as they square with established lines of attack on psychoanalysis, it will come as little surprise to readers of Sigmund Freud that these objections to the discipline also map closely, if not precisely, onto his critique of what, in a 'little didactic paper' from 1910, he calls '"Wild" Psycho-Analysis': the use of would-be psychoanalytic notions, diagnoses, and treatment by an individual who has not undergone psychoanalytic training.[1] The convergence of Freud's appeal against wild analysis with popular objections to the sanctioned, non-wild version – and even with critiques of analysis by trained analysts – proves an important precedent in the history of the practice. Without wishing to reduce psychoanalysis to a symptom of its own unease, we might say that in its early days, what Freud calls his 'scientific psychology' first begins to comprehend itself, to confront its own demons, in objects it marks as *not*-psychoanalysis – in the case of wild analysis, Freud insists, a bowdlerised imitation. If Freud 'invents' wild analysis in an effort to isolate and preserve his science from its own potential pitfalls, then the very notion of wild analysis provides us with a striking way of asking about the limits of psychoanalysis. It is in the close encounter between psychoanalysis and this undisciplined other, an encounter close enough to spur Freud to found the International Psychoanalytical Association the same year, that psychoanalysis first comes into contact with its own vital edges.

In the clinical case reported in Freud's essay on '"Wild" Psycho-Analysis', a middle-aged divorced woman had sought him out following a consultation with a physician who claimed to derive his diagnosis – anxiety states resulting from a lack of sexual satisfaction – from Freud's own insights. Describing the case and listing his objections to the physician's recommendations – that the woman in question either resume relations with her husband, take a lover, or else seek satisfaction by other available means – Freud accuses this 'wild' analyst of a radical misconception of 'psychosexuality'; of ignoring, that is, the manifold 'psychical factors' that make sexual life irreducible to 'coitus or its analogy' (Freud, 1957a, p. 223, p. 224). Surprisingly perhaps, it is not the physician's unruliness or arbitrariness of thought that Freud objects to but the reductive simplicity of his thinking, belying what, for psychoanalysis, is the untidiness and incorrigibility of human sexuality. The wild analyst, it seems, was not quite wild enough – not sufficiently attentive to the wildness of the unconscious – for Freud. Yet this physician's tame conception of sexual life allows Freud to recognise and claim his own defiance of limits, grasped through an encounter with a clinician who, rather than going too far, has not gone far enough: as Freud says, 'He [the clinician] cannot have remained unaware [...] that psycho-analysis is commonly reproached with having extended the concept of what is sexual *far beyond its usual range*.' (Freud, 1957a, p. 222 our emphasis). By marking itself off from a 'wild' other, psychoanalysis stakes a claim to certain transgressions of its own.

The title of this book, *Wild Analysis: From the Couch to Cultural and Political Life*, takes its cue from the longstanding relationship of psychoanalysis to its own practical and theoretical limitations, the confrontation, configuration and expression of which proves a fertile source of insight and possibility across the discourses of analysis. The original concept of wild analysis can be understood, from a twenty-first-century perspective, as a cover for the question of where psychoanalysis ends and its 'wild' counterparts – potentially some of its sharpest interlocutors – begin. The book proposes to reopen the question of wild analysis by exploring psychoanalytic ideas at their limits, arguing from a diverse range of perspectives that the thinking produced at these limits – where psychoanalysis strays into other disciplines, and vice versa, as well as moments of impasse in its own theoretical canon – points toward new futures for the discipline. Pursuing the question of wild analysis, then, is an act of estrangement: an effort to draw psychoanalytic thought out of its comfort zones and into territories Freud himself designated as obscure and resistant, the 'grey' and 'shadowy' hinterland of female sexuality and the 'unplumbable' (*unergründliche*) navel of the dream being two key examples (Freud, 1961c, p. 226; Freud, 2010, p. 101). The book's twelve chapters trace fault lines, dissonances and new resonances in established psychoanalytic theory, often by moving its insights radically further afield. These chapters take on sensitive and difficult topics in twentieth-century cultural and political life, including representations of illness, forced migration and the experiences of refugees, and questions of racial identity and identification in post-war and post-apartheid periods, as well as contemporary debates surrounding the Enlightenment and its modern invocations, the practice of literary critique and forceful or 'paranoid' reading. Others explore more acute examples of psychoanalysis going astray, such as models of education and research informed by the insights of psychoanalysis, or instances where psychoanalysis strays into taboo political and cultural territory, as in Freud's compelling remarks on cannibalism.

Wild Analysis is rooted in a concrete historical effort to engage psychoanalysis beyond the couch, which took the form of a postgraduate research forum held at Birkbeck and Queen Mary, University of London. 'Psychoanalytic Thought,

History and Political Life' was founded in 2001 by the historian and psychoanalyst, Daniel Pick, and the feminist scholar, Jacqueline Rose, in response to what both perceived as the demand for a new order of politically engaged thinking in the wake of 11 September 2001. In their 'Preface' to this book, Pick and Rose describe the work of the forum, and its commitment to staging new conversations between psychoanalysis and the contemporary political and cultural moment. This book gathers together some of the work by participants in that forum, showcasing the work of a new generation of psychoanalytic thinkers whose work extends and reformulates some of the key questions that brought psychoanalysis and the humanities together in the opening decades of the twenty-first century.

As much as it addresses questions that psychoanalysis helps us to formulate regarding the cultural and political life of recent decades, the book also explores how the discourse of psychoanalysis manages its own internal pressures, shaped, in turn, by pressures – historical, political and cultural – from beyond the clinical sphere. One of the touchstones of this book is the idea that psychoanalysis, as a science of the unconscious, of the slips and resistances of the human mind, inevitably, and perhaps uniquely, became a science of its own resistances. The wildness in psychoanalysis is not just the unruliness of its objects – sexuality, memory, the dream – but its efforts to comprehend what Shoshana Felman calls its own 'unthought' (Felman, 1982, 10). This wildness resides in the way later thinkers and clinicians including Leo Bersani, Christopher Bollas, André Green and Jean Laplanche make use of the dilemmas and impasses of psychoanalytic thinking, refusing to exclude the insights, discourses and practices of psychoanalysis from scrutiny, and putting the resulting critiques of psychoanalysis to work just as fruitfully as established theories.

Stephen Frosh claimed in 2010 that 'psychoanalysis holds something significant for all the other disciplines – specifically, a capacity to theorise subjectivity in a way that is provocative and unique, through reference to the unconscious' (Frosh, 2010, p. 36). Indeed, he claims that

> psychoanalysis has had a contentious but productive history of engagement with the intellectual world outside the clinic, specifically with the humanities and social sciences, since its inception; and it is still a widely used yet also controversial element in the critical armoury of those working in these disciplines.
>
> (Ibid., pp. 4–5)

This may remind us of Freud's own utopian vision in which psychoanalysis becomes a 'meta-discipline' for the humanities and the social sciences:

> As a 'depth-psychology', a theory of the mental unconscious, it can become indispensable to all the sciences which are concerned with the evolution of human civilization and its major institutions such as art,

religion and the social order. It has already, in my opinion, afforded these sciences considerable help in solving their problems. But these are only small contributions compared with what might be achieved if historians of civilization, psychologists of religion, philologists and so on would agree themselves to handle the new instrument of research which is at their service.

(Freud, 1959, p. 248)

While this scenario was never fully realised – and any discipline claiming such a privileged position should surely elicit mistrust – psychoanalysis has always attracted researchers and scholars from the arts and the social sciences. From Theodor W. Adorno to Judith Butler, from Herbert Marcuse to Juliet Mitchell and Joan Scott, from Frantz Fanon to Edward Said, from Laura Mulvey to Louise Bourgeois – sociologists, historians, artists, cultural critics and philosophers – have all used psychoanalysis as part of an attempt to imagine a better world, as well as to bring about political change.

In 1977, within the field of literary studies, Shoshana Felman inaugurated a famous 'turn' – a turn from what she called the 'vulgar', or literal, 'application' of psychoanalysis to literature, to a form of reading that recognised the mutual 'implication' of literature and psychoanalysis in each other (Felman, 1977a, p. 5; Felman, 1982, p. 8). In 'vulgar' reading, according to Felman, 'literature is submitted to the authority, to the prestige of psychoanalysis'; '[w]hile literature is considered as a body of *language*—to be *interpreted*—psychoanalysis is considered as a body of *knowledge*, whose competence is called upon *to interpret*' (Felman, 1977a, p. 5). Challenging this master–slave relationship between psychoanalysis and literature, Felman instead encouraged us to place them alongside each other on a more equal footing. As others have observed before us, the relationship between psychoanalysis and literature runs deep – after all, psychoanalysis deals in the life of psychical fictions.[2] Yet, despite this kinship, a number of the chapters in this book reveal that psychoanalysis and literature are also apt to probe the limits of each other. For both Coles and Tyson, literature can help to take psychoanalytic thinking to its outermost limits, to forms of insight (about the status of knowledge, or the mind of the infant) that Freud himself found difficult to tolerate.

Furthermore, this capacity to engage with their own wildness, with the insights of one discipline estranged and revivified by the other, renders psychoanalysis and the humanities a potent discursive alliance, one that engages deeply and sometimes uncomfortably with the reaches and residues of individual and collective psychic life. Although psychoanalysis has long occupied a precarious position between the sciences and the humanities, in this important sense it can provide insight at moments when scientific epistemologies are found wanting, or when they leave us lost for words. As the philosopher Bruno Latour remarked in his Gifford Lectures on the twenty-first century climate crisis, 'the sciences are now and will remain from now on so intermingled with the entire culture that we need to turn to the humanities to understand how they really function' (Latour, 2017, p. 4). Whether by examining the novels of Elena Ferrante or Virginia Woolf, the brutal theatre of Sarah Kane, or the debates emerging around the academic culture of 'critique', the humanities allow us to work through some of the resistances we find, not just in the political and cultural discourses of the moment but in the canons of psychoanalytic literature too. In the wake of a new century, in the wilderness of an old one, the effort to comprehend our unfolding cultural and political realities remains as pressing as ever.

Wild analysis, wild history

To situate this book's approach in the history of the term '"wild" psycho-analysis' is both important and revelatory. In 1914, following his split with Jung (and just prior to his split with Adler), Freud published an article on 'The History of the Psychoanalytic Movement' in which he left no room for doubt regarding who exactly has the authority to decide on the boundaries of psychoanalysis:

> Although it is a long time now since I was the only psycho-analyst, I consider myself justified in maintaining that even today no one can know better than I do what psychoanalysis is, how it differs from other ways of investigating the life of the mind, and precisely what should be called psychoanalysis and what would better be described by some other name.
> (Freud, 1957b, p. 7)

Staking a bizarre (if not unsurprising) claim to the sole right to decide what psychoanalysis is and what it is not, Freud appears, at this moment in 1914, to set a stark limit on the disciplinary borders of psychoanalysis, excluding as '"wild" psycho-analysis' any practice that could reasonably be shown to be not truly Freudian.

In their glossary of psychoanalytic terms, *The Language of Psychoanalysis* (*Vocabulaire de la psychanalyse*, 1967), Jean Laplanche and Jean-Bertrand Pontalis define 'wild psycho-analysis' as 'the procedure of amateur or inexperienced "analysts" who attempt to interpret symptoms, dreams, utterances, actions, etc., on the basis of psycho-analytic notions which they have as often as not misunderstood' (Laplanche and Pontalis, 1973, p. 480). The term here would seem more to suggest clinical inexperience than outright ignorance, and yet the question of who decides, who legislates, on the inexperience or ignorance of the analyst takes us to the heart of the problem of authority. Within the official, sanctioned version of psychoanalysis, we find some genuinely eccentric forays into clinical practice, straying to a greater or lesser degree from more conventional, established therapeutic techniques. How would we describe, for example, a case in which an analyst feeds a hungry patient with a piece of herring, as Freud did with his 'Rat Man' (1909)? How, beyond simply unorthodox, might we define the relationship between the first American psychoanalyst, A. A. Brill, and his longstanding patient, Mabel Dodge Luhan, in which the two dined and holidayed together? (Everett, 2016). What, if not a case of analysis run wild, was Melanie Klein's insistence that a young evacuee's vindictive fantasies against Hitler during the Second World War were fantasies of 'destroying the bad Hitler inside Mummy' (Klein, 1998, p. 225)? Or Jacques Lacan's institution in 1967 of the procedure he called 'the pass',[3] which, symbolically inverting Freud's binding of analytic practice to institutional recognition when he founded the IPA, shifted the authority to determine her readiness for practice onto the individual psychoanalyst (see Safouan, 2000). Although these moments in psychoanalytic history may not constitute instances of '"wild" psycho-analysis' in Freudian terms, they nonetheless underscore the uncertainty surrounding the borderline between the unorthodox and the wild. Where from one angle 'wild analysis' might be located in these seemingly eccentric or unorthodox departures from the authorised canon of psychoanalysis, there has also been, over the last century, a proliferation of clinical models that, while variations on the 'talking cure', have in many cases transformed its founding principles beyond recognition.[4] Although none of us, as editors of this book, are practicing psychoanalysts, it feels important to note the difference in what is at stake between the clinical setting – where 'wild analysis' might shade into more troubling or downright abusive practices masquerading under the banner of the 'talking cure' – and the terrains of history, literature and culture.

In 1985, Roy Schafer argued that scientific debates concerning the criteria for defining 'wild analysis' in the clinical setting are in fact 'pseudo debates':

> One must acknowledge the fundamental propositions one has accepted as true before beginning a critique of wildness. This acknowledgement is required because there can be no theory-free and method-free vantage point from which to assess in some absolute manner competing approaches and the often diverse phenomena to which they give rise or which they require to be emphasized.
>
> (Schafer, 1985, p. 277)

If 'wild analysis' cannot serve as a scientific tool for discrediting the opponents of psychoanalysis, then it becomes empty rhetoric deployed in interminable squabbles between different schools of thought. In other words, after more than 100 years of 'pseudo debates' over what precisely 'wild analysis' might be, the concept has almost entirely lost its currency. The more we explore and stretch it, the more 'wild analysis' starts to look like a useful, if intriguing, ruse. Yet by exploring where psychoanalytic discourse frays at the edges – struggling with its own writing, its relationship to fiction and other discourses, and its political implications in the face (and the aftermath) of violence and catastrophe – this book offers a reappraisal, even a re-appropriation, of the term. Wild analysis began, we suggested, as a gesture to what psychoanalysis was not: as its negative and as a means of approaching and naming its own discontents. Yet like all negatives, it serves to affirm something unique and vital to psychoanalysis. By recuperating the concept of 'wild analysis', we aim to foreground the extent to which psychoanalysis is vitalised by its contact and engagement with the limits of its own knowledge. This means confronting the stakes, risks and dangers of psychoanalysis in its clinical and discursive forms, both of which plumb the depths of human fragility, and the problem of the analyst's hermeneutic authority. As such, to speak of wild analysis, also means, for us, valorising what was perhaps the original 'wildness' of psychoanalysis – free association, the untameable movement of meaning that Jean Laplanche called the 'anti-hermeneutics' of psychoanalysis (Laplanche, 1996).

Let us take the case of 'psychohistory' as an example of 'wild analysis'. Historians have long been suspicious about the application of psychoanalysis in the field of history, though some historians, in particular post-war psychobiographers, have sought to use psychoanalysis as a legitimate analytical tool. Erik Erikson's monumental biography of Luther (1958) and Walter Langer's *The Mind of Adolf Hitler* (1972) are perhaps the most famous examples of the effort, predominantly in the United States, to use Freudian thought in the understanding of historical moments as well as, with arguably less success, to psychoanalyse historical figures (Pick, 2012; Roper, 2012). In the 1960s and 70s, the Columbus Centre, the subject of Chapter 10 of this book, made a more sophisticated effort to put psychoanalytic thought to use in the effort to comprehend historical and political phenomena that had so heinously marked the twentieth century up to that point. The literature of psychobiography, however, quickly acquired a bad reputation, becoming a symbol for second-rate historical work and a cautionary tale for why psychoanalysis and history should ostensibly be kept apart. Applying psychoanalytic concepts in an effort to understand the behaviour of historical actors, especially prior to the modern age, has frequently been considered 'wild analysis' and a *faux pas* for the professional historian. A common perception was – and still is – that while historians seek to know the facts (what 'really' happened in the past), psychoanalytic tools ultimately serve to complicate this question by privileging psychic truth over other forms of knowledge.

This distinction between history and psychoanalysis has been challenged recently by Joan Scott (2012), who suggested that psychohistory failed because 'for the most part, [it] selected aspects of psychoanalytic theory that are least challenging to history's epistemology' (Scott, 2012, p. 68). Psychohistorians, Scott argues – like those 'vulgar' literary readers described by Felman – instrumentalised psychoanalysis, which they viewed as mere 'equipment or tools for approaching the past' (Ibid.). But the 'application' approach was only one way of reading Freud in the field of history, and as Scott and others have shown, there are better ways to think of how psychoanalysis can usefully augment the craft of the historian.

In the work of the medieval historian, Lyndal Roper, for example, we can see a more nuanced understanding of the role psychoanalysis might play in understanding the past. As a medievalist who uses psychoanalysis to analyse the pre-modern world, Roper is perhaps more vulnerable than most to the accusation of performing an anachronistic 'wild analysis' of history. But as she explains, psychoanalysis helps her

> to approach an understanding of early modern people which does more than treat them as colourful psychic primitives from a carnival world; which takes individual subjectivity seriously enough to be able to pose the difficult question of what, precisely, is historical in subjectivity.
>
> (Roper, 1994, p. 12)

The dilemma for the historian of the pre-modern is that psychoanalysis is 'a historical creation of the nineteenth century', and yet 'makes universalist claims about human psychological functioning which seem irreconcilable with the study of history' (Ibid., pp. 12–13). However, she writes:

> I think we simply need to refuse this apparent dilemma. All theories have their histories, and psychoanalysis, like Marxism, another child of the nineteenth century, is constantly changing. It does not endanger the status of the historical to concede that there are aspects of human nature which are enduring, just as there are aspects of human physiology which are constitutional.
>
> (Ibid., p. 13)

It is precisely such a refusal that we wish to champion in this book. Refusing the false dilemma of historical particularity and the ostensible autonomy of disciplines, we examine moments of estrangement, tension and unease within psychoanalytic accounts of historical, cultural and political life, in the uses and institutions of psychoanalytic ideas beyond the consulting room, as well as fruitful points of tension within the psychoanalytic discourse.

This book, like the discussions at the Psychoanalytic Thought, History and Political Life forum, is marked by an awareness of and consequent effort to resist the temptations of positivism and reparation.[5] Both Daniel Pick and Jacqueline Rose have used the insights of psychoanalysis to write powerfully and memorably on the imaginaries of violence and the failures of imagination of states. Along with writers, analysts and historians including Sally Alexander, Barbara Taylor, Lyndsey Stonebridge, Stephen Frosh, Matt ffytche, Patricia Gherovici, Dagmar Herzog, Dominick LaCapra, Élisabeth Roudinesco, Judith Butler, and others, they have shown us the unique forms of insight that arise in the unscripted encounter between psychoanalysis and historical, cultural, and political life. More recently, essays in non-academic publications, such as Eli Zaretsky's writing on Donald Trump, 'populism', and 'mass psychology', or an article in *Prospect Magazine* by Susie Orbach on the urgent need for psychoanalytic thinking in the age of Trump, suggest a more widespread resurgence and reappraisal of psychoanalysis as an invaluable source of insight into the drives that underpin our political present (Orbach, 2018; Zaretsky, 2018; Zaretsky, 2017; Zaretsky, 2016). Taking our inspiration from these writers and others, this book, like the forum out of which it arose, is committed to facilitating new and ever more challenging encounters between psychoanalysis and the cultural and political life of our times.

The book is divided into four sections, the titles of which are taken from a selection of landmark publications in twentieth-century psychoanalysis. What follows is a brief introduction to these four remarkable texts and the chapters grouped around them in this volume.

A note upon the mystic writing pad

It is no revelation to say that Freud's struggles to identify his psychology with the scientific epistemologies of his day brought him closer to the resources and repertoires of literature.[6] From the nomenclature of Freud's most famous 'complex' and his use of illustrative examples from literature, to contemporary re-examinations of the object lessons of Antigone and Hamlet,[7] literature and psychoanalysis are longstanding interlocutors whose history in the last century has been one of variously forgetting and remembering one another, each magnetised to the other's capacity to ask questions – as Felman so memorably puts it – otherwise (Felman, 1977a).

In his 1925 paper, 'Notiz über den »Wunderblock«',[8] translated by Strachey as 'A Note Upon the Mystic Writing Pad' (Freud, 1961a), Freud finds himself in the grip of an analogy that, throughout the twentieth century, has refused to let psychoanalysis go. Setting out to present his model of memory, that is, Freud ends up talking about writing. The *Wunderblock*, which had appeared on the market shortly before the essay's publication, is a children's toy that, for Freud, perfectly replicates the mechanics of human memory: the layering of a wax slab, a sheet of wax paper and a final top-sheet of celluloid to protect the wax paper, allows words or images scored into the pad to be visible on the wax paper. While lifting it immediately erases the marks, they remain imprinted in a 'permanent trace' in the underlying wax slab, even while the pad can be re-inscribed an infinite number of times. Memory, Freud explains, is paradoxical in much the same way, combining an infinite capacity for impression and the ability to leave a permanent trace. And yet, remarks Freud, 'the analogy would not be of much value if it could not be pursued further than this' (Freud, 1961a, p. 230). It sometimes seems as though the analogy gets ahead of Freud, gesturing to places where he cannot follow. It is impossible for us, in the early twenty-first century, to read Freud's essay 'before' the influence of deconstruction, prior to the Derridean unconscious and its preverbal graphic traces, or to the Lacanian one, structured, famously 'like a language' (Lacan, 1999, p. 48; Derrida, 1972). When Freud describes the two-handed use of the *Wunderblock*, one hand lifting the paper, the other hand writing, his figure anticipates the now-classic idea of the unconscious as an agency undercutting the fantasy of psychic as well as authorial sovereignty, evoking the 'enigmatic signifiers' of Laplanche (Laplanche, 1999). The idea Freud conceives, and his analogy would go on to reproduce on ever more complex scales, is that we are being written and unwritten even while we write our own lives.

In its efforts to pinpoint and configure new objects of knowledge such as the mnemic system, the hysterical symptom, and the unconscious, psychoanalysis often finds its conceptual limits in the limits of an analogy or metaphor such as that of the mystic writing pad. What begins as a descriptive term, a residue of the processes of conceptualisation, can easily settle into a rigid determinism. 'Metaphors', writes Hans Blumenberg, 'are fossils that indicate an archaic stratum of the trial of theoretical curiosity' (Blumenberg, 1997, p. 82). Where analogy calls attention to what metaphor would obscure – the condensation of multiple imaginative possibilities, a productive failure of empirical description – it also allows us to move both ways between its poles: in the case of Freud's mystic writing pad, from a description of memory through writing to a description of writing via memory. Like a kind of *Traumarbeit* or dream work playing out in its written discourses, psychoanalysis required the forging of a new written discourse with its own orders of thinking and its own aesthetics that brought it closer to fiction and, in places, endowed it with a new and sometimes problematic theoretical force. The founding allegory of Oedipus is perhaps the most bracing example of the deterministic power of myth and literary symbolism – what Rachel Bowlby has called 'Freudian mythologies' – in the entire psychoanalytic canon (Bowlby, 2009). Freud himself wrote elsewhere that 'The ego is an organization characterized by a very remarkable trend towards unification, towards synthesis' (Freud, 1959, p. 196). In search of new epistemologies for non-empirical, elusive objects, we could say, the discourse of psychoanalysis found itself subject to a similar drive, exploiting the synthetic power of myth to organise its own impulses and intuitions.

It is this organisation of desire in the theoretical writings of psychoanalysis that the three chapters in this section each approach from different angles. In the book's first chapter, 'D. W. Winnicott and the finding of literature', Elizabeth Sarah Coles reads Winnicott's critique of the synthetic force of psychoanalytic interpretation alongside what she argues is a powerful alternate discourse on aesthetic relationship in his best-known writings on creative and cultural experience. Testing the limits of two terms he puts to, often, enigmatic use ('finding' and 'creating'), the chapter argues that Winnicott's vindication of resistant, incomprehensible and dissatisfying objects in both early infant and adult cultural life, offers critical practice in the humanities – and critical readings of literature in particular – a curious and unexpected ally in its recent search for alternative approaches and forms of critical writing.

Eschewing a chronological approach to psychoanalytic writing, the book's second chapter, 'Project for a Scientific Psychology: The Impossibility of a Text', by Manuel Batsch turns to the earliest incarnations of what Freud would call his 'metapsychology'. In his chapter, Batsch traces some of the earliest attempts of psychoanalysis to get to grips with the nature of its objects – in particular, the model of human memory suggested by the peculiar symptomatology of hysteria. Analysing Freud's and his readers' attempts to fit the logics of hysterical memory into neurological and hermeneutic methodologies, and engaging with Jacques Derrida's reading of the Freudian text, the chapter proposes that the 'fertile impossibility' of this text marks out the way for a new genre of theoretical writing in psychoanalysis – the essayistic and fragmentary metapsychology. Both these first chapters ask what is being done – and what might potentially be done – with the objects of psychoanalysis at the level of the theoretical text.

The final chapter in this section, Shahidha Bari's '"Where had she walked thus and whither was she going?": Freud, Ferrante and Feet in Jensen's *Gradiva*', pursues one of Freud's most famous forays into literary fiction, his retelling and psychoanalytic reading of Wilhelm Jensen's novella, *Gradiva: Ein Pompejanisches Phantasiestück* (1903), just three years after its publication. The chapter traces some of the fictions Freud tells himself in the process, concerning the agencies of another of his impossible objects: feminine sexuality. Arguing for the resistances of Jensen's story to Freud's efforts to instrumentalise it for a reading of male fantasy, Bari proposes that what his use of the story betrays is in fact Freud's anxieties concerning the ability of psychoanalysis to contain woman's errant desire, her capacity to wander beyond the limits of its frameworks. The chapter turns to the Neapolitan novels of Elena Ferrante, an author known for her interest in psychoanalysis, arguing that Ferrante offers us an alternative account of feminine volition.

Mass psychology

One of the main dilemmas of Freud's famous text *Massenpsychologie und Ich-Analyse* (1921) is how to translate its title. There is almost a consensus that Strachey's decision to use the term 'group psychology' rather than 'mass psychology' in his translation to English is problematic because the German title locates Freud's work within a tradition of nineteenth-century 'crowd psychology' (e.g., Le Bon, Tarde) while Strachey's choice of the English word 'group' evokes few or none of these associations. However, as Daniel Pick argues, it is important to view Strachey's decision within the context of a politically charged set of debates around the meaning of the crowd/mass/mob/group/herd, and to consider the ambiguous and slippery political connotations of each of these terms:

> The familiar dilemmas of translating Freud are on this occasion part of a wider conundrum about the implications of a whole range of terms and contrasts running through the history of thought on groups and crowds. We are aware of the tendentious nature of the habitual contrasts: crowd

versus mob; mass versus individual; elite versus mass; leader versus followers, group versus herd. For Freud, however, something powerfully real is certainly at stake in group psychology; as a concept it is no mere chimera to be discarded; however shadowy its exact nature. Freud ponders the best group designation. If human beings are social animals, then of precisely what kind?

(Pick, 1995, p. 48).

Contrary to nineteenth-century social scientists, for whom the psychology of the masses bordered on an obsession, Freud offered psychoanalysis as a way to imagine group experience as the core of the human condition rather than a pathology of marginalised peoples – or peoples perceived as marginalised by hegemonic cultures – who came together and constituted a 'dangerous' political power. Viewed from this perspective, Freud's essay does not so much contribute to the 'crowd psychology' tradition, with its problematic tendency to project class hatred onto 'the masses', but rather shifts the terms of this debate altogether.

In her introduction to J. A. Underwood's new translation of 'Mass Psychology and the Analysis of the "I"' (2004), Jacqueline Rose suggested that Freud's text

> centres on two great social institutions, the army and the church, and two intensely intimate conditions – being in love and hypnosis in which, to use his own formula, we are dealing with "if the expression be permitted" a "mass of two".
>
> (Rose, 2004, p. xi)

In Freud's account, love and hypnosis are mechanisms that facilitate the formation of political institutions such as the army and church, providing the psychical tools through which individuals become soldiers and believers. These institutions' great challenge is to make masses into groups and prevent groups from turning into masses. However, Rose argues, by 'their very ability to generate unquestioning sacred loyalty, these intuitions inevitably turn groups into masses, even if of a different kind'. In other words, they are 'microcosms of what they most fear' (Ibid., p. xii). By revealing the precarious foundations of these political institutions, Freud's text simultaneously exposes the irrational forces underpinning the very attempt to distinguish between 'masses' and 'groups'.

One of the problems with the term 'mass' in its English usage, is the extent to which it has been used to prop up a fantasy of an anonymous and incoherent 'mass' – 'the masses' – which itself contributes to a failure to consider the rights and political and economic needs of particular groups of individuals within a democratic society. But even if we agree that 'mass psychology' and 'group psychology' are complementary terms rather than opposite ones, the temptation to favour the term 'mass psychology' in an attempt to explain

Trump, Brexit, the rise of populism, and even what some commentators describe as a post-truth era (as if there had ever been a 'pre-truth' or indeed a 'truth era') is greater than ever. Contemporary historians are tireless in their efforts to understand whether what we are witnessing in the twenty-first century is a new kind of political crisis or a return of the repressed from mid-twentieth century Europe. We have seen a resurgence of interest among some commentators in Adorno's post-war writings on mass psychology, racism, and the authoritarian personality, as though his thinking offered some key tools, if not prophecies, for understanding the present. It was Adorno who, in the aftermath of the Second World War, emphasised the usefulness of Freud's turn to the nineteenth-century 'hypnotic tradition' in understanding the formation of groups. In his seminal article, 'Freudian Theory and the Pattern of Fascist Propaganda' (Adorno, 1951), Adorno not only claims that 'Freud believes that the bond which integrates individuals into a mass, is of a *libidinal* nature' (Ibid., p. 121), but that specifically in the Fascist tradition, 'the techniques of the demagogue and the hypnotist coincide with the psychological mechanism by which individuals are made to undergo the regressions which reduce them to mere members of a group' (Ibid., p. 123).

Thus, in his attempt to understand the rise of Donald Trump, historian Peter Gordon returns to Adorno's 'Authoritarian personality', concluding that

> the attempt to describe Trumpism with the pathologising language of character types only works as a defense against the deeper possibility that Trump, far from being a violation of the norm, may actually signify an emergent norm of the social order as such.
>
> (Gordon, 2016)

Eli Zaretsky suggests we follow Adorno's 'Freudian Theory and the Pattern of Fascist Propaganda' in order to grasp that in the age of Trumpism, 'the narcissism in question is not only Trump's. More important is that of his followers, who idealise him as they once, in childhood, idealised themselves' (Zaretsky, 2018). Mass psychology in the Freudian sense is about a group of people identifying with the leader, but it is also about a group of people identifying with a narcissistic image of themselves as a group: hence, the success of Trump's slogan, 'Make America Great Again' understood by many as a not-so-covert call to 'Make America White Again'. Writing about the phenomenon of group psychology in *Civilization and Its Discontents*, Freud wrote that: 'It is always possible to bind together a considerable number of people in love, so long as there are other people left over to receive the manifestations of their aggressiveness' (Freud, 1961b, p. 114). Groups – whether in the shape of nations, institutions, or political parties – are founded as much on the basis of a hatred of those that they exclude, as on the basis of a professed love for those that they include. Coining the term the 'narcissism of minor difference', Freud described the 'relatively harmless' competition between the 'Spaniards and the Portuguese [...] the North Germans and the South Germans, the English and the Scotch' (Ibid.). But if Freud's apparent ease with such national competition feels somewhat ill-placed in the aftermath of recent referendums in Britain, and the rise of far-right nationalism globally, Freud was already of course painfully aware of the forms of hatred produced through such processes of group formation. By the end of the paragraph that begins with the 'relatively harmless' competition between the 'Spaniards and the Portuguese' comes the chilling observation that, through the same logic, 'the dream of a Germanic world-dominion called for anti-semitism as its complement' (Ibid., p. 115).

The chapters in this section of the book suggest that defining the boundaries of the group – for Freud, for Adorno, and for us today – is a task that is intimately connected to questions of race and gender.[9] The categories of race and gender have haunted the history of mass psychology, especially in contexts where racialised narratives of history were founding political and national myths. In the first chapter of this section, Nicky Falkof tells the story of scaremongering or 'moral panic' surrounding alleged 'Satanism' in South Africa during the late 1980s and early 1990s. These were the last years before the fall of the apartheid regime, where it was already possible to see its imminent collapse. Born of a fear of losing established racial privileges and racial hegemony, 'South Africa's satanic panic was particular to its context and symptomatic of the multiple anxieties that characterised white life' (p. 40).

Anxiety about Satanism in South Africa was characterised by false stories, rumours, and conspiracy theories circulated by the press about Satanic groups that were said to commit all manner of violent acts. This historically acute case of moral panic is similar in many respects to early-twentieth-century cases of mass psychology, which were always derived from collective anxieties that simultaneously registered and sought to disavow historical facts – in this case the imminent collapse of the apartheid regime under pressure from black South Africans' demand for political justice. Indeed, in the place of these anxieties, the 'uncanny white Satanist', appeared as a 'fetishized' figure, 'a figure that was both terrifying and familiar, emerging from within the white world rather than from the frightening outside' (p. 46). Psychoanalytically speaking, Falkof argues, the 'disavowal of black people's agency and the legitimacy of their claims in favour of the fetishisation of imaginary threats allowed white people to once again turn away from black South Africans' increasingly powerful calls for justice and equality' (p. 46). Far from representing a mere delusion or an utter detachment from reality, white South Africans' moral panic about Satanism in the 1980s can in fact be read as a significant symptom of the real political situation in South Africa at this moment in history. The process of 'turning a blind eye' (Steiner, 1985) to the real political situation of South African apartheid was itself part of the psychical and political process through which white South African society established and maintained itself as the dominant political community. What this case reveals so powerfully, is that denial in its different forms – moral panic, repression, fetish, hysteria – are not symptoms of a hegemonic community but the very precondition for its existence (Hall and Pick, 2017).

Shifting our attention from apartheid South Africa to America in the era of Jim Crow, Ian Magor's chapter focuses on a now neglected Hollywood film, *Pinky*, released in 1949. At the centre of the film stands Patricia 'Pinky' Johnson, a light-skinned woman of mixed racial heritage who 'passes' as white while studying nursing in New England, where she falls in love with a white doctor. Refusing his proposal of marriage, she leaves the North and returns to the South where she grew up, only to face new racial obstacles and boundaries. Magor's piece problematises some of our contemporary assumptions about the interchangeability of identities – namely, the plasticity of races, ethnicities and religions according to our own personal plan of self-making. Magor's chapter draws attention to the fact that, for many people in history and in contemporary society, universalism operates as a violent demand that seeks to erase and to render unliveable those identifications and identities that fall outside of the racist, sexist and heteronormative assumptions of the dominant culture.

Laura Mulvey famously analysed the logic of the 'male gaze' that dominated Hollywood for so long. Hollywood films, she argues, offer feminine bodies as 'objects' that serve masculine processes of identification. As Magor shows, this process of group making was, and very often still is, not an option for black women: 'The space which the black male might still have to identify with the male hero is ostensibly closed off to the black female viewer' (p. 57). The cinema as space where one can fantasise one's life as different by identifying with narratives from the big screen, is a privilege that cannot always be bought for the price of a cinema ticket. It was Frantz Fanon who captured this failure of identification in the cinema. Invited to identify with on-screen representations of black men, Fanon's self-recognition in a black character at the same time produces a painful *misrecognition* – one which he anticipates: 'I cannot go to a film without seeing myself. I wait for me' (cited in Chapter 5, p. 54).

Post-colonial thinkers, including Fanon, Edward Said, Gayatri Chakravorty Spivak and Achille Mbembe, have contributed a great deal to our understanding of race as a group-maker. Working with and against psychoanalysis, they have explored its origins in nineteenth-century racial sciences as well as revealing the opportunities provided by Freud and others for emancipation from the colonial gaze. Within this tradition – but also stretching its scope – Marita Vyrgioti focuses on a topic often overlooked by Freudian scholars: his references to cannibalism. Rather than providing a thoroughgoing theory of cannibalism (as he did in the case of incest relations, for example), Freud's position on cannibalism 'emerges sporadically, in footnotes, in emotionally invested texts, and through a writing of significant obscurity' (p. 68). Reconstructing the cannibalistic discourse of the nineteenth century and exploring Freud's engagement with it, Vyrgioti argues that Freud 'found in the colonial imagery of the cannibal trope an entry point to critique the hegemonic, Christian colonial subjectivity by identifying the ritualistic repetition of cannibalism in the Eucharist' (p. 68). For Freud, Vyrgioti argues, cannibalism is a site for exploring the colonial violence of Christianity against its others, Jews included. Vyrgioti's close reading of Freud's references to cannibalism sheds new light on the identification processes at the core of violent acts of group-making. The group, she argues, 'revives the ambivalence felt by the prehistoric sons towards the primal father, but due to its incapacity to "murder and devour" the leader, as the sons once did, the group projects outwards any aggression originally felt for the leader' (p. 76). Rather than signifying the omnipotence and self-confidence of the group, this political violence towards the group's 'other' exposes the ambivalent and ambiguous nature of its foundation. As Freud himself put it in 'Mass Psychology', 'the cannibal, as we know, has a devouring affection for his enemies and only devours people of whom he is fond' (Freud, 1955, p. 105).

The location of cultural experience

In his 1967 essay 'The Location of Cultural Experience', D. W. Winnicott wrote that 'Freud did not have a place in his topography of the mind for the experience of things cultural' (Winnicott, 1971, p. 95). Freud, wrote Winnicott, 'used the word "sublimation" to point the way to a place where cultural experience is meaningful, but perhaps he did not get so far as to tell us where in the mind cultural experience is' (Ibid.). Taking as his epigraph a quotation from the Indian poet Rabindranath Tagore, 'On the seashore of endless worlds, children play', Winnicott recounts his adolescent bafflement at the meaning of the poet's words, but observes that, regardless of meaning, the quotation stuck: it 'found a place in me'. Recalling his own distinctly unsubtle knowingness upon first becoming 'a Freudian', Winnicott describes, with characteristic wariness, his own 'Freudian' reading of the poem: 'I knew what it meant'. The psychoanalytic interpretation of the poem's symbolism unfolds with a knowing predictability and an almost crushing heavy-handedness:

> The sea and the shore represented endless intercourse between man and woman, and the child emerged from this union to have a brief moment before becoming in turn adult or parent. Then, as a student of unconscious symbolism, I knew (one always knows) that the sea is the mother, and onto the seashore the child is born. Babies come up out of the sea and are spewed out upon the land, like Jonah from the whale. So now the seashore was the mother's body, after the child is born and the mother and the now viable baby are getting to know each other.
>
> (Ibid., pp. 95–96)

Presented as a near-parody of the worst excesses of 'Freudian' interpretation, Winnicott's brief account of his foray into poetic interpretation conveys the dull predictability of his own youthful symbolic literalism, the 'endless intercourse' and the babies 'spewed out upon the land', suggesting the wild analyst's repeated collapsing of the multivalent ambiguities of poetic language into what Shoshana Felman would surely describe as 'vulgar' interpretation (Felman, 1977b). The rapid movement from Tagore's 'seashore of endless worlds' to the Freudian analyst's vulgar insistence on 'endless intercourse', leaves the reader feeling bereft, stripped of the realms of possibility suggested by the poetic language.

Unsatisfied by this exercise in Freudian interpretation, Winnicott describes his own shift from the position of masterful knowing to a 'state of not-knowing', a state which, Winnicott suggests, might have more in common with our actual experiences of cultural life than the traditional Oedipally fixated Freudian interpretation of literature and art (Winnicott, 1971, p. 96). For Winnicott, Tagore's image of children playing on the seashore – on the limit – of endless worlds, is put to better use when we read it, not as a symbolic statement of the infant's Oedipal relationship to the mother's body, but instead as a hint at the commonality between cultural experience and the childhood world of play. Psychoanalysts, blindsided by their fixation on instinctual life, have 'failed to state with comparable clearness or conviction the tremendous intensity of these non-climactic experiences that are called playing' (Ibid., p. 98). Shifting the focus away from a form of reading that homes in on the unconscious desires hidden – more or less disguised – within the artwork, Winnicott instead sets out to explore the question of where in the mind (or outside it) cultural experience might be located. For Winnicott, cultural experience is 'an extension' of childhood play, and it is located 'in the potential space between the individual and the environment' (Ibid., p. 99, p. 100). Neither a product of individual fantasy, nor belonging solely to the realm of external reality, this 'potential space is at the interplay between there being nothing but me and there being objects and phenomena outside omnipotent control' (Ibid., p. 100).

As Elizabeth Sarah Coles argues in the first chapter of this book, Winnicott's resistance to the violence of Freudian interpretation appears alongside a compelling alternate discourse on creativity and aesthetic experience that anticipates a number of contemporary interventions in the world of literary studies on the so-called 'limits of critique' (Felski, 2015). In a characteristically understated fashion, there is also a compelling political dimension to Winnicott's account of the location of cultural experience. Hesitating over his own use of 'the word "culture"', Winnicott nonetheless resists the association with highbrow *Kultur*, describing instead an 'inherited tradition' that constitutes the 'common pool of humanity, into which individuals and groups of people may contribute, and from which we may all draw' (Winnicott, 1971, p. 99). Although the reference to the 'inherited tradition' inevitably and perhaps uncomfortably evokes Jungian archetypes, the 'third area' of cultural experiencing is, for Winnicott, a 'common ground', an implicitly democratic, shared space that 'transcends personal experience' and opens the individual up to that 'common pool of humanity' (Ibid., p. 96, p. 100, p. 99).

The question of the location of shared, democratic cultural spaces, as well as the question of how we read or interpret cultural experiences, are both central to the chapters in this section of the book. In '"Little Mussolini" and the "parasite poets": Psychoanalytic Pedagogy, Modernism, and the Illegible Child', Helen Tyson examines the figure of the child in psychoanalytic writing, progressive pedagogy, and modernist writing from the 1920s and 1930s. Contrasting Dora and Bertrand Russell's vision for their progressive school with the portrait of progressive schooling as imagined in Virginia Woolf's 1931 novel *The Waves*, and viewing both in the context of contemporary psychoanalytic accounts of children's education, this chapter examines the fraught political fantasies attached to discussions of democratic education in the period. The figure of the child, Tyson argues, is an overdetermined, and frequently obscure or even illegible, figure that stages a conflicting set of anxieties about the role of the unconscious in political life, and in British democracy, in the early decades of the twentieth century.

In 'Exposed to the Other: Responding to the Refugee in Caroline Bergvall's *Drift*', Catherine Humble places D. W. Winnicott's Second World War squiggle games alongside the line poems presented in Caroline Bergvall's contemporary mixed-media artwork *Drift*, arguing for the powerful effects of both the squiggle game and the line poem in bearing witness to the traumatic experiences of both the Second World War evacuee and the contemporary refugee. In this chapter, Winnicott's celebration of states of not-knowing and his insistence on the value of shared creative encounters, are brought to bear on our contemporary refugee crisis. Humble reads the strangely resistant line poems in *Drift* as staging the limits of our capacity to represent human trauma, arguing that in her refusal to represent either the idealised or demonised refugees whose images circulate daily in the press and on social media, Bergvall demands a different kind of response to the polarised sympathy or disgust solicited by the Murdoch press. For Humble, Bergvall's drawings demand that the reader respond not with what Winnicott called 'clever and apt interpretations' (Winnicott, 1971, p. 117), but instead with what he describes as a form of receptive resonance. These drawings not only demand an ethically responsible and 'non-coercive kind of witnessing' (p. 119), but they also, Humble argues in conclusion, bear witness to the unconscious of history.

Refusing the bifurcated and ahistorical vision of contemporary media representations of refugees, Bergvall's line drawings demand that the reader or viewer take up a position of ethical care towards the other. It is this same tendency on the part of the Western media to split our visual world into the good and the bad, the virtuous and the demonised, that concerns Theo Gordon in his chapter, 'Between the Acts, or, Melanie Klein and the Representation of People with AIDS'. In this chapter, Gordon uses Melanie Klein's writing on paranoia and splitting to explore the paranoid visual representations of people with AIDS in 1980s tabloid journalism, where images of figures such as the heartthrob Rock Hudson were split between a 'before' and 'after' shot, encouraging viewers, as Gordon puts it, to 'read illness in the difference between two images' (p. 129). In this analysis, the tabloid journalist occupies the position of the Kleinian infant, splitting the visual field into 'good' and 'bad' objects, fuelling a vicious circle of cultural paranoia and homophobia in relationship to HIV and AIDS. As Gordon argues, Klein's analysis of her ten-year-old child evacuee, Richard, and his drawings, can be usefully redirected towards an analysis of the paranoid circulation of violence in the visual iconography surrounding the AIDS epidemic.

At the same time, Gordon explains, in the world of art criticism, a theoretical debate erupted concerning the extent to which artistic practices might disrupt the 'symbolic impasse' whereby the visual depiction of the person with AIDS immediately 'collapsed into phobic referents that were stymying the efforts of AIDS activism to shift public conversation around the epidemic' (p. 136). For Gordon, it is in a work like Zoe Leonard's Strange Fruit that we might find an example of the kind of artwork that both registers the historic and continued violence wrought upon people with AIDS, while simultaneously offering a powerfully reparative holding space in which to process that violence. For Leo Bersani, Melanie Klein's theory of reparation was complicit in a 'culture of redemption' in which 'art redeems the catastrophes of history' (Bersani, 1990, p. 22). Contrary to Bersani, Gordon rereads Kleinian reparation as an artistic practice that refuses to forget both historic and continuing forms of socio-political violence.

The suppressed madness of sane men

In her 1950 book *On Not Being Able to Paint*, Marion Milner described her attempt, on 5 August 1939, to capture in paint an approaching storm on the West Sussex coast. Struggling to paint the scene, Milner produced instead a free drawing in charcoal, finding afterwards that she had 'made the thunder bird of the New Mexican Indians, spreading right across the sky, also a huge shadowy Indian drum and a snake rising up out of the sea' (Milner, 2010a, p. 20). It was only much later, Milner recounts, that she 'noticed the significance of the date when the free drawing "Thunder over the Sea" […] had been made, with its great Indian war drum looming in the sky': 'The date showed that it had been only a matter of days between the making of the drawing and the bursting of the storm of war over the whole of Europe' (Ibid., p. 165). The storm, Milner recognises, 'which all this while I had been treating as a private and inner one, was not only that' (Ibid.). *On Not Being Able to Paint* traces what Milner describes as the 'monsters within and without', demons that haunt Milner both internally and externally, traversing and unsettling the borders between the historical landscape of the 1930s and 1940s and the inner life of the aspiring artist and psychoanalyst.

The question of borders is central within Milner's writing, a form of writing that extends the limits of psychoanalysis, demonstrating how psychoanalytic insight challenges the boundary between psyche and history, as well as offering a powerful account of both the pleasures and the perils of moments in which boundaries appear to break down. Turning, on a number of occasions and in different publications, to George Santayana's description of 'the suppressed madness of sane men', Milner's writing explores both the 'cosmic bliss' and the 'catastrophic chaos' experienced at moments when the boundary between individual and social world begins to blur or even to break down (Milner, 1987, p. 96; Milner, 2010b, p. xliv). For Milner, the blurring of boundaries between the 'I' and the 'not-I' is, as for Winnicott, central to our experiences of play and creativity – it can be a form of ecstasy, but it can also be experienced as a form of madness.

'The suppressed madness of sane men' seems a fitting subtitle for a section of the book that, returning to the opening question of the limits of psychoanalysis, also explores what the uses of psychoanalysis might be for an analysis of history, of madness, and of politics. All three of these concluding chapters are concerned with limits – from the limits of psychoanalysis as a tool for the study of history, to the limits of what a spectator can bear in the contemporary theatre, to the limits of enlightenment thinking. In 'Nazism's Inner Demons: Psychoanalysis and the Columbus Centre (1962–1981)', Danae Karydaki explores the limits to which psychoanalysis might extend as an analytic tool, and considers the challenge psychoanalysis poses to the limits of reason and enlightenment thought. Responding to Perry Anderson's claim, in 1968, that, although Britain was home to a 'flourishing' clinical practice, the impact of psychoanalysis on British culture had been 'virtually nil' (Anderson, cited by Karydaki, in Chapter 10, p. 147), Karydaki's investigation into the archives of the Columbus Centre at the University of Sussex suggest that a number of historians working in Britain in this period were in fact deeply committed to psychoanalysis as a tool for historical research.

Established by David Astor and Norman Cohn in 1966, amidst a utopian post-war commitment to new forms of education pioneered at the University of Sussex, the Columbus Centre, as Karydaki reveals, set out to employ psychoanalysis as a tool for studying, in Astor's words, 'man's capacity to destroy his fellow beings without rational motives' (Astor, cited by Karydaki in Chapter 10, p. 147). The centre deployed psychoanalytic ideas in an attempt to understand the unconscious processes of dehumanisation at work in Nazi Germany, in Apartheid South Africa, in the sixteenth- and seventeenth-century witch-hunts, and in the persecution of Roma people across Europe. Despite Cohn's later hesitation about not having, as he put it, used psychoanalysis 'sensibly', Karydaki demonstrates the unique contribution made by this underexplored body of work (Cohn, cited by Karydaki in Chapter 10, p. 159). Distinguishing the work of the Columbus Centre from the contentious and speculative arena of 'psychohistory', Karydaki makes a compelling case for the value of a 'critically engaged employment of psychoanalysis in the study of history', which, 'can break a well-established stereotype that the Nazis were mad, exceptionally sadistic and a unique type of perpetrators' (p. 160). Responding to Hannah Arendt's infamous portrait of Adolf Eichmann as embodying the 'banality of evil' rather than its monstrous pathology, Karydaki demonstrates that 'the Arendtian and Freudian readings of history are not', despite Arendt's own reservations about psychoanalysis, 'mutually exclusive' (p. 160. See also Rose, 2016). Although mindful of the risks of trivialising or normalising evil, Karydaki concludes by noting that the resistance to this kind of psychoanalytically informed historical work lies more fully in our own fear of finding 'Nazism's inner demons' within ourselves (p. 161).

For the architects of the Columbus Centre, psychoanalysis presented itself as a unique tool with which to comprehend the unconscious mechanisms at work in history. In 'Reaching Into the Blind-Spot: Rape, Trauma and Identification in *Blasted*', Leah Sidi explores the unique insights that psychoanalysis might yield when confronted with the theatre of Sarah Kane. Bringing Sandor Ferenczi's understanding of trauma to a reading of the controversial and much misunderstood play, *Blasted* (1995), Sidi argues that rather than ignoring the mental consequences of sexual violence, as a number of critics have suggested, this play constitutes a devastating attempt to enact the inner life of a rape victim. Psychoanalysis, in this chapter, does not simply offer one of any number of alternative ways of reading the stage, rather it brings to light otherwise inaccessible truths about the impact of sexual violence on an individual's mental life. By reading *Blasted* through Ferenczi's mimetic model of trauma, in which the victim 'mimetically incorporate[s] the thoughts and feelings of the aggressor' (Leys, cited by Sidi in Chapter 11, p. 170), Sidi makes sense of Kane's otherwise baffling decision to shift the focus of attention in this play from the rape victim, Cate, to her assailant, the misogynistic, racist, homophobic tabloid journalist, Ian. By shifting the focus of the play to Ian's paranoid and phobic fantasy world, Kane, in Sidi's interpretation, asks the audience to experience the mental world of a trauma victim, in which the survivor's own sense of her self is shattered and invaded by the thoughts and feelings of the aggressor. While, in Karydaki's chapter, psychoanalysis offers a unique lens through which to expose the unconscious fantasies at work in historical acts of violence, for Sidi too, psychoanalysis yields an insight into the inner demons of trauma not otherwise visible to critics.

Both Karydaki and Sidi explore acts of violence that challenge the limits of reason, exposing a madness lurking beneath the veneer of our own forms of so-called sanity and enlightenment reason. In our final chapter, D'Maris Coffman weighs up the battles that have raged around the meaning of enlightenment over the past 230 years and considers the position of psychoanalysis in relation to these arguments. Responding to Steven Pinker's 2018 polemic, *Enlightenment Now: The Case for Reason, Science, Humanism, and Progress*, which trumpeted the rehabilitation of

'Enlightenment values' in our present-day, Coffman offers an urgently needed return to the historical question: 'What is Enlightenment?' Tracing the emergence of this question in the historically specific setting of the Berlin Enlightenment, Coffman argues that we need to consider 'The Enlightenment' as 'milieu, movement (or project), process, and stance' – as neither 'revolutionary [n]or even always innovatory' (p. 182). In a salient reminder to Pinker *et al*, Coffman notes a pervasive 'confusion of tongues' in contemporary articulations of so-called enlightenment values: 'Kant was, especially in his answer, an apologist for an enlightened despot – a revelation which would no doubt come as a surprise to Pinker and his allies, who see in the Enlightenment the genesis of liberal democracy' (p. 185). Both critics and advocates have, as Coffman notes, appropriated the idea of the Enlightenment for differing and divergent political ends.

'Freudianism', Coffman argues, 'may be the most problematic child of the Enlightenment' (p. 186). Viewed by its champions as a means of liberating the patient from their suffering, psychoanalysis has also, of course, been criticised as a tool of Western, patriarchal, bourgeois, heterosexual normalisation. And yet, Coffman argues, it is by considering the Enlightenment as a critical stance or a form of hermeneutics that we might find value in both the idea of enlightenment and in psychoanalysis today.

For Coffman, one of the most serious dilemmas we face as intellectuals, historians and critics is 'the extent to which our scholarly milieu group is implicated in contemporary social and material realities or in our own mental habits' (p. 189). Drawing an analogy with the problem of 'parallel processing' as witnessed in the training of psychoanalysts – where candidates in training inadvertently reproduce their difficulties with their patients with their supervisors – Coffman suggests that historians might learn from the analytic solution to this dilemma. In psychoanalytic training, group supervision provides a space in which the forms of repetition that appear in parallel processing can be analysed by the 'milieu group'. Proposing that we see the scholarly community as just such a milieu group, Coffman argues for a more thorough 'commitment to self-reflection on the extent to which the discursive logics of the public sphere reproduce, unwittingly or not, the hierarchical relations of the participants' (p. 189. See also Bion, 1961). It is, for Coffman, only by preserving the integrity of our 'institutionally protected public spaces' that we might maintain any 'hope for civil society' (p. 189). Despite the difficulties of group psychology described in a number of chapters in this book, Coffman draws these chapters to a conclusion with a powerful articulation of the value of groups and institutionally protected public spaces for the continued functioning of the scholarly community.

Wild analysis may have been conceived by Freud as a moment in which psychoanalysis threatens to go awry, but, as the essays gathered in this book demonstrate, wild analysis might also describe moments in which psychoanalysis stumbles upon uncomfortable truths about culture, politics, and society. These essays mark our collective belief that it is via psychoanalysis that our study of history, culture and politics might gain access to insights that remain otherwise inaccessible, providing an invaluable source of critical reflection as we plunge further into the twenty-first century.

Notes

1 Remark made in a letter to Sándor Ferenczi dated October 27, 1910 (Ferenczi and Freud, 1993, p. 229). Throughout this introduction we use both Freud's term '"Wild" Psycho-Analysis', from his 1910 paper (Freud, 1957a), and the more general term 'wild analysis', as used by Jean Laplanche and J. B. Pontalis in *The Language of Psychoanalysis* (1973, p. 480).
2 See for example Rachel Bowlby (2007), Maud Ellmann (1994), and Shoshana Felman (1977a).
3 Lacan's term for the 'pass' is derived from 'the passage to the desire to be an analyst' (Lacan, 1995, p. 10).
4 For psychoanalytic critiques of cognitive behavioural therapy, see Leader (2008), and Cohen (2013).
5 Christopher Bollas warns against the dangers of such temptations in his introduction to the public conversation between Jacqueline Rose and Edward Said on the Israel-Palestine conflict. See Said (2004).
6 Shoshana Felman (1977a) and Maud Ellmann (1994) have had a particularly strong impact on discussions of psychoanalysis and literature, and the multiple entanglements between the Freudian metapsychology and literary example and technique.
7 See for example Janet Adelman (1992), Judith Butler (2000), Simon Critchley and Jamieson Webster (2013), Jacques Lacan (1997).
8 Published in *Internationale Zeitschrift für Psychoanalyse* 11 (1925), 1, and Sigmund Freud, Gesammelte Schriften 6, 415.
9 The Authoritarian Personality was published as part of the Studies in Prejudice Series, edited by Max Horkheimer and Samuel Flowerman. As Stephen Frosh (2016) has recently shown, from their Marxist perspective, they were much motivated by the need to develop one universalistic explanation for anti-Semitism and racism, i.e., to provide an explanation in which anti-Semitism is a symptom for the general problem of racism under a capitalist structure. But Frosh convincingly argues that their argument was problematic, partly because some particularities of the Jewish history and anti-Semitism kept haunting the project.

Bibliography

Adelman, J. (1992) *Suffocating mothers: fantasies of maternal origin from Hamlet to The Tempest*. New York and London: Routledge.
Adorno, T.W. (1951) 'Freudian theory and the pattern of fascist propaganda'. In A. Arato and E. Gebhardt, (1978) *The essential Frankfurt School reader*. Oxford: Blackwell.
Bersani, L. (1990) *The culture of redemption*. Cambridge, MA: Harvard University Press.
Bion, W. R. (1961) *Experiences in groups and other papers*. London: Tavistock Publications.
Blumenberg, H. (1997) 'Prospect for a theory of non-conceptuality', *Shipwreck with spectator: paradigm of a metaphor for existence*. Cambridge, Mass.: MIT Press.

Bowlby, R. (2007) *Freudian mythologies: Greek tragedy and modern identities*. Oxford: Oxford University Press.
Butler, J. (2000) *Antigone's claim: kinship between life and death*. New York: Columbia University Press.
Cohen, J. (2013) *The private life: why we remain in the dark*. London: Granta.
Critchley, S. and J. Webster (2013) *Stay, illusion!: the Hamlet doctrine*. New York: Verso Books.
Derrida, J. (1972) 'Freud and the scene of writing', *Yale French Studies* 48, 74–117.
Ellmann, M. (ed.) (1994) *Psychoanalytic literary criticism*. London: Longman.
Erikson, Erik H. (1958) *Young man Luther : a study in psychoanalysis and history*. London: Faber.
Everett, P., ed. (2016) *Corresponding lives: Mabel Dodge Luhan, A. A. Brill and the psychoanalytic adventure in America*. London: Karnac Books.
Felman, S. (1977a) 'To open the question', *Yale French Studies* 55 (56), 5–10.
Felman, S. (1977b) 'Turning the screw of interpretation', *Yale French Studies* 55 (56), 94–207.
Felman, S. (1982) *Literature and psychoanalysis: the question of reading: otherwise*, Baltimore and London: Johns Hopkins University Press.
Felski, R. (2015) *The limits of critique*. London and Chicago: University of Chicago Press.
Ferenczi, S. and S. Freud (1993) *The correspondence of Sigmund Freud and Sándor Ferenczi*, ed. Eva Brabant, Ernst Falzeder and Patrizia Giampieri-Deutsch, trans. Peter T. Hoffer, Cambridge, Mass.: Harvard University Press, 3 vols., vol. I.
Freud, S. (1955) 'Group psychology and the analysis of the ego'. In *The standard edition of the complete psychological works of Sigmund Freud*, ed. J. Strachey; trans. J. Strachey and A. Freud, with A. Strachey and A. Tyson, London: The Hogarth Press and the Institute of Psychoanalysis, 24 vols., vol. XVIII.
Freud, S. (1957a) "Wild" psycho-analysis. In *The Standard Edition of the Complete Psychological Works of Sigmund Freud*, ed. J. Strachey; trans. J. Strachey and A. Freud, with A. Strachey and A. Tyson, London: The Hogarth Press and the Institute of Psychoanalysis, 24 vols., vol. XI.
Freud, S. (1957b) On the history of the psycho-analytic movement. In *The standard edition of the complete psychological works of Sigmund Freud*, ed. J. Strachey; trans. J. Strachey and A. Freud, with A. Strachey and A. Tyson, London: The Hogarth Press and the Institute of Psychoanalysis, 24 vols., vol. XIV.
Freud, S. (1959) 'The question of lay analysis'. In *The standard edition of the complete psychological works of Sigmund Freud*, ed. J. Strachey; trans. J. Strachey and A. Freud, with A. Strachey and A. Tyson, London: The Hogarth Press and the Institute of Psychoanalysis, 24 vols., vol. XX.
Freud, S. (1961a) 'A note upon the mystic writing pad'. In *The standard edition of the complete psychological works of Sigmund Freud*, ed. J. Strachey; trans. J. Strachey and A. Freud, with A. Strachey and A. Tyson, London: The Hogarth Press and the Institute of Psychoanalysis, 24 vols., vol. XIX.
Freud, S. (1961b) *Civilization and its discontents. The standard edition of the complete psychological works of Sigmund Freud*, ed. J. Strachey; trans. J. Strachey and A. Freud, with A. Strachey and A. Tyson, London: The Hogarth Press and the Institute of Psychoanalysis, 24 vols., vol. XXI.

Freud, S. (1961c) Female sexuality. In *The standard edition of the complete psychological works of Sigmund Freud*, ed. J. Strachey; trans. J. Strachey and A. Freud, with A. Strachey and A. Tyson, London: The Hogarth Press and the Institute of Psychoanalysis, 24 vols., vol. XXI.

Freud, S. (2010), *The interpretation of dreams: the complete and definitive text*, ed. and trans. J. Strachey (1955), New York: Basic Books.

Frosh, S. (2010) *Psychoanalysis outside the clinic: interventions in psychosocial studies*, Basingstoke: Palgrave Macmillan.

Frosh, S. (2016) 'Studies in prejudice: Theorising antisemitism in the wake of the Nazi Holocaust'. In *Psychoanalysis in the age of totalitarianism*, eds. Matt ffytche and Daniel Pick. London: Routledge.

Gordon, P. E. (2016) 'The authoritarian personality revisited: reading Adorno in the age of Trump', *b20* [online: https://www.boundary2.org/2016/06/peter-gordon-the-authoritarian-personality-revisited-reading-adorno-in-the-age-of-trump/].

Hall, C., and D. Pick (2017) 'Thinking About Denial', *History Workshop Journal* 84, 1–23.

Klein, M. (1998) *Narrative of a child analysis*. London: Vintage.

Lacan, J. (1995), 'Proposition of 9 October 1967 on the psychoanalyst of the school', trans. R. Grigg, *Analysis* 6, 1–13.

Lacan, J. (1997) *The seminar of Jacques Lacan, book vii: the ethics of psychoanalysis 1959–1960*, ed. J-A. Miller, trans. D. Porter. New York and London: W. W. Norton and Company.

Lacan, J. (1999) *Seminar* XX. New York: Norton.

Langer, W. C. (1972) *The mind of Adolf Hitler*. New York: Basic Books.

Laplanche, J. (1996) 'Psychoanalysis as anti-hermeneutics', *Radical Philosophy* 79, 7–12.

Laplanche, J. (1999) *Essays on otherness*. London: Routledge.

Laplanche, J., and J. B. Pontalis (1973) *The language of psychoanalysis*, trans. D. Nicholson-Smith. London: Hogarth Press and the Institute of Psycho-Analysis.

Latour, B. (2017) *Facing gaia: eight lectures on the new climatic regime*. Cambridge: Polity Press.

Leader, D. (2008) *The new black: mourning, melancholia and depression*. London: Penguin.

Milner, M. (1987) *The suppressed madness of sane men: forty-four years of exploring psychoanalysis*. London: Tavistock Publications.

Milner, M. (2010a) *On not being able to paint*. London: Routledge.

Milner, M. (2010b). *In the hands of the living god: an account of a psycho-analytic treatment*. London: Routledge.

Orbach, S. (2018) 'Misogyny on the couch: why it's time to let psychoanalysis into politics', *Prospect Magazine* [online: https://www.prospectmagazine.co.uk/arts-and-books/susie-orbach].

Pick, D. (1995) 'Freud's group psychology and the history of the crowd', *History Workshop Journal* 4 (1), 39–62.

Pick, D. (2012) *The pursuit of the Nazi mind: Hitler, Hess, and the analysts*. Oxford: Oxford University Press.

Roper, L. (1994) *Oedipus and the devil: witchcraft, religion and sexuality in early modern Europe*. London: Routledge.

Rose, J. (2004) 'Introduction'. In S. Freud, *Mass psychology and other writings*, trans. J. A. Underwood. London: Penguin.

Rose, J. (2016) 'Total belief: delirium in the West'. In *Psychoanalysis in the age of totalitarianism*, eds. Matt ffytche and Daniel Pick. London: Routledge.
Safouan, M. (2000) *Jacques Lacan and the question of psychoanalytic training*. Basingstoke: Macmillan.
Said, E. (2004) *Freud and the non-European*. New York: Verso Books.
Schafer, R. (1985) 'Wild Analysis', *Journal of the American Psychoanalytic Association* 33, 275–299.
Scott, J. W. (2012) 'The incommensurability of psychoanalysis and history', *History and Theory* 51 (1), 63–83.
Steiner, J. (1985) 'Turning a blind eye: The cover up for Oedipus', *International Review of Psycho-Analysis* 12, 161–172.
Winnicott, D. W. (1971) *Playing and reality*. London: Psychology Press.
Zaretsky, Eli (2016) 'American id: Freud on Trump', *Huffington Post* [online: https://www.huffingtonpost.com/eli-zaretsky/american-id-freud-on-trum_b_10105596.html].
Zaretsky, E. (2017) 'The three paradoxes of populism and Freudian mass psychology', *History Workshop*, [online: http://www.historyworkshop.org.uk/the-three-paradoxes-of-populism-and-freudian-mass-psychology/].
Zaretsky, E. (2018) 'The Mass Psychology of Trumpism', *LRB Blog* [online: https://www.lrb.co.uk/blog/2018/09/18/eli-zaretsky/the-mass-psychology-of-trumpism/].

Part 1

The mystic writing pad

Chapter 1

D. W. Winnicott and the finding of literature

Elizabeth Sarah Coles

In an interview in 2003, the poet Jorie Graham posed the following question: 'Will a communal action—via a writer's and a reader's meeting on the page—create a tenable "we"?'[1] Graham was reflecting on where meaning happens in her poems and to whom exactly it belongs: whether what she calls a reader's 'instinct' is what sets the limits of description, or whether it is instinct that is bound by a 'communal action' of literature, belonging to neither reader nor writer but placing intangible demands on both. Graham's question echoes several lines of inquiry in the recent history of literary studies that seek to recast the bonds between form and social life.[2] Yet it is at the intersection of literary and psychoanalytic theory that we come closest to her immediate concerns: where to ask about the 'we' of reading and writing is to ask about the emotions, fantasies and instincts summoned or suspended on the printed page; and where thinking about the creation of 'we' from 'I' (and 'I' from 'we') might compel us to ask another question, with which Graham ends her remarks: 'Can that "we" combat our capacity for destruction and self-destruction?'.[3]

Psychoanalysis has long understood that with the beginning of a 'we' comes the beginning of thought.[4] For the British psychoanalyst and paediatrician, Donald Woods Winnicott (1896–1971), the bond between 'we' and 'I' at the deepest keel of cognition is one of the raisons d'être of psychoanalysis, both as a communal action and a mode of conversation. Throughout his working life, however, Winnicott would return to the problem of just how communal, how equitable, this action can ever really be – or what kind of conversation really goes on between an interpreting analyst and a patient, between interpretation and its objects. It is a problem that runs on a parallel current to Winnicott's ideas on how conversation with the world – how a shared world, we could say – first becomes possible in the life of the infant; how others come to exist for us, beyond what Martin Heidegger, in his late critique of psychoanalysis, called the 'container mind' (Heidegger, 2001, p. 90; p. 227–228). What joins Winnicott's writings on the 'nursing couple' with his vision of the analytic pair is his concern for how a 'we' ever becomes real in the first place – and the sometimes radical consequences when it doesn't.

This essay returns to questions that have long shaped Winnicott's legacy in the literary humanities, the undisputed centrepiece of which is his 'transitional object' and the repertoire of 'transitional phenomena' through which the baby begins to comprehend difference.[5] Beyond infancy and throughout adulthood, the ontological and psychic distinction between 'me' and 'not-me' is a distinction whose precariousness, whose gradations and whose consequences cross from aesthetic and religious experience to the shakier contingencies of social and political life: how we use and talk about the objects of human culture, how we are able (and unable) to agree on their meaningfulness, are questions in Winnicott that understand the tenability of culture in terms of the tenability of relationship. Imagining the kind of object *literature* might be, reflecting on contemporary and future conversations between literature and its interpretation, this essay brings Winnicott's notions of what he calls 'object-relating' into dialogue with his critique of the relationships of interpretation, in which he consistently emphasises relationships of language. What these elements share, and where the one lends itself to a reading of the other, is a tantalising and troubling distinction that Winnicott himself never clearly or finally theorises, and which offers a powerful set of terms for rethinking the interpretive conversations of literary criticism. The terms Winnicott uses, which together form the central axis of this essay, are the object lesson of 'finding' and its would-be counter-experience, the psychic action he calls 'creating'.

Winnicott's roughly drawn account of 'finding' and 'creating' – experiences that, for the child as much as for the psychoanalyst, occupy the tenuous ground between fantasy and action – offers an aesthetics that is far less straightforward than Winnicott's more explicit remarks on culture and the work of art would seem to suggest. A reappraisal of Winnicott's aesthetics in light of his thinking on interpretation and interpretive language is now particularly pressing: the concerns converging in recent years around the written discourses of literary criticism, the established vogue for so-called 'critique', and the vagaries of what Paul Ricoeur famously called the 'hermeneutics of suspicion', have begun to make a problem of the discipline's own interpretive conversations (Ricoeur, 1970). From its deterministic commitment to exposure and narrow affective range, to the seductive appeal of the broad-stroked, forceful intelligibility Eve Kosofsky Sedgwick calls 'strong theory', the problem of 'critique' is something the literary humanities has only recently begun to get to grips with (Sedgwick, 2003, p. 133). Psychoanalysis, on the other hand, has long been conversant with its own unease regarding interpretation, beginning in the dialogues of Sigmund Freud and Sándor Ferenczi, placed securely on the agenda in the Controversial Discussions of the 1940s, and theorised most forcefully in the late work of Jean Laplanche (Ferenczi, 1988; Laplanche, 1996, 1999). While I will not be suggesting that the current pull against critique is a direct legacy of psychoanalysis, I want to propose that Winnicott's accounts of interpretive and early object-relating can, in unexpected ways, help to clarify what kind of object literature might be for those of us whose task is to describe it; what kind of 'we' might be at stake in its reading; what it is in literary works that certain forms of critical reading appear to betray, denature or deny, and what that might say about the contradictory lures and responsibilities of reading literature.

Critique and creative imagination

In her 2003 volume, *Touching Feeling*, Sedgwick makes a case for the overriding 'feeling' of contemporary literary criticism, going one step further than Ricoeur's 'suspicion' by speaking in terms of 'paranoia'. The signature affect of criticism in the wake of deconstruction, 'paranoid reading' has, Sedgwick says, 'limited the gene pool of literary-critical perspectives and skills' (Sedgwick, 2003, p. 144). Yet its distaste for surprise, its surprising disavowal of curiosity, means paranoid reading makes it 'less rather than more possible to unpack the local, contingent relations between any given piece of knowledge and its narrative/epistemological entailments for the seeker, knower or teller' (Ibid., p. 124). What is at stake, Sedgwick suggests, is *possibility* – both vis-à-vis the object of reading and, by extension, in the reader's own self-relation. Invoking possibility again, she notes that the hermeneutics of suspicion is 'widely misunderstood as a mandatory injunction rather than a possibility among other possibilities': suspicion turns possibility into an action that closes down possibilities in its wake (Ibid., p. 125). Sedgwick's language also evokes Ricoeur, who asked of the hermeneutics of psychoanalysis: 'does not this discipline of the real, this ascesis of the necessary, lack the grace of imagination, the upsurge of the possible?' (Ricoeur, 1970, p. 36). Suspicion can unleash deterministic and graceless truths. Finding wherever it seeks, it culls where most it could cultivate.

In the wake of Sedgwick's essay, several critics have linked the culling of possibility to specific argumentative qualities that turn a key legacy of the hermeneutics of suspicion, the practice of 'critique', into a heavy-handed and formulaic operation. Isobel Armstrong homes in on the excision of textual ambiguity, and with it ambiguous emotional states, from the pedagogies and practices of criticism (Armstrong, 2000). Citing a range of rebarbative examples, Lisa Ruddick writes of the determined contemporary vogue for 'deadness or meanness', the normative coldness and cruelty of a critical discourse that leaves its own workings unexamined ('In the name of critique, anything except critique can be invaded or denatured' (Ruddick, 2015, p. 71)). In her influential 2015 work, *The Limits of Critique*, Rita Felski argues that 'suspicious' styles of reading 'can be stultifying, pushing thought down predetermined paths and closing our minds to the play of detail, nuance, quirkiness, contradiction, happenstance'. By these means, Felski says, the critic 'conjures up ever more paralysing scenarios of coercion and control' (Felski, 2015, p. 34). Sedgwick's 'strong theory' is now more than ever being construed as a theory of force; its vehement interest in exposing the object – doing so 'strongly', convincingly – renders such writing indifferent to the object.[6] It is also, by the same token, a theory of *seduction* approximating Ferenczi's sense of the term: a discourse, a tongue, seducing and seduced by its own strength of argument.[7]

Yet if wider calls for a 'post-critical' writing go largely unheeded, it is perhaps because the force of argument is something that continues to satisfy – authors arguably more than readers – and that both force and satisfaction now rank among the highest points of value in critical discourse.[8] While what is and is not of value for literary criticism is a question answerable only by way of literature, the arguments emerging against critique can be understood to express a psychoanalytic problem, a problem to which Winnicott's thinking in particular offers a vivid set of theorisations and imaginative possibilities. Since Freud first theorised the transference, psychoanalysis has been alert to the allure of forceful and compelling interpretive stories. In his clinical diary, Ferenczi accuses Freud of 'artificially provok[ing]' the very transference effect he interprets, by dint of a hermeneutic authority Ferenczi argues should be 'mutual' (Ferenczi, 1988, p. 93). The issue here is not the transference – which we might say is, de facto, both artificial and a provocation – but the question of an unchecked or at least un-confessed hermeneutic authority; as opposed to a subjective centre or 'I' that, in the words of Augustine's famous confession, glaringly psychoanalytic *avant la lettre*, has 'become a problem to [itself]' (Augustine, 1961, p. 239).[9] At the heart of Ferenczi's insistence on openly discussing the transference and countertransference is a belief that the psychoanalytic cure is only a solution – only really cures – if and because it also remains a problem; interpretation can only do its work, he seems to suggest, if the interpretation's authority is in doubt from the start.[10]

Winnicott's attitude to interpretation could not have been clearer. In an essay on 'Interpretation and Psychoanalysis' (1968) he tells us, citing the same impasse as Ferenczi, that 'there are analysts who in their interpretative role assume a position which is almost unassailable so that if the patient attempts to make a correction the analyst tends rather to think in terms of the patient's resistance than in terms of the possibility that the communication has been wrongly or inadequately received' (Winnicott, 1989, p. 208). Winnicott's concern is for the preservation not just of possibility but of a driven interpretive precariousness, reflected in his wariness about cultivating what he calls elsewhere 'an intermediate area in which play can take place, and then inject[ing] into this area or inflat[ing] it with interpretations which in effect are from [his] own *creative* imagination', a wariness that led him to 'retain some outside quality by not being quite on the mark or even by being wrong' (Winnicott, 1971, p. 102; Winnicott, 1965, p. 167). He also observes that 'by the language we use [with a patient] we show our natural interest in [the] matter', which includes the tonal and lexical engagement, perhaps even the mirroring, of one 'language' in another (Winnicott, 1971, p. 104). The language of analysis has a precarious relationship to possibility, including the possibility of relationship itself. This precariousness is linked to the faculty he calls '*creative imagination*', an index in Winnicott both of relationship and – as above – its jeopardy, hence the unilateral and unchecked force implicit in 'injecting'. At stake in interpretation, then, is the preservation of a 'we', an essential element of which is the linguistic and psychic non-reducibility of one to the interpretations of the other; the possibility of resistance that is not already pre-empted, as Jacques Derrida warned, by the interpretation of resistance (Derrida, 1998).

Winnicott's written style has been said to sustain a similar position. Anne Clancier and Jeanine Kalmanovitch suggest that, in keeping with his commitments in the consulting room, '[t]hanks to his creative style, Winnicott provided only part of the organisation of his ideas: the rest he left to the reader to create' (Clancier and Kalmanovitch, 1987, p. 66). We begin to get a sense of the double potentiality of 'creating' and the 'creative': something that can be liberating, vital and above all relational, and a form of aggression that shares traits (self-satisfaction, closure to possibility, non-relation) with the vagaries of suspicion. In the context of his developmental theories, Winnicott's notion of creating is bonded at the deepest level to the experience he calls 'aliveness' in our relationships with the world; yet the experience of creating must eventually touch its own limits, must encounter some resistance, if the reality and aliveness of others is to get a look-in. We might say that some element or experience keeps 'creative imagination' from collapsing into fantasy, a fantasy incapable of perceiving its own edges or, perhaps just momentarily, 'becoming a problem' to itself.[11] In what is an undeniably complex theoretical arrangement in Winnicott – one which does leave much 'creating' to the reader – the condition of possibility for 'creative living' is the same as what ultimately sets limits on it: the complementary experience Winnicott calls '*finding*'.

Found objects

In 'The Location of Cultural Experience' (1967), Winnicott describes 'found' objects in the following terms:

> Yet for the baby (if the mother can supply the right conditions) every detail of the baby's life is an example of creative living. Every object is a 'found' object. Given the chance, the baby begins to live creatively, and to use actual objects to be creative into and with.
>
> (Winnicott, 1971, p. 101)

Recalling the *objet trouvé* of twentieth-century modernism, the 'found' object lends itself to creative appropriation as though lying in wait for it (in Winnicott's terms, 'lying around *waiting* to be found', Winnicott (1965, p. 181)). What this means is that the object must be freely available, permissive in its receipt of associations, and participating in shared reality only to the extent that anyone and everyone can appropriate it too (see Bollas, 1987). Interpretation, we saw, can strive to be similarly accommodating: 'Psychotherapy', Winnicott says, 'is not making clever and apt interpretations; by and large it is a long-term giving the patient back what the patient brings' – a response *in kind*, we could say (Winnicott, 1971, p. 117). The baby whose mother's face mirrors his internal states enjoys a similar sensation of a world 'in rapport' with his projections (ibid., p. 113). And yet in his discussion of the mirror-role of the mother, Winnicott introduces a caveat to the child's 'creation' myth, the belief that he made, and commands, the world: creative capacity is about 'a significant exchange with the world, a two-way process in which self-enrichment alternates with the discovery of meaning in the world of seen things' (ibid.). Replace 'discovery' with 'finding' here and we have the beginnings of the paradox of finding and creating in Winnicott: that the 'finding' of meaning includes the recalibration and refusal (as well as the receipt) of projections, and that, provided the infant first experiences 'creating' her world, this recalibration and refusal is as essential to a tenable 'we' as the primary fantasy of creation. After the infant has 'created' the world, the lesson of finding is a lesson in the reality of others.

One of the first times Winnicott ventures the finding/creating distinction is in his essay 'On Communicating and Not Communicating' (1963).

> In health the infant creates what is in fact lying around waiting to be found. But in health *the object is created, not found*. [...] A good object is no good to the infant unless created by the infant. Shall I say, created out of need? Yet the object must be found in order to be created. This has to be accepted as a paradox, and not solved by a restatement that, by its cleverness, seems to eliminate the paradox.
> (Winnicott, 1965, p. 181)

At this point, Winnicott's terms appear to collapse in on one another in a paradox he tells us not to do anything with. The object must be created by the infant, yet the object must be found in order to be created; the fantasy of creation is made possible by – and experienced as simultaneous with – the reality of finding something already created, an unconscious Freudian fort/da game in which the reel is, let's say, both 'gone' and 'there!' at once. Winnicott's knotty little paradox bears a striking correspondence to the etymology of 'finding': the verb *invenire* is the root of 'to find' as well as 'to invent'; the twin experiences co-depend, as at the level of fantasy, to the point of collapse.[12] Yet where 'found' objects are a pretext for their creation by the infant, they are also a gentle rebuttal of his private 'creation' myth: created, *not* found, or found to be *not created* by the infant. A 'found' object can signify subjective availability but it can also belong to the category of phenomena that pertain to 'shared reality', a reality established as such by its refusal and recalibration of creative projections – or as Winnicott says elsewhere, by 'get [ting] in the way' (crucially, the infant's own experience of '*not being found*', his own power of refusal, is of equal, if not greater, importance in establishing his stake in 'shared reality', see Winnicott (1965, p. 211)). The experience of availability (or 'object-relating', as Winnicott calls it) 'can be described in terms of the subject as an isolate'. What marks the shift to what he calls 'object *use*' is the addition of 'features that involve the nature and behaviour of the object,' which 'must necessarily be real in the sense of being a part of shared reality, not a bundle of projections [...] but as a thing in itself', of which Winnicott emphasises 'the object's independent existence, its property of having been there all the time' (Winnicott, 1971, p. 88).

It is this quality of realness as established by 'finding' – by something 'in the way', real 'in the sense of being a part of shared reality' – that comes to bear on the question of literary interpretation: its conversation with the work of literature, the operations of force and fantasy in that conversation, and, as Winnicott described in the case of his patients, its affective consequences for readers and interlocutors in whose 'we' the work of language participates. As a hermeneutic object, language sets some basic terms of its own. A 'found' object par excellence, language is happened-upon in a shared, public world, belonging to the other in ways that recall and repeat its early acquisition by the child; this re-discovery is an inexhaustible pretext for invention that, at the same time, continually undermines the unconscious fantasy of creation. Like Winnicott's transitional object, language allows both infant and adult to 'weave other-than-me objects into the personal pattern' (Winnicott, 1971, p. 3). In Julia Kristeva's memorable tableau, language is gifted to the child by others whose own autonomy it comes to symbolise as well as endlessly re-enact: the child's belief in language is a leap of faith that matches and meets – while also inevitably falling short of – his belief in the existence of others (Kristeva, 2009).[13] Repeating this original misrecognition and the faith it gives rise to, the gift of language for the linguistic individual is defined, at least in part, by its irreducibility to both the giver and receiver of the gift: by its forms of 'autonomy and life', by its shifting and widening public sphere, by its 'property of having been there all the time'. Its universalising capacity to pertain, to *belong*, both permits creativity and prohibits totalising 'creation'.

If language is always already 'found', then what does it matter if interpretive discourses have become more interested in 'creating' the work of literature than in finding and re-finding its operations; more taken by what confirms their suspicions than by what, in diffuse or precise forms, continues to elude them? One of the vocations of literature – and contemporary literature in particular, perhaps – has been to showcase and magnify the paradoxes and double binds of language, at the heart of which is the dilemma of autonomy and belonging, finding and creating. Considering the case of literature and what the 'finding' of language might mean for interpretation and criticism, I return now to Winnicott and to the complex emotional drama underpinning the finding of objects beyond our control.

Love, destruction and the case of literature

In 'The Use of an Object' (1969) Winnicott outlines how, just as the baby depends on his mother's responsiveness in order to feel real, so that real or 'true self' (as Winnicott calls it) becomes a social self among equally real others through the mother's survival of his aggression – his response, that is, to the small sparks of dissent, the everyday non-compliances, that introduce him to a non-creatable other. It is a movement, Adam Phillips has said, 'from seeing himself through the other, to seeing the other' (Phillips, 1988, p. 130). Its denouement arrives as follows:

> after "subject relates to object" comes "subject destroys object" (as it becomes external); and then there may come "object survives destruction by the subject." But there may or may not be survival. A new feature thus arrives in the theory of object-relating. The subject says to the object: [...] "Hullo object!" "I destroyed you." "I love you." "You have value for me because of your survival of my destruction of you." "While I am loving you I am all the time destroying you in (unconscious) *fantasy.*" Here fantasy begins for the individual. The subject can now *use* the object that has survived.
>
> (Winnicott, 1971, p. 90)

Perhaps the most important lesson in Winnicott's vignette of object love is that it is not only the object's reality that is at stake in its survival (or not) of unconscious fantasy. What is also at stake is its 'value for me' – 'You have value for me *because* of your survival of my destruction of you'. The experience is marked by the same collapsed causality we saw in 'finding' and 'creating' objects: 'destroyed because real, becoming real because destroyed (being destructible and expendable)'. The price of this reality must be paid, Winnicott says, 'in acceptance of the ongoing destruction in (unconscious) *fantasy*' (Ibid.).

When we say a work of literature has 'value for me', might we think about literary value as bound up in a similar dilemma? What might it mean for an act of language (in or as literature) to 'survive' us? If love of an object includes – and, for psychoanalysis, always involves – a destructive wish, then, Winnicott's logic goes, that destructiveness can only be felt because the object is capable of surviving it. At the kernel of this logic is an admission that loving is only possible if and because its object survives. The price of loving literature might, finally, be the paranoid and punitive impulses of critique, expressions of the darker hues of human psychic life; yet the lesson of Winnicott's genealogy of human 'value' is that the highest point of such value, and the very genesis of object love, is the experience of the object's excess, resistance and survival of our uses, the refusal of an unconscious wish to create it in our image.

Winnicott's stated views on art, it should be noted, pull strongly against these ideas. In his brief formulations on the artwork, Winnicott hands it over wholesale to the realm of subjectivity and to an untroubled fantasy of creation: 'I enjoy it because I say I created it [...] This is mad, but in our cultural life we accept the madness' (Winnicott, 1989, p. 57–58). He adds the following justifications: 'the fact is that an external object has no being for you or me except in so far as you or I hallucinate it' and 'it is only what you create that has meaning for you' (ibid., p. 54; Winnicott, 1987, p. 95). In the realm of aesthetics, we might be led to believe, we have no use for – perhaps even no possibility of – the object lesson of finding; art is only meaningful insofar as it placates what Leo Bersani and Ulysse Dutoit call 'appreciatively appropriating subjects' (Bersani and Dutoit, 1993, p. 5).

On the subject of poetry, however, Winnicott seems to have other ideas. Referring to a patient's 'great interest in poetry', Winnicott notes that 'fantasying was about a certain subject and it was a dead end. *It had no poetic value*' (the italics are Winnicott's, 1971, p. 35). In his numerous remarks on poetry and poems, Winnicott evokes a phenomenon defined by its evasion of capture and categorisation, a cultivated excess of its own expressed form; he links these qualities to the sovereign singularity of the patient's language, which the language of interpretation should attempt to preserve (Coles, 2014). Yet returning to Winnicott's remarks on 'survival' (which implicitly equate what has not been created by the infant with what he is unable to 'destroy'), there are other elements to be considered vis-à-vis poetics. Poetry in the late twentieth and early twenty-first centuries has come to rely increasingly on haphazard operations, material and non-material elements that challenge the kind of object literature can be understood to be. Contemporary poets such as Anne Carson, Susan Howe, Tom Raworth and Mary Ruefle, among others, play with the contradictory allegiances of sound and text, multiple drafts and versions, errata, erasure and randomisation (the generation of 'found' lineation using a random integer generator, a twenty-first-century incarnation of 'potential literature').[14] The normalisation of copying, citation and other forms of appropriation alongside more traditional expressions of literary creativity, while a challenge to established notions of authorship, deliberately multiplies the experience of 'finding': the singular, single-authored work quickly announces itself (or allows itself to be discovered) as anything but that, amalgamating source texts, readings and revisions in the same literary object.[15] In the case of live and recorded readings, performance introduces other unpredictable elements to verse, prose and other literary installations relying on the contingencies of physical and vocal presence. Performance aesthetics pose a unique challenge to the experience of literature as an object to be 'hallucinated' by bringing speakers' real time into the equation, or by including multiple media and haphazard elements that diffuse, contradict or sabotage the narrative possibilities of vocal action on-stage.[16]

Literature has always been exposed to agencies beyond the provisional, fantasised 'we' of author and reader, from the accidents and presences of voice and staging, to the material and political circumstances of its production. The keenness of some contemporary literature to make a feature out of these contingencies only ratchets up the challenge for readers and makes the hermeneutics of suspicion look sorely at a loss. Yet such elements also remind us that the emotions of frustration, destruction, bewilderment and love are not only high-points of literary value and attachment. They can also be the confessional centre – rather than the unacknowledged centre of gravity – of *criticism*: interpretation that makes a problem out of its own desire, that confesses and enjoys where the object strays from, refuses or 'gets in the way' of its designs.

Returning finally to language, and in contrast to his remarks on the work of art, Winnicott seems to find the experience of being played and controlled by words both compelling and tantalising. Describing the workings of his own theoretical vocabulary, he makes the following mercurial observation, ascribing to language a capacity for realness that situates it deep in the 'found' world:

> we can use words as we like, especially artificial words like counter-transference. A word like "self" naturally knows more than we do; it uses us and can command us.
>
> (Winnicott, 1965, p. 158)

Some words or some quality of words, he hints, cannot be 'created'. Frustrating our attempts to command them, surviving our desired destruction, appropriation or suppression of their autonomy, they occupy the open field of 'shared reality'. The point is not that words or even particular formations of words agree or disagree, so to speak, with our uses of them. The point is the value we place on their 'found' forms of life, on our individual and cultural attachments to where they belong, by turns frustratingly and thrillingly, to others.

In the interview quoted at the start of this essay, Jorie Graham has more to say on the relationships of reading, saying of poems specifically that they 'don't want to make the reader "agree". They don't want to move through the head in that way. They want to go from body to body' (Graham, 2003). Such a movement includes any number of bodies, voices and timbres, through public 'madness' and private dissent, through words that have 'been there' – and that continue to be sounded – 'all the time'.[17] Love need not exclude such discord any more than loving literature depends on the production of agreement. Perhaps it lies in finding literature, losing it, and finding it again elsewhere.

Acknowledgements

This essay is dedicated to Marina Voikhanskaya.

This project has received funding from the European Union's Horizon 2020 research and innovation programme under the Marie Sklodowska-Curie grant agreement No 887344.

Notes

1 Graham (2003).
2 See James (2015) on 'the social lives of form', a review of three recent studies addressing the complex and contingent relations between literary, social, and political forms. Among the works reviewed by James is Derek Attridge's *The Work of Literature* (Attridge, 2015), which argues that any examination of literature's social and political efficacies must engage with the 'affective and somatic as well as [...] intellectual' experience of texts, whose meaning is bound to the bodily 'event' of their reading (p. 7).
3 For example, Blasing (2007) has written on the 'public, emotional power of language' as the guarantor of the private lyric 'I'. In Blasing's psychoanalytically oriented account, 'an individuated speaker is heard in a language that foregrounds the materiality of the linguistic code and resists an individual will' (p. 28): the lyric 'I' is a creation of the linguistic 'we'.
4 See Sigmund Freud's essay 'Negation' (1925) in Freud (1961), p. 253, and Wilfred Bion's essay 'Theory of thinking' (1961) in Bion (1967) for discussions of how hunger and other examples of lack set in motion the capacity for abstract thought.
5 The establishment of this reading of Winincott comes in the wake of Adrian Stokes' influential account of post-Kleinian visual aesthetics, in which the artwork receives and contains projected impulses (see Harris Williams, 2014). Winnicott's terms appear in his landmark essay 'Transitional Objects and Transitional Phenomena' (Winnicott, 1971, pp. 1–25).
6 See Marielle Macé's account of the emotional economy of reading, what she calls a 'pas de deux' in which empathy, embodied experience and even estrangement are only falsely separable from hermeneutics (Macé, 2011, p. 190).
7 See Coles (2014), pp. 65–71.
8 E.g. Hoy (2004) and Ulmer (2002), pp. 83–110. See also Anker and Felski (2017 pp. 5–7.).
9 This of course anticipates the project of deconstruction with regard to interpretation, a project that shares its own non self-centred subject with Lacanian psychoanalysis. Jacques Derrida's 'circumfession', in the autobiography co-written with Geoffrey Bennington, plays on the original self-problematising spirit of Augustine's *Confessions* (Bennington and Derrida, 1993).
10 There is a long tradition of critiquing interpretation in psychoanalysis, including but not limited to: E. Balint (1968), M. Balint (1968), Khan (1974), Lomas (1987), Bollas (1989), pp. 77–116; Bollas (2007).
11 Discussing what he also calls 'creative imagination', the philosopher and theologian Henri Corbin offers a similar distinction, placing fantasy ('an exercise of thought without foundation in nature') on the side of 'madness' (Corbin, 1969, p. 179).
12 Thanks are due to Amador Vega for bringing this shared etymology to my attention.
13 Shoshana Felman, perhaps in tension with Winnicott, has called interpretation a 'gift of language' (Felman, 1987, p. 119).
14 See e.g. Carson (2013) and 'By chance the Cycladic people' in Carson (2016) for two examples of Carson's use of randomisation software (e.g. https://www.random.org/integers/ accessed 18.09.2017) to produce accidental lineation and formatting. For examples of the deliberate use of errata and erasure in contemporary poetry, see Howe (1990), Raworth (1996), and Ruefle (2006). See also Levin Becker (2012) for a ludic account of 'literature in the conditional mood' in the wake of the Oulipo group.
15 For discussions of literary appropriation, see Goldsmith (Goldsmith, 2011, pp. 109–124) and Perloff (2012).

16 For example: performances of Anne Carson's 'Possessive used as drink (me): a lecture on pronouns in the form of 15 sonnets' (2006), excerpts from which are published in *London Review of Books*, Vol. 32, No. 19, 7 October 2010, and No. 21, 4 November, 2010, and can be viewed at: http://playgallery.org/video/recipe/ (accessed 20.09.2017).
17 For a nuanced consideration of the public and social residues of the lyric 'I,' see Blasing (2007).

Bibliography

Anker, E. S. and R. Felski (2017) *(eds) Critique and postcritique*. Durham and London: Duke University Press.
Armstrong, I. (2000) *The radical aesthetic*. Oxford: Blackwell.
Attridge, D. (2017) *The work of literature*. Oxford: Oxford University Press.
Augustine, Saint (1961) *Confessions*, trans. R. S. Pine-Coffin. Harmondsworth: Penguin.
Balint, E. (1968) *Before I was I: psychoanalysis and the imagination*, ed. J. Mitchell and M. Parsons. London: Free Association Books.
Balint, M. (1968) *The basic fault: therapeutic aspects of regression*. London: Tavistock Publications.
Bennington, G. and J. Derrida (1993) *Jacques Derrida*, trans. Geoffrey Bennington. Chicago: University of Chicago Press.
Bersani, L., and U. Dutoit (1993) *Arts of impoverishment: Beckett, Rothko, Resnais*. Cambridge, Mass.: Harvard University Press.
Bion, W. (1967) *Second thoughts*. London: Heinemann.
Blasing, M. K. (2007) *Lyric poetry: the pain and the pleasure of words*. New Jersey: Princeton University Press.
Bollas, C. (1987) *The shadow of the object: psychoanalysis of the unthought known*. London: Free Association Books.
Bollas, C. (1989) *Forces of destiny: psychoanalysis and human idiom*. London: Free Association Books.
Bollas, C. (2007) *The Freudian moment*. London: Karnac Books.
Carson, A. (2013) *Red doc*. London: Jonathan Cape.
Carson, A. (2016) *Float*. London: Jonathan Cape.
Clancier, A., and J. Kalmanovitch (1987) *Winnicott and paradox: from birth to creation*, trans. A. Sheridan. London: Tavistock Publications.
Coles, E. (2014) 'Psychoanalysis and the poem: on reading in Sándor Ferenczi and D. W. Winnicott', *New Formations* 83, 64–78.
Corbin, H. (1969) *Alone with the alone: creative imagination in the Sufism of Ibn 'Arabi* (1958), trans. R. Manheim. Princeton: Princeton University Press.
Derrida, J. (1998) *Resistances of psychoanalysis* (1996), trans. P. Kamuf. Palo Alto: Stanford University Press.
Felman, S. (1987) *Jacques Lacan and the adventure of insight: psychoanalysis in contemporary culture*. Cambridge, Mass.: Harvard University Press.
Felski, R. (2015) *The limits of critique*. Chicago: University of Chicago Press.
Ferenczi, S. (1988) *The clinical diary of Sándor Ferenczi* (1932), ed. J. Dupont, trans. M. Balint and N. Z. Jackson. Cambridge, Mass.: Harvard University Press.

Freud, S. (1961) 'Negation' and 'The ego and the id'. In *The standard edition of the complete psychological works of Sigmund Freud*, ed. J. Strachey; trans. J. Strachey and A. Freud, with A. Strachey and A. Tyson, London: The Hogarth Press and the Institute of Psychoanalysis, 24 vols., vol. XIX.

Goldsmith, K. (2011) *Un-creative writing: managing language in the digital age*. New York: Columbia University Press.

Graham, J. (2003) 'The art of poetry No. 85', interview by T. Gardner, *The Paris Review*, Spring 2003, no. 165.

Harris Williams, M., (2014) *(ed.) Art and analysis: an Adrian Stokes reader*. London: Karnac Books.

Heidegger, M. (2001) *Zollikon seminars: protocols – conversations – letters*, ed. M. Boss, trans. F. Mayr and R. Askay. Evanston: Northwestern University Press.

Howe, S. (1990) *Singularities*. Middletown, CT: Wesleyan University Press.

Hoy, D. C. (2004) *Critical resistance: from poststructuralism to post-critique*. Cambridge: MIT Press.

James, D. (2015) 'The social lives of form', *Public Books*, 10 January 2015.

Khan, M. R. (1974), *The privacy of the self*. London: The Hogarth Press.

Kristeva, J. (2009) *This incredible need to believe* (2007), trans. B. B. Brahic. New York: Columbia University Press.

Laplanche, J. (1996) 'Psychoanalysis as anti-hermeneutics', *Radical Philosophy* 79.

Laplanche, J. (1999) 'Interpretation between determinism and hermeneutics'. In J. Fletcher (ed.), *Essays on otherness*, trans. L. Thurston. London: Routledge.

Levin Becker, D. (2012) *Many subtle channels: in praise of potential literature*. Cambridge, Mass.: Harvard University Press.

Lomas, P. (1987) *The limits of interpretation*. London: Penguin Books.

Macé, M. (2011) *Façons de lire, manières d'être*. Paris: Gallimard.

Perloff, M. (2012) *Unoriginal genius: poetry by other means in the new century*. Chicago: University of Chicago Press.

Phillips, A. (1988) *Winnicott*. London: Fontana Press.

Raworth, T. (1996) *Clean and well lit: selected poems 1987–1995*. New York: Roof Books.

Ricoeur, P. (1970) *Freud and philosophy: an essay on interpretation* (1965), trans. D. Savage. New Haven: Yale University Press.

Ruddick, L. (2015) 'When nothing is cool'. In A. Bammer and R-E. Boetcher Joeres (eds.) *The future of scholarly writing*. New York: Palgrave Macmillan.

Ruefle, M. (2006) *A little white shadow*. Seattle: Wave Books.

Sedgwick, E. K. (2003) *Touching feeling: affect, pedagogy, performativity*. Durham: Duke University Press.

Ulmer, G. (2002) 'The object of post criticism'. In H. Foster (ed.) *The anti-aesthetic: essays on postmodern culture*. New York: New Press.

Winnicott, D. W. (1965) *The maturational processes and the facilitating environment*. London: The Hogarth Press.

Winnicott, D. W. (1987) *Babies and their mothers*, ed. C. Winnicott, R. Shepherd and M. Davis. Cambridge, Mass.: Perseus Publishing.

Winnicott, D. W. (1989) *Psycho-analytic explorations*, ed. C. Winnicottet al. Cambridge, Mass.: Harvard University Press.

Winnicott, D. W. (1971) *Playing and reality*. London: Tavistock Publications.

Chapter 2

Project for a scientific psychology
The impossibility of a text

Manuel Batsch

Introduction: an epistemological coup

In the 1990s the endeavour to ground psychoanalysis in neuroscience pushed a group of psychoanalysts and neuroscientists to institute their research around a new discipline that they called neuro-psychoanalysis. The study of the relationship between psychoanalysis and neuroscience pre-existed the emergence of neuro-psychoanalysis. By giving a formal frame to their field, the aim of the neuro-psychoanalytic movement was more specifically to translate the psychic apparatus into an observable neural apparatus in order to integrate psychoanalysis into neuroscientific research on subjectivity. In other words, the neuro-psychoanalytic agenda can be understood as a sort of epistemological coup by which psychoanalysis would become a branch of neuroscience and more specifically of a neuroscientific approach to subjectivity. The very term 'neuro-psychoanalysis', in placing the neurone before the psyche, seems to attest to a desire to subject the psychical to the neuronal.[1]

The effort to legitimise or to challenge the attempted takeover of metapsychology by neuro-psychoanalysis has given rise to a resurgence of interest in Freud's pre-analytic neurological writings. The upholders of neuro-psychoanalysis have been trying to situate the true origins of Freud's intellectual journey not in the clinic, where Freud treated his hysterical patients, but in the neurological laboratory. From this angle, I want to suggest that Freud's 'Project for a Scientific Psychology' (hereafter the Project) (Freud, 1950[1895]) is a pivotal text because it articulates a neurological model of the mind and a clinical explanation of hysteria. To my mind the Project is also crucial because, despite being so central to the controversy surrounding the continuity between Freud's neurological and psychological periods, it remains a thorn in the side of both the followers and adversaries of neuro-psychoanalysis. It is precisely this aspect of the Project that I want to explore here: a text indigestible and un-exploitable for the sake of an epistemological argument about Freud. I describe the Project as an impossible text because it is at the juncture between neurology and psychology,

DOI: 10.4324/9781003200765-3

between causality of brain functioning and the teleology of the symptom's meaning, and yet it resists being integrated to any of these categories. The Project is neither a physiological model nor an account of hysteria; rather, it is a writing in which hysteria storms into the vocabulary of neurology.

The impossibility of the Project manifests itself most obviously in Freud's refusal to publish it. Starting from this point, I will argue that far from being a failure, Freud's abjuration of his manuscript marked the invention of metapsychology as a new category of theoretical texts characterised by their incompleteness. My main intention here is to show that Freud's Project reveals late-nineteenth-century scientific writing to be in conflict with Freud's increasing recognition of an unconscious mode of thinking. This interpretation is in contrast with a neuro-psychoanalytic reading, which I argue aims to expel hysteria from metapsychology in order to transform it into a form of discourse more readily assimilable by neuroscience.

'A kind of madness'

Why did Freud abandon the writing of the draft that was published posthumously in Strachey's *Standard Edition* under the title of 'Project for a Scientific Psychology'?

The Project is an epistolary text that appeared in Freud's letters to Fliess. The trace of its genesis and its abandonment can therefore be followed in these letters. On 27 April 1895, Freud wrote that he was 'caught up in The Psychology for Neurologists' and that he had 'never before experienced such a high degree of preoccupation' (in Masson, 1985, p. 127). On 8 October 1895, Freud sent the two first parts of a draft that he had written at the speed of the train that had brought him back from Berlin to Vienna, carried away by the enthusiasm of one of his 'conferences' with Fliess. The fruit of intense intellectual research, sustained by the use of cocaine, the Project soon became, in Freud's eyes, an aberration. On 29 November 1895, Freud described renouncing the draft to Fliess:

> I no longer understand the state of mind in which I hatched the psychology; cannot conceive how I could have inflicted it on you. I believe you are still too polite; to me it appears to have been a kind of madness.
>
> (Ibid., p. 152)

It seems that readers of the Project can easily share the impression of 'madness' that Freud attributed to his own endeavour. Indeed, many commentators have pointed out the strangeness or the almost abnormal difficulty of this text. Jean Laplanche wrote of the 'uneasiness of the contemporary reader' who 'begins wondering whether he has not been swallowed up by some monstrous pseudo-scientific machine' (Laplanche, 1976[1970], p. 31). In his introduction, Ernst Kris stressed the difficulty of the Project (Kris, 1954, p. 27). Isabel Knight described the 'embarrassment' of 'psychoanalytic traditionalists' and the uneasiness of 'humanist sympathizers' in the face of 'a document at once so dense and so cryptic' (Knight, 1984, p. 340).

The strangeness generated by the reading of this text derives partly from its formalism, which can appear out of date. This anachronism plays at two levels. Commentaries on these two types of anachronisms have established two main justifications for Freud's renunciation of the Project. The first is that the neurological machinery imagined by Freud rests on the scientific theories of his time. Freud's intention, expressed at the very beginning of the Project: 'to furnish a psychology that shall be a natural science' (Freud, 1950[1895], p. 295), inscribes the text in the physiological perspective of the Helmholtz school. The 'oath' of this positivist movement that developed from the 1860s onwards in German-speaking universities, was summarised by Du Bois-Reymond as 'to put in power this truth: No other forces than the common physical chemical ones are active within the organism' (Du Bois-Reymond, 1927). Thus, the Project combines an energetic approach with the anatomical discovery of the neurone that had just been introduced by Waldeyer in 1891.

The anachronism of the scientific knowledge on which Freud developed his text is at the root of the first justification for the failure of the Project:

> Freud had realised that the current state of neuroscientific knowledge was such in 1895 that his physiological and anatomical speculations were in fact *pseudo*scientific explanations and –ironically – that he was on far more solid ground scientifically if he confined himself to a *psychological* language.
>
> (Solms, 1998, p. 7)

This could be named the 'positivist explanation'. It supposes that if, at the time of Freud, the limitations of the neuropsychology justified abandoning the Project, the progress of neuroscience would make the working of the mind accessible to physical methods.

In other words, there is nothing necessary in the impossibility of the Project; it is, on the contrary, just a matter of timing: one day the advancements of neuroscience would overcome this impossibility. The hypothesis put forward by Mark Solms and more generally by the neuro-psychoanalytic movement is that such a day has now arrived: the 'neuroscience of the mind has developed to such an extent in the decades since Freud's death in 1939 that the situation that he confronted in 1895 has now reversed itself' (Solms, 1998, p. 9). Thus neuro-psychoanalysis presents itself as the continuation of Freud's Project and claims this after a century of confinement to natural sciences.

The second anachronism within Freud's work is the sense that the Project is a pre-analytic draft and that at this stage Freud's models were more physiological and neurological than psychological. It is this impression that Janet Malcom expressed when she described the Project as Freud's 'strenuous, doomed effort to give a physiological source to the psychological phenomena he was discovering' (Malcom, 1981, p. 26). In his introduction to *The Interpretation of Dreams*, James Strachey expressed a similar opinion: describing the Project as a set of 'elaborate physiological explanations', Strachey described how, as time passed, Freud's 'interest was gradually diverted from neurological and theoretical on to psychological and clinical problems' (Strachey, 1953, p. xviii). Isabel Knight has described this view as the 'orthodox opinion' of Freud's Project (Knight, 1984, p. 355, n. 2).

Such a reading of the Project as a somehow 'pre-Freudian' text leads to the second justification for the abandonment of the draft, this being the idea that the study of the psyche exceeds the frame of naturalistic science: 'the *Project* stands as the greatest effort Freud ever made to force a mass of psychical facts within the framework of a quantitative theory, and as the demonstration by way of the absurd that the content exceeds the frame' (Ricœur, 1970[1965], p. 73). This idea could be called the hermeneutic reading because it argues that only an interpretative framework can account for subjective facts. Like the positivist standpoint, it identifies that the objects studied in the text exceed the conceptual framework through which they are described. However, unlike the positivist view, the hermeneutic reading supposes that no degree of progress in neuroscience could compensate for it. In other words, and paraphrasing the title of one of Paul Ricoeur's chapters, the impossibility of the Project is the impossibility of 'an energetics without hermeneutics' (Ibid., p. 69).

The difficulty for Freud's positivist commentators arises from their need to justify Freud's departure from the language of naturalistic science. Against their view, I think that this departure is not only due to the limitation of nineteenth-century neuroscience. Moreover, I defend the idea that, already in the Project, Freud 'both preserves and overthrows the language of naturalistic sciences' (Friedman and Alexander, 1983, p. 304). Indeed, under the guise of the energetic and neuronal model developed in the Project, Freud's metapsychology already begins to appear in this text. To use Paul-Laurent Assoun's formulation: 'the neuronal model developed here is already transformed into a metapsychology' (Assoun, 2009 p. 502, my translation).[2]

The uneasiness of the hermeneutic commentators towards this text is due to the fact that it forces them to acknowledge the biological heritage of Freud's theory and, as such, they are tempted to reject it from the Freudian corpus, as if Freud's giving it up were evidence that the Project was a theoretical dead end. Against this view, I propose that the impossibility of the Project is a fertile impossibility. It could be said that Freud's main discovery in writing this draft was its very impossibility: the discovery that some empirical psychological phenomena resist any conceptual formalisation. Freud's metapsychology would be a continual attempt to describe those phenomena; as such, the Project in its impossibility can be read as a precursor of the whole metapsychological research.

I would like to offer a third explanation for Freud's abandonment of the Project. Unlike the neuro-psychoanalytic perspective that posits the central problem raised by the Project as 'the nature of the relationship between the brain and the mind' (Solms, 1998, p. 1), I read it as an attempt to formalise the functioning of memory as it appears in the clinic of hysterical patients. Following Jacques Derrida's commentary on Freud's text, I will try to resituate Freud's abandonment of the Project in a larger intellectual history, in which rational approaches studied objects that could not be apprehended through the grid of empirical observations or meanings. In the case of Freud, this object is the functioning of memory in hysteria. I propose that what is at stake in Freud's Project is not so much the creation of a model of the mind but more importantly a description of the kinds of memories that cause hysteria. Hence, the strangeness triggered by the reading of the Project might come not only from its anachronism but also more fundamentally from the strangeness of the memories it tries to describe – or more precisely from the fact that those memories resist formalisation: an awkwardness of scientific language in the face of hysteria.

A memory without objects

To read the Project as an attempt to formalise memory, it is necessary to return to Jacques Derrida's comprehension of the text. Derrida perceived that the model of memory exposed in the Project 'is remarkable as soon as it is considered as a metaphorical model and not as a neurological description' (Derrida, 1978[1967], p. 252). Remarkable because its prototype is 'borrowed not from spoken language or from verbal forms, nor even from phonetic writing, but from a script which is never subject to, never exterior and posterior to, the spoken word' (Ibid., p. 249). In the Project, Freud describes memory as an interplay of differences existing between neurones. This metaphor suggests a form of writing that 'makes what we believe we know under the name of writing enigmatic' (Ibid., p. 250). This writing is enigmatic because it is made of traces.

Derrida sought to distinguish between the sign and the trace. He understood the sign to be the element of a nomenclature: an object that classifies meaning and which is observable in itself, in its essence. The essence of the trace, on the other hand, cannot be exposed because it finds its origin in differences: the trace appears in the differences between objects. The nature of these objects, in which the trace becomes manifest is almost contingent and secondary. In Derrida's reading of the Project, the neurone corresponds to the sign. The neurone can be observed under the microscope as an empirical reality. The trace however can never be observed because it is made of the difference between the activated neurones. Without differences in the way neurones are activated, memory would be paralysed. It is the difference 'which is the true origin of memory, and thus of the psyche' (Derrida, 1978[1967], p. 252).[3] Thus, Derrida's reading of the Project shows a model of mental life in which memory is not formed of empirical objects. It is not an archival storage facility as it is not the qualitative memory that is described in the Project, but a contrivance capable of registering differences. In reality, it would be the whole psyche that confronts us with non-empirical objects since memory 'is not a psychical property among others; it is the very essence of the psyche' (Derrida, 1978[1967], p. 252).

This reading has a fundamental and somehow ironic consequence: in his attempt to furnish a natural science for the study of mental life, Freud discovered a description of the psyche that escaped natural science: instead of an anatomical chart (or any form of observable nomenclature), a script of absences. When Freud turned the positivist light on in the darkroom of the psyche, the ghost of the trace had already escaped the room. The fact that the description of the mind led to a non-empirical 'psychical writing' constitutes, I believe, the first great innovation of the Project.

Derrida's reading of the Project led him to argue that in a peripheral but persistent way, Freud had conceived memory as a form of writing with no points of origin. This view is intellectually stimulating but I believe it neglects the clinical significance of Freud's Project and ultimately it brings us back to a hermeneutic reading of the text. If as I have been trying to argue, the Project is an impossible text – by which I mean a text that resists both a hermeneutic and a positivist reading – it is I think owing to the knot it makes with the clinic of hysteria. In the next part of this essay I will explain how Freud's account of hysterical memories reveals the true sense of memory as psychic writing. A form of writing that does not account for the subject's behaviour and that is not a text waiting to be interpreted. The metaphor of memory with a form of writing offers an image of memory as a series of potentialities that manifest themselves through effects of meaning at times incomplete and at times excessive.

Transcendental lies

The description of memory as psychical writing helps us to understand the clinic of hysteria and in particular the way hysterical memories are deceived by sexuality. In the second part of the Project, Freud tries to understand the nature of those hysterical memories that escape the control of the ego. According to him, what characterises these reminiscences is sexuality. Some sexual reminiscences get around the ego defence mechanisms and trigger in the mental apparatus pathological defences, in other words *symptoms*. Amongst the ideas that produce a distressing affect in the ego, only sexual ideas seem to have the power to generate neurotic symptoms. What is the nature of this power contained in some sexual memories? To answer this question, Freud proposed the theory of the proton pseudos.

According to James Strachey, the term proton pseudos

> occurs in Aristotle's *Prior Analytics* (...), a work dealing with the theory of the syllogism which was later included in what came to be called the *Organon*. The chapter deals with false premises and false conclusions, and

the particular sentence asserts that a false statement is the result of a preceding falsity ("*proton pseudos*").

(Strachey, 1966, p. 352, n. 1)

Ola Andersson has shown that even though he had borrowed the term from Max Herz's 'critical psychiatry', Freud had not been influenced by Herz's views (Andersson, 1962, pp. 196–197).

Proton pseudos could be translated from the Greek as 'first lies'. Andersson proposed that the 'lie' was an indication of 'the "false connection" occurring between the affective state of the hysteric and the "symbol" when a "sexual idea" had been "repressed"' (Ibid., p. 196). Indeed, at first glance the clinical exploration of hysteria showed that the connection between an idea and an affect appeared '(1) *unintelligible*, (2) *incapable of being resolved by the activity of thought*, (3) *incongruous*' (Freud, 1950[1895], p. 348). Freud's famous stroke of genius was to reveal, in the face of scientific prejudices, that what seemed *unintelligible* and *incongruous* – like the dream or the hysterical symptom – had its own logic, the logic of the primary process. Hence, the logic of the hysterical memory would be one of displacement.

What excludes the hysterical memory from the secondary process, and therefore from the '*process of thought*', is 'the special psychical determinant from natural characteristic of sexuality' (Ibid., p. 353). This natural characteristic of sexuality is the retardation of puberty. When he wrote the Project, Freud had not yet theorised infantile sexuality and so he assumed that 'no sexual experiences produce any effect so long as the subject is ignorant of all sexual feeling – in general, that is, till the beginning of puberty' (Ibid., p. 333). In such a way that after puberty a sexual memory 'arouses an affect which it did not give rise to as an experience' (Ibid., p. 356). That some memories contain a hidden sexual charge constitutes the essence of the hysteric lie. On 15 October 1895, Freud had 'revealed' to Fliess this 'great clinical secret': 'Hysteria is the consequence of a presexual *sexual shock*' (Masson, 1985, p. 144). The proton pseudos is a sexual Trojan horse that deceives the control of the ego: ideas that 'unexpectedly release unpleasure, and the ego only discovers this too late. It has permitted a primary process because it did not expect one' (Freud, 1950[1895], p. 358). The power of the proton pseudos comes from the fact that they release a sexual affect similar to the one of an actual experience: the ego is not capable of distinguishing between what is perceived and what is hallucinated. Hence, the terrifying situation of the hysteric would be that ideas imprisoned in her inner life act as an external sexual assailant.

A way to understand the fact that Freud characterised the hysterical sexual memory as *proton*, as a *first*, could be that it is the *primary* process which produces those memories. Ideas produced by a primal mode of thinking disturb the process of thought. The hysteric is like a somnambulist whose waking thoughts are invaded by dream images: ideas of a hallucinatory kind barge in, in the middle of verbal ideas.[4] As the proton pseudos are excluded from the process of thought, they are ideas that are not thought but enacted. With the proton pseudos, Freud described ideas whose meaning escapes the mind but that are instead acted through the body, which becomes the scene of the hysteric's private theatre.

Precisely because of this theatricality of the symptom, hysterics have been accused of faking. The other side of the same idea was to present hysteria as the only possible protest against patriarchy (Showalter, 1987). In fact from the angle of the hysterical proton pseudos, the first victim of the hysterical lie, or the one to whom the protests are addressed, is the hysteric herself. The proton pseudos is not a subjective lie but, as noted by Jean Laplanche, what is 'at stake is a transition from the subjective to a grounding – perhaps even to a transcendental – dimension: in any event a kind of objective lie inscribed in the facts' (Laplanche, 1976[1970], p. 34). It is the transcendental nature of the proton pseudos that resolves the contradiction concealed in this term: the *proton pseudos* can be both *lie* and *primary* because it is inscribed in the psychic destiny of the subject. The hysterical symptom does not aim to deceive and it does not aim to protest. The hysterical symptom is the expression of a peculiar kind of memory – the proton pseudos – that reveals how sexuality has been inscribed in the inner life of the subject.

The peculiarity of the proton pseudos rests on the nature of memory understood as a form of psychical writing that is not made of signs but of differences, and that becomes a slippery object for natural science in as much as it resists direct observation. The proton pseudos falls within this psychical writing: it is the form taken by a hysterical memory that is not an archive and whose observation has always escaped, even the subject to whom it belongs. The abandonment of the Project is not the failure to describe the functioning of the mind because of the limitations of late nineteenth-century neurophysiology but, rather, the discovery of a new genre of theoretical texts whose incompleteness demonstrates the very nature of hysterical memories. Far from being a failure, the Project is the starting point for a new way of writing memory. However, when he wrote the Project, Freud still believed in his *neurotica*: he held on to the reality of the seduction scene, reawakened at puberty to produce a neurosis. He had not yet discovered the form of reality created by unconscious phantasies and their consequences, as beautifully summarised by Laplanche: 'what is repressed is not the memory but the fantasy derived from it or subtending it' (Laplanche, 1976[1970], p. 102). This is, I believe, the main reason for the impossibility of the text of the Project: the attempt to describe a trace as an archive. The tension of the Project exists because Freud had identified the strange nature of hallucinatory ideas that are the outcome of psychical reality but was obliged to translate them into the realm of scientific discourse.

To speak of memory in terms of 'hallucinations' or 'transcendental lies' raises a serious political issue, since it could be read as a negation of the external reality of abuses. However, I don't think my reading of Freud's Project excludes the political dimension of psychopathology. What I have tried to emphasise is how this cryptic text points to the difficulty of capturing and describing certain experiences verbally. In her paper, 'Trauma, Recognition, and the Place of Language', Juliet Mitchell raised the question of why theories of trauma 'revert to neurophysiological models' if they 'regard the breaching event as the originary trauma'. Indeed, 'there can be nothing biologically causative about a rape or a mother's death or about their possible effects' (Mitchell, 1998, p. 124). Mitchell's hypothesis is that it is not 'because we cannot conceptualize the psyche at the level of a traumatic experience' that 'we engage with natural science explanations' but rather 'because they echo our existential experience' (Ibid., p. 124). Through clinical cases, Mitchell shows how in a traumatic experience, the subject is withdrawn from reality at the level of his or her own verbal language. Hence, the use of biological models rather than psychological ones would reflect the fact that a trauma forces the subject outside of his/her language and that traumatic experience leaves its mark on a non-verbal level.

Conclusion: the witch

In the Project, Freud identified hallucinatory ideas that coexist with perceived ideas. In order to describe the functioning of those hallucinatory ideas, Freud proposed a model of the psyche whose functioning is illuminated by Derrida's concept of trace. A psyche that is not made of *objects-ideas* observable in their positivity, but rather of *facilitations-ideas*, which exist only in their difference from other facilitations. It follows that memory and the act of recollection is not the excavation of an archive but the transcription of past facilitations from the activation of the present.

To give an account of hysteria, Freud put forward a concept of pre-sexual sexual memories that he names the proton pseudos. I have used the description of the proton pseudos to argue for an understanding of memory as a dynamic mode of thinking in which perceptions are transformed into ideas whose meaning is never present to consciousness. The hysterical symptom confronts the subject with representations that are both transcendental archives and immanent transcriptions. The hysterical symptom would in fact be the expression of the very functioning of a memory that produces meaning through the effects of gaps. This probably explains the universal character of hysteria: 'every adolescent must carry the germ of hysteria within him' (Freud, 1950[1895], p. 356) wrote Freud and what makes of hysteria 'not *a* disease but *the* disease in its pure form, the one, which is nothing in itself but is likely to take the shape of every other disease' (Swain, 1994, p. 53, my translation).[5] Through this great plasticity of forms, the hysteric transcribes every other disease in the hallucinatory code of infantile sexuality, and in such a way that the hysteric continuously enacts the ideas that horrify him.

'The mind of the hysterical patient is full of active yet unconscious ideas; all her symptoms proceed from such ideas', Freud would write almost twenty years after the Project (Freud, 1912b, p. 262). The failure of the Project resulted partly from the attempt to describe these active unconscious ideas in a model that ignored the dynamic unconscious.

A few months after abandoning his text, in a letter to Fliess dated 13 February 1896, Freud coined the term metapsychology: 'I am continually occupied with psychology – really metapsychology' (in Masson, 1985, p. 172). Freud's metapsychological endeavour will resume the question discovered in the Project: how to describe a form of memory that operates beyond the archive memory? Freud will try to describe the transcendental lie that the hysterics were enacting in their convulsions, in a kind of theoretical trance, which, enigmatically enough, he would name in one of his last texts, quoting Goethe's *Faust*, 'the witch metapsychology': 'We can only say: "So muss denn doch die Hexe dran!" (*"We must call the Witch to our help after all!"*) - the Witch Meta-psychology' (Freud, 1937, p. 225). Hence, the other name for metapsychology is borrowed from a great literary work. Literature and metapsychology: two alternative forms of knowledge to rational discourse, and the figure of the witch, who appears as the incarnation of the knowledge of a subjective past revealed by hysteria.

To reintroduce a positive neuronal model into the Project implies the removal of the esoteric figure of the witch and the abandonment of any attempt to formalise a form of knowledge carried by hysterical memories. The relevance of the Project is its use of neurology to invent a system of notation for hysterical memory. The impossibility of this text: its difficult categorisation, its resistance to traditional forms of rational discourses and its incompleteness are characteristics that demonstrate the sexual and unobservable nature of those memories. The Project therefore makes way for metapsychology understood not as a theory of the mind but as the production of texts that attempt to formalise the unconscious.

Notes

1 A sign of this subjection is the fact that in common with neuroscience, the language in which the great majority of neuro-psychoanalytic papers have been published is English, whereas psychoanalytic publications have managed to maintain a much greater diversity of languages.
2 'C'est bien en effet un modèle "neuronique" qui est là développé, mais déjà "méta-psychologisé"'.
3 Approaching the question of memory from another perspective the philosopher Clément Rosset has reached very similar conclusions. He pointed out that to forget is not the disappearance of a memory but rather a mental state in which each memory appears undifferentiated. In such a way, Rosset has argued, that it would be impossible to distinguish between a state of total amnesia and a state of total reminiscence (Rosset, 1977, pp. 18–20).
4 'One shuts one's eyes and hallucinates; one opens them and thinks in words' (Freud, 1950[1895], p. 339).
5 'L'hystérie n'est pas *une* maladie, elle est *la* maladie à l'état pur, celle qui n'est rien par elle-même mais susceptible de prendre la forme de toutes les autres maladies'.

Bibliography

Andersson, O. (1962). *Studies in the Prehistory of Psychoanalysis*. Stockholm: Svenska Bokförlaget.
Assoun, P.L. (2009). *Dictionnaire des Oeuvres Psychanalytiques*. Paris: Presse Universitaire de France.
Derrida, J. (1976[1967]). *Of Grammatology*. Baltimore; London: Johns Hopkins University Press.
Derrida, J. (1978[1967]). *Writing and Difference*. London: Routledge.
Du Bois-Reymond, E. (1927). *Zwei Grosse Naturforscher des 19. Jahrhunderts: Ein Briefwechsel Zwischen Emil Du Bois-Reymond und Karl Ludwig*. Leipzig: J. A. Barth.
Freud, S. (1912). A Note on the Unconscious in Psycho-Analysis. In *The Standard Edition of the Complete Psychological Works of Sigmund Freud*, Volume 12. London: The Hogarth Press and the Institute of Psycho-Analysis.
Freud, S. (1937). Analysis Terminable and Interminable. *The Standard Edition of the Complete Psychological Works of Sigmund Freud*, Volume 23. London: The Hogarth Press and the Institute of Psycho-Analysis.
Freud, S. (1950[1895]). Project for a Scientific Psychology. *The Standard Edition of the Complete Psychological Works of Sigmund Freud*, Volume 1. London: The Hogarth Press and the Institute of Psycho-Analysis.
Friedman, J., and Alexander, J. (1983). Psychoanalysis and Natural Science: Freud's 1895 Project Revisited. *The International Review of Psycho-Analysis* 10: 303–318.
Knight, I.F. (1984). Freud's "Project": A Theory for Studies on Hysteria. *Journal of the History of the Behavioural Sciences* 20, October 1984.
Kris, E. (1954). *Introduction to the Origins of Psycho-Analysis*. London: Imago.
Laplanche, J. (1976[1970]). *Life and Death in Psychoanalysis*. Baltimore; London: Johns Hopkins University Press.
Malcom, J. (1981). *Psychoanalysis: The Impossible Profession*. New York: Knopf.
Masson, J.M. (1985). *The Complete Letters of Sigmund Freud to Wilhelm Fliess, 1887–1904*. Cambridge, MA; London, England: Belknap.
Mitchell, J. (1998). Trauma, Recognition and the Place of Language. *Diacritics*, 28. 4: 121–133.
Ricoeur, P. (1970[1965]). *Freud and Philosophy: An Essay on Interpretation*. New Haven and London: Yale University Press.
Rosset, C. (1977). *Le Réel Traité de l'Idiotie*. Paris: Les Editions de Minuit.
Schaeffer, J. (1986). Le Rubis a Horreur du Rouge. Relation et Contre-Investissement Hystériques. *Revue Française de Psychanalyse*, 50, May–June: 923–944.
Showalter, E. (1987). *The Female Malady: Women, Madness and English Culture, 1830–1980*. London: Virago.
Solms, M. (1998). Before and After Freud's Project. *Annals of the New York Academy of Sciences*, 843, May 1998: 1–10.
Strachey, J. (1953). Editor's Notes, Preface and Introduction. In *The Standard Edition of the Complete Psychological Works of Sigmund Freud*, Volume IV. London: The Hogarth Press and the Institute of Psycho-analysis.
Strachey, J. (1966). Editor's Notes, Preface and Introduction. In *The Standard Edition of the Complete Psychological Works of Sigmund Freud*, Volume I. London: The Hogarth Press and the Institute of Psycho-Analysis.
Swain, G. (1994). *Dialogue avec l'Insensé*. Paris: Gallimard.

Chapter 3

'Where had she walked thus and whither was she going?'

Freud, Ferrante and feet in Jensen's *Gradiva*

Shahidha Bari

In May 1938, on the eve of Freud's expulsion from Vienna and flight to London, his colleague August Aichhorn, with one eye on posterity, persuaded photographer, Edmund Engelman, to record the contents of the original consulting rooms at Berggasse 19 (Joel Sanders Architect, 2015). Engelman's images capture the cluttered office, the familiar couch draped with oriental rugs and piled with cushions, the dark walls unevenly clad with pictures, engravings and artefacts – among them, the image of Gradiva. Gradiva hangs adjacent to and above the couch, regal in a bas-relief plaster cast and browned with age. Her upright Roman figure is carved in profile, her hair pinned low and head bent forward as she hurries, pacing everlastingly onward. The speed of her movement is suggested in the folds of her gown which are thick and numerous, cumbersomely swirling around her eager stride. Her skirt is gathered in one hand, drawn up to clear the ankles and to expose her feet: one pressed flat, the other arched in motion, toes pushing off from the ground beneath her.

But Gradiva holds an important place in Freud's thinking, as well as in his consulting room. In his 1906 essay, 'Delusions and Dreams in Jensen's *Gradiva*' (Freud, 2001a), a brief and focused study of Wilhelm Jensen's short novel of 1903, Freud reads the story of *Gradiva* as an elaboration of the writer's psyche. The scholarship around the essay has often attended to it as a persuasive example of the interconnection of psychoanalysis and fiction, recognising the novel as an exercise in male fantasy. But Freud's effusive account of it also reveals how easily fantasy can marginalise female experience. In this way, the figure of Gradiva poses a challenge to psychoanalysis, both presenting an emblem of Freud and marking the elision of femininity. This essay examines the place of *Gradiva* in Freud's thinking and argues that while Gradiva's story invites Freud's analysis of male fantasy, it also betrays his anxieties about the waywardness of women and the ability of psychoanalysis to contain them through the instruments of interpretation and diagnosis. Finally, the essay updates Freud's reading of Jensen's novel by looking to the work of Elena Ferrante – a contemporary writer with

DOI: 10.4324/9781003200765-4

acknowledged interests in psychoanalysis – counterpoising the fictional account of male desire with an alternative expression of female will.

The image of Gradiva is important to Freudian psychoanalysis. Ernest Jones noted how fervent analysts, eager to follow in Freud's footsteps, would emblazon their consulting rooms with replicas of the engraving, the girl easily transformed into the cipher of their intellectual affiliation (Jones, 1953–7, p. 342). Today, at 20 Maresfield Gardens, Freud's Gradiva hangs over the entrance to the study, but at Berggasse 19, the plaster cast was positioned at the foot of the couch, her profile turned to the patient, as though she were striding inexorably toward them, her head bent in assenting acknowledgement. In the 1937 film of Freud at home, commissioned by Marie Bonaparte and narrated by Anna Freud, the camera's unsteady lens darts around the room, swooping down on the analyst's accoutrements – the sphinx, the Egyptian plough, the family photographs – resting only momentarily on Gradiva's bas-relief, strangely vigorous in the stillness of the empty analytical setting. 'Gradiva' intones Anna Freud gravely – but Gradiva is unmistakeable. Freud himself had not mistaken her when he spotted her sculpted form in the Vatican museum in September 1907, a year after his essay was published. Writing home to his wife, he observed that he had recognised there a 'dear familiar face' (Freud and Freud, 1992, p. 267).

In Jensen's story, an ardent young architect by the name of Norbert Hanold grows infatuated with an engraving displayed in a museum in Rome that depicts a woman walking vigorously.[1] He names her Gradiva after Mars Gradivus, the Roman god of war who strides into battle. Later, acquiring a plaster cast of the image, Norbert displays it on the wall of his study, contemplating it daily, until the figure penetrates his dreams, becoming the stuff of fantasy. One night, dreaming of Gradiva amidst the ruins of Pompeii, Norbert determines to travel there, convinced he will encounter her spectre on the site of the lost city. True to his dream, he does, indeed, encounter a woman walking vigorously – only she reveals herself not as an apparition of Gradiva, but instead the now adult form of Norbert's childhood playmate, Zoë Bertgang. Over the course of the novel, Zoë, quietly and calmly, awakens the archaeologist from his dreams and delusions, gradually reconciling him to his real life. Unsurprisingly, Freud latched onto the story eagerly, perceiving it as a model of psychoanalytically sympathetic fiction. In Jensen, he had found a novelist to revere: creative writers, he observed, could be 'valuable allies' for psychoanalysis, providing in their fictions evidence that 'is to be prised highly, for they are apt to know a whole host of things between heaven and earth of which our philosophy has not yet let us dream' (Freud, 2001a, p. 8).

If there is a certain modesty here in the casting of psychoanalysis as the handmaiden to the profundity of writers, it is undercut by the confidence with which Freud construes Jensen's novel as a pre-eminently psychoanalytical enterprise. Lis Møller asserts that Freud reads the novel purposefully, 'with the intention of pronouncing *Gradiva* the ally of psychoanalysis' and positioning it 'as one long defence of the dream theory' (Møller, 1991, p. 31). But there are aspects of Jensen's novel that enable this alliance too. The parallels are striking and obvious: Norbert, for instance, dreams of Pompeii, just as Freud too invokes the image of a ruined city in *Civilisation and its Discontents*. For Freud, the wreckage of Ancient Rome, buried deep underground, contrasts to the retentive terrain of mental life where 'nothing which has once been formed can ever perish' (Freud, 2001b, p. 69). But Jensen's story exemplifies this too: the return of the lost childhood friend is evidence of the irrepressible past. Gradiva is the manifestation of an infantile libidinal attachment that lastingly shapes adult desire. Incarnated as Zoë, she is also proof of the efficacy of the psychoanalytic method, walking Norbert out of fantasies of ruin and leading him safely back into the present. When he hails Gradiva in Latin, Zoë patiently insists he address her in modern German.

A gratified Jensen himself addressed Freud in the spring of 1907, writing congenially 'I can agree without reservation that your paper has completely divined and done justice to the intentions of my little book'. In an intriguing exchange of letters, Jensen airily attributed his 'depiction of psychical developments' to 'poetic intuition' rather than deliberate intention, but Freud replying eagerly probed further, seeking out the origin of Jensen's story and the object of Norbert's dream (Fletcher, 2013, p. 1001). He issued a stream of personal questions: 'Where is your own person hiding in the story and how far back does the material reach into your life?' (Ibid., p. 1004). Curiously, nothing in the information provided by Jensen seemed to signal the diagnosis to which Freud nonetheless proceeded when he theorised that the figure of Gradiva derived from the author's forgotten memory of a dead sister (Ibid., p. 1002). Why, then, did Freud read Jensen's *Gradiva* so determinedly against any authorial evidence?

Erica Davies offers one answer when she notes that 'Delusions and Dreams in Jensen's *Gradiva*', constituted 'the first full length application of psychoanalysis to a literary text' (Davies, 1998, p. 69). The stakes were high. Jensen's story triumphantly affirms Freudian thought when Norbert's fantasies are proved to be not the 'capricious products of his imagination but determined, without him knowing it, by the store of childhood impressions which he has forgotten, but which were still at work in him' (Freud, 2001a, p. 31). And yet more than this, the story extends beyond metaphors of archaeological ruins and models of infant memory, insofar as it stages the psychoanalytic method itself. The treatment for neurotic obsession is the therapy that Zoë offers up. She deploys a talking cure that induces the hero out of his delusion. In this respect, she is cast as the surrogate analyst, entrusted with the task of transforming pathological desire into civilised love. Joan Copjec acknowledges the radicalism of this gesture, noting that Gradiva's place at the foot of the couch also betrays the secret truth of the scene of analysis: a woman is 'clearly the end of the analytic search', she asserts (Copjec, 1984, p. 85). And this positing of the female analyst is no small accident here, Copjec suggests, since 'Delusions and Dreams in Jensen's *Gradiva*' follows in the wake of the case of Dora published in 1905.

Gradiva's triumph comes in the aftermath of Dora's failed analysis, and so Norbert's recovery under Zoë's care reaffirms the efficacy of a talking cure. She, unlike Dora, claims an active part in the patient's restoration. She is, in fact, writes Copjec, 'the agent of the cure, the analyst herself', and as such, she returns to Freud the analyst's lost credibility (Ibid., p. 87). Zoë's triumph remediates Freud's failure of Dora.

And yet the triumph claimed for Zoë can only ever be considered partial and qualified. Zoë is the analyst that lives up to her ancient Greek name: she is the Zoë (ζωή) that means 'life' and she serves to revive the delusional Norbert. But what she also restores to Norbert is the primacy of his sexuality at the expense of her own. In Freud's analysis of Jensen's novel, it is Norbert's identity to which Zoë tends, and it is his desire of which she is only the final expression. It is his pathology that she represents and his recovery that she aids. Accordingly, Mary Jacobus cites the case of Gradiva in her interrogative essay 'Is there a woman in this text?' (Jacobus, 1982). Jacobus concedes that Norbert's awakening to life provides Freud with an analogy for the awakening of 'strict psychiatry' to the existence of the unconscious, but Gradiva's role in this consigns her to victimhood (Ibid., p. 122). She joins the ranks of women who are the 'the mute sacrifice on which theory itself may be founded; the woman [who] is silenced so that the theorist can make the truth come out of her mouth' (Ibid., p. 118). Freud, Jacobus acknowledges, is not oblivious to his own implication in the interpretation of Jensen's novella, alert to the possibility that in reading the story in the light of his own theories, he might also read his theories *into* it, recovering from Jensen's fantasy only that which he sought to recover. But if the woman in the text is 'there,' Jacobus argues, then she is also 'not there', not its object, not its author, not even its primary concern (Ibid., p. 139). She serves to secure Norbert's recovery and confirm Freud's credibility and so she is the constitutor and guarantor of masculine identity, both within and beyond the frames of the text. Jensen's story takes her name but never accounts for her experience, construing her as only ever the object and exposition of a man's desire. She is, at once, over-determined and under-written.

And yet if, in the analytic scenario, the analyst claims for themselves an interpretive mastery, it is precisely the fantasy of this mastery that the figure of Gradiva punctures. As Sarah Kofman eloquently expresses it, 'le psychoanalyste ne détient ni la clef de l'oeuvre ni la verité: Il n'est past Zoé' (Kofman, 1974, p. 125). The psychoanalyst holds neither the key to the work nor the truth: he is not Zoë. Neither is he the life her name signals. Marilyn Manners argues that for both Jensen and Freud, the key concern of 'Delusions and Dreams in Jensen's *Gradiva* is not the life of Zoë so much as the revival of the repressed Norbert (Manners, 1998). He is, Manners suggests, a strange inversion – the archaeologist buried deep in his fantasy and Zoë, the statue he admires, is tasked with his excavation. And yet what of her own unexcavated desire? Gradiva never tells, and neither Jensen nor Freud consider it. Lacan issues this critique of Freud for whom 'there is no libido other than masculine. Meaning what? Other than that the whole field, which is hardly negligible, is thereby ignored. This is the field of all those beings who take on the status of the woman ...' (Lacan, 1985, p. 151). The asymmetric account of libido haunts Freudian scholarship and the literature with which it has engaged. Jacqueline Rose, taking up T.S. Eliot's query over the 'objective correlative' apparently lacking in *Hamlet*, points to the figure of Gertrude, the female sexuality that is the obscured cause, the play's 'inexpressible and inscrutable context' (Rose, 1996, p. 127). Jensen's novel and Freud's analysis similarly obscure Zoë's sexuality – they insistently turn her into stone. But it could just as easily be ash. In *Archive Fever*, Derrida, contra Freud, reads *Gradiva* not as the story of the delusion of men, but of the deletion of women, their footprints cast in the white hot ash of Vesuvius, an impression preserved for an archive that will not keep them (Derrida, 1996). Gradiva is a woman only imagined by men, but what remains of her, after Jensen plays out his fantasy in the ruins of Pompeii, is a sense of the hazard her sexuality poses and the power she possesses to provoke an ungovernable desire that is seemingly restrained only by analysis and in fiction.

This critical scholarship around Freud's essay exposes the force of his reading, the ways that it disfigures and deletes female experience. There is more to Zoë than Jensen's novel and Freud's analysis allows. In the story, she is the Roman girl in the gown who presents as a mystery awaiting decipherment. In Freud's essay though, she is the key that opens up the psyche – only not her own. On the wall of the consulting room, she is the constant companion to Freud's thinking. There, in stone, Gradiva's flowing gown is, ironically, made heavy and lined, impossibly unwieldy with its innumerable folds and furrows. There is something curious about this translation of cloth into stone that mirrors Freud's own distorted reading of female selfhood as male sexuality. How strange not to identify the fold with femininity, suggestive as it is of women's sexual organs? But Gradiva presents the opposite of the phallus and Freud overlooks it, determinedly seeing instead only the delusions and the dreams of the men who desire her. The girl in the dress is the object of Freud and Jensen's projection and this fictional representation of a woman is never permitted to give an account of herself. Instead, the story that bears her name is only a pathway into the pathology of others. But, she is, herself, the walker of paths, placing one foot after another, dauntless and unerring.

Tellingly, it is the gait, not the girl that preoccupies Norbert in the novel – something that he miraculously deduces from her stilled image alone. But how is it that a man could fall in love with a woman's walk? Freud has an answer to this when he configures a fetish as 'an effect of some sexual impression, received as a rule in childhood' (Freud, 2001c, p. 155). The foot, he explains is 'an age-old sexual symbol' (Freud, 2001c, p. 155). In an additional *footnote* of 1910, he further clarifies its phallic association: 'the foot represents a woman's penis, the absence of which is deeply felt' (Ibid., footnote 2). Jensen cannot resist the fantasies formed at a woman's feet. He launches into an account of Gradiva's 'maidenly grace' with an unimpeded imaginative license:

> With her head bent forward a little, she held slightly raised in her left hand, so that her sandaled feet became visible, her garment which fell in exceedingly voluminous folds from her throat to her ankles. The left foot had advanced, and the right, about to follow, touched the ground only lightly with the tips of the toes, while the sole and heel were raised almost vertically. This movement produced a double impression of exceptional agility and of confident composure, and the flight like poise, combined with a firm step, lent her the peculiar grace. Where had she walked thus and whither was she going?
>
> (Jensen, 2003, pp. 8–9)

When Norbert follows in the footsteps of the woman he adores, he tracks her movements and so betrays the impulse for surveillance beneath the supplication. This is revealing. To worship a woman is to demand to know her whereabouts, where she has come from and where she will go. Freud's analysis devolves into an investigation of Norbert's desire, but he is unable to register something more opaque and disquieting at the heart of the story. The mystery here is not just what women want (that old question that so famously foxes Freud), but where they go. Where is it that a woman might walk and where a man may not follow? Norbert's fantasy is predicated on the memory of a woman who has travelled freely beyond the purview of the man who desires her, leaving him frustrated and feverish. In Jensen's story, that freedom is imaginatively curbed with Zoë's return, but Freud too supplies an answer to the question of how you prevent a woman from straying beyond the tightly circumscribed limits of a fantasy. He turns her into stone and makes her a cipher for analysis itself. But at Gradiva's feet there is another story – about female desire, direction, ambition and volition – the depths of which not even Freud can begin to plumb.

So much of Jensen's novel and Freud's analysis is concerned with Gradiva's feet, that it is worth noting that in the consulting room plaster cast, she is depicted with the thinnest sandals, her soles neat and low. Gradiva strides forward, even though the history of women's footwear has been underpinned by an impulse to immobilise. This is most apparent in the aristocratic traditions of Chinese foot binding which begin in the eleventh century, but it is betrayed too in the narrowed vamp and badly distributed weight of modern heels (Bossan, 2004, p. 164). Free movement is not a prerequisite of women's footwear. And if the formulation of freedom as a literal right to come and go as you please might seem simple, it is also acute, since mobility is central to the language of woman's emancipation – the glass ceilings through which they break, the homes in which they are no longer expected to stay, the children they leave behind, the career ladders they struggle to climb. How women move matters. Mobility is both a feminist question and a metaphor too that reveals an anxiety about the waywardness of female desire. Freud asks what does woman want, but he might also ask where does a woman go, who could she love and what could she choose to leave behind?

Perhaps the answers to those questions are best provided by women themselves. If psychoanalysis is to make sense of the will of women, as well as the desire of men, its challenge is to extend its corpus to better incorporate the life (*zoë*) of women as it is told by women. Jensen seeks Gradiva in Pompeii and finds Zoë in modern Rome, but it is Naples, sprawling and unmanageable, that Elena Ferrante's two protagonists navigate in her novel, *My Brilliant Friend*. In this first novel of the tetralogy, Lila Cerullo and Elena (Lenu) Greco are the two children who venture into the basement of the local neighbourhood ogre, Don Achille, in search of their lost dolls. The opening vignette poses what the entire series explores, precisely this question of where women are permitted to go and what they might dare to do there. As the paths of their lives fork, Ferrante examines the choices of which the women avail themselves and the obligations that entrap them nonetheless. Lila, the daughter of the shoemaker, finds that her life stalls as her friend, Lenu, ascends social heights, a glittering, metropolitan and cultured world opening up before her. Lila is forced to find a different route out of the violent historic familial fractions of her small community. She imagines opening a shoe factory:

> 'A shoe factory?'
> 'Yes.'
> She spoke with great conviction, as she knew how to do, with sentences, in Italian, that depicted before my eyes the factory sign, Cerullo; the brand name stamped on the uppers, Cerullo; and then the Cerullo shoes, all splendid, all elegant, as in her drawings, shoes that once you put them on, she said, are so beautiful and so comfortable that at night you go to sleep without taking them off.
>
> (Ferrante, 2011, pp. 117–118)

As Lenu takes up Latin, Lila's fingers grow yellow and callused, stitching, gluing and labouring over the perfect prototype shoe with which to launch her business. Making shoes is not only a business, it is a form of invention here. The shoes that Lila imagines promise to generate revenue and elevate her standing, but they also feed her hungered imagination, fuelling her with a dream of freedom that might come of social mobility. The shoes that Lila dreams of making promise to lift her from her straitened, circumscribed life, taking her places other than home, forging pathways into a new world and new life. Revealing some of her drawings to Lenu, the latter is taken aback by the boldness and ingenuity of the designs, but also the limitless imagination they represent:

They were beautiful designs, drawn on graph paper, rich in precisely colored details, as if she had had a chance to examine shoes like that close up in some world parallel to ours and then had fixed them on paper. In reality she had invented them in their entirety and in every part, as she had done in elementary school when she drew princesses, so that, although they were normal shoes, they didn't resemble any that were seen in the neighborhood, or even those of the actresses in the photo novels

(Ibid., p. 116).

What Lenu discerns from these drawings are Lila's utterly original dreams, and she is awed both by their extraordinary ambition and frightened by their ingenuity. The shoes outwardly intimate an inner life carefully concealed and yet so rich and brilliant that Lenu is cowed by it. But Lila's opportunities are repeatedly curtailed, and at the end of the last novel, she is struck a final bitter blow when her young daughter is mysteriously lost. In the final few pages, Lila too goes astray. When Lenu returns to the village to seek her, she walks through the places of their childhood alone and consoles herself with an idea that Lila had 'broken her confines, and finally travelled the world' (Ferrante, 2014, p. 473). The lost dolls of their childhood are mysteriously returned to her, as though to suggest the completeness of a full circle, but they also repeat, in miniature, that larger question of where women go and how far they are ever able to leave the places from which they start. Ferrante's writing seeks to track this. She understands too that the question is not only one of where women go and what prevents them, but also how far they are permitted to tell their inward journeys at all. Ferrante has us follow the two women, tracking the complex circling and path crossing by which their bond is tightly woven, intimating how friendship is in the meeting and parting of ways, a constant recalibration of one to the other, but she also compels us to acknowledge a point beyond which we cannot venture. When Lila disappears, Ferrante allows her a final privacy that even she cannot penetrate.

Here, the limits of fiction are not unlike the limits of psychoanalysis – a discourse that Ferrante deeply respects. 'I love Freud', she writes 'and I've read a fair amount of him: it seems to me that he knew better than his followers that psychoanalysis is the lexicon of the precipice' (Ferrante, 2017, p. 122). But beyond the edge of the precipice, the writer and the analyst cannot go. 'Psychoanalysis' she concedes, 'is a powerful stimulus for those who want to dig inside, it can't be disregarded, it conditions us even when we reject it, it's the map for any treasure hunt amid the shadows of our body. A map, however, is only a map...' (Ibid., p. 124). Lila's final disappearance takes her off-grid. She is, at the last, curiously untrackable, as Ferrante herself sought to be in her insistent evasion of authorial identification. Pressed on the question of her identity, Ferrante cites the passage in *Totem and Taboo* where 'Freud tells of a woman who had forced herself not to write her own name any more. She was afraid that someone would use it to take possession of her personality. The woman began by refusing to write her own name and then, by extension, she stopped writing, completely...' (Ibid., p. 84). To give one's name is to hazard a kind of dispossession, to risk the trespass of others, an experience from which we might not ever be returned to ourselves unmarked.

Ferrante's familiarity with Freud reveals the same sympathy between fiction and psychoanalysis that Freud himself identifies in his fervent reading of Jensen's *Gradiva*. The Neapolitan novels present a counterpoint to Jensen's Pompeiian one, delineating a more complex portrait of women, but Ferrante writes with a certain wariness too, as if knowing how easily women's stories can be deleted and disfigured. *Gradiva* is proof of that. Zoë is turned 'Gradiva' and returned to 'Zoë' once more – but she is also 'Jensen' and 'Freud'. When she coaxes Norbert out of his delusion, it is an attempt at self-determination, an insistence that he register the particularity of the person she is, the language she speaks and the name she possesses. Freud's reading of the story registers this even as it overwrites it. In his essay 'Femininity', Freud remarks how a young woman 'often frightens us by her psychical rigidity and unchangeability. Her libido has taken up final positions and seems incapable of exchanging them for others. There are no paths open to further development; it is as though the whole process had already run its course...', but the figure of Gradiva is always poised mid-step, her destination yet to be determined (Freud, 2001d, p. 167). Footprints record the places where we once were, the routes taken and paths forged. They are only the barest trace of the life that leaves them behind. In Freud's consulting room, Gradiva is suspended in stone, always on the cusp of making her mark. 'Where had she walked thus and whither was she going?' asks Jensen, but where Gradiva treads, analysis cannot follow.

Note

1 For a full discussion of Jensen's story, see Rachel Bowlby, 'One foot in the grave: Freud on Jensen's *Gradiva*' in Bowlby (1992).

Bibliography

Bossan, M-J. (2004) *The art of the shoe*. New York: Parkstone.
Bowlby, R. (1992) *Still crazy after all these years: women, writing and psychoanalysis*. London: Routledge.
Copjec, J. (1984) 'Transference: letters and the unknown woman', *October* 28, 60–90.
Davies, E. (1998) *Maresfield Gardens: a guide to the Freud Museum*. London: Serpent's Tail.
Derrida, J. (1996) *Archive fever: a Freudian impression*, trans. E. Prenowitz. Chicago: University of Chicago Press.
Ferrante, E. (2011) *My brilliant friend*, trans. A. Goldstein. New York: Europa Editions.
Ferrante, E. (2014) *The story of the lost child*, trans. A. Goldstein. New York: Europa Editions.

Ferrante, E. (2017) *Frantumaglia: a writer's journey*, trans. A. Goldstein. New York: Europa Editions.
Fletcher, J. (2013) 'Gradiva: Freud, fetishism and Pompeian fantasy', *The Psychoanalytic Quarterly* 82 (4), 965–1011.
Freud, S. and E. L. Freud (1992) *Letters of Sigmund Freud*. New York: Dover.
Freud, S. (2001a) 'Delusions and dreams in Jensens's Gradiva', in J. Strachey *et al.* (ed.) *The standard edition of the complete psychological works of Sigmund Freud*, trans. J. Strachey and A. Freud, with A. Strachey and A. Tyson, Vol. 9. London: Vintage.
Freud, S. (2001b) 'Civilisation and its discontents' in J. Strachey *et al.* (ed.) *The standard edition of the complete psychological works of Sigmund Freud*, trans. J. Strachey and A. Freud, with A. Strachey and A. Tyson, Vol. 21. London: Vintage.
Freud, S. (2001c) 'Three essays on sexuality' in Strachey, J. *et al.* (ed.) *The standard edition of the complete psychological works of Sigmund Freud*, trans. J. Strachey and A. Freud, with A. Strachey and A. Tyson, Vol. 7. London: Vintage.
Freud, S. (2001d) 'Femininity', in J. Strachey *et al.* (ed.) *The standard edition of the complete psychological works of Sigmund Freud*, trans. J. Strachey and A. Freud, with A. Strachey and A. Tyson, Vol. 22. London: Vintage.
Jacobus, M. (1982) 'Is there a woman in this text?', *New Literary History* 14 (1), 117–141.
Jensen, W. (2003) *'Gradiva' and 'Delusions and dreams in Wilhelm Jensen's 'Gradiva'*, trans. H. Downey. Los Angeles: Green Integer Press, pp. 7–140.
Joel Sanders Architect (2015) *Berggasse 19: inside Freud's office with Diana Fuss*, Available at: http://joelsandersarchitect.com/berggasse-19-inside-freuds-office-with-diana-fuss/ (Accessed May 2017).
Jones, E. (1953–7) *The life and work of Sigmund Freud*. Vol. 2. New York: Basic Books.
Kofman, S. (1974) *Quatre romans analytiques*. Paris: Éditions Galilée.
Lacan, J. (1985) *Feminine sexuality: Jacques Lacan and the École Freudienne*, trans. J. Mitchell and J. Rose. Basingstoke: Palgrave.
Manners, M. (1998) 'The vagaries of flight in Hélène Cixous's *Le troisième corps*', *French Forum* 23 (1), 101–114.
Møller, L. (1991) *The Freudian reading: analytical and fictional constructions*. Philadelphia: University of Pennsylvania Press.
Rose, J. (1996) *Sexuality in the field of vision*. London: Verso.

Part 2
Mass psychology

Chapter 4

Psychoanalysis and Satanism
A case of moral panic in South Africa

Nicky Falkof

During the late 1980s and early 1990s, at a moment when the underpinnings of apartheid began to seriously falter, white South Africa experienced a potent moral panic around the apparent presence of white Satanists, imagined to be a powerful cult that threatened the stability of the nation. This essay is a reflection on the late apartheid Satanism scare. It offers a speculative argument for why psychoanalysis – or, more specifically, certain psychoanalytical concepts drawn from Freud's writings – can provide a useful conceptual frame for understanding the affective and ideological meanings of this peculiar historical episode, and of moral panics in general. More broadly, it gestures towards the potential of psychoanalysis to unsettle the fixity of certain paradigms and methodologies within the social sciences.[1]

Fears of Satanism in South Africa were deeply political and tied to challenges to white dominance. Ideas about the satanic menace, expressed in the pages of broadsheet newspapers and family magazines and repeated in the pronouncements of priests, politicians, parents, policemen and other 'moral entrepreneurs' (Becker 1995), were less a free-floating instance of urban legend than a concentrated manifestation of the affective consequences among whites of a perceived threat to whiteness.

Many scholars have written about the traumas of black life under apartheid. As a result, much is known about the curtailing of autonomy, family, hope and social mobility for black South Africans due to government programmes of so-called 'separate development' that entrenched segregation and maintained white dominance of South Africa. Less has been written about white people under apartheid.[2] My intention is not to claim that white South Africans were also 'victims' of apartheid. Rather, I am concerned with the way in which living under a system of legislated injustice warps even those who benefit from it. In line with Frantz Fanon, who observed that white oppressors were in their own way also subject to the 'psychoexistential complex' (1970, 12) that is a consequence of colonialism, I argue that white South Africans experienced their own set of psychoses, which were delusional and self-obsessional as well as reactionary. Whiteness under apartheid was paranoid, anxious and even hysterical. This is a common condition of racist injustice:

DOI: 10.4324/9781003200765-6

'Distorted relationships between oppressed and oppressors lead to and are partly a consequence of widespread mutually reinforcing psychic pathology on both sides of the divide' (Tabensky 2010, 78).

The pathological nature of white South African society, both during the final years of apartheid and in the decades since, lends itself to a psychoanalytic register. Achille Mbembe writes that we cannot properly understand the racialised colony unless we are able to account for its memory, with all the fantasy, terror, psychic work, loss and symbolism that that memory invokes (2015, 28). In order to do this we need an approach 'that is able to properly engage the affective and psychological components of the political phenomenon of racism' (Hook 2005, 485). In the discussion that follows, I show how ideas drawn from psychoanalysis can help to facilitate a reading of psychosocial formations that are a direct consequence of racism and colonialism.

Satan in South Africa

South Africa during the late apartheid period was a strained and anxious place. Between the early 1980s and 1994, when the African National Congress (ANC) took power in the first democratic elections, the country found itself in an almost constant state of turmoil as the struggle against racist white rule gained momentum and the legislative, bureaucratic and economic underpinnings of apartheid became increasingly unstable.

The ANC, demonised by politicians and the white press as a violent communist-terrorist group bent on the destruction of South Africa, gained ever more support among black South Africans. In 1985 President P.W. Botha declared a State of Emergency; the same year 'saw unprecedented levels of civilian unrest' (van der Westhuizen 2007, 16). The once robust South African economy began to falter. By the early 1990s economic and industrial leaders, realising that apartheid was bad for business, began to withdraw support from the state (van der Westhuizen 2007). Conservative churches also began to move away from the racist diktats of high apartheid (Kinghorn 1997). The global anti-apartheid movement became increasingly vocal and sports and cultural boycotts took their toll, with white South Africa becoming increasingly isolated. It was becoming clear that apartheid was unsustainable; however to many white people this looming change was nothing short of terrifying. According to a poll undertaken in 1991, 85 per cent of whites believed that white women would be routinely molested and that 'tribal violence' would become the norm under majority rule (Manzo and McGowan 1992, 16).

The Satanism scare emerged within this charged political climate. While similar scares occurred during this period elsewhere in the world, most notably in the US and UK (see Showalter 1997; Wright 1994; Richardson, Best, and Bromley 1991), South Africa's satanic panic was particular to its context and symptomatic of the multiple anxieties that characterised white life.

Satanism in South Africa was imagined as a violent, evil and dangerous cult. Satanists were accused of the worst crimes imaginable, from bestiality and baby rape to murder, drug-dealing, extortion and grave-robbing. Satanist groups were run by shadowy conspirators from 'overseas'. They undermined family, church and state, used popular culture to lure in the unsuspecting youth and were invisible to normal people but recognisable to each other through the use of arcane symbols.[3] They were infectious: like a virus, they invisibly attacked the healthy body of the state. Importantly, too, Satanists in late apartheid South Africa were almost exclusively figured as white. They were an *internal* threat: they emerged from within whiteness and, in many cases, they could be redeemed by becoming reborn Christians.

During this period hundreds of pamphlets and newspaper and magazine articles were printed detailing accusations or alleged cases of Satanism. Many of these included lists of warning signs for parents and teachers to watch out for. Adolescent behaviours that suggested satanic involvement included everything from listening to heavy metal and wearing black to feeling 'restlessness, fear, loneliness, anxiety, pride, depression, jealousy' or any other powerful emotion (van Zyl 1988, 15). Institutions lent credibility to the scare: in 1986 the University of South Africa held a conference on 'The Bible, The Church and Demonic Powers' in which it discussed the appropriate way for Christianity to respond to the satanic menace (*Star*, 3 July 1986). As late as 1992 the Education Department of Transvaal province produced a guide for teachers on dealing with 'Satanism and Occultism in the Classroom', which stated that 'the growth of Satanism poses a considerable threat to our national Christian heritage' (Transvaal Education Department 1992, 3). Stories of Satanist possession often included tales of how the affected people had been exorcised (*Star*, 7 April 1988), while recovering Satanists frequently confessed to journalists that they had been freed after becoming born-again Christians (*Huisgenoot*, 3 July 1986). Police made lurid claims about Satanist activity, like the 1990 allegation that they knew of eleven babies 'specially bred for sacrifice to the devil and ritually murdered by having their throats slit and their hearts cut out and eaten' (*Cape Times*, 19 May 1990). High profile ministers stated that youth involvement in Satanism was 'causing grave concern' within government (*Citizen*, 31 October 1990) and that Satanism and communism were the most significant problems facing the nation's youth (*Natal Mercury*, 2 July 1990). A special police body, the Occult-Related Crimes Unit, was set up to deal with the 'problem' of Satanism. In 1991 The Department of Home Affairs' annual report stated that 'programmes which positively portrayed possession or devil worship should not be shown on television' (*Argus*, 17 April 1991).

Despite persistent press coverage of the hideous crimes apparently perpetrated by Satanists, no real evidence of their existence was ever produced. No bodies were found to justify the claims about violent satanic murders; no financial proof of the illegal activities of Satanists was produced; no victims came forward to fortify the 'recovered' Satanists' tales of the physical and sexual abuse they were forced to perpetrate; no one was formally accused in a court of law of the extreme ends of satanic practice. Arrests of supposed Satanists were restricted to anti-social loners accused of minor infractions like smoking marijuana and drawing graffiti in graveyards (*You*, 14 November 1991). Police acknowledged that they '[hadn't] ever cracked a Satanism gang in this country' (*Weekend Post*, 22 June 1991).

The Satanism scare was overdetermined, a set of pathological responses to the anxiety surrounding social change that affected white South Africans during the last years of apartheid. At its core was an empty space into which collective neuroses could project images of imaginary threat; images that served particular purposes, as I illustrate in the final section of this essay.

Affect and moral panic

According to Stanley Cohen, who popularised the term, moral panic happens when

> a condition, episode, person or group of persons emerges to become defined as a threat to societal values and interest; its nature is presented in a stylised and stereotypical fashion by the mass media; the moral barricades are manned by editors, bishops, politicians and other right thinking people; socially accredited experts pronounce their diagnoses and solutions; ways of coping are evolved or (more often) resorted to; the condition then disappears, submerges or deteriorates and becomes more visible.
>
> (1972, 9)

This definition, which has become commonplace since the publication of Cohen's *Folk Devils and Moral Panics* in 1972, is useful for an analysis of South Africa's Satanism scare. In the same book Cohen discussed the idea of the folk devil, an 'unambiguously unfavourable symbol' (1972, 41) that often (although not, in his analysis, always) sits at the heart of the moral panic and becomes the repository for the fear, disgust, outrage and anger that the panic creates and/or condenses. The white Satanist in late apartheid South Africa is a paradigmatic example of this cultural figure.

However the notion of moral panic is not uncontested. While clearly useful for analyses of media and public reactions to various forms of social deviance,[4] it has also been the object of serious critique. Some scholars point to the 'negative normative judgement' (Hier 2002, 312) that can be inherent in defining an episode as a moral panic, calling the term a 'pejorative label' that tends to be used to 'explore topics which the researcher and his/her presumed audience often have an ideological vested interest in debunking or exposing' (Jenkins 2009, 36). Some suggest that the concept is not rigorous, that over-use in academic and political discourse has robbed it of much of its value (McRobbie and Thornton 1995, 560) and made it so easily transferable as to be almost meaningless (Rohloff and Wright 2010, 404). Others have criticised its tendency to oversimplify complex social phenomena (Watney 1988; Kitzinger and Miller 1998).

Much of the common analytical use of the notion of moral panic has been hamstrung by what one could call a disciplinary bias. Emerging from within progressive sociology and criminology, a notable proportion of research on moral panic emerges from a social scientific paradigm that is at pains to justify its conclusions as legitimate. Major scholars in the field have been concerned with 'constancies in the model' (Critcher 2003, 2) and with drawing distinct theories to prove that the concept is 'scientifically defensible' (Goode and Ben-Yehuda 1994, 41). The use of graphs and discussions of models place this body of literature within a discursive frame that is concerned to prove the 'science-ness' of social sciences (Latour 2000). Some – by no means all – of the literature on moral panics is embedded in a mode of knowledge production that does not always recognise the contradictory and emotional elements of social life. At its most extreme this desire for scientific legitimacy can lead to scholars reducing something as lurid, overdetermined and affective as a moral panic to a dry discussion about attributes that fails to account for the social power of these episodes.

One consequence of this is that we have a well-developed body of knowledge on how moral panics are spread and how they intersect with the media but less on the affective and symbolic features of the objects of these panics. Cohen himself, in his later work, writes that 'there have been [few] attempts ... to study groupings according to the content of the panics' (2011, 239). Critcher, also more recently (2011), suggests that moral panics contain important affective material and are part of the way in which we make sense of modernity. Following these theorists, I want to suggest that what is missing from much of the existing literature is analysis of, firstly, the content (as opposed to the form) of moral panics, and secondly, the affective and symbolic meanings within that content.[5] The language provided by psychoanalysis is a valuable tool for undertaking these tasks. Just as it taught us to pay attention to the symbolic meanings of language and of dreams (Freud 1991), ideas drawn from psychoanalysis can help us to think about these episodes in ways that take into account their narrative structures.

It is important to be clear that, in linking these ideas to historical events, I am not claiming to perform applied psychoanalysis on an entire culture. This is a speculative essay that attempts to engage existing conceptual tools to think through the psychic and affective states that may underlie a moral panic. Psychoanalytic ideas and terminology provide a set of metaphors that allow me to talk about these social formations. I follow the work of sociologists and anthropologists who, in Sara Ahmed's words, argue that 'emotions should not be regarded as psychological states, but as social and cultural practices' (2014, 9). Ahmed writes of the 'sociality of emotions' that 'it is through emotions, or how we respond to objects and others, that surfaces or boundaries are made' (2014, 10). In the case of South Africa's satanic panic, the depth and intensity of collective emotion associated with the threat of the mythical Satanist served to strengthen surfaces and boundaries that shored up the imagined wholeness of whiteness.

Psychoanalysis and Satanism

In this section I approach a number of well-known psychoanalytic concepts, suggesting the ways in which they can aid an understanding of the late apartheid Satanism scare as a collective response to threat, anxiety and ideological uncertainty.

One way to think about white responses to the weakening of apartheid is through the notion of repression, a condition that can emerge when 'an instinctual impulse … [meets] with resistances which seek to make it inoperative' (Freud 1957, 2977). Freud explains that repression occurs because of resistance to an instinct, which is internal, meaning that 'flight is of no avail, for the ego cannot escape from itself' (1957, 2977). When it is repressed as a consequence of trauma, this material tends to return in new, compromised forms (Freud 1962, 169–171). The return of the repressed is a process by which 'what has been repressed – though never abolished by repression – tends to reappear … in a distorted fashion' (Laplanche and Pontalis 1988, 398).

Repression is useful here since I am interested in affective processes and reactions to these: the fear rather than the actuality of loss of power and identity, a fear that could not be managed through governance, violence or other forms of agency that were familiar to white South Africans. Some reacted to impending change with concerns about their physical safety and economic wellbeing, alongside anxiety about the shape of a future South Africa. In other cases, however, responses to looming social change seemed bizarre and divorced from the political situation. For many, raised within a dramatic ideological climate that claimed civilisation and safety could only exist under white rule, the idea of a peaceful shift to democracy was quite literally unthinkable. Afrikaners in particular found it impossible to imagine the continued existence of God's 'chosen nation' under non-white rule (Manzo and McGowan 1992). The 'cyclical reinforcement of white fear [was] one of the vital ingredients for keeping the [National Party] in power' (van der Westhuizen 2007, 163). The fear of black peril (Ullmann 2005), the *swart gevaar* as it was known in Afrikaans, was potent, publicly acknowledged and skilfully manipulated by politicians, the media and cultural figures. But it was also premised on the idea that majority rule would never actually happen: if Afrikaners, and white people in general, held fast then South Africa would remain a white nation. Apartheid had done its work too well. As it began to wane, these conscious anxieties morphed, for many, into something unthinkable, a psychically inadmissible apocalypse. Long-held beliefs about the violence and chaos associated with black liberation were pressed to the back of the common consciousness because they had become too close, too overwhelming, too frightening, too threatening.

If we think of this shift as something akin to repression, then the Satanism scare can be understood as a symptom of that repression. Some white South African fears of the future, impossible to manage using existing mechanisms, were repressed. They then returned, distorted, in the shape of a different object: the phantasmic figure of the Satanist, which imagined the danger as coming from white people but nonetheless drew on longstanding beliefs about racial threat. Descriptions of satanic crimes mirrored the grotesque violence that appeared in whites' stories of African anti-colonial struggles. Events associated with black liberation elsewhere on the continent, like the Mau Mau uprising in Kenya, the French evacuation from Algeria and the Belgian retreat from Congo, 'were all deeply unsettling to whites in South Africa. Afrikaans newspapers provided full and often lurid accounts of these traumatic events. Fear of an equally violent catastrophe lay close to the core of Afrikaner thought' (Giliomee 2003, 120), but had never before come close to the core of Afrikaner reality.

Thus rather than an arbitrary object, the content of the moral panic, which coalesced around the signifier of the white Satanist, indicates the return of a repressed set of collective fears that had long been mobilised for political gain, and that became unmanageable in the face of social change. The Satanism scare revealed how impossible many whites found it to face a future that could only be imagined as deeply traumatising. Inducted by apartheid into a failure of collective imagination, many white people invested their affective energies into the panic surrounding Satanism, rather than – or in many cases as well as – thinking about the (apparently inevitable) nightmarish violence of majority rule.

Another set of concepts that can productively help us to think about Satanism at the end of apartheid, frequently linked by psychoanalysts (see for example Freud 1961), is the duo of fetishism and disavowal. These processes occur when external reality threatens to intrude into a belief on which the ego is predicated. Disavowal 'constitutes the defence against those anxiety-provoking external perceptions that endanger the knowledge of reality we have hitherto had' (Priel 1991, 21). In Freud's (notoriously problematic) design of infantile sexuality, disavowal refers to the male child's realisation that the mother does not have a penis and his subsequent refusal to admit this, as her lack suggests that he too may experience such a loss (1961, 151–152). Disavowal involves the relationship between knowledge and the concurrent refusal to know, the contradictory structure of '*Je sais bien mais quand même*', 'I know very well but all the same' (Mannoni 1985, 9–30). In Freud's explanation of fetishism, maternal lack is disavowed and some other visible object – hair, fur, shoes – replaces the missing phallus and becomes an object of sexual excitement (1961).

Without simply claiming that the imaginary Satanist was an object of white fetishist disavowal in the sense suggested above, we can think about some of the roles the Satanist played in late apartheid consciousness by examining its relation to the *mechanisms* of disavowal and fetishism, and to their imbrication in structures of power.

One of the many elements that underpinned apartheid's effectiveness was the governing fiction that white South Africans ruled by right rather than by violence, and that apartheid was an act of benevolent, paternalistic guardianship performed by altruistic and civilised whites for black people who were being permitted to 'separately develop' in line with their lesser capacities. By the mid-1980s this belief in the moral mandate of apartheid was becoming increasingly untenable, as black resistance increased across the country and the global anti-apartheid movement gained traction. What was disavowed here was the increasing legibility and volume of black South Africans' calls for freedom and justice, spurred by a level of international attention that added a renewed sense of legitimacy and threatened the justifications many whites depended on for their complicity with a brutal system. Fetishized in their place was the uncanny white Satanist, a figure that was both terrifying and familiar, emerging from within the white world rather than from the frightening outside. Segments of white South Africa looked away from autonomous black political action, which presented a genuine and significant danger to continued white rule, and towards the apocryphal figure of the Satanist, frightening and horrifying but coherent with rather than anathema to the ideas that upheld white South African political mythology.

Where the black resistance fighter threatened to reveal the weakness and delusion of the colonial beliefs underpinning white rule, the Satanist strengthened them, repeating a narrative that presented South Africa as a white Christian nation under attack from demonic forces that could only be beaten by prayer, adherence to the hierarchy and belief in the power of the community. Recalling Hall et al.'s claims about the hegemonic nature of the moral panic (1978), we can see in this instance the way in which panic served a political purpose. Disavowal of black people's agency and the legitimacy of their claims in favour of the fetishisation of imaginary threats allowed white people to once again turn away from black South Africans' increasingly powerful calls for justice and equality.

Finally I want to think briefly about Satanism in terms of hysteria. In classical psychoanalysis hysteria was understood as a disease of symbolism, which could be 'read' through its visible or audible physical symptoms. Juliet Mitchell notes that case studies of female hysterics were vital to the development of psychoanalytic ideas and led to 'understanding symptoms and dreams as wish fulfilment' (1996, 474). Hysteria was an illness 'in which the psychical conflict is expressed symbolically' (Laplanche and Pontalis 1988, 194). An hysterical symptom 'is an alternative representation of a forbidden wish which has broken through from the unconscious, whence it was banished, into consciousness – but in an "unrecognizable" form' (Mitchell 2000, 10). Such symptoms usually seem illegible and meaningless. They appear on the body of the hysteric and the psychoanalyst must interpret them in order to be able to read, and thus treat or cure, the condition.

Like hysteria, the sudden outbreak of Satanism fear involved an explosion of symbols and symptoms, which we can 'read' in order to understand its underlying causes. Stories of Satanism were littered with references to symbols: Satanic dens full of black candles allegedly made of human fat (*Personality*, 14 May 1990), peace signs, anarchy signs and other cryptic images scrawled on school walls and carved into teenage skin (Seale 1991, 19–40; Jonker 1997, 9), pentagrams and swastikas marked on graves (*Weekend Argus*, 19 May 1990), secret handshakes and code words known only to Satanists. South African Satanism was said to involve 'renouncing Christ, desecration of Christian symbols ... and the drinking of human blood in a blasphemous parody of the Eucharist' (Ivey 1993, 181). It existed in symbolic opposition to the white Christian nation, revealing by association the deep fissures within that set of myths.

It is unsurprising that white South African culture should have manifested its pathologies in this way. Afrikaner identity was created and invoked by a 'series of cultural symbols that established and constantly reaffirmed [it] as ... of Africa and the land, and as white' (Witz 2003, 11), and other white identities drew on this symbolic language to affirm their own embeddedness in whiteness and civilisation. Employing ideas drawn from studies of hysteria to think about the Satanism scare allows us to foreground the symbols – that is, the *content* – of the scare, and thus to reveal not just how the moral panic happened but also what it means for our understanding of the pathologies of whiteness in the late apartheid period.

The Satanist embodied a particular kind of threat, one that allowed white South Africans to believe that the apparent danger they faced was spiritual rather than political. If we consider Satanism in metaphorical rather than literal terms as a 'symptom' of a now-forgotten collective 'hysteria', we acknowledge the intensity and effects of the anxiety, outrage and terror that characterised often-repressed white fears of black majority rule, and thus the troubled and destructive nature of South African whiteness.

In closing, then, it is clear that it is important to consider the meaning as well as the spread of social phenomena like moral panics. In the case of Satanism in South Africa, such a consideration reveals the irrational beliefs and anxieties that underlay white identity in this period, and that persist in South Africa and elsewhere. This understanding is greatly enriched with reference to a psychoanalytic register that foregrounds the affective power of the panic. Traditional moral panic research needs to take more account of how these events make us feel as well as the symbolic content that comprises them.

Psychoanalysis and moral panic, particularly when used together, remain important tools for the analysis of the socio-cultural formations, identities, beliefs and behaviours that so powerfully shape lived experience. As critical and diagnostic implements that permit us to think about the affective structures that underlie the world we live in, they remain invaluable. To return to Derek Hook, the 'unprecedented violence' of the colonial encounter suggests that a psychological register is appropriate (2005, 479). We need psychoanalysis to understand moral panic, racism and the forces and experiences that underlie our collective histories of identity and ongoing struggles for social injustice.

Notes

1 My analysis of the South African Satanism scare draws on religious pamphlets, newspapers and magazine material from a ten-year period. Material was sourced using the SA Media database, a press cutting service hosted by the University of the Free State, and through manual searching of the press archives held by the National Library of South Africa. As SA Media does not collate full bibliographic detail for the material it collects, texts referred to in this essay have been referenced using source and date of publication, the only data that is consistently available throughout the corpus.
2 Notable exceptions include scholarship on the peculiarities of being white under apartheid (for example Wade 1993; Crapanzano 1985; Chidester 1991), and more recent work on the so-called Border War, the apartheid government's covert war against neighbouring states that offered support to the ANC, into which young white South African men were conscripted (Baines and Vale 2008; Batley 2007; Draper 2001).
3 As I have discussed elsewhere, the notion that deviant white people used secret symbolic languages in order to be visible to each other also appeared in related moral panics around Communism and white male homosexuality (Falkof 2015, 77–81; Falkof 2018a).
4 Moral panic has been used to explain fears around, for example, mugging (Hall et al. 1978), drug use (Linnemann 2010), single mothers (Ajzenstadt 2008), paedophiles (Critcher 2002), Muslims (Morgan and Poynting 2012) and role-playing games (Waldron 2005).
5 I have elsewhere (Falkof 2018b) discussed these critiques of moral panic theory in more detail.

Bibliography

Ahmed, S. 2014. *The Cultural Politics of Emotion*. s.l.: Edinburgh University Press.
Ajzenstadt, Mimi. 2008. 'Moral panic and neo-liberalism: the case of single mothers on welfare in Israel'. *The British Journal of Criminology* 49 (1): 68–87.
Baines, Gary F., and Peter Vale, eds. 2008. *Beyond the border war: new perspectives on Southern Africa's late-cold war conflicts*. South Africa: Unisa Press.
Batley, Karen, ed. 2007. *A secret burden: memories of the border war by South African soldiers who fought in it*. Johannesburg: Jonathan Ball.
Becker, Howard S. 1995. 'Moral entrepreneurs: the creation and enforcement of deviant categories'. In *Deviance: A Symbolic Interactionist Approach*, edited by Nancy J. Herman, 169–178. Dix Hills, NY: General Hall.
Chidester, David. 1991. *Shots in the streets: violence and religion in South Africa*. Boston: Beacon Press.

Cohen, Stanley. 1972. *Folk devils and moral panics: the creation of the mods and rockers*. Oxford: Martin Robertson.
Cohen, Stanley. 2011. 'Whose side were we on? the undeclared politics of moral panic theory'. *Crime, Media, Culture* 7 (3): 237–243.
Crapanzano, Vincent. 1985. *Waiting: the whites of South Africa*. London: Granada.
Critcher, Chas. 2002. 'Media, government and moral panic: the politics of paedophilia in Britain 2000–1'. *Journalism Studies* 3 (4): 521–535.
Critcher, Chas. 2003. *Moral panics and the media*. Buckingham; Philadelphia: Open University Press.
Critcher, Chas. 2011. 'For a political economy of moral panics'. *Crime, Media, Culture* 7 (3): 259–275.
Draper, Catherine. 2001. 'The border and beyond: an analysis of the post-border war discourses of families of ex-SADF soldiers'. Masters dissertation, Cape Town: University of Cape Town.
Falkof, Nicky. 2015. *Satanism and family murder in late apartheid South Africa: imagining the end of whiteness*. London: Palgrave.
Falkof, Nicky. 2018a. 'Sex and the devil: homosexuality, satanism and moral panic in late apartheid South Africa'. *Men and Masculinities*.
Falkof, Nicky. 2018b. 'On moral panic: some directions for further development'. *Critical Sociology*, October.
Fanon, Frantz. 1970. *Black skins, white masks*. London: Paladin.
Freud, Sigmund. 1957. 'Repression'. In *The standard edition of the complete psychological works of Sigmund Freud*, ed. J. Strachey; trans. J. Strachey and A. Freud, with A. Strachey and A. Tyson, London: The Hogarth Press and the Institute of Psychoanalysis, 24 vols., vol. XIV.
Freud, Sigmund. 1961. 'Fetishism'. In *The standard edition of the complete psychological works of Sigmund Freud*, ed. J. Strachey; trans. J. Strachey and A. Freud, with A. Strachey and A. Tyson, London: The Hogarth Press and the Institute of Psychoanalysis, 24 vols., vol. XXI.
Freud, Sigmund. 1962. 'Further remarks on the neuro-psychoses of defence'. In *The standard edition of the complete psychological works of Sigmund Freud*, ed. J. Strachey; trans. J. Strachey and A. Freud, with A. Strachey and A. Tyson, London: The Hogarth Press and the Institute of Psychoanalysis, 24 vols., vol. III.
Freud, Sigmund. 1991. *The Interpretation of Dreams*. London: Penguin.
Giliomee, Herman. 2003. *The Afrikaners, biography of a people*. London: Hurst and Company.
Goode, Erich, and Nachman Ben-Yehuda. 1994. *Moral panics: the social construction of deviance*. Oxford, UK; Cambridge, USA: Blackwell.
Hall, Stuart, Chas Critcher, Tony Jefferson, John N. Clarke, and Brian Roberts. 1978. *Policing the crisis: mugging, the state, and law and order*. London: Macmillan.
Hier, Sean P. 2002. 'Conceptualizing moral panic through a moral economy of harm'. *Critical Sociology* 28 (3): 311–334.
Hook, Derek. 2005. 'A critical psychology of the postcolonial'. *Theory & Psychology* 15 (4): 475–503.
Ivey, Gavin. 1993. 'The psychology of satan worship'. *The South African Journal of Psychology* 23 (4): 180–185.
Jenkins, Philip. 2009. 'Failure to launch: why do some social issues fail to detonate moral panics?' *British Journal of Criminology* 49 (1): 35–47.

Jonker, Kobus. 1997. *Satanisme en die tiener*. South Africa: Self-published.
Kinghorn, Johann. 1997. 'Modernisation and apartheid: the Afrikaner churches'. In *Christianity in South Africa: A Political, Social and Cultural History*, edited by Richard Elphick and Rodney Davenport. Berkeley, California: University of California Press.
Kitzinger, Jenny, and David Miller. 1998. 'AIDS, the policy process and moral panics'. In *The circuit of mass communication: media strategies, representation and audience reception in the AIDS crisis*, edited by David Miller, Jenny Kitzinger, Kevin Williams, and Peter Beharrell, 192–211. London: Sage.
Laplanche, Jean, and Jean Bertrand Pontalis. 1988. *The language of psychoanalysis*. Translated by Donald Nicholson-Smith. London: Hogarth Press.
Latour, Bruno. 2000. 'When things strike back: a possible contribution of "science studies" to the social sciences'. *The British Journal of Sociology* 51 (1): 107–123.
Linnemann, Travis. 2010. 'Mad men, meth moms, moral panic: gendering meth crimes in the midwest'. *Critical Criminology* 18 (2): 95–110. https://doi.org/10.1007/s10612-009-9094-8.
Mannoni, Octave. 1985. *Clefs pour l'imaginaire, ou, l'autre scène*. Paris: Seuil.
Manzo, Kate, and Pat McGowan. 1992. 'Afrikaner fears and the politics of despair: understanding change in South Africa'. *International Studies Quarterly* 36 (1): 1–24.
Mbembe, Achille. 2015. 'Terror and the postcolonial'. In *The colony: its guilty secret and its accursed share*, edited by Elleke Boehmer and Stephen Morton, 27–54. Chichester: Wiley-Blackwell.
McRobbie, Angela, and Sarah L. Thornton. 1995. 'Rethinking "moral panic" for multi-mediated social worlds'. *The British Journal of Sociology* 46 (4): 559–574.
Mitchell, Juliet. 1996. 'Sexuality and psychoanalysis: hysteria'. *British Journal of Psychotherapy* 12 (4): 473–479.
Mitchell, Juliet. 2000. *Psychoanalysis and feminism*. 4th ed. New York: Basic Books.
Morgan, George, and Scott Poynting, eds. 2012. *Global Islamophobia, Muslims and moral panic in the west*. Farnham, Surrey; Burlington, Vt.: Ashgate.
Priel, Beatrice. 1991. 'Disavowal in fiction'. *International Review of Psycho-Analysis* 18: 19–26.
Richardson, James T., Joel Best, and David G. Bromley, eds. 1991. *The satanism scare*. New York: Aldine de Gruyter.
Rohloff, Amanda, and Sarah Wright. 2010. 'Moral panic and social theory: beyond the heuristic'. *Current Sociology* 58 (3): 403–419.
Seale, Rodney. 1991. *Satanisme: die reg om the weet*. Menlo Park, South Africa: Hans Kirsten Uitgewery.
Showalter, Elaine. 1997. *Hystories: hysterical epidemics and modern culture*. New York: Picador.
Tabensky, Pedro Alexis. 2010. 'The oppressor's pathology'. *Theoria: A Journal of Social and Political Theory* 57 (125): 77–98.
Transvaal Education Department. 1992. *Satanism and occultism, section 1: guide for principles and teachers*. South Africa: Transvaal Education Department.
Ullmann, Christine. 2005. 'Black peril, white fear – representations of violence and race in South Africa's English press, 1976–2002, and their influence on public opinion'. PhD thesis, Köln: Universität zu Köln.
van der Westhuizen, Christi. 2007. *White power and the rise and fall of the national party*. Cape Town: Zebra Press.

van Zyl, James. 1988. *Know your enemy!* Stanger, South Africa: Faith in the Word Ministries.

Wade, Michael. 1993. *White on black in South Africa: a study of English-language inscriptions of skin colour.* Basingstoke: Macmillan.

Waldron, David. 2005. 'Role-playing games and the Christian right: community formation in response to a moral panic'. *The Journal of Religion and Popular Culture* 9 (1): 3–3.

Watney, Simon. 1988. 'AIDS, "moral panic" theory and homophobia'. In *Social Aspects of AIDS*, edited by Peter Aggleton and Hilary Homans. London: Falmer Press.

Witz, Leslie. 2003. *Apartheid's festival: contesting South Africa's national pasts.* Bloomington, Indiana: Indiana University Press.

Wright, Lawrence. 1994. *Remembering Satan.* London: Serpent's Tail.

Chapter 5

Reconstructing *Pinky*

Ian Magor

Upon its release in 1949, the film *Pinky* (1949) attracted large audiences and generated pages of newspaper comment. Despite being produced by Darryl Zanuck and directed by Elia Kazan it is little remembered today. The Cid Ricketts Sumner novel *Quality* (1946) on which it was based is less well-known still; and yet it is a book which contains some remarkably astute descriptions of the racialised gaze. One such takes place in the book's first encounter between the story's light-skinned heroine and a white, male station attendant, as he realises that the young woman in front of him has a black heritage. Upon recognising this he withdraws his previous offer of assistance. Ricketts describes how this is experienced by Pinkey:

> He had been just as he always was, no doubt, with—with people like her. A machine, implacable, blind, pitiless. And she—she was the thing the machine had passed over.
>
> (Sumner, 1946, p. 11)

The person looking is actually blinded to what he sees in front of him, forced by social conventions to re-interpret his vision, and thereby drain any humanity from the transaction. It is a gaze which also subverts logic: founded on the basis of the superiority of a skin colour and then, as here, its reliability as a signifier denied. The woman—now reduced to a 'thing'—has been pitilessly passed over, transferred from one classification to another, or more accurately, rejected as not belonging to a privileged category. This fictional character, Pinkey Johnson, has been discovered carrying out a form of trespass. The filmed adaptation of the story was able to place in still sharper focus the illogicality of this gaze, doing so at a time when America was confronted with the hypocrisy of its claims to be a beacon of freedom on the world stage, while running a two-tier, racially segregated system at home. The film was both a comment on this and part of an attempt to change public opinion. It demonstrates how fictional representations, such as this film, often carry a historical weight that is easily overlooked.

DOI: 10.4324/9781003200765-7

The film producer Darryl Zanuck acquired the screen rights to the novel, and in 1949 the movie, now titled *Pinky*, was released to general acclaim and box-office success. *Pinky* was seventh in the list of top-grossing films of 1949, and the most successful for Twentieth Century-Fox (Schatz, 1994, p. 6). Stormy weather on its opening day at New York's Rivoli Theatre on 29 September failed to prevent large audiences turning out, making it the venue's biggest matinee in ten years (Motion Picture Daily, 1949, p. 1), and the theatre began screenings at 8:30am to accommodate the crowds (Clark, 1997, p. 185). *Pinky* was the third in a cycle of five films, made and released within about a year of each other, tackling the subject of race. The first of the releases *Home of the Brave* was comprised of an all-male cast and the second, *Lost Boundaries*, was another story of racial passing, but with a narrative driven by male characters.[1] *Pinky* was, and still is, notable for its strong female core with all three of the principal actresses nominated for Oscars at that year's Academy Awards. It tells the story of a white-skinned, dual-heritage woman, Pinky[2] (Jeanne Crain), who has trained as a nurse in the North. While there, she has been in a relationship with a white doctor, Tom (William Lundigan), who is unaware of her black heritage and has asked her to marry him. Realising the implications of accepting and starting a family, Pinky has fled to the home of her grandmother, Aunt Dicey (Ethel Waters).[3] Appalled by the racism she sees, and feeling that she does not fit in, she decides to return to Tom. However, her plans are derailed by the illness of her grandmother's white matriarchal employer, Miss Em (Ethel Barrymore). Pinky is pressured into caring for Miss Em by Aunt Dicey and after a hostile introduction, the patient and her nurse come to respect one another. So much so, that when Miss Em dies, Pinky is the chief beneficiary of the will. This is contested by Miss Em's relatives on grounds of race, and Pinky is forced to go to court to fight her case. She wins, but this presents her with a dilemma of either staying on to run a segregated clinic as Pinky Johnson (Pinky thinks Miss Em wanted her to turn the house into a clinic), or starting a new life with her lover, passing as the white Mrs Thomas Adams, in Denver: a new life that will erase her previous history. She chooses to stay and run the clinic, thus sacrificing her relationship with Tom.

Screenwriter Philip Dunne was clear about the deliberate strategy of casting a recognisably white actress in the role of the passing lead. He insisted that 'the whole point was that she had to look absolutely white ... The message of the picture was very simple: People were wonderfully deferential to her until they found out and they turned completely, 180 degrees' (McBride, 2003, p. 490). Indeed, the casting of Jeanne Crain in the title role—although necessitated by the censorship and social mores of the time—works effectively in exposing the irrationality of the American system of segregation in force at the time of the film's release. This segregation was intimately bound up with fears relating to miscegenation.[4] The paranoid aspect of such fears was well illustrated when the light-skinned black actress Fredi Washington had to 'black up' for a romantic scene opposite the dark-skinned black actor Paul Robeson. Production Code administrators were afraid that the viewer would 'see' an instance of miscegenation, which was a strictly censored representation (Delson, 2006, p. 139). *Pinky* follows this tortured racist logic of superior and inferior beings—based on a heritage unreliably signified by skin colour—and reveals the dominance of racist anxiety about 'passing' in twentieth-century America. By showing this in the medium of cinema where the visual is prioritised, the discrepancy between what we see and what we are told is more difficult to disavow. The narrative takes the 'one-drop' rule of Jim Crow enforcement to its ultimate conclusion: this binary approach to classification shows, finally, how the system of apartheid contains the seeds of its own destruction. Moreover, the film also challenges the dominant male viewing position and conventional story structure. It asks viewers not only to align their gaze with a black woman but one who also rejects marriage to a white man. In the guise of a compromised melodrama, the film overturns a number of practices and processes that would become central to a psychoanalytical understanding of film. Such an understanding was based on an equivalence between the look of the camera and the white male gaze. By shifting the position of the audience's identification the film exposes the complicity of cinema itself in perpetuating the myth of the over-sexualised black woman.

Waiting and watching

> I cannot go to a film without seeing myself. I wait for me. In the interval, just before the film starts, I wait for me. The people in the theatre are watching me, examining me, waiting for me. A Negro groom is going to appear. My heart makes my head swim.
>
> (Fanon, 2000, p. 107)

The 'Negro groom' referred to ironically here by Fanon in 1951, calls to mind the image of the black slave Gus in D. W. Griffith's hatefully racist film *The Birth of a Nation* (1915). If it was this image that was causing Fanon's trepidation about what was to appear on the theatre screen, it was an image that also haunted the representation of black men in American cinema throughout the twentieth century. In Griffith's story, adapted from Thomas Dixon's novel *The Clansman* (Dixon, 1905), Gus, encouraged by the victory of the North in the Civil War and the enforced end of slavery in the South, asks his white former mistress to marry him. She refuses, runs away, he follows, and, reading this as a precursor to rape, she throws herself from a cliff to her death. After this visual assault on black sexuality, during the interwar years black actors were called upon to play little other than servants, petty criminals and buffoons (Bogle, 1994).[5] In waiting to see what the film will show of the black man, Fanon is painfully aware that irrational emotions could be called upon to make his head swim, knowing well how these effects will influence how he is seen by the rest of the audience—and even how he might regard himself—when the movie draws to a close. If what is shown on the screen is able to generate such identifications, what takes place within various kinds of viewer when a black female character is played by a white actress, with no use of blackface to act as a mask?

What is curious about many of the first reviews of *Pinky* is how little attention is paid to the fact that the eponymous role is played by a white woman. Leading critic Bosley Crowther, writing in the *New York Times* referred to the character as 'a girl with white skin but Negro blood' and credited Crain with 'giving a winning personality to the much-abused girl' (Crowther, 1949, p. 28). Given that the state of Virginia had the tightest legislation pertaining to miscegenation, it is not surprising that it was a reviewer from there who was more alert to the casting issues. Film critic Ralph Dighton classified Jeanne Crain as a 'native Californian of Irish descent who has specialised in "all-American Girl" portrayals'. He ruminated on how:

> There are love scenes between Jeanne and the white doctor who loves her enough to overlook her Negro blood. If "Pinky" were portrayed by a Negro, how would audiences react to her being kissed by white Bill Lundigan?
> Sometimes people will tolerate an idea where they wouldn't accept an actual fact.
> (Dighton, 1949, p. 13)

How far such ideas are tolerated is often as much a consequence of where and with whom a film is seen. In a piece written for *The Reporter* in 1949 specifically talking about the race cycle of films from earlier that year, Ralph Ellison (author of *Invisible Man*) exempts *Intruder in the Dust* as the only one of the quartet 'that could be shown in Harlem without arousing unintended laughter' (Ellison, 1995, p. 281). What Ellison also admits though is that each one of the films is 'worth seeing, and if seen, capable of involving us emotionally'. Because they are designed to work on the guilt of the white viewer, he registers a marked difference when they are shown to a predominantly white audience. There is a 'profuse flow of tears and the sighs of profound emotional catharsis heard on all sides' (Ibid., p. 280). Ellison's description of a 'catharsis heard on all sides', suggests that the experience of seeing white audiences emotionally affected by the film has a contagious effect on the black viewers. Ellison's approval of *Intruder in the Dust* was because through that film 'Negroes can make complete identification with their screen image' (Ibid., p. 281). Ironically, the general lack of opportunities for identification alongside the imposition of segregation in the cinema may have had the consequence of allowing black audiences to generate their own subversive responses to the mainstream white films they viewed. Ellison gestures towards this with his description of 'unintended laughter'. James Baldwin, on the other hand, was struck by aspects of white performance with which he could identify. Baldwin describes growing up and finding that white actors such as Sylvia Sidney and Henry Fonda moved him in profound ways that were not available when watching the belittling caricatures of black actors such as Stepin Fetchit and Manton Moreland (Baldwin, 1976, pp. 19–21). Baldwin's points of identification were the way that Fonda walked down a street and the feeling that he had of sharing a secret with Sidney. For an intellectual such as Baldwin these white models acted as a stark contrast to the 'excruciating, nearly incomprehensible stutter and drawl' of Fetchit (Rogin, 1996, p. 171). Baldwin said that he loathed the work of these actors but allowed for the possibility that others derived a certain truth from the 'comic, bug-eyed terror' they portrayed (Baldwin, 1976, p. 20). The American critic and author Mel Watkins makes a compelling case that black audiences revelled in the trickery which they saw in the performance of Fetchit, seeing him as emblematic of the Southern black quip 'Got one mind for white folks to see; 'nother for what I know is me' (Watkins, 2006, p. 22).

The black female spectator

Laura Mulvey's seminal article 'Visual Pleasure and Narrative Cinema' famously elaborates the concept of the 'male gaze'. Mulvey regards Hollywood as 'a world ordered by sexual imbalance, pleasure in looking has been split between active/male and passive/female. The determining male gaze projects its fantasy onto the female figure, which is styled accordingly' (Mulvey, 1975, p. 11). The unconscious anxiety which is aroused in the male viewer when confronted by the female body is managed in two main ways: the woman is glamourised to the extent that the look takes on the elements of a fetishistic scopophilia; or the spectator engages in a kind of sadistic voyeurism in which the male hero—with whom the viewer identifies—is responsible for an investigation of her character (Ibid., p. 14). Interestingly, in *Pinky*, when Tom is made aware of his partner's blackness he pledges to investigate his own character and attitudes. As a doctor he aligns himself with science, hoping that its methodologies will protect him from any belief in the inferiority of races. At the same time, he recognises that what we know to be the case can often be undermined by what exists deep down within ourselves: the irrational unconscious drives and projections which find their outlet in racist thoughts and actions. He immediately anticipates this creating problems for their relationship because he will not be able to 'cuss out' his future wife without her framing his reasons for doing so within a racial context. Already, what seconds ago was a story of two young people falling in love, has now become entwined in thoughts around the invalidation of scientific racism, unconscious prejudice, and threats to patriarchy. The black female body, as soon as it is placed centre screen, disrupts and destabilises the male gaze of classical narrative cinema.

So when Mulvey calls for a cinema that breaks the spell of illusion, that can 'free the look of the camera into its materiality in time and space and the look of the audience into dialectics, passionate detachment' (Ibid., p. 18), the focus of the camera on the black woman may work towards bringing this about for the white viewer. Ellison and Baldwin have already shown how Mulvey's 'passionate detachment' may have been imposed upon black cinema viewers through a failure to offer points of identification, and how this allowed a distance from the screen that created a freedom to analyse. Various black female theorists have shown how this is doubly so for black women. As the African American literature scholar Miriam Thaggert asks: 'With whom does a black woman identify, since neither the white male hero of a film nor the white woman who is only object, is a satisfying character with whom most black women can connect?' (Thaggert, 1998, p. 482). The space which the black male might still have to identify with the male hero is ostensibly closed off to the black, female viewer.[6] The feminist activist and scholar, bell hooks, asserts that 'Mainstream feminist film criticism in no way acknowledges black female spectatorship' (hooks, 1992, p. 123). What hooks demonstrates is how black women can override the split that Mulvey posits and which is crucial to her theory of an active/male and passive/female spectatorship. 'Black female spectators actively chose not to identify with the film's imaginary subject because such identification was disenabling' (Ibid., p. 122). hooks terms the way in which black women spectators were able to view the cinema as an 'oppositional gaze', making them critically aware of how film worked to construct white womanhood as the site of the phallocentric gaze, and thus able to choose to forego identification with either the victim or the perpetrator (Ibid.). What Mulvey sets out as a programme that needs to be taken up by women to deconstruct the binary opposition with which they were being presented, was for hooks a process that black women had been conducting since watching their first films. Confirming the centrality of *The Birth of a Nation* to American narrative cinema, she declares that 'as a seminal work, this film identified what the place and function of white womanhood would be in cinema. There was clearly no place for black women' (Ibid., p. 120). But this prohibition of black women, as hooks shows and Mulvey hints at, meant that the distance it created from full identification with the characters on screen granted a certain power to her gaze.

The whiteness of Pinky

The casting of Jeanne Crain in the role of Pinky was a deceptively radical choice, and successfully exposed the contradictions of American race laws and ideology. By using a white actress, it could be argued that the producers were complicit in perpetuating a system that excluded black actors from serious roles. It can be accepted that this was the case at the same time as suggesting that a light-skinned black actress such as Lena Horne might have complicated the desired identification with the white viewer. Importantly, the film was intended more for a white than a black audience.[7] The movie was marketed as a blockbuster and needed a white audience in order to achieve such success. Although this was the case in terms of numbers and financial return, the emotional investment of black audiences appears to have been far greater. When the film opened in Atlanta at The Roxy, the doors were opened at 8:30am and 'Negroes were lined up for blocks. More than sixty white people were also awaiting the opening'. There was a police presence because of threatened demonstrations but 'the balcony of Negroes and ground floor of whites applauded' what they saw (New York Times, 1949). The extra layer introduced by the casting of Crain enabled the white audience to see that in the illogical world created by the rules of segregation, and its insistence on 'pure blood', white skin, in and of itself, was no guarantee that a person could not be assigned to the category of Negro. Whatever Jeanne Crain as Pinky might be, she possesses none of the supposed Negro traits that form the regular Hollywood stereotype.

Film historian Donald Bogle was among those who saw the casting of Jeanne Crain as a shocking compromise and a racist tactic in itself, alleging that she made 'a far more successful movie but a far less honest one too' (Bogle, 1994, p. 152). But this idea of the white body being marked black was not as unusual as it might sound and look to us now. We need only remind ourselves that the leader of the National Association for the Advancement of Coloured People then was Walter White who began his autobiography 'I am a Negro. My skin is white, my eyes are blue, my hair is blond' (White, 1949). And Adam Clayton Powell, who represented Harlem in the House of Representatives, was light-skinned enough that he usually had to inform people that he was black. A 1948 *Ebony* magazine cover story estimated that there were around five million 'passers' and that each year saw up to 50,000 more passing into white society. Not only did this make white people wary of new neighbours, it discouraged them from looking too closely into their own family histories (Kelley, 2016). Valerie Smith, scholar of African American culture, captures why the figure of the mulatto is problematic for the racialised gaze: 'The light-skinned black body ... indicates a contradiction between appearance and "essential" racial identity within a system of racial distinctions based upon differences presumed to be visible' (Smith, 1994, p. 45). This means that sometimes, to accept the outward appearance of whiteness as a guarantee of the inherent quality of 'whiteness', bolsters the myths of racial difference. If the performance is convincing, and 'whiteness' accepted, this works towards reinforcing notions of white supremacy; if it is questioned, the correlation between actions and racial identity is then called into doubt.[8] So, in the film, Pinky's skin is an ambiguous and potentially misleading signifier. It is a subversion of what Fanon calls the 'racial epidermal schema' (Fanon, 2000, p. 84). Pinky must always be seen twice (Wald, 2000, p. 99). And if the skin is no guarantee of belonging to the race, then as Daniel Bernardi puts it: 'there are no white people per se, only those who pass as white' (Bernardi, 2001, p. xxi).

Whether or not an individual passed as white, however, was down to white eyes. We see this the first time that Pinky is (mis)recognised as white. This takes place on a train: Aunt Dicey puts Pinky in the black carriage but is overridden by a white train guard who moves her to the white carriage, thus setting off the series of events that see her receive a white schooling. A similar misrecognition resulted in the landmark ruling of *Plessy v. Ferguson* in 1896. It was this ruling which enshrined in law the legitimacy of offering segregated facilities and services for the supposed different races of 'whites' and 'coloured'. Whilst the ruling is regularly referred to for its centrality to Jim Crow segregation in the first half of the twentieth century, the fact that the plaintiff appeared to be white is rarely mentioned.[9] Homer Adolph Plessy was seven-eighths Caucasian and he chose to bring to the attention of the train guard that he was travelling in the carriage restricted to accommodating white passengers.[10] The 'impure' heritage of Plessy was not sufficiently marked by his skin but once alerted to it, the guard told him he should move and Plessy's refusal saw the matter eventually escalate to the Supreme Court. There are at least three major planks of twentieth-century racism supported in this ruling. Firstly, it gives full support to the 'one-drop' rule of a binary construction of race, where a person may only claim whiteness if they have no 'black blood' at all in their family history, and that if a person has any admixture whatsoever, for legal purposes they are to be treated as black. Secondly, it places the 'true nature' of a person in the heredity and biology of the corporeal body, so that a pale skin and Caucasian features do not define what race a person is declared to belong to. Thirdly, the way in which the laws of segregation were to be enforced was around the visual perception of the white—primarily male—bearer of the look, bestowed with the authority of the state or its organisations. Bizarrely then, the future decision about which carriage Plessy would ride in would be made by the same guard who had perceived him as belonging in the white carriage in the first instance. The onus, once again, would be on Plessy to declare himself. This must be seen as one of the reasons that such harsh punishment was meted out to any black people who broke the rules and particularly why so much rage was directed against the so-called 'mulatto'. The person of mixed race, whose heritage was not epidermically obvious presented the greatest threat to these binary positions.

Passing

Although as a melodrama *Pinky* plays up the transgression and danger of passing, the reality could be, for many, more prosaic. This is well captured in the 1929 novella *Passing*, written by Nella Larsen, where the story begins with Irene Redfield using the lightness of her coloured skin to enjoy the breeze of the Drayton's roof terrace, before going back to her major role as mother in a black family. Her passing was a matter of convenience and not a life choice. That said, the story does end with the outing of her friend Clare

Kendry. Clare Kendry has spent most of her adult life passing as white and has married a white man, who, upon learning of his wife's identity, rages: 'So you're a n****r, a damned dirty n****r!' (Larsen, 2014, p. 238). Once exposed, Clare (the name derived from the Latin clarus, referring to light and clarity) cannot continue as the person she is thought to be. Her figurative death only just precedes her actual death with a fall from the window. The words of her husband surely call to mind the exclamation which marks the opening of Fanon's 'The Fact of Blackness' in *Black Skin, White Masks* almost a quarter of a century later: '"Dirty n****r!" Or simply "Look, a Negro!"' (Fanon, 2000, p. 82). Larsen could also be seen as anticipating Fanon when Clare stands in front of the window immediately after she has been exposed by her husband, and her life is described as 'lying in fragments before her' (Larsen, 2014, p. 238). Fanon says that hearing the words "Dirty n****r", 'I burst apart' (Fanon, 2000, p. 82).

Both the film *Pinky*, and the novella *Passing*, show how the black body in and of itself carries limited meaning and that it is the contextualisation of the body that imbues it with significance. Judith Butler emphasises this point in her reading of Larsen's story in *Bodies That Matter*. Butler writes 'what can be seen, what qualifies as a visible marking, is a matter of being able to read a marked body in relation to unmarked bodies, where unmarked bodies constitute the currency of normative whiteness' (Butler, 1993, p. 170). In *Passing*, Irene changes little about herself when she dines in the Drayton other than her surroundings. Pinky presents a similar case. One of the admirable features of Pinky is that she accommodates herself in exactly the same manner wherever she happens to be. It is other people and social contexts that change her from one colour to another, often within the space of the same scene. Butler also stresses the role of a punishing super-ego. If the super-ego is instilled with a set of ideals that are socially instituted and maintained then it acts as a watching agency which employs social norms to 'sear the psyche' (Ibid., p. 182). Pinky's view of herself and her place in society is worked out in the film through her interactions with a range of social authorities in the form of the police, the courthouse, the hospital, the school, and above all through the institution of slavery and segregation. She declares that her decision to live as a black woman derives from the fact that a person cannot live without pride; the reverse of this is that the ego cannot live with the guilt with which it is assaulted by these forces of social regulation.

The cultural scholar Susan Courtney believes that 'reduced to its fundamental elements, the ultimate project of this film … is to make Pinky, and the viewer, see and accept her light-skinned body as being inescapably black' (Courtney, 2005, p. 173). It is certainly the intention of the white townspeople in the film to force Pinky to accept herself as black and live as other black people there do. It was important that, once recognised, they were forced to remain on the black side of the colour line in order to maintain its binary logic. Whether the viewer is made to accept Pinky as 'being inescapably black' is a question that demands a close reading of several key scenes in the film.

The denigration of Pinky

What happens when Pinky is recognised as black? When those who have not been able to see beyond/beneath her skin are made aware of her 'black blood'? This is when we see Pinky denigrated—made black, from the Latin root 'nigrate', to blacken or darken—before the eyes of the white characters in the film, for whom the denigration does amount to a lessening of her value. For the audience however, it is a cause for empathy; we see that Pinky is the same character, only re-contextualised. There are at least three such incidents in the film. In each case Pinky's deportment and attitude remain the same but the white representatives of power (re)place her in, what is for them, the correct category. Each instance involves the re-creation of a stereotype, so that as she passes from white to black she goes from being a victim of crime to a violent criminal, from a sexual innocent to a harlot, from a customer to a thief. In the second of these examples—innocence to wantonness—Pinky is walking home at night when two young white men approach her in their car and offer her a lift. They tell her that she should be particularly careful in that part of town, at which she corrects them, pointing out that it is her part of town because she is black. They are now transformed from would-be saviours to attackers.[11] In a scene that is explicit for its day—and it is arguable whether the censors allowed it to remain because the character was black—the men refer to her as a 'white dinge' and a 'swamp-rabbit'. They then trap her, hold her roughly, and molest her, commenting on her build. She gets away and flees through the cemetery, surely calling to mind, as pointed out by Courtney, all the women who have been abused and killed in slavery's long history (Ibid., p. 179).

When Pinky first runs away from the men they shine the headlight of the car on her thus revealing the outline of Jeanne Crain's legs through her dress. She is wearing a simple cotton dress but the headlight (transformed into a searchlight) makes it appear diaphanous. Pinky holds her knees together to try to prevent exposure but realises that there is no escape and this is only slowing her down. The invasive light beam operates here as signal of an imminent assault. And the projection of light to expose the body is perhaps a comment on one of the exploitations of cinema—though one which the filmmakers would bank on as an attraction for seeing the film as well[12]—a confession of its role in controlling and sexualising the sign of the black female body. If the male gaze looks at Jeanne Crain, the former Miss Pan Pacific and then known as 'Hollywood's number one party girl' (Long Beach Independent, 1955, p. 27), with the erotic investment that might be expected, what happens when that gaze is directed to view her as black? The men in the car react with visible excitement when Pinky declares to them that she is black. Clyde Taylor and Michael Rogin have each shown how the use of blackface was a vehicle for the indulgence of hidden desires (Rogin, 1996). Taylor thinks that the white audience is enabled to 'reenact the deflowering of Nordic nymphets' and then receive punishment in the guise of a 'Black alter ego' (Taylor, 1998, pp. 114–115). In a similar way, Pinky's switch to blackness allows for an explosion of sexual violence that is first thwarted and then turned into guilt when she flees, transformed in the guise of a white damsel in distress. The sexualisation of the black woman and the idea that she was available to the white man upon demand is captured graphically in a statement by Cole Blease, senator for South Carolina from 1925–31, who said he had 'very serious doubt as to whether the crime of rape can be committed upon a negro' (Blackmon, 2009, p. 305). Of course, slaveholders had the opportunity to rape the bodies which constituted their property, as a form of punishment or for their own gratification. Indeed, there was a direct benefit to the slave-owner if the woman became pregnant as a result of his sexual abuse. Legally, such children were black and fatherless. The result was a recurring cycle of slave labour and rape passing down the generations, not to mention the incestuous cross-race implications resulting from 'keeping things in the family'. As Jolie A. Sheffer writes, 'Miscegenation remained the ultimate social taboo in the South, even as its evidence was written on the faces and bodies of its enslaved population' (Sheffer, 2013, p. 14).

The scene in which Pinky is assaulted highlights the incessant sexualisation of the black body. It is also perhaps confessional in its implication of cinema and the support it gave to building such myths of black hypersexuality. This was again particularly graphically represented in *The Birth of a Nation*, in which Griffith pointedly laid the primary blame for the failure of reconstruction on the sexual appetite of the mulatto. The stability and hegemony of the white family is threatened by the mixed-race characters Silas Lynch and Lydia Brown. Each of them is consumed by a desire for sex with whites, thus threatening the identity of America, in Griffith's eyes, as a white man's nation. This vampiric desire is demonstrated most vividly when Lydia chews on her own fingers out of sexual anticipation. Such images had as devastating an impact on the opportunities for black actresses in the interwar years as the image of Gus for black actors. Those black actresses who did manage to avoid being cast as servants after Griffith's film, often only did so by taking on roles that emphasised their physical attractiveness and availability, usually as night-club singers or hostesses. This plagued the careers of Lena Horne, Dorothy Dandridge, and Hazel Scott, amongst many others (Cripps, 1977).

Pinky's next interaction with a man is when her fiancé arrives. They kiss in a straightforward manner but what lies behind the kiss is fabulously complicated and subverts the conventions highlighted by Mulvey. What we see on screen is a fairly standard Hollywood embrace with white Jeanne Crain in the grip of her white co-star. What the narrative informs us we are seeing is a mixed-race kiss which, with different casting, would have been the first of its kind in Hollywood. In the background, we see two young black children behind a fence. They can be seen as offering what Fanon refers to as the 'natural background' to the 'human presence' of the two lovers (Fanon, 1968,

p. 250). In one respect, these black faces serve to emphasise the whiteness of the actors; yet, at the same time, within the context of the film, they represent the heritage of Pinky and the racial marking of her descendants. Also, they are behind a fence, representing segregation, and placing them in a position of uncertainty. Pinky will be making a choice not just for herself but for her children as well: her choice will be their future. The two children seem to look directly at us, in a manner which the conventions of Hollywood cinema should prohibit. They place Pinky and Tom directly between us and the children, who are now effectively interrogating our gaze. On one level we can see that if we deny the rights of the couple to marry and have children we are erasing the children in the scene. On another level we have clear visual evidence that the offspring of such a marriage would be visibly different from the two children in the picture, thereby exposing the contradictions in the "one-drop" rule of racial classification.

Once Pinky has made her choice and moved Tom out of the picture, she has effectively allowed Pinky Johnson to live the life that Tom had told her would come to an end with her marriage to him (he tells her that there will be no more Pinky Johnson when she becomes Mrs Thomas Adams). The enigmatic ending of the film does leave us to question what she has won. She rings the bell of the clinic to bring an end to playtime. The bell at this time was particularly associated with liberty (it was used extensively during the Second World War to symbolise the quest for freedom for all peoples and was the emblem for raising money through liberty bonds) she looks up at the sky, mouths something inaudible, and is shrouded in light. There is then a long fade to black in which her face disappears, literally swallowed up by blackness, which is then maintained for fifty-five frames.[13] We then see 'The End', which here perhaps takes on a significance beyond the end of the film. It is the end of the line for the family of Pinky Johnson. If miscegenation laws forbid her from having a family with her white lover, then to abide by them means that she is condemned to have no children with her chosen partner. Racism and miscegenation laws have denied the viewer the traditional happy ending: there is at once triumph in the strong independent character we see—even if it is as the beneficiary of white money—but there is also an emptiness. The last line of the film actually refers to sterilisation and white sheets. The end of the novel sees the clinic burned down by members of the Ku Klux Klan; the movie offers a more positive denouement but it demands that the spectre of black female sexuality remains tightly buttoned up in a crisp white nurse's uniform.

Notes

1 The films which were released later than *Pinky* were *Intruder in the Dust* (1949) and *No Way Out* (1950).
2 The heroine of the novel is called Pinkey; in the film, she becomes Pinky. This does have curious echoes in the naming of the movie's producer Darryl Zanuck. He

should have been called Darrell, after the eponymous hero of *Darrell of the Blessed Isles*, a book his mother was reading during pregnancy. But, according to Zanuck, 'Darrell sounded like a girl, so they named me Darryl'. Zanuck also went on to name his eldest daughter Darrylina (Gussow, 1972).
3 In original scripts there were going to be indications that Pinky returned to her grandmother because she was pregnant. Jane White, who was brought in to help with the script, advised against this on the basis that 'we should avoid what amounts to another stereotyped concept that all young Negro women "get into trouble"' (Clark, 1997, p. 184).
4 This term was coined as part of a hoax pamphlet produced towards the end of the Civil War in 1863. The pamphlet alleged that the ultimate goal of the Republican Party was to encourage intermarriage between blacks and white until they were indistinguishable (Kaplan, 1949).
5 The place where Gus can be seen to feature again is in *King Kong* (1933), another misguided subhuman who had to be killed for his desire for the white female (Snead, 1994).
6 We can still accept James Snead's contention that the beauty of cinema is that it allows a 'polymorphic perverse oscillation between possible roles' (Snead, 1994, p. 23). The looser sense of identification, with the viewer doing more work, does mean that the black female viewer can more easily step outside of such identifications.
7 Darryl Zanuck described the aim of the film as being 'calculated to make every racist in the country mad as hell' (Mosley, 1984, pp. 327–328).
8 This was the actual background to the film *Lost Boundaries* where the family on which it was based were suspected not to be white by many of their neighbours but because they performed well as a 'good family' and were a part of the community, no issue was made of it.
9 For one of the fuller accounts of the case see (Bishop, 1977).
10 In a manner similar to some of the Civil Rights activists of the 1950s and 1960s, Plessy was drawing attention to legislation that might have otherwise gone unremarked. It is most likely that the guard would not have asked Plessy to move without being forced to make such a decision.
11 This is not straightforward. Their performance of chivalry may well have been the preamble to a sexual move on her, but the important fact is that they no longer feel it necessary to hide their real intentions.
12 *Variety* magazine did refer to this scene as 'an exciting sequence of attempted rape' (Variety, 1949, p.8).
13 This is a long time to hold the black screen and it is a device used at five other points in the film. Two are connected to the death of Miss Em and the other three are in each scene where she parts from Tom, indicating that blackness will end the relationship just as it ends the film.

Bibliography

Baldwin, J. (1976) *The Devil finds work*. London: Michael Joseph.
Bernardi, D. (Ed.) (2001) *Classic Hollywood, classic whiteness*. Minneapolis: University of Minnesota Press.
Bishop, D. W. (1977) 'Plessy v. Ferguson: A Reinterpretation', *The Journal of Negro History*, 62, pp. 125–133. https://doi.org/10.2307/2717173.
Blackmon, D. A. (2009) *Slavery by another name: the re-enslavement of Black Americans from the Civil War to World War II*. New York: Anchor Books.

Bogle, D. (1994) *Toms, coons, mulattoes, mammies, and bucks: an interpretative history of blacks in American films*. Oxford: Roundhouse.
Butler, J. (1993) *Bodies that matter: on the discursive limits of 'sex'*. New York: Routledge.
Clark, G. (1997) 'Cinema of compromise: Pinky and the Politics of Post War Film Production', *Western Journal of Black Studies*, 21, pp. 180–189.
Courtney, S. (2005) *Hollywood fantasies of miscegenation: spectacular narratives of gender and race, 1903–1967*. Princeton, N.J: Princeton University Press.
Cripps, T. (1977) *Slow fade to black: the Negro in American film, 1900–1942*. Oxford and New York: Oxford University Press.
Crowther, B. (1949) '"Pinky", Zanuck's Film Study of Anti-Negro Bias in Deep South, Shown at Rivoli'. *New York Times*, 30 September, p. 28.
Delson, S. (2006) *Dudley Murphy, Hollywood wild card*. Minneapolis: University of Minnesota Press.
Dighton, R. (1949) 'Controversial "Pinky" Holds Star's Career in Box Office Balance', *Daily Press (Newport News)*, 13 November, p. 13.
Dixon, T. (1905) *The clansman: an historical romance of the Ku Klux Klan*. URL http://catalog.hathitrust.org/api/volumes/oclc/9463484.html.
Ellison, R. (1995) *Shadow and act*, 1st Vintage International ed. New York: Vintage International.
Fanon, F. (1968) *The wretched of the earth*. New York: Grove Press.
Fanon, F. (2000) *Black skin, white masks*. London: Pluto Press.
Griffith, D. W. (1915) *The Birth of a Nation*. Epoch Producing Co.
Gussow, M. (1972) *Don't say yes until I finish talking: a biography of Darryl F. Zanuck*. New York: Pocket Books.
hooks, b. (1992) *Black looks: race and representation*. Boston, MA: South End Press.
Kaplan, S. (1949) 'The Miscegenation Issue in the Election of 1864', *The Journal of Negro History*, 34, pp. 274–343. https://doi.org/10.2307/2715904.
Kelley, N. M. (2016) *Projections of passing: postwar anxieties and Hollywood films, 1947–1960*. Jackson: U.P. of Mississippi.
Larsen, N. (2014) *Quicksand and Passing*. London: Serpent's Tail.
Long Beach Independent (1955) 'Jeanne Crain Likes Night Life, Says So', 18 March, p. 27.
McBride, J. (2003) *Searching for John Ford: a life*. London: Faber and Faber.
Mosley, L. (1984) *Zanuck*. London: Granada.
Motion Picture Daily (1949) 'Race Theme as Drama', 30 September, p. 1.
Mulvey, L. (1975) 'Visual Pleasure and Narrative Cinema', *Screen*, 16, pp. 6–18. https://doi.org/10.1093/screen/16.3.6.
New York Times (1949) '"Pinky" Atlanta Bow Calm', 18 November, p. 35.
Rogin, M. P. (1996) *Blackface, white noise: Jewish immigrants in the Hollywood melting pot*. Berkeley: University of California Press.
Schatz, T. (1994) *Boom and Bust: American Cinema in the 1940s, History of the American Cinema*. Berkeley: University of California Press.
Sheffer, J. A. (2013) *The romance of race: incest, miscegenation, and multiculturalism in the United States, 1880–1930*. New Brunswick, NJ: Rutgers University Press.
Smith, V. (1994) 'Reading the Intersection of Race and Gender in Narratives of Passing', *Diacritics*, 24, 43–57. https://doi.org/10.2307/465163.
Snead, J. A. (1994) *White screens, black images: Hollywood from the dark side*. New York: Routledge.

Sumner, C. R. (1946) *Quality.* New York: Bobbs-Merrill Co.
Taylor, C. (1998) *The mask of art: breaking the aesthetic contract – film and literature.* Bloomington: Indiana University Press.
Thaggert, M. (1998) 'Divided Images: Black Female Spectatorship and John Stahl's "Imitation of Life"', *African American Review*, 32, pp. 481–491.
Variety (1949) '"Pinky" Review', 5 October, p. 8.
Wald, G. (2000) *Crossing the line: racial passing in twentieth-century U.S. literature and culture.* Durham, N.C.: Duke University Press.
Watkins, M. (2006) *Stepin Fetchit: the life and times of Lincoln Perry.* New York: Vintage Books.
White, W. (1949) *A Man Called White: The Autobiography of Walter White.* London: Victor Gollancz.

Chapter 6

Freud and the cannibal
Vignettes from psychoanalysis' colonial history

Marita Vyrgioti

> *What is a cannibal who has eaten his father and mother?*
> *An orphan.*
> *And if he has eaten all his other relations as well?*
> *The sole heir.*
> S. Freud, *Jokes and their Relation to the Unconscious*
> (Freud, 1960, p. 153)

A rabbi and a parson agree to found a new common religion and set about listing the changes the other will have to make. The parson wishes to change the Sabbath service to Sunday, wants its language to be Latin instead of Hebrew, and he goes on to enumerate other concessions concerning Jewish ritual and religious observances. The rabbi agrees to them all, as though they were inessential, and has only one demand in return: Get rid of Jesus Christ.
Reik's account of a joke told by Freud at the 1913 Psychoanalytic Congress in Munich

(Reik, 1954, p. 19)

In his 1977 work, *Violence and the Sacred*, René Girard wrote that 'we are perhaps more distracted by incest than by cannibalism, but only because cannibalism has not yet found its Freud and been promoted to the status of a major contemporary myth' (Girard, 1977, p. 277). Girard's comment prepared the ground for contemporary anthropological texts that, emerging one after the other in the late 1970s, proposed that cannibalism has in fact been a myth of the hegemonic, colonising European arsenal that promoted the dehumanisation and primitivisation of aboriginal cultures to justify their extinction (Arens, 1979; Sahlins, 1979; Harris, 1977). Girard associates Freud's failure to explain cannibalism with the systematic misunderstanding of anthropologists who, distracted by the sensationalism of the ritual missed its structural value. Instead, Girard claims that had cannibalism found its Freud,[1] namely had it become incorporated in the psychic make-up of human subjectivity, the recognition of cannibalism's banality would make anthropological mythologies, sustained throughout colonialism, collapse. In this

DOI: 10.4324/9781003200765-8

essay, I argue that Freud had in fact found cannibalism. Yet having uncovered what was, for his contemporaries, an uncomfortable proximity between cannibalism and Christian imperial subjectivity, I suggest, his argument was necessarily silenced.

This essay identifies the moments where Freud drew on the imagery of cannibalism and, by contextualising them, it explores how behind this imagery lay an ideology of racial difference that informed and was informed by psychoanalysis. My argument is that Freud found in the colonial imagery of the cannibal trope an entry point to critique the hegemonic, Christian colonial subjectivity by identifying the ritualistic repetition of cannibalism in the Eucharist. However, the colonial vocabulary of cannibalism in Freud's psychoanalytic theory emerges sporadically, in footnotes, in emotionally invested texts, and through a writing of significant obscurity. Many of Freud's remarks about the cannibal trope remain inconclusive, arrested at the level of observation and description, delivered to the reader for interrogation. Therefore, I argue, the way in which Freud promoted the association of Christianity with the cannibal lexicon marks a postcolonial method of critique as a particular way of writing about the other.

The barbarity of European civility: cannibalism and racial representation

The relationship between psychoanalysis and anthropology has always been tense. In her work *The Subject of Anthropology*, Henrietta Moore frames this tension as a question of commitment to cultural variation (from the perspective of anthropology) and to psychic universality (from the point of view of psychoanalysis) (Moore, 2007). Moore proposes that one way of engaging with the interdisciplinary space between psychoanalysis and anthropology is, instead of engaging with the problem of universalism versus variation per se, to reflect on the 'more general dilemma of how to handle history—that is, how to explain the development of the individual in the context of an ongoing social/cultural system which itself changes over time and is subject to the workings of power' (Moore, 2007, p. 5). To explore how psychoanalysis—and Freud in particular—has engaged with anthropology and toyed with the racist smear of cannibalism, it is crucial to maintain an awareness of its historical context and transformations. Reading psychoanalysis from a postcolonial perspective entails an awareness of its historical, colonial baggage, part of which emerges out of Freud's theoretical engagement with colonial anthropology.

In his anthology on the history of Victorian anthropology, George Stocking shows that anthropological knowledge production supported and was supported by the structures of colonial settlement (Stocking, 1987). Providing a thorough analysis of the assumptions and doctrines of anthropology, Stocking outlines the paradox that although evolutionism theoretically implied that all cultures would naturally progress, unassisted, towards the top of the evolutionary ladder—moving away from their so-called state of savagery to a state of civilisation allegedly exemplified by European culture—in fact, this process was systematically hampered by British science and racial ideology. The anthropological comparative method 'required that [the so-called savages] should not have [progressed]; the evidence of ethnography and history showed that they had not; ethnocentric assumption suggested that they could not; and European expansion made it clear that they would not' (Stocking, 1987, p. 177). On a similar note, Ann Stoler argued that the racialisation of colonised peoples actively contributed to the making of the British self, by structuring the boundaries of respectability, gentlemanliness and the bourgeoisie to 'secure the tenuous distinctions of bourgeois rule' (Stoler, 2000, p. 97). The British self, then, was made in radical opposition to the aboriginal other, whose qualities were systematically constructed as incompatible with the civilised, white imperial subject (Stoler, 2000).

One aspect of nineteenth-century anthropological texts, often omitted from critiques that examine the impact of colonial anthropology in psychoanalysis by tracing tropes of racialisation (Brickman, 2003; Khanna, 2003), is the association of so-called aboriginal cultures with cannibalism.[2] For example, Edward Tylor, the founder of British cultural anthropology, believed that cannibalism was a practice of empowerment that put the cannibal in the position of a racialised other, not so much dangerous as innocent and naïve. In an anecdotal story about an English Merchant in Shanghai, Tylor wrote that 'he [the merchant] met his Chinese servant carrying home a heart and asked him what he had got there. He said it was the heart of a rebel, and that he was going to take it home and eat it to make him brave' (Tylor, 1920, p. 131). Similarly, another pioneer in the anthropological study of non-European cultures, John Lubbock, tied cannibalism to destitution, wretchedness and misery, thus implicitly elevating British life as a paradigm of freedom, nobility and sustenance:

> the true savage is neither free nor noble; he is a slave to his own wants, his own passions, imperfectly protected from the weather, he suffers from the cold by night and the heat of the sun by the day [...] hunger always stares him in the face, and often drives him to the dreadful alternative of cannibalism or death.
>
> (Lubbock, 1913, p. 586)

These should not be read as singular accounts or extreme exceptions embedded in works exploring the so-called 'primitive' cultures, but as a pervasive imagery shaping representations of the non-white body in the Western scientific discourse.

Traces of the racialised representation of the non-European are echoed when for instance, Freud, in opening his work *Totem and Taboo*, outlines his expectation of studying Australian aboriginals: 'we should certainly not expect that the sexual life of these poor naked cannibals would be moral in our sense', only to add that it appears that aboriginal cultures have taken great pains to institute their own methods for regulating incest, sexuality and kinship structures (Freud, 1955a, p. 2). Precisely because *Totem and Taboo* borrows its understanding of aboriginal cultures from colonial anthropology, Celia Brickman argued, it is a text that both problematically reiterates colonialist assumptions and 'sabotages the presumption of the superiority of the western mind held by the first generation of anthropologists' (Brickman, 2003, p. 52). Both Brickman and Khanna have traced the implications of Freud's use of colonial anthropology as inserting a racialised subtext in the model of human development: a distancing from qualities associated with 'darker races' and a progression towards a mature subjectivity 'whose unstated colour was white, just as its unstated gender was male' (Ibid., p. 72). Nevertheless, while the racial undertones of the psychoanalytic model of psychosexual development have been frequently exposed, the question of why Freud turned to the cannibal—or better, the question of what he does with this figure—requires some further investigation. If we follow Jacqueline Rose's reading of *Totem and Taboo* and ask what was at stake in Freud's engagement with the 'Australian exile', we find ourselves in the domain of a personal, as much as a theoretical, dispute between Freud and his disciple Carl Jung. For Rose, this dispute is a 'barely concealed conflict between the Aryan and the Jew' (Rose, 1999, p. 52). It is worth thinking then, to what extent this racialised conflict enters Freud's discussion of cannibalism and prehistoric origins in *Totem and Taboo*.

'When the saviour didn't come': *Totem and Taboo*'s cannibalism as a critique of Christianity

The relation between psychoanalysis and Jewishness has had a profound impact on the institutional politics of psychoanalysis, as well as the psychoanalytic theorisation of race. In *Hate and the Jewish Science* Stephen Frosh showed that Freud's negotiation of his Jewish identity was a lifelong process worked out through his writings; it informed the psychoanalytic subject, it inspired a theory of anti-Semitic racial hatred, and in cases like *Totem and Taboo*, it took the form of an intervention, shaped as a critical account of religion (Frosh, 2009, p. 41–42). Anti-Semitism was a concrete and racialised form of hostility in *fin-de-siècle* Vienna, which, alongside other prejudices, fostered the suspicious reception of psychoanalysis—even within psychoanalytic circles (Frosh, 2009). Freud's emphasis on sexuality, for instance, became a thorny issue for his Swiss, Christian colleagues: as George Makari notes, 'whispers had it that [Alfonse] Maeder', a psychoanalyst and close collaborator of Carl Jung, 'would dignify the claim that the Jews in Vienna were overly concerned with sex' (Makari, 2008, p. 276). According to Sander Gilman, the idea that Jewish sexuality was castrated and damaged was part of a chain of associations that constructed the male Jewish body as a hysteric, feminised other against which Christian masculinity was erected (Gilman, 1993, p. 152).[3] Nevertheless, Freud firmly rejected attempts to label psychoanalysis in racial terms (Frosh, 2009). The same did not hold true for Jung, who in his 1933 notorious editorial note at the *Zentralblatt fur Psychotherapie* wrote:

> The 'Aryan' unconscious has a higher potential than the Jewish; that is both the advantage and disadvantage of a youthfulness not yet fully weaned from barbarism. In my opinion it has been a grave error in medical psychology up till now to apply Jewish categories—which are not even binding on all Jews—indiscriminately to Germanic and Slavic Christendom. Because of this the most precious secret of the Germanic peoples—their creative and intuitive depth of soul—has been explained by a morass of banal infantilism, while my own warning voice has for decades been suspected of anti-Semitism.
> (Jung, 1970, p. 165)

In a letter to his Hungarian colleague Sándor Ferenczi in 1911, Freud wrote: 'there will surely be different world views [...] here and there. But there should be no distinct Aryan or Jewish science' (Gay, 2006, p. 239). Nevertheless, to safeguard the scientific and institutional consolidation of psychoanalysis, Freud appointed Jung as the first President of the International Psychoanalytic Association (IPA), founded in 1910. Despite the irritation of some of his colleagues on the grounds of Jung's anti-Semitism, Freud attempted to assure them that 'this Swiss will save us—will save me and will save you as well' (Freud quoted in Frosh, 2009, p. 43).

Nevertheless, Jung's *Symbols of Transformation* originally published as *Transformations and Symbols of the Libido* in 1912 began to shake Freud's hopes, foreshadowing the imminent rupture of the two men. Jung openly challenged fundamental Freudian ideas and advocated for the need to expand psychoanalysis beyond the study of the individual to the realm of myths and symbols (Jung, 1986). Jung aspired to explain how symbols were responsible for the formation of a 'collective spirit', a uniform collective human unconscious. Myths, he opined, would also offer access to the finite arsenal of unconscious 'primordial images', a term which in 1918 was substituted by the concept of the 'archetype' (Shamdasani, 2003, p. 297). Towards the end of *Transformations*, Jung argued that the model for understanding the image of the psychoanalytic self is Jesus Christ: 'from the point of view of psychology and comparative religion', Jung wrote, 'Christ [...] is a typical manifestation of the self' (Jung, 1986, p. 392). '[T]he self,' Jung argued, 'is an *imago Dei*'—it is made in accordance with God's image and 'cannot be distinguished from it empirically' (Jung, 1986, p. 392). Having read the manuscript twice and in the caring tone that characterised their relationship at that point, Freud responded: 'One of the nicest works I have read (again) is of a well-known author on the *Transformations and Symbols of the Libido* and added that 'sometimes I have a feeling that his horizon has been too narrowed by Christianity' (Freud, 1974, p. 459). Remarkably, the letter ended with a spirited condemnation of a father who becomes drawn—if not seduced—by the playfulness of his son: 'why in God's name did I allow myself to follow you into this field?' (Freud, 1974, p. 459). Jung's *Transformations* posed a provocation to Freud to follow a form of '"wild" psycho-analysis'. Unlike Jung, however, he did not pursue a comparative psychoanalytic study in myths and religion but turned instead to anthropological evidence about non-European cultures. If we read *Totem and Taboo* from the point of view of Freud's critique of Jung, an interesting twist appears. Freud's deployment of cannibalism can be seen as a specific strategy of exposing an aspect of Christian colonisation: namely, that the Christian subject proposed by Jung as a model of the psychoanalytic subject, was nothing more than a repetition of Christianity's unresolved relation with humanity's prehistoric, cannibalistic past.

According to Freud, cannibalism is a part of an unconscious memory shared by all humans. Cannibalism, in Freud's thinking, stands at the roots of the emergence of subjectivity and the social: in Freud's account of human prehistory, a horde of sons, motivated by incestuous wishes for their mother, murder their father and consume his body in act of primordial cannibalism: 'Cannibal savages as they were, it goes without saying that they devoured their victim as well as killing him' (Freud, 1955a, p. 142). The elimination of the father satisfied their hatred, but instead of giving them pleasure, it allowed the affection for the father to emerge along with feelings of guilt. Guilt from this act, therefore, became the 'beginning of so many things—of social organisation, of moral restrictions and of religion' (Ibid.). Jean-Luc Nancy and Philippe Lacoue-Labarthe build up on this basis the claim that this primal Father who is murdered and devoured is the visualisation of an 'absolute figure', which signifies the law and prohibition (Nancy and Lacoue-Labarthe, 1989, p. 201–202). Tracing the evolutionary schema of religion, Freud argues that the law of the primal father institutes early totemic religions around two prohibitions that structure and hold communities together: one must not kill and one must not eat the sacred animal (Freud, 1955a, p. 104).

In Freud's account, the sacred animal replaced the primal father, and is a concrete symbolisation of the prohibition of the law and of the taboo on incest (Freud, 1955a). God, says Freud, is an idea emerging from this sacred totem, which imposes the law and, through religious structures, ensures its observance. Christianity, however, proposed a method of 'allaying guilt': Christ, who in sacrificing himself, 'redeemed the company of brothers from original sin' (Ibid., p. 154). For Freud, 'the ancient totem meal was revived in the form of communion' and the 'Christian communion [...] is essentially a fresh elimination of the father, a repetition of the guilty deed' (Ibid., p.154–155). In drawing attention to the resemblance between the Christian ritual and a prehistoric myth, Freud challenges the colonial dichotomy between the Christian self and the savage one by pointing to a shared unresolved guilt that needs to be ritualistically purged.

Although Freud's perceptive account of Christianity was strategically produced 'to neatly eliminate anything Aryan-religious', as he wrote to his colleague and friend Karl Abraham, this does not mean that this disparaging critique occurred unambivalently (Freud, 2002, p. 183). An important source for Freud's critique was the early twentieth-century Christian anthropologist James Frazer who had castigated Christianity for its 'notional significance', arguing that in the last analysis it holds no universal truth for the genesis of the world. Frazer saw Christianity not as an unchallengeable and truthful religious doctrine but as just another system of thinking, an explanation of the world's origins, comparable to magical or scientific accounts (Lienhardt, 1993, p. 6). It is to Frazer that Freud turns in order to proclaim the proximity between Christianity and totemism when he writes: 'we can see the full justice of Frazer's pronouncement that "the Christian Communion has absorbed within itself a sacrament which is doubtless far older than Christianity"'(Freud, 1955a, p. 155). Freud repudiates the ownership of his reading of Christianity and adds in a footnote that: 'No one familiar with the literature of the subject will imagine that the derivation of Christian communion from the totem meal is an idea originating from the author of the present essay' (Ibid.). Overall, this implicit, anxious engagement with the critique of Christianity must be read alongside the fact that *Totem* became a troubling work for Freud—its completion came after the severance of his relationship with Jung and was followed by a period of depression, in which Freud 'began to feel uncertain of his case, a sure sign of his deep emotional engagement' (Gay, 2006, p. 326). The question that arises from this is, for a figure as austere and inquisitive as Freud: what was it that made the proximity between Christianity, totemism and cannibalism so uncomfortable?

The racialising logic of identification

Turning to Freudian psychoanalysis from a post-colonial perspective, one stumbles upon a plethora of colonial tropes employed to discuss non-Western cultures, which perpetuate a racialising logic that is yet to be fully explored. Significant contributions in this direction have emphasised the notion of 'primitivity' as imbuing the primary stages of individual development with a racialised subtext—as if development entails a growing out of savagery (Brickman, 2003). And additionally, the designation of female sexuality as a 'dark continent', adding a racialised dimension to femininity and sexual difference (Khanna, 2003). The cannibal trope and its place in psychoanalytic theory still remains unexplored, however. Freud pursued the implications of paternal cannibalism—as a practice which at once gave rise to, and was repudiated by, the social—by embroidering it into his metapsychology, silencing the provocative critique of Christianity and advancing the assumption that cannibalistic wishes are part of the human psyche: 'the instinctual wishes that [...] are born afresh with every child [...] are those of incest, cannibalism and lust for killing' (Freud, 1961b, p. 10). In the 1915 revision of the *Three*

Essays on the Theory of Sexuality Freud added a section asserting that the earliest stage of sexual development was the 'oral cannibalistic stage' that is informed by a 'relic of cannibalistic desires' (Freud, 1953, p. 159). In particular here, Freud asserts that what is expressed through the mouth, love and aggression, the pleasure derived from nutrition as well as sexual pleasure, are part of a phylogenetic heritage tied to the human condition. Oral cannibalism becomes the 'prototype' (Ibid., p. 198), Freud argued, for the mechanism of identification—a psychical process modelled on physical incorporation which is 'visualised'—to use Nancy and Lacoue-Labarthe's phrasing (Nancy and Lacoue-Labarthe, 1989, pp. 201–202)—as taking someone in, digesting and being physically as well as psychically formed by them. The cannibal trope is associated in Freud's writing with identification, with the fundamental process of acquiring one's self. The psychoanalytic subject is, therefore, constructed on the grounds of the universalisation of a racial, colonial trope.

This racialising logic appears strikingly in Freud's 1917 essay on 'Mourning and Melancholia', a text that uses melancholia—a self-destructive and self-consuming psychological condition—as a lens to explore processes of identification. In this essay, Freud offers insights on the structure of melancholia, a state of excessive asociality,

> painful dejection, cessation of interest in the outside world, loss of the capacity to love, inhibition of all activity, and a lowering of the self-regarding feelings to the degree that finds utterance in self-reproaches and self-revilings, and culminates in a delusional expectation of punishment.
> (Freud, 1957, p. 244)

In comparing mourning and melancholia, Freud points to two fundamental differences. Both mourning and melancholia are mechanisms of dealing with loss: in the former the individual is aware of the loss of a loved object, but in the case of melancholia, the loss is unconscious—'one cannot see clearly what it is that has been lost, and it is all the more reasonable to suppose that the patient cannot consciously perceive what he has lost either' (Ibid., p. 245). As a result, while in ordinary mourning it is 'the world [that] becomes empty' without the loved object, melancholia is an experience of a profound feeling of emptiness and impoverishment of the self (Ibid., p. 246). If the loss of the object entails a loss in the ego, melancholia exposes that an identification with the lost object must have taken place. What, then, is the nature of this identification?

For Freud the psychological development of the individual involves the transition from a primary narcissistic identification (where the ego wants to be like the object), into an object relation (where the ego wants to have the object). Melancholic identification is, therefore, a regression from an object-choice to a narcissistic identification and sheds light onto the nature of the process of primary identification and its fundamental ambivalence: melancholia 'is an excellent opportunity for the ambivalence in love-relationships to make itself effective and come into the open' (Ibid., p. 251). What melancholic identification exposes is the desire to cannibalise the object—to take it in and destroy it: 'the ego wants to incorporate this object into itself, and, in accordance with the oral or cannibalistic phase of libidinal development in which it is, it wants to do so by devouring it' (Ibid., p. 241). The ego turns against itself narcissistically and self-destructs, as Diana Fuss put it: 'turning identification's violent impulses completely inward, the ego consumes itself in an act of autocannibalism' (Fuss, 1995, p. 37).

By arguing that in melancholia the cannibalistic wishes of the primary narcissistic identification resurface and consume the ego, Freud theorises this psychological condition in racial terms. Equipped with cannibalistic wishes— alongside incestuous ones—the Freudian psychoanalytic subject is formulated on the assumption of a historical psychological continuity from the prehistoric primal crime to the 1920s Viennese unconscious. The ambivalent wishes against the primal father, Freud argues, have become repressed in the unconscious of humanity and affirm their existence in the intense self-consumption of the melancholic. In regressing to a cannibalistic stage of development, the melancholic re-enacts this prehistoric wish, to eliminate and become the father, but because of the taboo on cannibalism, the libido originally directed towards this object becomes distorted and is turned back against the melancholic herself. Abraham says Freud links the psychological inhibition with the loss of appetite, as a symbolic withdrawal from any form of nurturing incorporation (Freud, 1957, p. 241). Therefore, one might argue that the figure of the melancholic, linked as she is in Freud's thinking with a process of identification modelled on cannibalistic incorporation, unconsciously carries a form of guilt concerning this process of cannibalistic identity-formation that has been repressed from the social.

Nevertheless, in seeing melancholia as a 'pathology' which he opposes to the normal process of mourning, Freud reiterates a racial dichotomy between those individuals who are capable of recovering from loss through mourning, and those who in having cannibalised an object are confined to an asocial state, immersed in guilt and expecting punishment, just like the 'cannibal-savage' sons (Ibid). Thus, Freud's theory of melancholia is shot through with the colonial implications of the cannibal trope, reiterating a dichotomy in the European imaginary between mourning as a normative process of whiteness and melancholia as a pathology that makes the individual regress to a pre-historic, pre-social savagery and, implicitly, blackness.

Freud's theory of identification as an ambivalent relation to a lost object is informed, across his writings, by the colonial myth of humanity's prehistoric origins. Despite the exclusion of cannibalism from the social through the cultural institution of the taboo, cannibalistic wishes return and manifest their presence in the unconscious of the melancholic, colonial subject. Nevertheless, there is another layer embedded in Freud's theory of identification as a racialised psychological mechanism. For Freud, identification is an ambivalent desire to acquire another person's qualities. He therefore identifies 'an interesting parallel' in the belief of primitive peoples, and in the prohibitions based upon it, that the attributes of animals which are incorporated as nourishment persist as part of the character of those who eat them. As is well known, this belief is one of the roots of cannibalism and its effects have continued through the series of usages of the totem meal down to Holy Communion.

(Freud, 1961a, p. 29)

The Christian ritual of communion affirms Freud's hypothesis about the existence of an unconscious guilt emanating from the wish to collectively repeat a guilty deed—to consume the god's body in order to purge the guilt of having eaten him in the first place. Moreover, Freud offers an implicit political critique of an anti-Semitic aspect of Christianity, by decentring its claims of racial superiority through the recognition of a psychological resemblance with practices of religions that in the European Christian imaginary represented savagery and backwardness. Despite the ambiguous legacy of colonial thought, Freud's theory of identification insisted that Christian subjectivity, like all other forms of human subjectivity, is rooted in a history of cannibalistic identification.

In Freud's account of group psychology, the group—in this case the Christian church—revives the ambivalence felt by the prehistoric sons towards the primal father, but due to its incapacity to 'murder and devour' the leader, as the sons once did, the group projects outwards any aggression originally felt for the leader. Indeed, the group, like the worshippers of the Catholic church, is sustained by a symbolic consumption of the leader's body—an identification between the member's ego-ideal and the leader. Freud is also sketching the psychological mechanism of totalitarian groups: while the group is structured among the love of its members and the equal love of the leader for the members, the fundamental ambivalence of identification cannot be expressed within the group and is projected outwards. Hence Freud reminds his readers that the cannibal—the prototypical figure of identification—had 'a devouring affection for his enemies and only devours people of whom he is fond' (Freud, 1955b, p. 105). In this paradoxical phrasing, Freud explains that by making cannibalism a taboo, the group disowns precisely such a 'devouring fondness'. In other words, the group forgoes an aggressive wish to possess the other and refuse their psychic and physical separateness. What follows from Freud's theorisation is that groups such as the Catholic church depend on rituals that allow them to forgo these inner wishes, as they cannot be worked through otherwise. Above all, Freud laid out a psychological mechanism of identification, which although fragmented and unsystematic, nonetheless arose from an obscure and ambiguous use of the cannibal trope that held the association between possessing the other and a racialised violence which, at the same time, did not refrain from embodying a concealed, yet provocative, critique of hegemonic subjectivity.

Who is Freud's cannibal: obscure writing and postcolonial ethics

During the 1920s Freud channelled part of his intellectual activity in amalgamating many of his theoretical insights into a structural model of the self, in which the cannibal trope held an apparently marginal yet crucial role. The cannibal trope appears in these writings as an uncomfortable reminder of the racialised context amidst and against which psychoanalysis emerged. Soon afterwards, during the 1930s and the rapidly growing Nazi domination in Europe, Freud's early critical intervention about anti-Semitism and the role of Christianity would become both more urgently needed and more necessarily obscure (Frosh, 2009, p. 47). In a nod to the need to analyse and explain the emerging racial hatred against Jews, as well as to explore the tensions embedded in his own Jewish identity, Freud's characteristically pessimistic publications deconstructing religion emerged one after the other: *The Future of an Illusion* (1961b) with its association of religious belief and infantile feelings of helplessness, *Civilisation and its Discontents* (1961c) and finally, *Moses and Monotheism* (1964), a text in which the themes of totemism, cannibalism and Christianity return. In the second preface to *Moses and Monotheism*, Freud argued that the book discloses a truth about religion that cannot be said unless it is disguised: 'Not that I should have anything to say that would be new or that I did not say clearly a quarter of a century ago', in *Totem and Taboo*, but 'it has been forgotten in the meantime and it could not be without effect if I repeated it to-day' (Freud, 1964, p. 55). In exploring the history of Moses as an Egyptian outsider who founded the Jewish religion, Freud showed that religion is structured upon the repression of the foreignness of origins.

Moses and Monotheism can undoubtedly be regarded as a traumatic text, documenting Freud's personal experience of anti-Semitism and his reflections on Jewish identity (Yerushalmi, 1991; Frosh, 2009). It is also a record of how collective identity comes into being through religion, culture and tradition, and thus, as Edward Said claims, it deals with the inherent tensions in identity that prevent it from becoming consolidated into 'one Identity' (Said, 2003, p. 54). Moses, thus, as an Egyptian prince instead of a Hebrew orphan in Freud's reconstruction of the Biblical story, becomes the paradigmatic figure of how identity is fundamentally disrupted. Moses' status as an outsider embodies the explanation of why the Jewish tradition has—despite systematic oppression—eventually survived and why, although his murder was an act of savagery, the collectively held guilt has led Jews to refrain from subsequent acts of 'barbarism', and from the profound violence of 1930s nationalism (Freud, 1964, p. 55). On the other hand, the so-called progressive Christian religion, which came after Judaism and re-instituted the son, in the place of a father-religion, is a thinly veiled effort to absolve the collective guilt that weighed down on the Jews for years, which prevented them from violence. In affirming that it was the Jews who killed

Jesus, Paul exposed that in the anti-Semitic imagery Christian guilt was displaced and projected onto the figure of the Jew—who was therefore the guilty figure: 'You [Jews] killed our god!' (Ibid., p. 90). Moreover, Freud argues that what this negation did to the history of the Judeo-Christian religions was to replace 'the blissful sense of being chosen' to carry the guilt of the primal crime with the 'liberating sense of redemption' (Ibid., p. 135)—a sense of redemption that also freed the Christians from the guilt of their violent, cannibalistic and murderous instincts. But the flight from guilt necessitates the reliance on the sacrificial ritual of communion and the reiteration of a repressed act of prehistoric cannibalism (Ibid., p. 101). In drawing attention to the cannibalistic resemblance of the communion, Freud showed that anti-Semitism retains the prehistoric memory of cannibalism repressed, exposing the hypocrisy of Christian anti-Semitism. He also demonstrated why anti-Semitism as a racialised and religious hatred was a psychically less sophisticated response than the tolerance of the discomfort Christians experienced in their relations and interactions with Jews.

Overall, Freud's implicit critique of Christianity is informed by themes that boil down to questions of ethics: the ethics of Judaism's critique of Christianity, the ethics of Freud as a Jew towards his (former) Christian colleagues, and above all, the ethics of psychoanalysis as a form of writing about the self and of otherness. To challenge the foreclosure of the category of race, Freud employed *Moses* as an 'application of psychoanalysis' (Ibid, p. 10) that emphasised that there is a foreignness in every origin, as Moses' Egyptian identity proved. Linked to this notion was Freud's own racial foreignness as a Jew in an anti-Semitic world: this granted psychoanalysis its fundamental marginal status, as Said suggested (Said, 2003). Likewise, operating within this marginal space, Freud's reading of the history of religions revealed Christianity's obliviousness to its own repetition of 'primitive' cannibalistic rituals. The past, writes Freud survives in 'excellent replicas' (Freud, 1964, p. 84). In this way, Freud was pointing at something critical about the Christian unconscious without fully formulating it. His account of the proximity between Christian identity and cannibalism remained fragmented and arrested at the level of demonstration, overshadowed by a more powerful interrogation of Judaism's origins. We can assume that this obscurity was necessary due to socio-political reasons related to the obliterating violence of Nazism that was to come. Yet, I would like to propose that ultimately, the cannibal trope as a critique of Christianity should also be read as a postcolonial method of writing about the other. Freud's obscure use of the cannibal trope appears as a way of conveying psychoanalytic knowledge by indicating the precariousness of colonial dichotomies without reiterating the assumption that Christian subjecthood—like non-European subjecthood—is ever entirely transparent. This obscure writing from the margins is a postcolonial space in which to rethink psychoanalysis.

Conclusion

This essay began by challenging the view that Freud did not discuss the taboo on cannibalism, and showed that Freud's interest in the figure of the cannibal can in fact be situated alongside a psychoanalytic critique of race and racism. Freud draws on cannibalism as a colonial representation of racial difference to argue that social life depends on the repression of cannibalistic wishes. On the other hand, in modelling the process of identification upon cannibalistic wishes, Freud challenges the dichotomy between the hegemonic, white civilised subject and the racialised, cannibalistic other. Finally, contextualising Freud's references to the cannibal trope alongside vignettes from his own experience of anti-Semitism and his clash with Jung, I have argued that Freud turned to a racialised trope as a response to Christian anti-Semitism and has bequeathed us with an ethical, psychoanalytic writing of the racialised self and other, crucial for postcolonial thought.

Notes

1 While Freud is arguably the first psychoanalytic theorist to engage with the problem of prehistoric cannibalism, the theme was inherited and creatively incorporated in Melanie Klein's theory, coating processes of incorporation and introjection, with a colonial twist.
2 It was only after the mid-1970s that anthropological works began to systematically review the evidence provided for cannibalistic practices and rituals in the non-European cultures, revealing that cannibalism was strategically used to justify colonial exploitation.
3 The implication here is that in the popular early twentieth century imaginary circumcision equated castration (Gilman, 1993).

Bibliography

Arens, W. (1979) *The man-eating myth.* 1st ed. New York: Oxford University Press.
Bahun, S. (2014) *Modernism and melancholia: writing as countermourning.* Oxford: Oxford University Press.
Borch-Jacobsen, M. (1988) *The Freudian subject.* California: Stanford University Press.
Brickman, C. (2003) *Aboriginal populations in the mind.* New York: Columbia University Press.
Cheng, A. (2000) *The melancholy of race: psychoanalysis, assimilation, and hidden grief.* Oxford and New York: Oxford University Press.
Freud, S. (1953) 'Three essays on the theory of sexuality'. In *The standard edition of the complete psychological works of Sigmund Freud*, ed. J. Strachey; trans. J. Strachey and A. Freud, with A. Strachey and A. Tyson, London: The Hogarth Press and the Institute of Psychoanalysis, 24 vols., vol. VII.
Freud, S. (1955a) 'Totem and taboo'. In *The standard edition of the complete psychological works of Sigmund Freud*, ed. J. Strachey; trans. J. Strachey and A. Freud, with A. Strachey and A. Tyson, London: The Hogarth Press and the Institute of Psychoanalysis, 24 vols., vol. XIII.

Freud, S. (1955b) Group psychology and the analysis of the ego. In *The standard edition of the complete psychological works of Sigmund Freud*, ed. J. Strachey; trans. J. Strachey and A. Freud, with A. Strachey and A. Tyson, London: The Hogarth Press and the Institute of Psychoanalysis, 24 vols., vol. XVIII.

Freud, S. (1957) 'Mourning and melancholia'. In *The standard edition of the complete psychological works of Sigmund Freud*, ed. J. Strachey; trans. J. Strachey and A. Freud, with A. Strachey and A. Tyson, London: The Hogarth Press and the Institute of Psychoanalysis, 24 vols., vol. XIV.

Freud, S. (1960) Jokes and their relation to the unconscious. In *The standard edition of the complete psychological works of Sigmund Freud*, ed. J. Strachey; trans. J. Strachey and A. Freud, with A. Strachey and A. Tyson, London: The Hogarth Press and the Institute of Psychoanalysis, 24 vols., vol. VIII.

Freud, S. (1961a) The ego and the id. In *The standard edition of the complete psychological works of Sigmund Freud*, ed. J. Strachey; trans. J. Strachey and A. Freud, with A. Strachey and A. Tyson, London: The Hogarth Press and the Institute of Psychoanalysis, 24 vols., vol. XIX.

Freud, S. (1961b) The future of an illusion. In *The standard edition of the complete psychological works of Sigmund Freud*, ed. J. Strachey; trans. J. Strachey and A. Freud, with A. Strachey and A. Tyson, London: The Hogarth Press and the Institute of Psychoanalysis, 24 vols., vol XXI.

Freud, S. (1961c) Civilization and its Discontents. In *The standard edition of the complete psychological works of Sigmund Freud*, ed. J. Strachey; trans. J. Strachey and A. Freud, with A. Strachey and A. Tyson, London: The Hogarth Press and the Institute of Psychoanalysis, 24 vols., vol XXI.

Freud, S. (1964) 'Moses and monotheism'. In *The standard edition of the complete psychological works of Sigmund Freud*, ed. J. Strachey; trans. J. Strachey and A. Freud, with A. Strachey and A. Tyson, London: The Hogarth Press and the Institute of Psychoanalysis, 24 vols., vol. XXIII.

Freud, S. (1974) *The Freud/Jung letters: the correspondence between Sigmund Freud and C.G. Jung*, ed. W. McGuire; trans. R. Manheim and R. F. C. Hull. Princeton: Princeton University Press.

Freud, S. (2002) *The complete correspondence of Sigmund Freud and Karl Abraham 1907–1925*, ed. and trans. E. Falzeder. London: Karnac.

Frosh, S. (2009) *Hate and the Jewish science: anti-semitism, Nazism and psychoanalysis*. 2nd ed. New York: Palgrave Macmillan.

Fuss, D. (1995) *Identification papers: readings on psychoanalysis, sexuality, and culture*. 1st ed. London and New York: Routledge.

Gay, P. (2006) *Freud: a life for our time*. Revised. New York and London: Norton.

Gilman, S. L. (1993) *Freud, race and gender*. Princeton NJ: Princeton University Press.

Girard, R. (1977) *Violence and the sacred*, trans. P. Gregory. Baltimore: John Hopkins University Press.

Harris, M. (1977) *Cannibals and kings: the origins of culture*. New York: Random House.

Jung, C. (1970) 'The state of psychotherapy today'. In *Civilisation in transition: collected works*, 2nd ed. Vol. 10. Princeton NJ: Princeton University Press.

Jung, C (1986) *Symbols of transformation: an analysis of the prelude to a case of schizophrenia*, trans. R. F. C. Hull. 4th ed. London: Routledge.

Khanna, R. (2003) *Dark continents: psychoanalysis and colonialism*. Durham and London: Duke University Press.

Lienhardt, G. (1993) 'Frazer's anthropology: science and sensibility', *Journal of Anthopological Society of Oxford*, 24 (1), 1–12.

Lubbock, J. (1913) *Prehistoric times as illustrated by ancient remains and the manners and customs of modern savages*. 7th ed. London: Williams and Norgate.

Makari, G. (2008) *Revolution in mind: the creation of psychoanalysis*. London: Duckworth.

Moore, H. L. (2007) *The subject of anthropology: gender, symbolism and psychoanalysis*. Cambridge and Malden: Polity Press.

Nancy, J. L., and P. Lacoue-Labarthe. (1989) 'The unconscious is destructed like an affect', *Stanford Literature Review* 6 (2), 191–209.

Reik, T. (1954) 'Freud and Jewish wit', *Psychoanalysis* 2, 12–20.

Rose, J. (1999) 'Freud in the "tropics"', *History Workshop Journal* 47, 49–67.

Sahlins, M. (1979) 'Cannibalism: an exchange', *New York Review of Books* 26 (4), 46–47.

Said, E. (2003) *Freud and the non-European*. London: Verso.

Seshadri-Crooks, K. (1994) 'The primitive as analyst: postcolonial feminism's access to psychoanalysis', *Cultural Critique* 28, 175–218.

Shamdasani, S. (2003) *Jung and the making of modern psychology: the dream of a science*. Cambridge: Cambridge University Press.

Stocking, G W. (1987) *Victorian anthropology*. New York and London: The Free Press, A Division of Macmillan, Inc.

Stoler, A. L. (2000) 'Cultivating bourgeois bodies and racial selves'. In C. Hall (ed.) *Cultures of empire: colonizers in Britain and the empire in the nineteenth and twentieth centuries*. Manchester: Manchester University Press.

Tylor, E. B. (1920) *Primitive culture: researches into the development of mythology, philosophy, religion, language, art and custom*. 6th ed. Vol. 1. 2 vols. London: John Murray, Albemarle Street.

Yerushalmi, Y. H. (1991) *Freud's Moses: Judaism terminable and interminable*. New York and London: Yale University Press.

Part 3

The location of cultural experience

Chapter 7

'Little Mussolini' and the 'parasite poets'

Psychoanalytic pedagogy, modernism, and the illegible child

Helen Tyson

> There was nothing but praise for the up to date conditions & modern buildings. Yet perhaps when Dr. Crane undid his collar, & appeared […] stripped of ceremonial in the looking glass in the bath room, he may have thought in a moment of despondency & clarity, how much escaped his fingers, could not be accounted for. […] There were boys even now tossing uneasily on their beds. […] other forces […] thrust into his mind, & —Both he & Miss Damer must often have felt that […] though their […] methods were, modern, & their schools in every way up to date, something escaped.
> Virginia Woolf, draft for *The Waves* (1931) (Woolf, 1976, p. 26)

In May 1931 an article appeared in *The New Statesman and Nation* entitled 'Free Speech in Childhood'. This article, by Bertrand Russell about his and Dora Russell's Beacon Hill School located in the South Downs in West Sussex, insisted that although not 'completely free', the children at his newly founded progressive school did have 'complete freedom of speech' (Russell, 1931, p. 486). Invoking the authority of 'Freudian text-books', Russell went on to illustrate the peculiarly 'literary', as well as the democratic, benefits of this policy of 'free speech' (Ibid). Printing two poems produced 'by a syndicate' of children, Russell underscored the children's unique capacity to create poems 'suggested by the ordinary sights and events of their everyday life' (Ibid). Responding to Russell's article, one correspondent wrote in to denounce the practice of group composition as a form of 'séance', in which one 'little Mussolini' must be dictating to 'several little parasite poets, whose […] acquisitive faculties are being unhealthily exercised by this process of communal authorship' (Williams, 1931, p. 540). Barbara Low, a teacher, psychoanalyst, and feminist also wrote in to condemn the celebrated philosopher's utter failure to grasp the real impossibility, in psychoanalytic terms, of 'free speech', insisting instead on the enormous psychic difficulty of 'free speech' for the child (Low, 1931, pp. 606–607). A furious debate emerged in the letters pages of the *New Statesman and Nation* over the ensuing weeks, posing a number of questions about the relationship between psychoanalysis, education, and politics.

DOI: 10.4324/9781003200765-10

In the same year that Russell published his article on 'Free Speech in Childhood', Virginia Woolf published *The Waves*. '[T]his shall be Childhood; but it must not be my childhood,' Woolf wrote (Woolf, 1982, p. 236). In fact, as I show in this essay, Woolf's early drafts for *The Waves* reveal a direct engagement with the debates about childhood raised by experiments in new forms of progressive education. In this essay, I examine 'Childhood' as it was imagined in psychoanalytic, pedagogic, and modernist writing about progressive schooling. Following Michal Shapira's claim that British psychoanalysts made 'the understanding of children [...] key to the successful creation of social democracy' in wartime and post-war Britain, I too show how the figure of the child in the 1920s and 1930s was both invested with anxiety about the child's vulnerability to authoritarian politics and, at the same time, charged with the possibility that, subject to the right forms of education, the child might secure the future of democracy (Shapira, 2013, p. 1). The modernist child was a crucially overdetermined figure, a contested site for a number of opposing, and frequently contradictory, ideas about the meaning of the child in an age of nascent, yet imperilled, universal British democracy. Tracking a diverse range of modernist, psychoanalytic, and pedagogic writers in their frequently impassioned responses to early-twentieth-century progressive education, I argue that, for all of the thinkers explored in this essay, the figure of the child becomes fraught with a complex set of political fantasies invested in those Virginia Woolf describes as 'future citi[z]ens' (Woolf, 1976, 137). By staging and examining different accounts of both childhood and progressive education across psychoanalytic writing, pedagogy, and modernism in the 1920s and 1930s we can, I suggest, better understand what was at stake politically in this modernist fantasy of the child.

'[T]he last stronghold of the desire of adults to have power over others'? Psychoanalysis and education

In their correspondence between Bloomsbury and Berlin in 1924, James and Alix Strachey – central figures in the relationship between Bloomsbury modernism and psychoanalysis – returned repeatedly to the question of the relationship between psychoanalysis and education. In her account of the theoretical conflict that had 'showed its hoary head' in the Berlin Psycho-Analytical Society, Alix revealed one of the central conflicts that would dominate psychoanalytic debate for years to come: a debate between Melanie Klein and Anna Freud over whether or not the child psychoanalyst ought to exert educational 'influence' over the child (Meisel and Kendrick, 1986, p. 145; Freud, 1929, pp. 35–36). Describing Anna Freud as an 'open or secret sentimentalist', Alix found Klein's 'case' against the 'hopeless pedagogues' to be 'quite overwhelming': for Klein, the child was in possession, from early infancy, of a ferocious and demanding superego, the violence of which derives from the frustrations and destructive drives of early psychic life (Meisel and Kendrick, 1986, pp. 145–146). For Klein, the violently destructive urges that emerge from the infantile unconscious were caught up in an even more violent battle with a ferocious internal super-ego, a 'tyrannous' taskmaster whose brutality she would sum-up in the 1930s in the figure of an 'internal Hitler' (Grosskurth, 1987, pp. 163–182, pp. 321–33; Stonebridge, 2007, p. 25; Shapira, 2013, pp. 87–111). Rather than seek, as Anna Freud did, to tame, to educate, or (in Alix's words) to 'tone up' the infantile super-ego, Klein insisted that it was the role of the child psychoanalyst to analyse this despotic internal monster (Meisel and Kendrick, 1986, p. 147).

Negative reactions to Klein's analysis of children were Alix insisted, 'affective', rooted in moral, sentimental and romantic fantasies about childhood, rather than analytic experience (Meisel and Kendrick, 1986, p. 145). Describing a conversation with Lou Andreas-Salomé, who claimed 'that parents were the only proper people to analyse the child', Alix recalled 'a shudder run down my spine': 'It seems to me to be the last stronghold of the desire of adults to have power over others' (Ibid., p. 200). Reading Hermine Hug-Hellmuth's 'outpourings on the subject', Alix found 'a mass of sentimentality covering the old intention of dominating at least one human being—one's own child' (Ibid.). For Alix, the danger of blurring the lines between education and child analysis was that, under the guise of 'sentimentality', that 'old intention of dominating' and exerting 'power over' the child creeps in, producing a dangerously authoritarian confusion between analysis and education. Alix (unaware that Klein had in fact based her first papers on analysis of her own children) approved of Klein's apparently firm stance on the subject: 'She absolutely insists on keeping parental & educative influence apart from analysis' (Ibid., p. 201).

Alongside their discussion of the dangers of giving in to the 'old intention of dominating' the child, James and Alix Strachey also discussed, in their letters between Berlin and Bloomsbury, the pitfalls of new experiments in progressive, apparently psychoanalytically informed, pedagogy. James wrote to Alix with a cynical account of her nephew's experiences at the Malting House Garden School in Cambridge (Meisel and Kendrick, 1986, p. 205). The Malting House School had been established in 1924 by the inventor and speculator, Geoffrey Pyke, with the psychoanalyst Susan Isaacs as headmistress and chief researcher. The 'guiding idea' was, as John Forrester and Laura Cameron observe, 'that the children would be allowed to discover the natural world freely like little scientists, through the medium of fantasy and play' (Forrester and Cameron, 2017, p. 433). But, as John Rickman commented, among psychoanalytic circles,

> The question arose whether the freedom in this school might not have some of the quality of a 'pre-genital brothel' and so hinder the development of the cultural gains which are brought at the cost of erotic deprivation. Where would the energy for the sublimation necessary for cultural achievement come from if erotic satisfactions were not denied?
> (cited in Forrester and Cameron, 2017, p. 461)

Responding to James' letter, Alix wrote of the 'impossibility' of any such 'Psycho-analytical education':

> It all goes to confirm die [*sic*] Klein's view, which is that (1) Psycho-analytical education is an impossibility since it involves 2 contradictory processes a). necessary repression—of killing one's little friends & pumping over the porridge, etc., This is education; & b). the 'Abbau' [quarrying, mining, dismantling] of what is too violently repressed—from internal causes mostly, so that it is unavoidable—& the substitution of conscious condemnation for unc. repression. This is analysis.
> (Meisel and Kendrick, 1986, p. 209)

In Alix's analysis, educational reformers, in their desire to free the child from all forms of repression, sought an impossible form of education, rooted in a romantically naïve concept of the free child.[1] Alix's objection to this wild application of psychoanalysis to education was not simply the objection of a theoretical purist; it is also, as her comments on the 'old intention of dominating' and exerting 'power over' the child suggest, informed by a wider debate about the politics of progressive education in this period. In his account of Susan Isaacs' work at the Malting House school, Shaul Bar-Haim notes that debates about freedom in children's education in this period intersected with, and were overdetermined by, 'an acute crisis in liberal ideology' in the interwar period (Bar-Haim, 2017, p. 110). Indeed, what was at stake, politically, in these debates about free education, is thrown into stark relief in the correspondence which unfolded in the letters pages of *The New Statesman and Nation*, following Bertrand Russell's account of his and Dora Russell's experiment in progressive pedagogy.

In 1927, Dora and Bertrand Russell, inspired by other educational pioneers including Homer Lane, A. S. Neill, Maria Montessori, and Rachel McMillan, had opened Beacon Hill School on the South Downs in Sussex. In their published writings on the school, both Dora and Bertrand Russell stressed the centrality of democracy in the life of Beacon Hill School: the school, they wrote in the prospectus, was founded on the belief that 'Morality and reasoning [...] arise from the children's actual experience in a democratic group and never of necessity from the authority or convenience of adults' (cited in Gorham, 2005, p. 47). Dora Russell underscored the importance of self-governance by the children: 'The government of the school is in the hands of the School Council. Everybody belongs to this, from the Principal to the gardener, and every child who is 5 years old and over' (cited in ibid., p. 65). Looking back in 1980, Dora insisted that 'democracy was the basic principle of my school': 'Democracy', she elaborated,

> is also the vital element in education. Democracy defines each child as a unique individual who belongs, not to the State, or even to his parents, but first of all to himself. Education means his freedom and right, by his

own choices and interests, in relation to and out of what surrounds him, to create himself and not be manufactured by others, not to be treated as a 'thing' or a pawn.

(Russell, 1981, p. 211)

The Beacon Hill School was, as Deborah Gorham notes, 'always more Dora's project than Bertrand's, and after 1932 [when their marriage ended] it became exclusively and unequivocally hers' (Gorham, 2005, p. 41).

Bertrand Russell's 1931 account of the school was, nonetheless, a passionate articulation of the educational ideals underpinning the school—and it provoked a vehement debate. Insisting that the children at Beacon Hill had 'complete freedom of speech', and underscoring the importance of this free speech to democratic life, Russell wrote:

> The technique of psychoanalysis has been invented to undo the effects of the 'Hush! Hush!' policy by teaching people to say what hitherto they have only thought. We think it is rather a mistake to give people an expensive education in concealment resulting in nervous disorders, and then give them an expensive re-education to break down the concealment and possibly cure the nervous disorders. When children are left free as regards their language, they say from time to time such things as Freudian text-books assert that they must be thinking, but being able to express their thoughts freely, they are not obliged to give them some fantastic form and become to that extent out of touch with reality.
>
> (Russell, 1931, p. 486)

Citing the authority of 'Freudian text-books', Russell not only outlined his aim to rid the child of the kinds of 'nervous disorders' stemming from the 'Hush! Hush' policy of traditional education, but he also emphasised the specifically 'literary' outcomes of this policy of 'free speech' (Ibid., p. 487). In the article, Russell printed two poems produced by a 'sindicate' of children rather than a 'single author', emphasising that the children's freedom endowed them with a unique capacity for collective authorship of poems 'suggested by the ordinary sights and events of their everyday life' (Ibid.). Insisting that the children's collective poetic creations were a product of their uniquely free and organic relationship to their natural surroundings, Russell claimed that 'As regards literature, the children's diction is exact and expressive; their emotions clothe themselves spontaneously in appropriate language, and they do not acquire that bookishness which is the bane of artificial culture' (Ibid.). Although the two children's poems published alongside Russell's article deploy fairly conventional, even archaic, poetic diction, Russell nonetheless presents the poems as the products of direct experience (Ibid.). These young poets produce poems directly from experience and nature, 'and not', Russell insists, 'by imitation of some poet who imitated some poet who imitated some poet who imitated Homer' (Ibid.).

Russell's article inspired a fierce debate in the letters pages of the *New Statesman and Nation*. Responding to 'the practice at Beacon Hill of the communal authorship of poetry', one reader, W. E. Williams, wrote in to object: firstly, the poems produced must be 'suggested' by one of the teachers, and secondly, they must be the 'creation of one child', and one child only (Williams, 1931, p. 540). Insisting that 'the séance' must 'contain one poetic little Mussolini', the correspondent was adamant that 'the group must contain one real little poet and several little parasite poets, whose initiative and acquisitive faculties are being unhealthily exercised by this process of communal authorship' (Ibid.). Russell's idealistic espousal of the free child as a paragon of the possibilities of free speech and a model of spontaneous aesthetic purity was condemned for dangerously and 'unhealthily exercis[ing]' the fascistic susceptibilities of children, turning the scene of communal poetic composition into a miniature fascist state. Having indicted Russell with nurturing poetic dictatorship in the 'one real little poet', and of encouraging an unthinking passivity in the other 'little parasite poets', the correspondent then goes on, in somewhat paradoxical fashion, to accuse Russell of an excessive embrace of 'this democratic age':

> Can we begin too early to disclose to the children of this democratic age that some kinds of achievement are peculiarly personal and unique? [...] Was even such a crude form as the ballad really the product of a gang of hairy savages sitting round the camp fire after supper?
>
> I suppose I run the risk of being considered a fanatic, if I detect in a practice that Mr. Russell appears to applaud one more unconscious attempt to cramp creative personality in a society which too often fails to respect the necessary boundaries between sociological collectivism and aesthetic individualism (Ibid.).

In conclusion, as though putting the final nail in the coffin, the correspondent asked if the authors of the poems aren't 'far more addicted to "bookishness" than Mr. Russell knows, particularly to the verse of Mr. de la Mare?' (Ibid.). Walter de la Mare wrote both for and about children, elevating a Blakean idealised concept of the 'visionary' 'childlike' poet (De la Mare, 1919, p. 5, p. 9, p. 12). But, just as De la Mare's reliance on an archaic poetic vocabulary placed his poetry at odds with literary modernism, the implication in this letter is that, in spite of the claim that places the child poet as the font of originality, Russell's school reproduces a derivative version of childhood (and its accompanying aesthetic), at odds with the kind of 'aesthetic individualism' espoused by this critic.

For the psychoanalyst, teacher, and feminist Barbara Low, 'the two poems quoted by Mr. Russell as illustrative of the children's freedom from imitation' were 'by no means spontaneous expressions, but on the contrary, direct descendants of a whole host of poetry produced by those children's immediate predecessors, such as Walter De la Mare [and] Hilaire Belloc' (Low, 1931, p. 607).

Low, who had begun her career as a school teacher and lecturer in education, history and literature, was, in 1919, one of the founding members of the British Psycho-Analytical Society (Forrester, 2007, p. 49). In 1920 she wrote *Psycho-Analysis: A Brief Account of the Freudian Theory*, proposing the idea of the 'Nirvana principle' (which Freud would draw upon in *Beyond the Pleasure Principle*), and she would later become one of Anna Freud's most staunch supporters in the 'Controversial Discussions' (Freud, 1955, p. 56). As well as being active in the Fabian Society, Low was also secretary of Dora Marsden's Freewoman Discussion Circle, and a close friend of the modernist writers D. H. Lawrence and Dorothy Richardson (Bland, 2001, p. 271; Clarke, 1996, pp. 75–76). She was acquainted with both Dora and Bertrand Russell, but this did not stop her from launching a fervent attack.[2] In her first letter to *The New Statesman and Nation*, Low condemned Russell's utter failure to grasp the impossibility of any such 'free speech'. Summarising what she understood to be Russell's 'main thesis'—'that the human being in the state of childhood is perfectly capable of, first, *knowing* his own thoughts and feelings; secondly, *expressing* those thoughts and feelings in an appropriate fashion'—Low described her 'considerable shock' at finding such a celebrated 'philosopher, psychologist and sociologist reiterating the cheap catchwords of "popular" writers and speakers' (Low, 1931, p. 606).

> Has his experience [...] really taught him that 'Freedom' is a magic gift scattered lavishly on every new-born infant? Has he no recollection of his own early life and its inner development? Has he no realisation of the internal checks to mental and emotional freedom which do not vanish merely by facility in speech, nor even by the removal of external prohibitions?
>
> (Ibid., p. 607)

Responding to Russell's apparent claim 'to have achieved the miracle of eliminating from the deepest recesses of the human soul some of its profoundest emotions', Low cited Samuel Butler as a 'better guide in these matters' (Ibid.). Butler's portrait of a soul tormented by the internal wranglings and conflicting demands and prohibitions of its own 'former selves', was, Low insisted, 'Not quite so simple a picture [...] of the human soul as is Mr. Russell's, painted in the rose colour of "Freedom"' (Ibid.). In bitingly satirical style, Low ridiculed 'Mr. Russell's' naïve 'dream' of 'free' education, pointing to the absurdity of assuming that by 'eliminating all conventions and taboos imposed by the adults', one might allow 'the rising generation to express all that they wish and—hey, presto!—the next generation will evolve as "Free" human beings' (Ibid.).

As the hesitations in the Stracheys' responses to the Malting House School demonstrate, and as Low's objections to the Beacon Hill School make clear, for these psychoanalysts, the advocates of new forms of progressive education had been misled by a 'popular', perhaps even 'wild', belief that 'nervous disorders' are caused solely by a form of externally imposed social repression that might be alleviated or even removed by a freer form of education.[3] For Low, however, the 'human soul' was populated by forms of intrapsychic conflict that refuse any such easy separation of what lies inside and outside of the mind. Low writes:

> I suggest to Mr. Russell that the technique of psycho-analysis (concerning which, by the way, he makes a new and remarkable definition hardly to be accepted by psycho-analysts) would reveal to him the difficulty of 'free' speech and still more of 'free' thinking, even when all external taboos are removed.
>
> (Ibid.)

Insisting on the *difficulty* of free speech 'even when all external taboos are removed', Low offers a portrait of the child in which the child's psychic life is not transparent either to himself or herself, or to others. The child, in Low's account, is an altogether more complex, conflicted and enigmatic being.

In Russell's romantic portrait of free childhood, he makes a crucial set of links between the child's freedom from external taboos, the child's unique access to an 'exact and expressive' form of language, and the idea of the school as a miniature democracy. W. E. Williams' criticisms of the Beacon Hill School seem to have been founded predominantly on a liberal objection to a perceived assault on poetic individualism by a form of 'collectivism' that, in Williams' interpretation, threatens to collapse into fascism. Refuting the 'existence of a poetic Mussolini', Russell responded to Williams' accusations by reasserting that the process of communal poetic composition was 'co-operative', not fascistic.[4] Nonetheless, although the process of group composition was evidently rooted in the desire to inculcate democratic co-operative as opposed to fascistic politics, Russell's image of childhood does fall back on a troublingly evasive fantasy of childhood as a refuge from the difficulties and divisions of language and society.

As both Jacqueline Rose and Daniela Caselli have argued, the figure of the child that dominated the cultural imagination of the early twentieth century relied upon an adult fantasy of childhood which placed 'the innocence of the child and a primary state of language and/or culture in a close and mutually dependent relation' (Rose, 1993, p. 9; Caselli, 2009, pp. 127–128). Russell's claim about the 'exact and expressive' diction of his child poets is just one instance in a long tradition in which the child is viewed as having unique access to an unmediated and pure form of language. As Rose pointed out, we use this fantasy of the child

> to hold off a panic, a threat to our assumption that language is something which can simply be organised and cohered, and that sexuality, while it

cannot be removed, will eventually take on the forms in which we prefer to recognise and acknowledge each other.

(Rose, 1993, p. 10)

For Caselli, this fantasy of the child 'comes at the price of collapsing political self-reflectivity in favour of identifications that are troubling because posited beyond the realm of analysis' (Caselli, 2010, p. 246). Bertrand Russell may have sought to inculcate his young charges with a love of co-operative co-existence, but his naïve theory of the natural and spontaneous transparent expressivity of childhood veers dangerously close to an evasive fantasy of the child as a refuge from the difficulties of language, society and politics.

In Russell's account of the Beacon Hill School, his idealisation of the child's unique possession of a form of language that gives immediate and transparent access to the natural world is, as Low stresses, a fantasy that masks the truth of language as a site of rupture and difficulty. In contrast to Russell's fantasy of a childhood free from all forms of external and internal constraint, Low insists upon a portrait of psychic life characterised by division and conflict. And, in contrast to Russell's fantasy of a childhood in perfect possession of an 'exact and expressive' form of language that gives the child direct access to the objects of the real world, Low emphasises the difficulty of the child's relationship to language (Russell, 1931, p. 487). Low does not spell out the political implications of this account of childhood, but her insistence on the 'difficulty of "free" speech and still more of "free" thinking', is by no means a rejection of Russell's democratic ideals (Low, 1931, p. 607). For Low, the child is just as crucial in securing the future of democracy. But rather than paint a rose-tinted fantasy of childhood freedom and democracy, Low's portrait of the child's complex and conflicted internal world highlights the child's vulnerability in relationship to the destructive drives that cut across the terrains of psychic life and politics in the interwar period.

The psychoanalytic portrait of the child as dominated by destructive drives and conflicts contributed, in this period, to an urgent need to acknowledge and understand the relationship between the 'war inside' and the 'war outside' (see Riley, 1983; Walkerdine, 1998; Shapira, 2013). As fascism began to rear its ugly head across Europe, psychoanalysts increasingly stressed the porous boundary between internal and external hatred and conflict, locating the origins of destructive drives and psychic conflicts in the mind of the child. Low's correction to Bertrand Russell is part of a wider psychoanalytic movement that insists, contrary to Russell's romantic idealism, upon the need to confront and to analyse, rather than ignore and repress, the destructive drives and conflicts of the child's inner life. Increasingly in the 1930s, psychoanalysts began to insist that the confrontation with one's own destructiveness was a crucial step on the path to securing a precarious democracy. For Melanie Klein, as for D. W. Winnicott and for other child psychoanalysts in this period, the failure to acknowledge one's own hatred would only result in its more violent re-emergence elsewhere: disavowal, in Klein's model of the psyche, leads to projection, whereby the individual's inner destructiveness is projected onto figures in the outside world, driving a vicious cycle of destruction and aggression.[5] The democratically responsible individual must learn to tolerate and understand his or her own hatred, in order to become less vulnerable to authoritarian politics. By failing to acknowledge this psychoanalytic portrait of the child's inner life, Russell consequently failed to address the relationship between inner destructiveness and conflict, and the forms of aggression, mastery and struggle at work in the wider world of early 1930s Europe.

'Future citi[z]ens'

In 1931 Virginia Woolf published *The Waves*, a novel fraught with anxieties about the precarious nature of co-operative democracy, the threat of fascism, and the destructive aspects of group relationships formed in childhood. Woolf, like Barbara Low, contrasts (and in her final text replaces) the idealism of the progressive pedagogues with a more complex, troubled, and enigmatic portrait of childhood. *The Waves* begins with the voices of six children in the garden at a co-educational nursery and boarding school. As Jessica Berman writes, '*The Waves* has long been recognized as Woolf's most poetic rumination on the problem of commonality', and it can also be read, alongside *The Years* (1937), *Three Guineas* (1938), and *Between the Acts* (1941), as one of Woolf's most sustained meditations on the rise of fascism in Britain and Europe in the late 1920s and early 1930s (Berman, 2001, p. 140). *The Waves* also, I want to argue, begins by focusing these questions about community, commonality, and fascism, in childhood.

In his 2015 introduction to *The Waves*, David Bradshaw pointed out the strikingly progressive nature of the co-educational nursery school in Woolf's novel: noting the parallels with other contemporary experiments in progressive education, he suggested similarities both with Bedales, 'the first co-educational boarding school in England' (Alix Strachey's school), and with the Portman Hall School, a 'co-educational, non-sectarian, and non-socially segregated' school founded by the 'feminist and educationalist Barbara Leigh Smith Bodichon' (Bradshaw, 2015, p. xvii). In 1934 Woolf's own Hogarth Press published Reginald Snell's *Progressive Schools: Their Principles and Practice*, which included an extensive discussion of 'The Psychological Approach' to progressive schooling and included a discussion of the Malting House School and the Beacon Hill School, alongside A. S. Neill's more famous progressive school, Summerhill (Pekin, 1934, p. 33, p. 36). In the drafts for *The Waves*, Woolf described the headmaster Dr Crane and the schoolteacher Miss Damer dwelling on how 'modern' their 'methods' are, 'their schools in every way up to date' (Woolf, 1976, pp. 26–27). One passage describes 'Miss Lamberts celebrated school on the East Coast' (Ibid., p. 119). 'There was', Woolf writes, 'nothing but praise for the up to date conditions & modern buildings'; 'visitors to the school were shown the method of washing plates by electricity', while the 'Innumerable children [...] now began to be called "future citi[z]ens"' (Ibid., p. 26, p. 137). Regardless of whether or not we can trace the co-educational nursery school in the final text of *The Waves* to any specific historical model, the drafts indicate that Woolf was responding directly to the rise of progressive pedagogy, reflecting the stress on 'modern' 'methods', the turn to co-education, and the belief that new and progressive forms of education might equip the 'future citi[z]ens' of democratic society (Ibid., p. 26, p. 137).

The early drafts of *The Waves* make it clear that Woolf was interested in the new forms of progressive pedagogy on trial at schools like Beacon Hill. Although Woolf's friend David 'Bunny' Garnett sent his son, Richard, to Beacon Hill, in her autobiographies Dora Russell lamented that 'the Bloomsbury set [...] treated the school as matter for merriment', suggesting that Woolf may have been amongst those who, like Barbara Low, were critical, or at least mocking, of the Russells' venture (D. Russell, 1981, pp. 26–27). In *The Waves*, in place of Bertrand Russell's naïve embrace of the 'free child' in possession of a uniquely and spontaneously expressive language, Woolf in contrast offers us a portrait of the child as an enigmatic figure riven by conflict and aggression. The headmaster Dr Crane surveys his 'modern' and 'up to date' schooling methods, but he also frets 'in a moment of despondency and clarity, how much escaped his fingers, could not be accounted for' (Woolf, 1976, p. 26). For Woolf, as for Barbara Low, 'something escape[s]' the progressive pedagogue and his 'up to date' methods (Ibid.). In contrast to Bertrand Russell's idealised 'exact and expressive' child poets, Woolf embraces a modernist aesthetics of difficulty and obscurity. She also offers, despite her notorious ambivalence about psychoanalysis, a strikingly Kleinian portrait of childhood. It is, I want to suggest in this final section, by staging and examining the differences between Woolf's and Russell's 'future citi[z]ens' that we might begin to grasp the political desires that are at stake in these contested imaginings of the playgrounds of democracy.

Woolf was famously ambivalent concerning psychoanalysis. Although, from 1924 onwards, she and her husband Leonard Woolf became the chief publishers of psychoanalysis in England, she nonetheless appears to have refused to read Freud with any seriousness until after his death in 1939. And yet, despite her reservations about 'Freudian Fiction', there is a case to be made for the striking parallels that exist between Woolf's writing and that of Melanie Klein (Woolf, 1988a). While Woolf was writing *The Waves*, her friend Alix Strachey was translating Klein's first book, *The Psycho-Analysis of Children*, which was published by the Hogarth Press in 1932, just one year after *The Waves*. In the 'Preface', Klein thanked 'Mrs. James Strachey' and 'Mr. Strachey for the great assistance which their stimulating hints and suggestions have given me in its composition' (Klein, 1932, p. 12). It has not so far been recognised, however, that in the 'Translator's Note' to the first edition of *The Psycho-Analysis of Children*, Alix Strachey also thanked Virginia

Woolf's brother, the psycho-analyst Adrian Stephen, for his assistance with the translation (Ibid., p. 13).[6] This reinforces Elizabeth Abel's suggestion that the 'amateurish knowledge' of 'Freud and the psychoanalysts', which Woolf claimed came from 'superficial talk' alone, may have had a distinctly Kleinian colouring (Woolf, 1979, p. 36; Abel, 1989, p. 20). In any case, by 1939, when, on a 'wild wet' evening in March, she was a guest at the 'Great Psycho Analysts Dinner'— the Twenty-Fifth Anniversary Dinner of the British Psycho-Analytical Society— Woolf evidently knew enough to be 'set upon & committed to ask to dinner Mrs. Klein' (Woolf, 1988b, p. 208). Woolf's engagement diaries, housed in the University of Sussex Special Collections, contain two separate entries for appointments with 'Mrs Klein'—one on Tuesday 14 March, and another on Saturday 25 March 1939 (Monk's House Papers; see Figures 7.1, 7.2, and 7.3).

Woolf described her dinner with 'Mrs Klein' in her diary:

> Mrs Klein dined [...] A woman of character & force & some submerged—how shall I say—not craft, but subtlety: something working underground. A pull, a twist, like an undertow: menacing. A bluff grey haired lady, with large bright imaginative eyes.
>
> (Ibid., p. 209)

Abel, pursuing an 'intertextual' relationship rather than one of 'influence' between the two thinkers, notes the 'link between the person and the theory': 'Klein's psyche, in this rendition, is isomorphic with her representation of the psyche; primitive forces work underground; a Minoan-Mycenean civilisation, more tumultuous than Freud's threatens to engulf a superstructure (and perhaps the viewer as well)' (Abel, 1989, p. xvi, p. 19).

In the drafts for *The Waves*, the waves that echo throughout the novel are figured as the 'prostrate forms of mothers', who, 'in their flowing nightgowns', spawn 'innumerable children':

> Many mothers & before them many mothers, & again many mothers, have groaned, & fallen [...]. Like one wave, [...] succeeding another. Wave after wave, endlessly sinking & falling as far as the eye can stretch. And all these waves have been the prostrate forms of mothers, in their flowing nightgowns, with the tumbled sheets about them holding up, with a groan, as they sink back into the sea.
>
> (Woolf, 1976, p. 7)

Every wave, Woolf wrote, 'cast a child from it; before it sank into the obscure body of the sea' (Ibid., p. 10). Woolf describes the 'innumerable children' in tones of abject ambivalence:

> The little bodies wriggled & turned & twisted, curiously mobile & restless, uneasy, ill-directed, shooting out arms & legs,—for there could be no

'Little Mussolini' and the 'parasite poets' 97

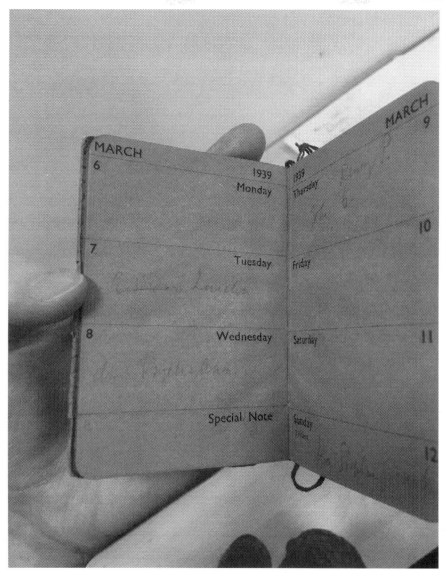

Figure 7.1 Virginia Woolf engagement diaries, Monk's House Papers, University of Sussex Special Collections, SxMs-18/4/41
Source: Reproduced with kind permission from the Society of Authors as the Literary Representative of the Estate of Virginia Woolf.

98 The location of cultural experience

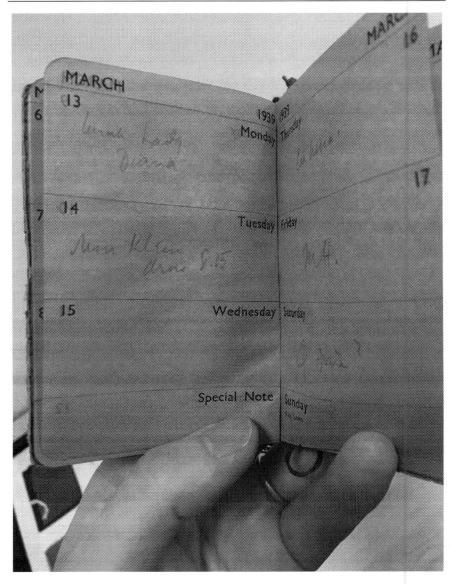

Figure 7.2 Virginia Woolf engagement diaries, Monk's House Papers, University of Sussex Special Collections, SxMs-18/4/41
Source: Reproduced with kind permission from the Society of Authors as the Literary Representative of the Estate of Virginia Woolf.

'Little Mussolini' and the 'parasite poets' 99

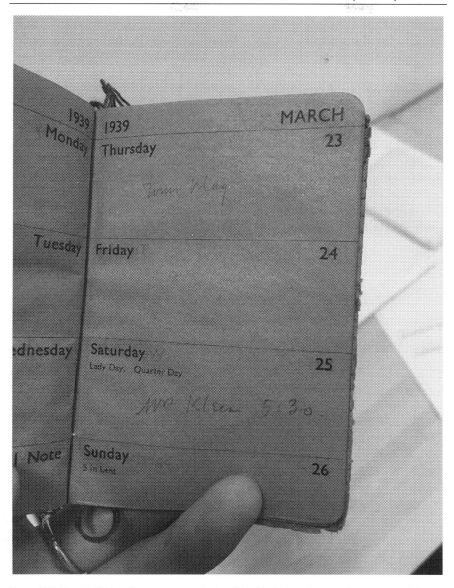

Figure 7.3 Virginia Woolf engagement diaries, Monk's House Papers, University of Sussex Special Collections, SxMs-18/4/41
Source: Reproduced with kind permission from the Society of Authors as the Literary Representative of the Estate of Virginia Woolf.

doubt that these whiffs of spray, these pinkish balls, were, now that the light burnt a little clearer, [...] new born babies, tossed [...] from the top of the waves, cast off by the rapidity of the sea—To a sardonic eye [...] nothing could have been more ridiculous & base than [...] the worm like, eel like, half conscious yet blindly impulsive & violent actions of these little bald ~~brats~~ [above: animals]. And soon the beach was covered with their markings. Soon they were staggering across the sand, & leaving foot prints [...].

(Ibid., p. 62)

'The beach', Woolf concludes, 'was black with them' (Ibid.).

The tone of this 'surreal fantasy' of maternal 'fecundity [...] tinged [...] with disgust', is, as Alison Light notes, coloured by Woolf's troubled attempts to include the voices of a diverse social spectrum in the novel (Light, 2007, pp. 202–203). But it is also tempting to connect the 'obscure' maternal 'body' of the sea in Woolf's novel with Melanie Klein's contemporaneous efforts to delve into what Freud had described, infamously, as that 'grey' and 'shadowy' realm of the pre-Oedipal relationship to the mother (Freud, 1961, p. 225). Not only is the novel haunted by this ambivalent maternal origin, but *The Waves* also echoes Klein's portrait of the turbulent emotional life of childhood: the narrator of the drafts describes how 'Jealousy & hatred already ravaged' the new-born babies writhing on the beach, and protests 'I am not laying too great a stress upon all this. I am not exaggerating the intensity of children's feelings!' (Woolf, 1976, p. 7, p. 14). Klein burrowed back into the earliest moments of the infant's psychic life, controversially positing a violent, passionate emotional and fantasy life in the child. Sounding very much like Klein and her followers as they argued their case for this passionate life against the detractions of sceptics, Woolf writes that 'there is nothing more certain than that children are tortured by jealousy & love, long before they know their names' (Ibid., p. 14).[7] 'People ~~say that children are happy~~', Woolf writes: 'They forget the terrible revelations; the faces that look out from behind leaves' (Ibid.).

Woolf, like her contemporaries in the British Psycho-Analytical Society, emphasises the passion, violence and destructiveness of children's feelings. She shares with psychoanalysts like Klein an understanding of childhood as both violent and destructive, and also as vulnerable to the lures of fascistic politics. Throughout *The Waves* the group ties formed in early childhood threaten to subsume the six voices within an oceanic oneness that resembles fascism (McIntire, 2005). Like Low, however, Woolf also stresses the obscurity and complexity of the child's inner life. In place of the idealised portrait of childhood found in Bertrand Russell's account of the Beacon Hill School, Woolf situates childhood as a site of precarious struggle for a new form of democratic selfhood. For Woolf, as for Low, the conflicts, violence, and passionate intensities of childhood cannot, and indeed must not, be denied, but rather confronted as part of a struggle for new forms of democratic life, for the 'future citi[z]ens'.

'For Hannah Arendt', Jacqueline Rose writes, 'every new birth is the supreme anti-totalitarian moment' (Rose, 2018, p. 79). 'Beginning', Arendt writes in the final pages of *The Origins of Totalitarianism*, 'is identical with man's freedom'; and 'This beginning is guaranteed by each new birth' (Arendt, 2004, p. 616). Every new birth, by opening a new and crucially unpredictable set of possibilities, represents a refusal of the oppressive and insidious logic of totalitarian power. The 'worm like, eel like, half conscious yet blindly impulsive [...] brats' that appear in the drafts of *The Waves* figure Woolf's anxieties in this period about both children's and adults' vulnerability to 'blind' impulse and to the violent fascisms of the 1930s. But, the 'curiously mobile & restless, uneasy, ill-directed' bodies of Woolf's infants also, like Arendt's new births, invoke the possibility of anti-totalitarian resistance. Although Woolf notes that, to a 'sardonic eye', the 'twisting babies' might appear as 'ridiculous & base', animalistic and violent, 'bald brats', nonetheless the image of the 'little bodies' wriggling and twisting 'curiously mobile & restless, uneasy, ill-directed, shooting out arms & legs' captures precisely that sense of unpredictability that Hannah Arendt found so valuable in each new birth. There is something inscrutable and unpredictable in Woolf's image of the 'twisting babies', which eschews the forms of personal and political domination that Woolf goes on to trace in the ensuing novel.

For Woolf, as for Arendt, there is something valuable in the uncertainty and unpredictability of each new birth, but there is also something valuable in the ways that this infantile mind resists easy interpretation. As the 'twisting babies' of the drafts begin to emerge as distinct individuals, Woolf's narrator asks 'What geography can one make of the soul?' (Woolf, 1976, p. 23). But the image that emerges is one of the child's inner life as stretching into an 'unfathomable pit in the centre':

> If [one could] [...] sketch a plan of the soul, there would be a pit [...] which opens on profundity, a so deep [...] it would show a [...] little figure with its roots going so deep, so deep, into such an unknown layer, that if it is not to be sucked in & drawn into blackness, it must have tentacles attached to the world above.
>
> (Ibid.)

For Woolf, the illegibility of the child stands as something that refuses to be subsumed within that vision of oceanic oneness that *The Waves* nonetheless yearns for. The 'unintelligible infant' is, I suggest in conclusion, an overdetermined figure, a vehicle for a number of conflicting uncertainties about political and psychic life in 1930s Europe. But while the infant is viewed by both Woolf and Klein as a figure riven by a violent and destructive emotional life, it is also, in Woolf's writing, a site of potential resistance to the forms of violence that cut across the historical landscape of 1930s Europe.

Notes

1 On Isaacs' responses to these criticisms, and for more detailed accounts of the school, see Forrester and Cameron, 2017; Bar-Haim, 2017.
2 See Zytaruk and Boulton (1981, p. 310, p. 311, p. 312, p. 490, p. 589) and D. Russell (1975, p. 219).
3 As Forrester and Cameron note, Susan Isaacs, 'upon learning of the existence of Russell's school, had drafted a letter offering cooperation'. However, she was also critical of Russell's published writing on education, criticising *On Education, Especially in Early Childhood*, see Forrester and Cameron (2017, pp. 448–449, p. 467).
4 On the co-operative movement see Webb (1891); Woolf (1921); Gurney (1996); Berman (2001, pp. 123–130).
5 On Winnicott's contribution to this tradition, see Alexander (2016).
6 The reason, presumably, that Adrian Stephen's involvement has not been noticed, is that the 'Translator's Note' is omitted from the 1975 edition of *The Psycho-Analysis of Children*, which was 'revised in collaboration with Alix Strachey by H. A. Thorner' (Klein, 1932, p. 13; Klein, 1997, pp. viii–ix).
7 On the controversies surrounding Klein's work see King and Steiner (1992).

Bibliography

Abel, E. (1989) *Virginia Woolf and the fictions of psychoanalysis*. Chicago: University of Chicago Press.
Alexander, S. (2016) 'D. W. Winnicott and the social democratic vision', in M. ffytche and D. Pick (eds), *Psychoanalysis in the age of totalitarianism*. London: Routledge, pp. 114–130.
Arendt, H. (2004) *The origins of totalitarianism*. New York: Shocken.
Bar-Haim, S. (2017) 'The liberal playground: Susan Isaacs, psychoanalysis and progressive education in the interwar era', *History of the Human Sciences* 30 (1), 94–117.
Berman, J. (2001) *Modernist fiction, cosmopolitanism, and the politics of community*. Cambridge: Cambridge University Press.
Bland, L. (2001) *Banishing the beast: feminism, sex and morality*. 2nd edn. London: Tauris Parke.
Bradshaw, D. (2015) 'Introduction', *The waves*, ed. by David Bradshaw. Oxford: Oxford University Press, pp. xi–xxxix.
Cameron, L. (2006) 'Science, nature, and hatred: "finding out" at the Malting House Garden School, 1924–29', *Environment and Planning D: Society and Space* 24, pp. 851–872.
Caselli, D. (2009) *Improper modernism: Djuna Barnes' bewildering corpus*. Surrey: Ashgate.
Caselli, D. (2010) 'Kindergarten theory: childhood, affect, critical thought', *Feminist Theory* 11, 241–254.
Clarke, B. (1996), *Dora Marsden and early modernism: gender, individualism, science*. Ann Arbor: University of Michigan Press.
De la Mare, W. (1919) *Rupert Brook and the intellectual imagination*. London: Sidgwick and Jackson.
Forrester, J, (2007) '1919: psychology and psychoanalysis, Cambridge and London – Myers, Jones and Maccurdy', *Psychoanalysis and History* 10 (1), 37–94.

Forrester, J. and L. Cameron (2017) *Freud in Cambridge*. Cambridge: Cambridge University Press.
Freud, A. (1929) 'On the theory of analysis of children', *International Journal of Psycho-Analysis* 10, 29–38.
Freud, S. (1955) Beyond the pleasure principle. In *The standard edition of the complete psychological works of Sigmund Freud*, ed. J. Strachey; trans. J. Strachey and A. Freud, with A. Strachey and A. Tyson, London: The Hogarth Press and the Institute of Psychoanalysis, 24 vols., vol. XVIII.
Freud, S. (1961) 'Female sexuality'. In *The standard edition of the complete psychological works of Sigmund Freud*, ed. J. Strachey; trans. J. Strachey and A. Freud, with A. Strachey and A. Tyson, London: The Hogarth Press and the Institute of Psychoanalysis, 24 vols., vol. XXI.
Gorham, D. (2005) 'Dora and Bertrand Russell and Beacon Hill school'. *Russell: The Journal of Bertrand Russell Studies* 25, 39–76.
Grosskurth, P. (1987) *Melanie Klein: her world and her work*. London: Karnac.
Gurney, P. (1996) *Co-operative culture and the politics of consumption in England: 1870–1930*. New York: Manchester University Press.
King, P. and Steiner, R. (eds) (1992) *The Freud—Klein controversies 1941–45*. London: Routledge.
Klein, M. (1932) *The psycho-analysis of children*, trans. A. Strachey. London: Hogarth Press.
Klein, M. (1997) *The psycho-analysis of children*, trans. A. Strachey; rev. H. A. Thorner. London: Vintage.
Light, A. (2007) *Mrs Woolf and the servants*. London: Penguin.
Low, B. (1929) 'A note on the influence of psycho-analysis upon English education during the last eighteen years', *International Journal of Psycho-Analysis* 10, 314–320.
Low, B. (1931) 'Letters: free speech in childhood', *New Statesman and Nation* 1 (17), 606–607.
McIntire, G. (2005) 'Heteroglossia, monologism, and fascism: Bernard reads The Waves', *Narrative* 13 (1), 29–45.
Meisel, P. and Kendrick, W. (eds) (1986) *Bloomsbury/Freud: the letters of James and Alix Strachey 1924–1925*. London: Chatto and Windus.
Pekin, L. B. [Reginald Snell] (1934) *Progressive schools: their principles and practice*. London: Hogarth Press.
Riley, D. (1983) *War in the nursery: theories of child and mother*. London: Virago.
Rose, J. (1993) *The case of Peter Pan; or, the impossibility of children's fiction*. 2nd edn. Philadelphia: University of Philadelphia Press.
Rose, J. (2018) *Mothers: an essay on love and cruelty*. London: Faber & Faber.
Russell, B. (1931) 'Free speech in childhood', *New Statesman and Nation* 1 (14), 486–488.
Russell, D. (1981) *The Tamarisk Tree, Volume 2: My School and the Years of War*. London: Virago.
Shapira, M. (2013) *The war inside: psychoanalysis, total war, and the making of the democratic self in postwar Britain*. Cambridge: Cambridge University Press.
Stonebridge, L. (2007) *The writing of anxiety*. Basingstoke: Palgrave Macmillan.
Walkerdine, V. (1998) 'Developmental psychology and the child-centred pedagogy: the insertion of Piaget into early education', in J. Henriqueset al (eds), *Changing the subject: psychology, social regulation and subjectivity*. 2nd edn. London: Routledge, pp. 153–202.

Webb, B. (1891) *The co-operative movement in Great Britain*. London: Sonnenschein.
Williams, W. E (1931) 'Letters: free speech in childhood', *New Statesman and Nation* 1 (15), 540.
Woolf, L. (1921) *Socialism and co-operation*. London: Leonard Parsons.
Woolf, V. (1976) *The waves: the two holograph drafts*, transcr. and ed. J. W. Graham. London: Hogarth Press.
Woolf, V. (1979) *The letters of Virginia Woolf, volume 5 1932–35*, ed. N. Nicolson and J. Trautmann. London: Hogarth Press.
Woolf, V. (1982) *The diary of Virginia Woolf, volume 3, 1925–30*, ed. A. O. Bell and A. McNeillie. London: Penguin.
Woolf, V. (1988a), *The essays of Virginia Woolf*, ed. A. McNeillie and S. N. Clarke, London: Hogarth Press, 6 vols., vol. III.
Woolf, V. (1988b) *The diary of Virginia Woolf, volume 5, 1936–41*, ed. A. O. Bell and A. McNeillie. London: Penguin.
Woolf, V. *Virginia Woolf engagement diaries*, Monk's House Papers, University of Sussex Special Collections, SxMs-18/4/41.
Zytaruk, G. J., and J. T. Boulton (eds) (1981) *The letters of D. H. Lawrence: volume II, June 1913 – October 1916*. Cambridge: Cambridge University Press.

Chapter 8

Exposed to the other
Responding to the refugee in Caroline Bergvall's *Drift*

Catherine Humble

Reading *Drift* for the first time feels a bit like opening someone's private diary. Crammed with sketches, photos, torn sentences, and everyday thoughts, the small book almost swells in your hand with its wayward force. In *Drift*, the French-Norwegian mixed media poet, Caroline Bergvall, combines abstract line drawings, a reworking of the medieval poem 'The Seafarer', a report on a present-day refugee incident, and her own prose diary entries, to explore historical sea migrations from medieval times to the present day. Thrown between hard clarity and wild abstractions, the reader is alternately anchored and bewildered. We enter a space that is at once private and deeply exposing.

Of central importance to *Drift* is an event of forced migration that took place in March 2011 that became known as the 'left-to-die boat' case, and which Bergvall documents in her third chapter entitled 'Report'. In chilling factual prose, Bergvall tells how seventy-two African refugees were left to drift in the Mediterranean Sea for fourteen days, despite numerous official sightings of their boat. Drawing on archival evidence and survivors' testimony, Bergvall records the traumatic details of the sea migration in which sixty-three people were left to die. The callous loss of life reverberates throughout *Drift* like an absent presence that haunts the book.

Accompanying her book, Bergvall has also performed *Drift* in an extraordinary visual-sound poem.[1] Joined by screen visuals and live percussion music, Bergvall stands before a shifting, drifting digital text of her work, chanting the poetry cycles from *Drift*. Her body judders, her words stutter, as if the poet herself is battered by the storm at sea—or by mental anguish. You don't so much watch the performance of *Drift* as give way to its mesmeric force. The book is similarly immersive. Central to both the performance and book version of *Drift* is visual representation, and it is the visual image that opens the book; before we get to any written word, the reader encounters a series of sketches, each one made up of fine lines in spiral or solid block shapes.

This chapter will focus on the sketches that open *Drift*, exploring the role of visual representation in bearing witness to the traumatic experiences that the refugees underwent in the left-to-die boat case. Yousif Qasmiyeh, a

DOI: 10.4324/9781003200765-11

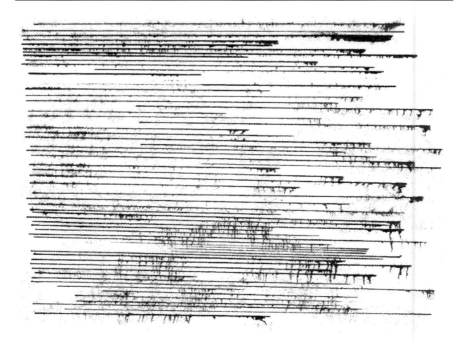

Figure 8.1 'Lines 11', ink on paper, from '(16 Drawings)'
Source: Reproduced in *Drift* (Nightboat Books, 2014). Permission granted by Caroline Bergvall.

Palestinian refugee writer, has recently claimed that 'reading and thinking about refugee issues' means we have to 'offer ourselves to new modes of seeing' (Qasmiyeh, 2017a); Bergvall's drawings form a response to this demand, inviting the reader into new ways of seeing and responding to the experiences that contemporary refugees have undergone. My argument is two-fold. First, I will look at how the drawings of *Drift* work at a liminal state of representation—between evoking representations of the left-to-die boat incident and forestalling the reader's capacity to represent. I am especially interested in how this liminal state of representation—this incitement to see and not see—bears witness to a certain traumatic liminal experience in the left-to-die boat refugees.

Second, and concurrently, the chapter will explore the role of witness, considering the relationship between the refugees' first-hand testimonies, Bergvall's transformation of these testimonies through her drawings, and the kinds of positions that we as readers are asked to take up as witnesses to the traumatic event. In thinking about visual testimony, I will turn to Donald Winnicott's squiggle game—the process of drawing that's carried out between a patient and an analyst, where the analyst bears witness to the mental distress expressed through drawing. Winnicott first began using the process of drawing that became known as the squiggle game in his work with World War II evacuees; though a very different historical context to the current refugee crisis, I am interested in the parallels that arise between using drawing to approach traumatic experiences in these different displaced groups. It is my hope that some of the psychoanalytic insights that arise from Winnicott's squiggle game, and from the context in which it developed, can help us to respond in searching ways to the traumatic experiences of the refugees conveyed through Bergvall's drawings.

Report: the left-to-die boat case

> The forensic principle: that every action or contact leaves a trace. I decide to use the narrative of the journey and its harrowing drift, the story told by the survivors and corroborated by the forensic findings.
> (Bergvall, 2014, p. 134)

So Bergvall describes her documentation of the left-to-die boat incident in her archival chapter entitled 'Report'. Here, Bergvall relays key findings from a research project entitled 'Report on the "*Left-To-Die Boat*"', carried out by the Forensic Oceanography group at the Centre for Research Architecture at Goldsmiths, University of London.[2] The Goldsmiths Report uses digital records of the refugees' boat taken from radar images, and extensive interviews with refugee survivors, to track the journey of the left-to-die boat. In preparing *Drift*, Bergvall spent some time with the team of researchers exploring their findings, and her 'Report' is a truncated version of the Goldsmiths Report; I will provide a brief summary of it here.

In the early hours of the morning on 27 March 2011 in Tripoli, Libya, Bergvall states, seventy-two Sub-Saharan refugees from the nearby camp—the majority from Ethiopia, some from Nigeria, Ghana, Sudan, and Eritrea—boarded a small rubber boat and set sail for the Italian island of Lampedusa.[3] The refugees were handed a GPS, a compass and satellite phone, and enough fuel, they were told, to make it to the Italian island in about eighteen hours; they were given no food or water (Ibid., p. 72). 'At the moment of departure, they contested being forced to travel in such a vessel', says Bergvall, 'With little choice, they embarked' (Ibid., p. 71).

After eighteen hours at sea, the refugees were not even halfway to Lampedusa and about to run out of fuel; their GPS batteries were failing (Ibid., p. 73). A French Rescue Army aircraft soon arrived, survivors recall. It took photos of the boat and disappeared. Drawing on the radar images gathered by the Goldsmiths group, Bergvall explains that at least thirty-eight naval ships were in the waters close to the refugee boat during the days it was left to drift. At that time, as part of the military operations in Libya, NATO was enforcing an arms embargo in the central Mediterranean Sea, which placed the boat in the most highly surveyed area of sea in the entire world (Ibid., p. 74).

In their written testimony, survivors state that late in the evening of 27 March a helicopter bearing the words 'Rescue Army' approached them:

> It circled around 4–5 times and came close. It came very close to us down, we showed them our babies, we showed them we finished oil, we tell them please help us.
> I think we saw them take pictures.
>
> (Ibid., p. 76)

The helicopter left without providing assistance. In the middle of the night, the refugees approached two fishing boats asking for help. They steered away (Ibid., p. 77). The same helicopter reappeared, state survivors, this time it 'lowered eight bottles of water and small packets of biscuits' and 'left again' (Ibid., p. 77).

On the morning of 28 March, the motor ran out of fuel. The boat drifted in stormy conditions for ten days, during which time the passengers began to die. On the sixth day at sea a military ship approached, saw the dead bodies, and left without providing assistance. Daniel Haile Gebre, a surviving refugee interviewed by the Oceanography group, said:

> They circled around us, three times, until they came very close, 10 meters. We are watching them, they are watching us. We are showing them the dead bodies. We drank water from the sea to show them we were thirsty. The people on the boat took pictures, nothing else.
> We knew that we would die little-by-little.
>
> (Ibid., p. 80).[4]

During the last days at sea, almost all the surviving refugees had lost consciousness or were seriously ill. On the tenth day at sea without provisions the boat drifted back onto a Libyan shore. Of the seventy-two passengers nine survived (Ibid., p. 81).

On viewing the refugee

It is significant that the historical 'Report' is introduced in a chapter that comes *after* the drawings that open *Drift*. By opening with drawings instead of words, *Drift* tacitly registers the important role of visual medium in representations of today's refugee crisis; it also hints at the limits of verbal language to express the extreme experiences that this group of refugees underwent, as if verbal communication has given up in the face of such human damage. That the historical 'Report' comes *after* the drawings also invites two readings of the opening images. At first, we read the drawings afresh, outside the context of the left-to-die boat incident. But then we return to the drawings after reading the 'Report', which encourages a more historically attuned reading of them. Yet to order these readings *first* and *second* is to suggest a chronological order that the book eschews. The reading experience of *Drift* is more circular than linear; the echoic structure and montage form of the book steers the reader in diverse directions, so that our reading becomes one of a circling return.

The sketches that open *Drift* combine flat line images with others that have a spiralling, errant excess. Read in the context of Bergvall's 'Report', the drawings can evoke historically situated representations. The levelled lines that sometimes turn in and back on themselves in chaotic twists could depict the sea, the wind, the storm into which this group of refugees helplessly sailed. The images seem ghostly. Echoes, perhaps, of these finished lives. The drawings themselves migrate. They drift—one into the other. They bring to mind ECT graphs, heartbeats flatlining. Human lives expiring. In her diary section of *Drift* entitled 'Log', Bergvall reflects upon her process of creating the book and directly relates her drawings to the left-to-die boat incident, comparing her sketches to 'imaging sonars or spectrographs' (Bergvall, 2014, p. 147)—the systems used by Rome Maritime Rescue Co-ordination to record the location of the refugees' vessel. Her 'graphic work' she says, 'emerges from tracking' (Ibid., p. 153). Evoking imaging sonars, the drawings bring to mind the digital representations of the refugee vessel that were so callously ignored.

If visual representation is crucial to Bergvall's book, it is partly because vision was so critical to the circumstances of the abandoned boat people: the people who were so dreadfully hyper-seen and unseen. It was precisely the decision on the part of numerous authorities to turn a blind eye, to ignore what they could *see*, that led to the unthinkable suffering and loss of life. Bringing to mind the military ship that 'circled around us, three times [...]. We are watching them, they are watching us', Bergvall's spiral drawings invoke the gaze of the maritime authorities. As the reader traces the lines that loop and sweep about, we follow the field of vision of the military ship, its encircling look. And in so doing, we are made to form a disturbing identification with the perpetrators of neglect, what Ruth Leys calls an 'imitative-identificatory' relationship with the perpetrator (Leys and Goldman, 2010, p. 658).[5]

Visual representation has been crucial to the western view of the present-day refugee crisis, with popular perceptions of today's forced migration framed primarily through media images. Media organisations sell papers by telling human stories, Daniel Trilling reminds us, and so they have a strong interest in manipulating readers' sympathy with shocking images of refugees (Trilling, 2016). One week *The Sun* will print the now famous image of the dead Syrian boy Aylan Kurdi swept up on a Turkish beach, tugging at the reader's sympathy; the next week it'll show a mob of young black African men scrambling at a Calais fence: these men are out to invade your home, destroy your safety, is *The Sun*'s ignoble message (Ibid.).[6] On seeing a photo of a small dinghy crammed with ailing migrants, today's social media reader might feel momentary heartache, before being propelled onto the next tweet. There's also notably a certain 'ideal refugee' who's more visible in the western media, according to Elena Fiddian-Qasmiyeh (2016a, p. 459); children and mothers from Syria and the Western Sahara are 'hypervisible in the press', she says, whereas black male youths and 'other refugees from across the Middle East, North Africa, Southeast Asia, and farther afield have been rendered invisible "as" refugees deserving of protection' (Ibid., pp. 459–460).

In avoiding a direct representational depiction of the refugee, Bergvall's drawings demand a different kind of response than idealisation, identification or sympathy. The stance of sympathy, Susan Sontag warns, can at best be distancing, at worst self-congratulatory: 'Driven by a fantasy of benevolence and self-piety, these forms of compassion create a [comfortable] separation between oneself and the situation of the other' (Sontag, 2003, p. 91).[7] While the flood of migrant media images might have galvanised some change, says Trilling, the oversaturation of photojournalism on the refugee crisis has led to atrocity's normalisation, leaving readers with compassion fatigue (Trilling, 2016). In contrast, Bergvall seeks an affect that sticks. Her images 'insist on being seen' (Bergvall, 2014, p. 157). Her aim, she says, is to 'jolt' the reader out of the 'the fog of incessant newsrush and quick apparitions and swift forgetting' (Ibid.). And she does so not through identification but disorientation. While the drawings evoke associations of meaning, they eschew any clear human image with which the reader might *identify*. An image I can see *myself* in (if only as a fellow human being). Or my family, my children. As Emmanuel Lévinas reminds us, human relations based on identification ultimately operate to confirm oneself; they are a form of self-recognition (Lévinas, 1969, p. 159). In identifying with the dead Syrian boy—as the reader's son or family member—the reader incorporates the other into their world, and in so doing, negates the extreme otherness of the traumatic situation. Through identification, however pitiful the photographic image of the dead boy left at sea might be, it fails to fully other and disturb: it leaves the reader feeling untouched, complete. In contrast, Bergvall's abstract drawings take the reader outside their familiar modes of visual recognition, provoking a feeling of de-signification. The images work against identification to unsettle and undo the reader.

In psychoanalytic thought, 'representation' arises from the early meeting of the infant's chaotic drives with a 'good enough object' (Levine, Reed, Scarfone, 2013, pp. 6–15): that is, with the presence of a reliable other who can hold and contain the infant's drives, their excessive forces get transformed into representations (for instance, the child's unchanneled drives are met with the stable object of the mother, which produces in the child the psychic representation of satisfaction). In 'Fear of Breakdown', Winnicott suggests that traumatic breakdown in cognition takes place when the maternal object or holding environment that confirms the subject is lacking or fails in various ways, and so the subject's capacity for internal holding and representation breaks down (Winnicott, 1974).[8] As commentators have variously noted, the contemporary refugee will often undergo extreme trauma; one might think about this trauma in terms of the radical breakdown of the refugee's stable objects and holding environment (home, safety, family), producing failures in cognition. In *Drift*, the reader is asked to bear witness to something of the refugee's traumatic experience through the breakdown in visual representation in the line drawings.

In Bergvall's line drawings, the breakdown of visual representation reverses Fiddian-Qasmiyeh's notion of the 'western gaze'—the way in which media images turn refugees into objects of the western look (Fiddian-Qasmiyeh, 2016b). As Lévinas argues, exposure to one's own otherness provokes a sense of responsibility for the other (Lévinas, 1969, pp. 152–168, 256). The point I want to stress here is that the reader is not invited to identify with the refugee, but is rather compelled to respond ethically to the otherness and vulnerability of the refugees' situation.

Return to blankness: Bergvall's flat line drawing

Bergvall's line drawings consist of two kinds of images, what I call the *flat line drawings*—the fine lines that form block shapes, and the *spiral drawings*: those with a more circular, spiralling form. In the flat line drawing reproduced in Figure 8.2, the repeated lines of the sketch appear to emanate movement:

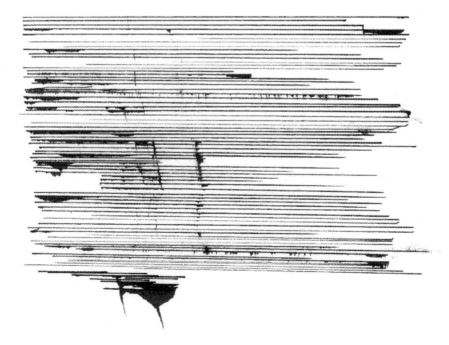

Figure 8.2 'Lines 12', ink on paper, from '(16 Drawings)'
Source: Reproduced in *Drift* (Bergvall, 2014). Permission granted by Caroline Bergvall.

they have a kinetic appearance. Bergvall makes this link, connecting the 'movement' of the refugee with the movement of her sketches: 'The growing reality of collective departures and arrivals would need to be experienced as dynamic pattern formations', she writes (Bergvall, 2014, p. 140). A distinctive experience of today's forced migrant is that they move yet end up nowhere, notes Lyndsey Stonebridge (Stonebridge, 2015, p. 1347). They remain in the limbo state of the camp or adrift at sea. In the repeated lines that foster the effect of movement, but a movement that fails to change, that does not arrive at a settled or secure place, the drawings stage the permanent interim space of statelessness. The reader experiences a stuckness in time and place, a limbo state. This would be to read the drawing mimetically, at the level of meaningful representation (like the other historically meaningful associations of the sonar image, the limbo state, etc.) However, the drawing also provokes a response outside of semantic meaning.

The line drawing also appeals to our senses rather than our sense making. By opening a book that Bergvall has explicitly described as a poetry collection, the drawings ask, in part, to be read as poems, or what I would like to call *line poems*. Through a reversal of the sonar image where sound gives rise to vision, in the line drawing above, the visual elicits imagined registrations of sound. Seeing becomes sounding. 'Drawing must be understood as engaging a rhythm', says Jean-Luc Nancy (Nancy and Armstrong, 2013, p. 70), and so Bergvall's lines evoke beats in the reader's mind, differentiations. A mental rhythm. Bergvall describes the lines of her sketches as 'engaging in short dances that release other spatial rhythms. They start to behave like the faint trackings of sounds' (Bergvall, 2014, p. 147). Read in the context of a poetry book, the condensed shape brings to mind a sonnet form, the regular lines held within a tight and mostly ordered form hints at poetic meter (the slight line indentation at each third section of the poem hints at a stanza change, with a final trailing couplet). Yet poetic meter is also undercut in the flat lines that evoke single steady beats or pulses (in place of a variant rhythm). The blurrings and blottings that emerge—the line-endings that coagulate and the clusters of line clots—might be heard as hard, elongated beats or pulsations. A repeated throbbing beat trails down the centre of the page.[9] Importantly, these irregular pulsations refuse to cohere into clear semantic associations. The pulsing beats appeal to our senses. They connect to us on a visceral rather than a verbal and semantic level.

I would like to suggest that these line blots attest to something outside of representation: to the formlessness of trauma. As we have seen, for a number of psychoanalytic thinkers, trauma exceeds semantic representation. Trauma is an event that shatters our cognitive capabilities, leading to 'a general enfeeblement and disturbance of the mental capacities', says Freud (Freud, 1955). Developing Freud's definition, Cathy Caruth defines trauma as an overwhelming event that exceeds conscious understanding and verbal communication (Caruth, 1995, pp. 3–6). 'To be traumatised', Caruth writes, 'is precisely to be possessed by an image or event' (Ibid., pp. 4–5), and so in their insistent return, Bergvall's images bear the repetitive, possessive mark of trauma. A traumatic event 'brings us to the limits of our understanding' says Caruth (Ibid., p. 4), and we can similarly read the blurrings and blottings of Bergvall's sketches as staging limits—the limits of any clear verbal or visual representation of the traumatic experiences of the refugees.[10] In the above drawing, there is a thing like quality to the line clumps redolent of Freud's hard 'thing' presentations of the unconscious—the early sensory images that make up unconscious psychic functioning. For Freud, the visual is developmentally and topographically more primary than the verbal (Freud, 1997, pp. 513–514). Unconscious contents are first present as what he calls indeterminate visual *things*, and in the system preconscious these 'thing-presentations' become attached to 'word-presentations' and thus 'represented' (*Wortvorstellung*) (Freud, 1957).[11] The thing presentations re-emerge when representation breaks down in the face of trauma. In the drawing above, where the lines start to clot and congeal, becoming hard and thing-like, they testify to the thing presentations of traumatic states.

In *Drift*, the images bear witness to unrepresented aspects of the refugee's traumatic experience, and Bergvall anchors them in the historical specificity of the event. Read within the context of the left-to-die boat incident recounted in Bergvall's 'Report', the reader is able to transform the abstract lines into representational meanings specific to the historical event—e.g. of the refugee's movement, their limbo state, the sonar image. We are encouraged, as we saw in the squiggle drawing, to think about the meaning of the perpetrator's look, and in so doing to reflect on how we, as readers, might be collusive in the look that fails to do anything. Engaging with the left-to-die boat incident in this way—at the level of cognition, meaning, and identification—our reading of the drawings accords with what Ruth Leys describes as the 'mimetic model' of trauma (Leys and Goldman, 2010, pp. 658–660): an approach to history that retains some interpretive distance and perspective on scenes of trauma, considering issues of human agency and meaning such as what it might mean to identify with perpetrators of harm.

But the images also mark a shift into affective experience, which is not in my view a retreat from the world, but a way of engaging more affectively with the world. In her work on the 'turn to affect', Leys has been critical of those who see affect as fundamentally independent of intention and meaning (Leys, 2011). And yet, the drawings of *Drift* are especially powerful precisely because they combine representation *and* affect. In confronting the drawings, the reader is encouraged to think in meaningful ways about the refugee event, but also to feel helplessly exposed in the face of something unrepresented, approaching an experience closer to Caruth's 'collapse of understanding' and 'blankness' that is the force of trauma. In reading Bergvall's drawings, we are able to convert dissociated affects into meaningful representations *and* we receive unrepresented affects that can't be transformed into meaning. The 'turn to affect' (ibid) here is thus not an abrupt turn away from representation. Rather, unrepresented affect co-exists with representational meanings, where both express different aspects of the left-to-die boat experience.

This is the double reading that the drawings incite, and which Bergvall herself alludes to, offering as she does interpretations of the drawings in terms of the historical specificity of the left-to-die boat incident, while acknowledging that the event breaks down any settled, comprehensive representation: 'To separate, to leave someone, is to leave everything. Everything planned, known, secured, released, fine-tuned, structured, achieved is now upended in a way that exceeds comprehension' (Bergvall, 2014, p. 158). Her own process of creating *Drift* was a 'return to blankness' (Ibid., p. 148), Bergvall notes, as she explores the refugees' sense of 'being lost', which 'shut down the field of thinking, of sensing, and choosing one's tracks'; it is what she calls 'unimaginable' (Ibid., p. 149). The images in *Drift* occupy a liminal space between the represented and the unrepresented, offering a form of containment for the unrepresentable aspects of the refugee experience.

Visual testimony: Winnicott's work with evacuees

In bearing witness to the unrepresented trauma of the refugee, Bergvall's drawings contain interesting parallels with Winnicott's squiggle. In the squiggle game, Winnicott would make a mark on a piece of paper and hand it over to the child with the invitation to 'make it into anything' (Winnicott, 1968, p. 301). The child would add lines, and the analyst would respond by drawing their own lines. The purpose of the game, Winnicott claimed, was to allow the child the capacity for 'communication of significance' of life experiences in a visual form (Ibid., pp. 301–302). In the squiggle game, drawing is a means of creatively reaching out to the other, communicating meanings and experiences at the limits of representation. In *Therapeutic Consultations*, Winnicott repeatedly states that the children's drawings express what is 'unthinkable' (Winnicott, 1971b, pp. 83, 86). He writes, 'the important thing is not my talking so much as the fact that the child has reached something' (Ibid., p. 69).

The squiggle drawings take place within what Winnicott calls 'the transitional space' (Winnicott, 1971a, p. 5)—the psychical space in which the infant explores its creative relation to the world. The transitional space is what Winnicott calls an 'intermediate territory' between 'inner psychic reality' and 'the external world' (Ibid.); that is, the squiggle drawings negotiate a relationship between the internal and external world. It is in the transitional space that the young infant first works out a relationship of *connection with* and *separation from* the adult other or primary care giver: through the drawing, the child emotionally reaches out towards the other person with the expectation of a response—a witness. In this space, the interaction with the other is visual, tactile and aural—it is mostly pre-verbal (Ibid., p. 2, 4). Importantly, in later life the transitional space can be occupied by the arts, what Winnicott calls the 'cultural field' (Ibid., p. 13). Winnicott states, 'it is assumed that no human being is free from the strain of relating inner and outer reality, and that relief from the strain is provided by an intermediate area of experience which is not challenged (the arts)' (Ibid.). It is useful here to stress that Winnicott's account of the transitional space is not a theory of artistic creation. Instead, the transitional space is about everyday modes of creative communication; it is an account of what he calls 'creative living' (Ibid.). Likewise, Bergvall's *Drift* is so affecting precisely because it fosters a *creative aliveness*. It offers a participatory experience. Encountering *Drift*, one might be said to enter a space of creative living.

One reason why it is an especially enriching endeavour to bring the drawings of *Drift* in relation to the squiggle drawing, is that Winnicott first started to use drawing in his practice while working with a socially displaced group—the evacuated children of World War II (Farley, 2012, p. 426)—another group of migrants. Appointed Consultant Psychiatrist to the Government Evacuation Scheme in Oxford in 1940, Winnicott worked with evacuees who had left their homes because of air raids (Phillips, 2007, p. 62; Winnicott, 2011, p. 1). In the 'Introduction' to the 2012 edition of Winnicott's *Deprivation and Delinquency*, Winnicott's widow and former co-worker Clare Winnicott writes:

> The evacuation experience had a profound effect on Winnicott because he had to meet in a concentrated way the confusion brought about by the wholesale break-up of family life, and he had to experience the effect of separation and loss, and of destruction and death [...]. There is no doubt that working with deprived children gave a whole new dimension to Winnicott's thinking and to his practice.
>
> (Winnicott, 2011, pp. 1–3)

Evacuation became pivotal for Winnicott's thinking about the relationship between the human and the social environment, leading to his interest in what he called 'environmental provision' (Ibid., p. 78, 89). 'During the war, of course, it would be increasingly difficult to ignore the pressure of outside reality' (Phillips, 2007, p. 77), writes Adam Phillips in his account of Winnicott's growing engagement with the social. In his 'Letter to the British Medical Journal' entitled 'Evacuation of a Small Child', written in December 1939, Winnicott states that 'children without homes start off as tragedies' (Winnicott, 2011, p. 12). Being torn from one's home because of external social forces, says Winnicott, can cause a breakdown in conscious understanding: 'it can in fact amount to an emotional black-out' (Ibid., p. 12), a void of cognition and feeling amounting to trauma. It is significant that Winnicott's paper, 'The Evacuated Child', started off as a national radio broadcast that constituted an appeal. 'Taking someone into your home is very different to letting someone into your house' (Ibid., p. 35), Winnicott said, in his address to the nation. The psychoanalyst implored foster parents and listeners at large to bear witness to the 'child who has suddenly been uprooted, seemingly turned out of his own home [...]. They will have a limited capacity to keep alive and *represent* their past experiences', he said (Ibid., p. 40; my italics). Addressing listeners in the first person *you*, Winnicott's radio broadcast exerted an ethical demand: to bear witness to the evacuees' extreme distress that they themselves struggled to represent.

In bringing together Winnicott and Bergvall, it is important to recognise that the situation of World War II evacuees is by no means equivalent to that of the contemporary refugee. Any simple elision of the two is clearly reductive. Cautioning against a tendency of some journalists to distil the history of refugees to a glorified history of British humanitarian help, Jessica Reinisch criticises the historical reductionism of making different migration situations interchangeable (Reinisch, 2016). There is clearly no straightforward line to be drawn between the evacuees of World War II and contemporary refugees, instead one must recognise the similarities and differences, as well as the historical connections, between the two situations.[12] To start with, evacuation in World War II was an official wartime government scheme, which meant that the children were taken on relatively smooth, controlled and legal journeys, accompanied by a teacher who knew them and provided some continuity. This stands in stark contrast to the often perilous journeys across vast stretches of land, sea and geographic borders, that forms the flight of today's refugees—clandestine journeys that are precariously arranged, often with no clear destination in sight. It is also notable that Winnicott's migrants were all children, whose internalisation of home would have been very precarious; they were torn away from home at a point of actual dependence—and of course this is also the case for child refugees today. Importantly, World War II evacuees did not suffer physically destitute states, and in contrast with today's refugees, for the most part they were welcomed into their new homes. The differences are far reaching. But there are, I believe, some important historical and affective parallels. Like refugees today, the evacuee migrants were in states of mental and geographic transition, experiencing a loss of home and family because of outside political circumstances. Some evacuees also witnessed the devastating destruction of their hometowns and other people's lives in the bombings. For the World War II evacuees, the trauma of their radically ruptured lives often disturbed their verbal comprehension. Not only is this an experience that is sometimes shared by today's refugees, but a major problem for today's refugees is that way that they are silenced and ignored.

While it wasn't until 'Transitional Objects and Transitional Phenomena' in 1953 that Winnicott first mentioned the squiggle game, and his case studies on the game weren't published until 1965, 1968 and 1971 (Winnicott, 1965, 1968, 2012), it is significant that Winnicott first began the practice of drawing with children while overseeing Oxfordshire hostels for particularly disturbed evacuees (Farley, 2012, p. 428).[13] As Lisa Farley has shown, in between the pages of Winnicott's 1945 hostel notebook held at the Wellcome Library are a dozen drawings, a couple of which bear the names of young children, and some of which show the mark of Winnicott's hand (Ibid., p. 427). While Winnicott provided little published commentary on these drawings, their very presence demonstrates his use of visual testimony in reaching out to the evacuees.[14] It seems that Winnicott found something about drawing brought the evacuees nearer to their traumatic experience of war and loss of home than words could express. In spending time with evacuees, Winnicott became increasingly convinced of the child's need for a witness to receive experiences that may not be easily expressed in words, 'a witness to the affective force of the experiences that defied literal or immediate representation' (Ibid., p. 420).

Bergvall and Winnicott: the demand to witness

Figure 8.3 'Lines 6', ink on paper, from '(16 Drawings)'
Source: Reproduced in *Drift* (Nightboat Books, 2014). Permission granted by Caroline Bergvall.

Bergvall's sketches appear not as complete images, but as processes: the drawings appear as rough or unfinished, incomplete. This is particularly the case for the more chaotic, spiralling drawings. In their state of process and incompletion, and in their contact with formlessness, the drawings open up a transitional space of connectedness with the reader. As Farley puts it, Winnicott read the drawings that emerged in the transitional space as 'affective forces' of unsymbolised experiences *seeking expression* and response (Farley, 2012, p. 420, 442). As lines in process, Bergvall's drawings are *on their way towards* the reader, they open up. As unfinished, the sketches make demands on the reader: to participate and respond to their incompletion, to respond not with what Winnicott calls 'clever and apt interpretations' but with receptive resonance (Winnicott, 1971a, p. 117). The drawings demand a dynamic, involved response. Like the analyst engaged with the squiggle game, the reader is made to receive these sketches with acknowledgement before knowledge.

While the squiggle game helps us think about the demand to witness provoked by Bergvall's drawings, one must not overlook the differences between Winnicott's and Bergvall's use of drawing. One way in which the squiggle game appears to depart from Bergvall's sketches is the tendency of the game to reach representation. The squiggle that turns into a snake, for example—a recurrent image in the case studies of *Therapeutic Consultations in Child Psychiatry* (Winnicott, 1971b, pp. 10, 33–39), with clear sexual overtones, giving rise to specific interpretations. Bergvall's drawings are more abstract and unsymbolised, much more resistant to direct representation and interpretation. However, it is not insignificant that in his squiggle case studies some of Winnicott's more traumatised patients create 'messy' and 'abstract' drawings that don't clearly represent anything (Ibid., pp. 74, 77, 80, 154, 155).[15] And while some critics have suggested that the squiggle game is only applicable to the neurotic who is able to represent, not the traumatised subject (Abram, 2016, p. 494), I think this overlooks the significant place of trauma in the squiggle game. In the squiggle case studies documented in *Therapeutic Consultations in Child Psychiatry*, Winnicott repeatedly speaks of the 'trauma' to which the drawings approach (1971b, pp. 83, 87, 120).[16] He also makes it clear that arriving at finite interpretations of the image is not the sole purpose of the squiggle game. The squiggle is 'simply one way of getting into contact with the child', he says, a 'communication at a deep level' (Ibid. p. 3). 'Reaching something', Winnicott says, 'is more important than the child's communication' of clear pictorial representations (Ibid., p. 67). More than forming meaningful interpretations of the drawings then, reaching some kind of mental affect (even if, or especially if, it is an effect of dissociation) is the real, vital connection at stake. After Winnicott, Green suggests that the *cathexis* of representation—an investment in the *process of looking for meaning*—is more important than arriving at an actual represented content. The same can be said of Bergvall's images, where it is the process of looking for meanings which brings us into contact with the unpresented affect—the 'emotional black-out' (Winnicott, 2011, p. 12).

For both Bergvall and Winnicott then, drawing can approach unrepresented mental states. Yet the position of witness is also different in Bergvall's and Winnicott's use of drawing. Winnicott's drawing process was a subjectively engaged witnessing; he would often initiate the drawing and offer himself as support for it. Not so for Bergvall, whose drawings weren't created in direct participation with the refugees, rather they form her own response to the 'Left-to-Die-Boat Report' and its survivor interviews. In this way, Bergvall stands as second-hand witness to the first-hand written testimonies. Does this then problematise Bergvall's role as witness? Is her own visual representation simply an act of appropriation? These are crucial ethical questions, not least because they lead us to confront the complexities of what it means to bear witness to trauma. Bergvall is self-conscious about her position as second-hand witness: in *Drift* she 'relays the [Goldsmiths] report's complex piece of memorialisation, interpretation and investigation', (Bergvall, 2014, p. 134). Bergvall is always clear that *Drift* is a constructed testimonial narrative, that she plays an interpretive role in the creation and reception of the left-to-die boat testimony. Mindful of Spivak's critique of the Western writer who 'speaks for' the subaltern, I would like to suggest that Bergvall's drawings refuse to treat the refugee as the object of study *over there*, as something that knowledge should be extracted from and brought back *here*. [17] Treating today's refugee as a positive object of knowledge, claims Agnes Woolley, is dangerously complicit with the oppressive operations of the British asylum adjudication system, which demands of forced migrants 'empirically verifiable narratives' that fit with the asylum system's idea of the 'deserving refugee' (Woolley, 2014, p. 20). Instead of an eye-witness account of so-called 'empirical facts', Bergvall's drawings bear a different kind of witness—to mental states and human affects. In turn, they encourage in the reader a non-coercive kind of witnessing: opening our receptivity to affective experiences that are not conscious nor empirically verifiable. In a kind of relay of witnesses that corresponds to what Shoshana Felman calls a 'chain of witnesses', the reader is positioned as *witness to the witness to the witness* (Felman, 2014, pp. 48–68). And this chain logic says something about the very nature of bearing witness to trauma: that for trauma to be acknowledged, it demands the other and others in their open receptivity.

This demand for a receptive witness is also central to Winnicott's squiggle drawings—his awareness of the need for a witness to the other's traumatic experience. As we have seen, in the squiggle drawings witnessing is in part attentiveness to what *cannot be said*—to what Caruth calls the 'impossible saying' of testimony (Caruth, 1995, p. 10). Likewise, the unrepresented effect of Bergvall's drawings registers the refugees' experiences that cannot be known or seen directly, but where their unconscious force requires a response in the reader. Rather than forge a polarised distinction between the unrepresented and the represented, I would like to suggest that Bergvall's line drawings—like some of Winnicott's squiggle drawings—are in process, *on their way towards representation*. As we have seen, the drawings can provoke historically situated associations in the reader, but they don't fully settle on these meanings. In this way, the images work like Winnicott's 'root of symbolization' (Winnicott, 1971a, p. 234)—the shift that takes place within the transitional space from self-enclosure *towards* symbolic communication, without arriving at stable meanings. The reader can partially transform the rawness of the traumatic traces present in the images into meaningful representations, as we've seen, and these are important, visually bringing to life and making us think about the historical meanings of the left-to-die boat case. Yet these associations only ever skirt around, never fully transform, the unrepresented affect, the emotional blackout, at the core of the drawings that testifies to the unrepresented trauma of the left-to-die boat people.

In bringing together historically situated representations and the unrepresented in this way, Bergvall's drawings do not encourage a reading of the refugees' traumatic experiences that is universal and timeless, outside of historical meaning. Indeed, we might also do well here to ask the wider question of what we mean by representing history. Never simply an unmediated channel to the historical past, history is always a transformation of past events, a tension between internal and external reality. It is the interplay, the dialogue set up between internal and external, affective and material, unrepresented and represented, that's so fundamental to Bergvall's project in *Drift*. Yet what's especially powerful about the line drawings, what really sticks, is how they register traces of mental affect—of an emotional blackout. When today's asylum system depends so much on uncovering a unilateral historically accurate version of events, the drawings offer an alternative space for the refugees' experience—a space that's more hospitable to mental affect than the restrictive frameworks in which the refugees' experience is coerced within the asylum adjudication system. In this way, the images are historical in Winnicott's sense of 'history taking', which 'does not mean the collection of facts' (about the patient's past), but the capacity to 'make contact' with a 'significant area of distress' that is not yet thinkable (Winnicott, 1971b, p. 125). More than forming an 'accurate history' (Ibid., p. 220), Winnicott is interested in making contact with mental experiences that are outside conscious understanding.[18] And so, along with the 'empirical' historical account of the refugee incident where meaning and consciousness preside, *Drift* registers *another form of history*—receptiveness to the unconscious, psychical effects of the event. In bearing witness to what eludes conscious representation in the refugee boat incident, we might call this bearing witness to the *unconscious of history*.

Notes

1 Accompanied by screen visuals by Swiss artist Thomas Koppel and live percussion by Ingar Zach, Bergvall performed *Drift* in various venues across the UK in 2014. The performance was produced by Penned in the Margins (Chivers, 2014).

2 The 'Report on the "Left-to-Die-Boat"' is compiled by The Forensic Oceanography project at the Centre for Research Architecture, Goldsmiths, University of London. The report includes interviews with all the survivors. Of the nine survivors, Daniel Haile Gebre could speak English proficiently and did not need a translator (Heller et al., 2014, p. 655). For the obligation to rescue passengers in distress, see article 98 (1) of the United Nations Convention on the Law of the Sea, quoted in *Forensis* (Heller et al., 2014, p. 655).
3 By March 2011 Libya had been at civil war for a month. The Libyan leader Muammar Gaddafi's previous agreement with Europe to tighten border controls disintegrated and many refugees began to leave detention camps, fleeing the country's chaos.
4 The Italian and Maltese Maritime Rescue Coordination Centers, and NATO forces present in the area, were informed of the distress of the boat and its location. Despite the legal obligation to render assistance to people in distress at sea enshrined in several international conventions, none of these forces intervened. As well as holding those responsible for the crime of non-assistance, the aim of the Forensic Oceanography's Report was to draw greater attention to migrant deaths in the Mediterranean and the impunity that surround perpetrators of human rights violations committed against migrants at sea (Heller et al., 2014).
5 Here, my argument concurs with Leys's stress on the important role of the psychical mechanism of identification in the experience of trauma, which she claims 'affect and trauma theorists' ignore (Leys and Goldman, 2010, p. 670).
6 Susan Sontag refers to 'those professional, specialised tourists known as journalists [...] "If it bleeds, it leads" runs the venerable guideline of tabloids and twenty-four-hour headline news shows—to which the response is compassion, or indignation, or approval, as each misery heaves into view' (Sontag, 2003, p. 16).
7 On the dangers of "sentimental voyeurism", see also Rose (1998, p. 52, 54).
8 In *Beyond the Pleasure Principle*, Freud describes trauma as that which breaks the mind's protective shield: 'We describe as "traumatic" any excitations from outside which are powerful enough to break through the protective shield' (Freud, 1955, p. 16). Developing this line of thought, Levine, Reed, and Scarfone argue that the failed connection between the subject and object (the self and the other) leaves the subject with an 'unrepresented' mental state (Levine, Reed, Scarfone, 2013, pp. 6–15).
9 Along with Antony Rowland, I am mindful of the ethics of close reading in relation to real-life atrocities, which can entail a reduction of real-life suffering to an exercise in practical criticism. Yet considering how visual and poetic form approaches certain human experiences registered at the limits of representation, and avoiding a generalised reading of trauma, does, I believe, require careful textual attention (Rowland, 2015, pp. 69–83).
10 Challenging this account of trauma, Ruth Leys objects to the notion that trauma can't get into language and representation. For Leys, to say that a trauma is unrepresentable is to dangerously forestall conversation about it, to render the victim passive, paralysed in the face of a trauma that can never be overcome (Leys, 2011, pp. 266–298). See also Rose (1998, p. 43).
11 César Botella elaborates on the transformatory capacity of the primary psychic functioning of sensory images in his account of 'regredience': the regredience of the word presentation to the thing presentation, or 'topographical regression' (Botella, 2014, pp. 911–936).
12 Tony Judt draws a line from World War II to the present refugee crisis (Judt, 2010, p. 9).
13 Winnicott never undertook regular psychoanalysis with the hostel children, rather he interviewed the particularly distressed evacuees (Winnicott and Britain, 1944, p. 104).

14 In 'The Problem of Homeless Children' Winnicott notes the importance of 'drawing and painting' in working with the evacuees (Winnicott, 1944, p. 107). In 'Hate in the Counter-transference' Winnicott reflects on his use of drawing with one particularly disturbed evacuee (Winnicott, 1947, p. 199). In his hostel notebook of 1945, Winnicott writes a note to himself to 'see drawings' produced in one interview with a child named George (Farley, 2012, p. 428).
15 See especially the cases of Ashton and Robert (Winnicott, 1971b, pp. 47–161, 89–105).
16 See especially the cases of Robert and Alfred (Winnicott, 1971b, pp. 89–105, pp. 110–127).
17 Subaltern refers to the social group that is socially, politically, and geographically outside of the hegemonic power structure of the colony and of the colonial homeland.
18 Speaking of his patient Mark for instance, Winnicott writes, 'Although I knew a good deal about him it would have been valueless to have worked on the basis of this knowledge' (1971b, p. 273).

Bibliography

Abram, J. (2012) *Donald Winnicott today*, ed. J. Abram. London: Routledge.
Abram, J. (2016) 'Commentary on "The arms of the chimeras" by Béatrice Ithier', *International Journal of Psycho-Analysis* 97 (2), 489–501.
Abram, J. (2007) *The language of Winnicott: a dictionary of Winnicott's use of words*. London: Karnac Books.
Berger, J. (2005) *Berger on drawing*. County Cork: Occasional Press.
Bergvall, C. (2014) *Drift*. New York: Nightboat Books.
Botella, C. (2014) 'On remembering: the notion of memory without recollection', *International Journal of Psycho-Analysis* 95 (5), 911–936.
Caruth, C. (1995) *Trauma: explorations in memory*. Baltimore: Johns Hopkins.
Chivers, T. (2014) 'Tour dates for Caroline Bergvall: *Drift* announced', *Penned in the Margins*. Available at: http://www.pennedinthemargins.co.uk/index.php/2014/05/tour-dates-for-caroline-bergvall-drift-announced (Accessed: 23 June 2018).
Farley, L. (2012) 'Squiggle evidence: the child, the canvas, and the "negative labour" of writing history'. In J. Abram (ed.) *Donald Winnicott today*. London: Routledge.
Felman, S. (2014) 'Fire in the archive: the alignment of witnesses'. In J. Kilby and A. Rowland (eds.) *The future of testimony*. London: Routledge, pp. 48–68.
Fiddian-Qasmiyeh, E. (2016a) 'Representations of displacement from the Middle East and North Africa', *Public Culture* 28, 457–473.
Fiddian-Qasmiyeh, E. (2016b) 'Panel one: refugees now—representations and perspectives', *Placeless people—what can history tell us about today's refugee crises?* Birkbeck, University of London, 20 June. Available at: http://backdoorbroadcasting.net/2016/06/placeless-people-what-can-history-tell-us-about-todays-refugee-crises/ (Accessed: 29 June 2018).
Freud, S. (1955) 'Beyond the pleasure principle'. In *The standard edition of the complete psychological works of Sigmund Freud*, ed. J. Strachey; trans. J. Strachey and A. Freud, with A. Strachey and A. Tyson, London: The Hogarth Press and the Institute of Psychoanalysis, 24 vols., vol. XVIII.
Freud, S. (1957) 'The unconscious'. In *The standard edition of the complete psychological works of Sigmund Freud*, ed. J. Strachey; trans. J. Strachey and A. Freud, with

A. Strachey and A. Tyson, London: The Hogarth Press and the Institute of Psychoanalysis, 24 vols., vol. XIV.
Freud, S. (1997) *The interpretation of dreams*, ed. T. Griffith; trans. A. A. Brill. London: Classics of World Literature.
Green, A. (2016) *Andre Green at the squiggle foundation: revised edition*, ed. Jan Abram. London: Karnac Books.
Heller, C. and Pezzani, L. and SITU Research. (2014) 'Report on the *Left-to-Die Boat*', *Forensis: the architecture of public truth*. London: Sternberg Press and Forensic Architecture, pp. 637–655.
Judt, T. (2010) *Postwar. A History of Europe since 1945*. London: Vintage.
Kinnahan, L. A. (2011) 'An interview with Caroline Bergvall', *Contemporary Women's Writing* 5 (3), 232–251.
Kristeva, J. (1980) *Desire in language: a semiotic approach to literature and art*. New York: Columbia University Press.
Lévinas, E. (1969) *Totality and infinity*. Pittsburgh: Duquesne University Press.
Levine, H. and Reed, G. and Scarfone, D. (eds.) (2013) *Unrepresented states and the construction of meaning: clinical and theoretical contributions*. London: Karnac Books.
Leys, R. (2011) 'The turn to affect', *Critical Inquiry* 37, 434–472.
Leys, R. and Goldman, M. (2010) 'Navigating the genealogies of trauma, guilt, and affect: an interview', *University of Toronto Quarterly* 79 (2), 656–679.
Nancy, J. L. and Armstrong, P. (2013) *The Pleasure in drawing*. Oxford: Oxford University Press.
Oxford Dictionaries. (2012) 'Witness, def.1', in *Oxford dictionaries*. Available at: https://en.oxforddictionaries.com/definition/witness (Accessed: 19 August 2018).
Phillips, A. (2007) *Winnicott*. London: Penguin.
Qasmiyeh, Y. M. (2017a) 'In conversation: Yousif M. Qasmiyeh on language and liminality', *Asymptote Journal*, 15 February 2017. Available at: https://www.asymptotejournal.com/blog/2017/02/15/in-conversation-yousif-m-qasmiyeh-on-language-and-liminality/ (Accessed: 17 June 2018).
Qasmiyeh, Y. M, and Ammann, O. (2017b) 'The multiple faces of representation', *Refugee hosts*. Available at https://refugeehosts.org/2017/09/15/the-multiple-faces-of-representation/ (Accessed: 17 August 2018).
Reinisch, J. (2016) 'Panel two: lessons from history', *Placeless people—what can history tell us about today's refugee crises?*Birkbeck: University of London, 20 June. Available at: http://backdoorbroadcasting.net/2016/06/placeless-people-what-can-history-tell-us-about-todays-refugee-crises/.
Rose, G. (1998) 'Beginnings of the Day: Fascism and Representation', in *Modernity, Culture and the Jew*, ed. Bryan Cheyette and Laura Marcus. Oxford: Polity Press.
Rowland, A. (2015) 'Reading holocaust poetry: singularity and Geoffrey Hill's "September Song"', *Textual Practice* 30 (1), 69–88.
Sontag, S. (2003) *Regarding the pain of others*. London: Hamish Hamilton.
Stonebridge, L. (2015) 'Statelessness and the poetry of the borderline: André Green, W.H. Auden and Yousif M. Qasmiyeh', *Textual Practice* 29 (7), 1331–1354.
Trilling, D. (2016) 'Panel one: refugees now—representations and perspectives', *Placeless people—what can history tell us about today's refugee crises?*Birkbeck, University of London, 20 June. Available at: http://backdoorbroadcasting.net/2016/06/placeless-people-what-can-history-tell-us-about-todays-refugee-crises/.

Winnicott, D. W. (1947) 'Hate in the counter-transference'. In *Through paediatrics to psychoanalysis: collected papers.* London: Karnac Classics, 1975.

Winnicott, D. W. (1953) 'Transitional objects and transitional phenomena: a study of the first not me possession', *International Journal of Psychoanalysis* 24, 89–97.

Winnicott, D. W. (1965) 'A clinical study of the effect of a failure of the average expectable environment on a child's mental functioning', *International Journal of Psychoanalysis* 46, 81–87.

Winnicott, D. W. (1968) 'The squiggle game', in C. Winnicott, R. Shepherd, and M. Davis (eds.) *Psychoanalytic explorations.* London: Karnac Books, 1989, pp. 301–302.

Winnicott, D. W. (1971a) *Playing and reality.* London: Psychology Press.

Winnicott, D. W. (1971b) *Therapeutic consultations in child psychiatry.* London: The Hogarth Press and the Institute of Psycho-Analysis.

Winnicott, D. W. (1974) 'Fear of breakdown', *International Review of Psycho Analysis* 1, 103–107.

Winnicott, D.W. (1975) *Through Paediatrics to Psychoanalysis: Collected Papers.* London: Karnac Classics.

Winnicott, D.W. (2012) *Deprivation and delinquency.* London: Routledge.

Winnicott, D. W. and C. Britton (1944) 'The problem of homeless children'. In *Through paediatrics to psychoanalysis: collected papers.* London: Karnac Classics, 1975.

Woolley, Agnes (2014) Contemporary asylum narratives: representing refugees in the Twenty-First Century. Basingstoke: Palgrave Macmillan.

Chapter 9

Between the acts, or, Melanie Klein and the representation of people with AIDS

Theo Gordon

Prologue: the past in the present

In 2013, Ian Bradley-Perrin and Vincent Chevalier created *Your Nostalgia is Killing Me!* for PosterVirus, an agitprop affinity group of AIDS ACTION NOW! based in Toronto, Canada.

Designed to be shared on the internet and plastered over the streets, the poster shows a computer-generated bedroom, wallpapered with repetitions of General Idea's *Imagevirus* graphic and figures drawn in Keith Haring's signature style. The walls are adorned with reproductions of North American

Figure 9.1 Vincent Chevalier and Ian Bradley-Perrin, *Your Nostalgia is Killing Me*, 2013. Digital Print
Source: © Vincent Chevalier and Ian Bradley-Perrin. Used with permission.

DOI: 10.4324/9781003200765-12

AIDS activist graphics from the late 1980s, including those by the Silence = Death Collective and Gran Fury, as well as a photograph of Justin Bieber wearing an ACT UP (AIDS Coalition to Unleash Power) t-shirt, and United Colours of Benetton's notorious jumper advert of the person with AIDS David Kirby on his deathbed. Inspired by Richard Hamilton's 1992 computer-generated remake of *Just what is it that makes today's homes so different, so appealing?*, which had incorporated General Idea's *Imagevirus* as a decorative domestic feature, Bradley-Perrin and Chevalier aimed to critique the commodification and canonisation of the history of the AIDS epidemic in North America as a crisis of the past, and point to the necessity for continued activism in the present. The HIV/AIDS pandemic, their poster reminds the viewer, is far from over (Visual AIDS, 2013).

The poster's provocative tagline, expressing the artists' concern that discussions of 'the past' of AIDS activism 'foreclosed a possibility of experience in the present', caused considerable controversy when Ted Kerr shared the poster online, via Facebook, with ACT UP New York alumni (Kerr, 2014). Avram Finklestein describes how, despite the artists' intent to critique 'the social media machinery that helps spin cultural memory into memes', the image 'sparked a flash fire' amongst those who had lived through the 1980s and 1990s (Finklestein, 2017, p. 208). For these survivors, it seemed to attack the 'sense of accomplishment that also acts as a balm to help soothe the terrible sacrifices' of this period (Ibid., p. 210). On 1 March 2014, Visual AIDS convened a panel at New York Public Library that brought Bradley-Perrin and Chevalier together with Finklestein and the writer John Wier, amongst a 'vibrant crowd', to enable discussion about the poster and to foster dialogue between people differently affected by the HIV/AIDS crisis across time (Bradley-Perrin, 2014).

As the controversial reception of *Your Nostalgia is Killing Me!* demonstrates, the stakes are extremely high in any consideration of the history of the HIV/AIDS epidemic. For not only is it an ongoing worldwide crisis with particular sociopolitical contexts in each country, but everyone who has ever been affected by HIV/AIDS, each in their particular way, carries with them their own experiences and memories, which are often inflected by the history of stigma and violence against people with HIV/AIDS. Further, any discussion of histories of HIV/AIDS, either before or after the 'pharmaceutical threshold' in 1996 that saw significant changes to the epidemic, runs the risk of fossilising the recent past and obscuring the continuing urgency of the present (Pearl, 2015, p. 2). This chapter considers the past and present of HIV/AIDS afresh. I discuss the violence of media coverage, in the US and the UK, in light of psychoanalytic theory, exploring how Melanie Klein's work on paranoid-schizoid mechanisms elucidates the coding of social violence within representations of people with AIDS. I consider how Zoe Leonard's sculptural work *Strange Fruit* (1992–1997) prompts a reassessment of Klein's concept of reparation as a process of representation that can make histories of violence available as a resource for contemporary sociopolitical life.

Splitting in the field of vision

Klein's theory of the paranoid-schizoid position elucidates the splitting of the visual field in the representation of people with AIDS (PWA), and the paranoia informing – and projected onto – these images. In *Narrative of a Child Analysis*, Klein records in expansive detail her clinical work with Richard, an anxious and paranoid little boy that she analysed during the Second World War (Klein, 1998). Richard's case, which Klein also discusses in 'The Oedipus Complex in the Light of Early Anxieties' in 1945, is remarkable for the wealth of visual material produced by the analysand and for the importance that Klein gives to his drawings in her interpretations of his anxiety (Klein, 1975b). In her work with Richard, Klein offers intriguing insights into the ways that processes of paranoid splitting, introjection and projection shape the visual field.

Richard created a series of images consisting of 'starfish shape' patterns of red, purple, blue and black, that for Klein symbolise his father, mother, brother and himself in turn.

Discussing one such picture, 'Drawing V', with Klein, which shows one side of clear light blue and the other as a mixture of the four colours, Richard free-associated that the image looked like a 'very horrid' bird where the light blue in the top right became a crown, the purple below its eye, and the adjacent purple and red sections its beak (Ibid., p. 388).

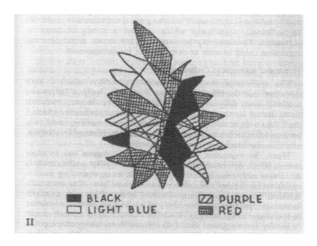

Figure 9.2 Reproduction of a drawing by 'Richard'
Source: Melanie Klein, 'The Oedipus Complex in the Light of Early Anxieties', in *The Writings of Melanie Klein, Volume I*, ed. Roger Money-Kyrle et. al., New York: Free Press, 370–419 (p. 379). Courtesy of the Melanie Klein Archive and the Wellcome Library. © Melanie Klein Trust.

128 The location of cultural experience

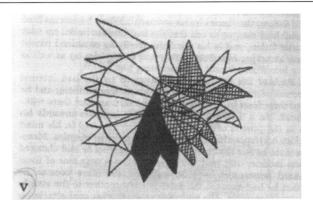

Figure 9.3 Reproduction of a drawing by 'Richard'
Source: Melanie Klein, 'The Oedipus Complex in the Light of Early Anxieties', p. 389. Courtesy of the Melanie Klein Archive and the Wellcome Library. © Melanie Klein Trust.

Klein offered the interpretation of the bird as his persecuting mother, manifest as 'greedy and destructive' with her beak (Ibid.). The composition of the beak in red and purple, the colours representing Richard and his brother Paul, suggested 'Richard's projection onto his mother of his own (as well as his brother's) oral sadistic impulses' (Ibid.). Klein observes how the drawing demonstrates 'the defences by means of splitting and isolating' of good and bad objects that characterise paranoia, one side showing projection of destructive aggression onto a representation of the mother in an array of colours, the other a patch of uninterrupted blue symbolising the ideal mother (Ibid.).

'Drawing V' is thus significant for its clear rendering of difference in the visual field, perpetually enacting a split in two that is recombined in one. The fracture between the two sides expresses a paranoid imperative to keep loved objects apart from hated objects, a fearful division that is fundamentally unstable. In her *Narrative*, then, Klein describes the creation of a split image, one side showing a terrifying image as a locus onto which the subject paranoiacally projects all the aggression that they feel is coming from outside but is in fact coming from within, and the other side showing an idealised image free of blemishes and held up as a model of virtue. Klein's interpretation of the feared image of the mother, filled out with Richard's own aggression through patches of vivid red and purple, reveals how the mother is represented only as an effect of his violence against her. It is this creation of a split image, or diptych, that is an important effect of paranoia in the visual field. We can observe paranoia, the return of a projected death drive, in the creation of a divide between two photographs of the same person with AIDS. As Klein exposes how paranoid fear manifests between two representations overdetermined by destructive phantasy, so the pairing of photographs of PWA urges us to take a paranoid stance by suggesting that we can read illness in the difference between two images.

As the AIDS crisis was unfolding in the United Kingdom and the United States at the beginning of the 1980s, sections of the tabloid media used the trope of splitting to exacerbate the potential fears around this unknown illness. Notable examples include a double page spread in the British tabloid the *Sunday People* from May 1983 showing two photographs with the screaming title, 'What the Gay Plague did to Handsome Kenny', and much of the coverage of Rock Hudson's death in October 1985, as in the *Los Angeles Times*, which was reproduced as a prop in Steven Soderberg's biopic of Liberace, *Behind the Candelabra* (2013).

The two images of Kenny, one showing the swelling of his facial features, are bound together by the promise of 'pictures that reveal disturbing truth about AIDS sickness [sic]' prompting the viewer to oscillate between the images, reading such 'truth' in the difference between two representations of the same body. Similarly the *Los Angeles Times* comments that Hudson's AIDS 'moved the world', suggesting that disease is represented in the difference between the two pictures as an evident truth on Hudson's aged visage. A

Figure 9.4 Bright Eyes, Stuart Marshall. 1984, UK, SD video, colour, sound
Source: Courtesy of LUX, London.

130   The location of cultural experience

Figure 9.5 Los Angeles Times, 2 October 1985
Source: Copyright © 1985. Los Angeles Times. Used with Permission.

great deal of literature has been written on the role photographic representations have played in perpetuating stigmatising stereotypes of people with AIDS (Grover, 1992; Gagnon, 1992; Crimp, 2002; Watney, 1987). All agree that the photograph is a particularly problematic medium for PWA representation due to its co-optation by reactionary factions of the press early in the epidemic. Grover thus characterises the early image of the illness as 'the moribund *AIDS victim*, who was also (magically) a demon of sexuality, actively transmitting his condition to the "general population" even as he lay dying off-stage' (Grover, 1992, p. 33). Klein's theory of splitting provides an interpretative framework through which to think the AIDS diptych as a representational trope overdetermined by paranoia. The juxtaposition of two images of a person with AIDS 'before' and 'after' enacts the form of paranoid splitting described in Klein's analysis of Richard's drawings, of an image as an effect of aggression.

No doubt these images in the *Sunday People* and *Los Angeles Times* incited a complex maelstrom of affects, both for journalists and readers, including sympathy, fascination, compassion, disgust and anxiety. Yet the recurrence of the trope of splitting suggests a concentration of paranoia in this maelstrom, a compulsion, which is impossible to satisfy, to identify the truth of illness between images. The division solicits the reader to pour over the contrast, heightened through juxtaposition, between the image of illness, as a problem of the objectified other, and the image of health. The visual field is divided not only into 'before' and 'after', but, in Klein's terms, 'good' and 'bad', and, as in Richard's drawings, this split is accompanied by dread that one could swiftly become the other, as in the apparent ease of Kenny's physical transformation across the pictures. The difference between the two photographs is key, but so is the suggestion of slipperiness between them. Thus Hudson's AIDS 'moved the world' as the first time the 'general public' realised that a Hollywood figure they identified with could become ill from a disease supposedly confined to the socially marginalised. The splitting of representation is unstable, yet in its voyeuristic insistence on the signifiers of infection it serves also to contain PWA as 'other' in opposition to any meaningful intervention in the crisis. Roger Hallas explains the deadly effects of such voyeurism as 'homosexual bodies were put on display as a traumatising threat to the general public, while traumatised queer lives were discounted', the gulf between paranoid representation and reality causing many unnecessary deaths (Hallas, 2010, p. 17).

Stuart Marshall's 1984 video *Bright Eyes* attempts to historicise the *Sunday People*'s feature on Kenny, the narrator observing that the newspaper has 'taken up a question that has troubled the medical profession since the last century: how does one form a true picture of an illness?' Marshall invokes the intertwined histories of photography and medicine as an actor dressed in full Victoriana reads aloud an 1859 article from *The Lancet* proclaiming that 'photography is so essentially the art of truth'. The video continues to show examples of photographic identification of pathological types from Havelock Ellis's categories of perversions from *The Criminal*, including two examples of 'an hysteric'.

Inching his way toward psychoanalysis with Josef Breuer in *Studies on Hysteria*, Sigmund Freud describes how the hysteric literalises metaphor physically through bodily conversion symptoms, whilst treatment for hysteria is dependent on the 'talking cure' which allows 'the strangulated affect' of the subject to 'find a way out through speech' (Breuer and Freud, 2001, p. 181, p. 17). If photographs as 'objective' evidence served to silence the pictured subject, then it was Freud's endeavour to let the subject speak and to listen anew, for, as psychoanalysis tells us, the claim to reality is always over-determined by the power of the phantasy realm. Freud founded psychoanalysis on his discovery that hysteria confounds any simple relation between symptom and sign, against understandings of the visibility of illness (Rose, 1986). Marshall invokes the pathologising history of attempts to define perversion and hysteria through photography, pointing out that photographic representations of people with AIDS cannot hold the 'truth' that they claim.

For Martha Gever, Marshall's video reveals how the discourse of medicine can invoke 'representations that claim to reproduce reality' as 'strategies to

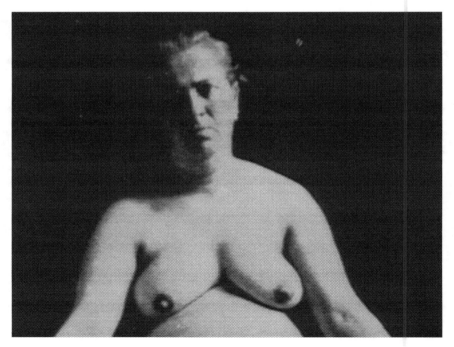

Figure 9.6a Bright Eyes, Stuart Marshall. 1984, UK, SD video, colour, sound
Source: Courtesy of LUX, London.

Figure 9.6b Bright Eyes, Stuart Marshall. 1984, UK, SD video, colour, sound
Source: Courtesy of LUX, London.

identify and classify physical phenomena', so making apparent 'the components that constitute disease – either individual or social – in the form of visible evidence' (Crimp, 2002, p. 117). The danger lies in the disavowal of paranoid phantasies in the visual. Klein's theory of splitting as an attempt to manage an endogenous dread shows how these tabloid images are overdetermined by anxiety, exposing the transparency of the photographic signifier as filled in by the fantasies of journalist and viewer alike (Klein, 1975c). The *Sunday People*'s violent proposition is that the truth of AIDS lies in the gap between the 'idealised' and 'terrifying' images of Kenny. It is our continued task to question how representations of illness might engage ideologically regressive fantasies. The diptych functions by appealing to betweenness, inviting the reader to fill in the representational gap with their most extreme fantasies of the horror of deathly sexuality.

The split in the AIDS diptych thus figures as both a defence against the anxiety of paranoia and an incitement to fear and hatred, so enacting what Lyndsey Stonebridge describes as the 'vicious circle' of Klein's paranoid anxiety (Stonebridge, 1999, p. 42). Splitting in the field of vision, the attempt to concretise the identification of PWA, was paralleled in the possibility of societal splitting in the creation of quarantine camps, a frightening eventuality that Gregg Bordowitz remembers as close to being realised in the United States (Bordowitz, 2002, p. 31). Sarah Schulman recalls that in 1985 persecutory stigma reached a fever pitch in New York City with the targeting of the bathhouses: 'suggestions of quarantine began to circulate. People with AIDS faced severe housing and job discrimination as the press fuelled unbounded fears and paranoia on a daily basis' (Schulman, 1994, p. 110). At this moment Republican bastion William F. Buckley called for the mandatory tattooing of PWA, supposedly to contain the spread of the HIV virus, by providing a visual signifier that would split off and isolate certain people away from the general population, aiming to render them sexually secluded (Buckley, 1986).

In *My Own Private Germany*, Eric Santner observes 'a disturbing rise of expression of paranoia in the United States' as increasingly constitutive of American subjectivities since the end of the Cold War, despite Richard Hofstadter's observation of its prevalence across the political history of the nation (Santner, 1994, p. xiii; Hofstadter, 1964/2008). Santner suggests we understand paranoia as a *'crisis of symbolic investiture'*, an anxious persecutory state precipitated by internally troubled power and the failure of a symbolic order to be performatively upheld as it crumbles from within (Santner, 1994, p. 26). For Santner, the symbolic order functions through performative investiture, and when this becomes insufficient or undermined an excess of sexuality breaks out (Ibid., p. 61). Richard Meyer charts the symbolic construction of Hudson's image, observing his outing via his AIDS diagnosis and death as a moment of crisis that destabilised this cultural fantasy. Across the fifties Hudson's 'starbody' became the epitome of heterosexual masculinity, an 'expansive landscape of the masculine', yet Meyer notes that the power of his appeal also lay in a certain desexualisation and feminisation of his figure as the 'gentle giant' of the big screen (Meyer, 1992, p. 260). In the diptych, Hudson's idealised beauty is destabilised as merely a performance of a symbolic heterosexual ideal, a phantasy 'good object' exposed as paranoid construct.

In *Epistemology of the Closet*, Eve Kosofsky Sedgwick takes instabilities of knowledge as generative of culture, describing 'the closet' as a binary construct of homo/heterosexual definition that claims 'pretended knowingness' of orientations (Sedgwick, 1990, p. 12). Epistemological uncertainty creates a paranoid demand for clarity and normative categorisations in opposition to a more mature, depressive conception of subjectivities. Sedgwick situates her argument in the media reportage of homosexuality and AIDS, noting the 'violently contradictory and volatile energies' of 'homo/heterosexual definition' that manifest in 'every morning's newspaper' in the United States (Ibid., p. 54). For Sedgwick such frenzied paranoid attempts to separate categorically the hetero and the homo reveal the absurdity of 'anybody's urbane pretence at having a clear, simple story to tell about the outlines and meanings of who and what are homosexual and heterosexual' (Ibid., p. 54). Sedgwick's project is to deconstruct the ways such structural binarism is 'hammered most fatally home' in the cultural sphere (Ibid., p. 12). Rock Hudson's AIDS diptych, landing fatally home on the mat in the morning paper, is a key example of paranoid splitting in the visual field, the split showing a need to keep phantasmatic images apart, as the borderline between the Hollywood hunk and the person with AIDS becomes increasingly unstable, upsetting the symbolic order. Hence the revelation of his illness was the moment the press declared that AIDS could strike anyone. So *Life* announced in July 1985 that 'now no one is safe from AIDS', and *Time* in August 1985 wrote of AIDS as 'a growing threat', asking, 'now that the disease has come out of the closet, how far will it spread?'

This paranoid question implies that it could go right to the top, even reaching the president himself. If Hudson's identity was a sham, dissolved in the moment of his outing, could not the same happen to other Hollywood stars – perhaps even his contemporary, Ronald Reagan, by now the ultimate figure of power in the country? Leo Bersani persuasively links phobic reactions to people with AIDS in the UK and the USA to the epidemic's tragic literalisation of the potentially self-shattering effect of sexuality, in which the rectum is 'the grave in which the masculine ideal of proud subjectivity is buried' and hence that of phallic power as well (Bersani, 1987, p. 222). Paranoid anxieties about the continuation of Reagan's performance of office precipitate splitting in the field of vision, a futile attempt to stabilise structured power in photographic images. We can expose this structure by placing the Hudson diptych in an expanded field between representations of Reagan as the cool-movie-star-you-can-rely-on, an image he traded on throughout his entire political career, and Alon Reininger's photograph of Ken Meeks, the winner of the World Press Awards in 1986.

In the expanded field, the stability of the AIDS diptych is once more exposed as on the brink of collapse. Sedgwick observes how the reality of an incoherence of hetero/homo desires and identities leads to a crisis of the symbolic order, engendering a reflexive return of paranoia. This resulted in renewed investment in violent attempts to categorise and separate the homosexual and heterosexual, the 'bad' and the 'good', the ill and the healthy.

AIDS, activism and reparation

It was upon viewing a mournful response to the AIDS crisis, Stashu Kybartas's 1987 video *Danny*, that Douglas Crimp came to the realisation that representations of PWA as 'desperately ill, as either grotesquely disfigured or as having wasted to fleshless, ethereal bodies', function as '*phobic* images, images of terror of imagining the person with AIDS as still sexual' (Crimp, 2002, p. 106). Paranoia in the visual field, phobia of a deathly sexuality, was manifest in the splitting in representations of PWA in the media. This inhibited the capacity of images of PWA to signify in multiple ways, trammelling into a paranoid stability (AIDS = gay = death) wherein the 'truth' of illness

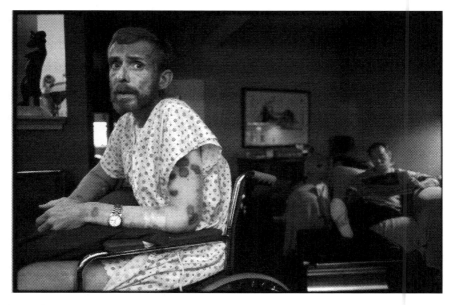

Figure 9.7a Alon Reininger, *Ken Meeks PWA*, 1986
Source: © Alon Reininger/Contact Press Images.

was simultaneously declared as evident in the visible signs on the body and conjured in the fantasy gap between images. In November 1988, the New York City chapter of the AIDS Coalition to Unleash Power (ACT UP) staged a protest at the exhibition *Nicholas Nixon: Pictures of People* at the Museum of Modern Art, demanding '*no more pictures without context*', angry at Nixon's photographs of people with AIDS nearing death (Grover, 1992, p. 39). On the back of this protest, Crimp wrote,

> We can perhaps agree that portraits of people with AIDS created by the media and art photographers alike are demeaning, and that they are over determined by a number of prejudices that precede them about the majority of people who have AIDS – about gay men, IV drug users, people of colour, poor people.
>
> (Crimp, 2002, p. 99)

Crimp explains how photographic representation, rather than displaying a signifier open to interpretation, had paranoiacally collapsed into phobic referents that were stymying the efforts of AIDS activism to shift public conversation around the epidemic.

Between the acts 137

Figure 9.7b David Pollack, Tired of Losing? Ronald Reagan, 1968 Presidential Primary Campaign Poster, 1968.
Source: Copyright © Getty Images.

The artistic and activist task was to find ways to intervene in this symbolic impasse, and practices that developed to contest culturally dominant, paranoid determinations of signifiers are an important legacy of the AIDS crisis. Writing in the catalogue for *Art AIDS America*, an exhibition that was rejected by 100 museums in the United States before opening at the Tacoma Art Museum, Washington in 2015, Jonathan Katz posits that 'strategic, fully self-conscious positioning' and the 'denial that any work is identical with its maker's life, meanings or intentions' are key legacies of AIDS in American art (Katz and Hushka, 2015, p. 31, p. 26). Katz connects such artistic innovations to the rise of the culture wars at the turn of the 1990s, in which right wing politicians censored artists such as Andreas Serrano and Robert

138 The location of cultural experience

Figure 9.7c Detail, *Los Angeles Times*, 2 October 1985
Source: Copyright © 1985. Los Angeles Times. Used with Permission.

Mapplethorpe whose representational works were deemed profane and perverse, describing how artists responded by creating works that were 'the material obverse of a recognisable image of either homosexuality or AIDS' (Ibid., p. 27). Zoe Leonard's *Strange Fruit* is one artistic project that confounds such recognition. In doing so, *Strange Fruit* explores how we might understand the legacies of the historical violence against people with AIDS in our present moment.

In 1992, Leonard began sewing back together the discarded skins of oranges, bananas, grapefruits and avocados that she had eaten.

She continued to sew zips, buttons and fasteners onto these husks to create her 'strange fruits' until 1997, living between India, New York, Alaska, and Provincetown, Massachusetts (Leonard, 2010, p. 63). Leonard had been active in ACT UP/New York, working on needle exchange programmes and the Women's Caucus, and was a founding member of the artists' collective fierce pussy, but by 1992, and after the death of her friend the artist David Wojnarowicz, Leonard became 'tired and sad' and left New York City (Ibid., p. 62). All 295 pieces of *Strange Fruit* were purchased by the Philadelphia

Figure 9.8 Zoe Leonard, *Strange Fruit*, 1992-97. Orange, banana, grapefruit, and lemon skins, thread, buttons, zippers, needles, wax, sinew, string, snaps, and hooks. 295 parts: Dimensions variable. Installation view, Whitney Museum of American Art, New York, 2018.

Source: © Zoe Leonard. Courtesy the artist, Galerie Gisela Capitain, Cologne and Hauser & Wirth. Philadelphia Museum of Art: Purchased with funds contributed by the Dietrich Foundation and with the partial gift of the artist and the Paula Cooper Gallery, 1998. Photograph by Ron Amstutz.

Museum of Art in 1998, and were on show in Leonard's 2018 mid-career retrospective, *Zoe Leonard: Survey* at the Whitney Museum of American Art. Its title echoing colloquial jibes against queers as 'fruits', and Billie Holliday's haunting ballad in which she sings of black bodies hanging from Southern trees after lynchings by whites, Leonard's empty fruit cases sit bathetically in the art gallery, gradually withering and decaying over time.

These strange fruits have not fallen from the tree onto the gallery floor. The juicy fruit contained inside the empty skins has been consumed and the normally discarded remnants reassembled and patched up with needle and thread. Connecting the piece to Leonard's loss of so many friends in the AIDS crisis, which 'decimated the community around her', Margaret Iversen sees the work as 'driven not by nostalgia but by separation, loss, and desire' (Iversen, 2017, p. 41). Olivia Laing argues that *Strange Fruit* 'isn't activism' but that it 'deals with some of the same forces', as it takes 'the pain of exclusion and loss and isolation and holds them, quietly' (Laing, 2015, p. 260). Leonard's work registers violence against people with AIDS through non-referential representation, recuperating the everyday detritus of fruit skins and making them strange by sewing each husk up into an empty case. Each fruit holds its own body in its empty repair, as an evocative metaphor for all those bodies that were lost in the socio-political crisis of AIDS.

If photographic representation of people with AIDS was overdetermined by prejudice, collapsing the signifier, then Leonard's fruits show the fragile, broken skin of singular forms in a connotation of bodily destruction and loss. The concept of reparation holds particular significance in Klein's work, as she identifies the 'depressive position' as the necessary developmental stage for the infant as it moves out of the paranoid-schizoid position, where it realises that the 'good' and 'bad' breasts are combined in the figure of the whole mother, and so the baby attempts to make reparation to the mother for the violence that it imagines it has done to her (Klein, 1975a, p. 271). Reparation has come under fire as one of the most normative aspects of Kleinian theory, because of its ameliorative, and hence exculpatory, effects on destructiveness (Bersani, 1990). *Strange Fruit* questions this understanding of reparation in significant ways. To the extent that Leonard's work is reparative, in her process of literally sewing back together ripped and fragmented fruit skins, each strange fruit continues to bear witness to the violence of their consumption. In her repurposing of rubbish Leonard makes apparent the marks of repair in large stiches of brown thread and plastic buttons that patch together where the skins were torn apart.

This is reparation that continually holds aggression in its very form, as the seams between each fragment of skin precisely show the impossibility of repairing or undoing the irrevocable rips in skins of fruits that are gone, eaten, consumed.

In *Powers of Horror*, Julia Kristeva locates Klein's paranoid-schizoid position within the abject, the between subject and object that must be discarded for the 'I' function to hold, exemplified in bodily excretions and waste (Kristeva, 1982). Leonard takes such abject matter and reforms it, showing through reparation how undoing and destructiveness cannot be undone. *Strange Fruit* complicates any dogmatic split between the paranoid-schizoid and depressive positions by maintaining the violence of loss in the creation of a work of art. Leonard's work is an important example of artistic practices that render the irrevocable violence enacted on people with AIDS and those around them. By poignantly preserving destruction in its form, *Strange Fruit* makes apparent the persistence of the trauma of loss, as a resource for our political moment.

Epilogue: paranoid and reparative, now

In 1990, Leo Bersani critiqued Melanie Klein alongside Marcel Proust as proponents of 'the redemptive power of art', which he condenses into the aphorism, 'experience destroys: art restores' (Bersani, 1990, p. 7, p. 14). In

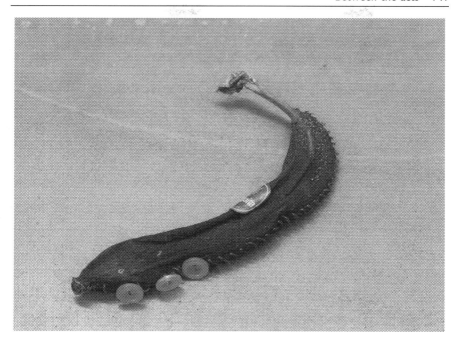

Figure 9.9 Zoe Leonard, *Strange Fruit* (detail), 1992-97. Orange, banana, grapefruit, and lemon skins, thread, buttons, zippers, needles, wax, sinew, string, snaps, and hooks. 295 parts: Dimensions variable.
Source: © Zoe Leonard. Courtesy the artist, Galerie Gisela Capitain, Cologne and Hauser & Wirth. Philadelphia Museum of Art: Purchased with funds contributed by the Dietrich Foundation and with the partial gift of the artist and the Paula Cooper Gallery, 1998. Photograph by Graydon Wood.

polemical voice, he argues that Klein's theory of artistic creativity as reparation in the wake of violence serves a diminished and conservative culture in which 'art redeems the catastrophes of history' (Ibid., p. 22). In Bersani's decrying of the regressive view that 'because of the achievements of culture, the disasters of history somehow do not matter', we hear him denounce the idea that art could in any way compensate for all the losses of the sociopolitical and historical cataclysm of the AIDS crisis (Ibid.). Clearly there can be no compensation. Yet Bersani's critique must not foreclose the possibility for Kleinian insight into the in-formation of aggression in representations of people with AIDS. This understanding is integral to appreciate the paranoid determination of people with AIDS in the media, and to decipher the representation of political violence in *Strange Fruit*. Leonard's work insinuates a political practice of reparation that holds destructiveness without tipping into the sentimentality or nostalgia of the culture of redemption.

Eve Kosofsky Sedgwick takes up the question of reparation in 'Paranoid Reading and Reparative Reading', first published in 1997. Sedgwick describes Klein's paranoid-schizoid position as one of 'terrible alertness to the dangers posed by the hateful and envious part-objects that one defensively projects into, carves out of, and ingests from the world around one', an unstable persecutory state 'marked by hatred, envy and anxiety' of a barely-perceptible other (Sedgwick, 2003, p. 128). Sedgwick questions paranoid reading strategies, understood as the pursuit of a singular monolithic theory that obscures the multivalency of cultural artefacts, as representing only '*a* way, among other ways, of seeking, finding and organising knowledge' (Ibid., p. 130). She notes Guy Hocquenhem's assertion, following Freud's description of paranoia as repressed homosexuality in his case history of Judge Schreber (Freud, 2001), that analysis of paranoid states has particular use in revealing 'how homophobia and heterosexism work' (Sedgwick, 2003, p. 126). Sedgwick points out how, as a result, 'by the mid-1980s' paranoia had become both a 'privileged *object* of antihomophobic theory' as well as a 'uniquely sanctioned methodology' in emergent queer studies and AIDS activism (Ibid., p. 126).

The imperative to challenge the pervasive socio-cultural paranoia and homophobia of the epidemic was a factor in the prevalence of 'paranoid reading'. Sedgwick argues for the transition from paranoid to reparative reading practices, taking inspiration from the 'ethical possibility' built into Klein's understanding of the depressive position as 'a guilty, empathetic view of the other as at once good, damaged, integral, and requiring and eliciting love and care' (Ibid., p. 137). Yet any 'reparative reading' of the histories of HIV/AIDS must not ignore the most extreme manifestations of paranoia and violence witnessed in the epidemic. Such a process would not result in artworks and art histories that redeem and close the story on political crisis, the outcome Bersani objects to, but would rather make space for the most painful violence of HIV/AIDS whilst keeping these narratives open, both to reflect the ongoing epidemic and make space for future change.

On 17 December 2015, the Tacoma Action Collective performed an intervention in the exhibition of *Art AIDS America*, staging a 'die-in' of silent bodies on the floor of the gallery space surrounded by posters announcing 'stop erasing black people' (ArtForum, 2016). The group were angered that, while HIV/AIDS continues to affect African-Americans disproportionately in the United States, of the 107 artists in the exhibition only 5 were black (Kerr, 2016). The protest led to the exhibition changing form to feature a more diverse line-up, introducing the work of 15 new artists of colour when it was next mounted at the Bernard A. Zuckerman Museum of Art in Kenneshaw, Georgia. The exact details of this moment of tension are too intricate to explore at length here; I refer to this intervention and its repercussions as an example of how histories of HIV/AIDS cannot be static or monolithic, or white or male, but rather have to be in process, shifting and opening representational space for all those who have been and still are affected by the epidemic. Such histories and 'reparative' cultural practices must be able to hold historical and contemporary violence and injustice in their very form.

Bibliography

ArtForum (2016) 'Tacoma museum meets with protesters who staged "die-in" to protest lack of artists of color in AIDS exhibition', *ArtForum News*, 6 January. https://www.artforum.com/news/tacoma-museum-meets-with-protesters.whostageddie-in-to-protest-lack-of-artists-of-color-in-aids-exhibition-57191. Last accessed 4/9/2018.

Bersani, L. (1987) 'Is the rectum a grave?', *October* 43, 197–222.

Bersani, L. (1990) *The culture of redemption*. Cambridge, Massachusetts: Harvard University Press.

Bordowitz, G. (2002) 'Interview #004'. *The ACT UP Oral History Project*, 17 December. http://www.actuporalhistory.org/interviews/images/bordowitz.pdf Last accessed 4/9/2018.

Bradley-Perrin, I. (2014) 'Ian Bradley-Perrin at the NYPL: "The failures of the past are still with us"'. *In the Flesh*, 3 March. http://www.inthefleshmag.com/dyke-about town/ianbradleyperrin-at-the-nypl-the-failures-ofthe-past-are-still-with-us/ Last accessed 3/9/2018.

Breuer, J. and S. Freud (2001) Studies on hysteria. In *The standard edition of the complete psychological works of Sigmund Freud*, ed. J. Strachey; trans. J. Strachey and A. Freud, with A. Strachey and A. Tyson, London: The Hogarth Press and the Institute of Psychoanalysis, 24vols., vol. II.

Buckley, W. F. (1986) 'Crucial steps in combating the AIDS epidemic: identify all the carriers', *New York Times*, 18 March.

Crimp, D. (2002) *Melancholia and moralism: essays on AIDS and queer politics*. Cambridge, Massachusetts: MIT Press.

Finklestein, A. (2017) *After silence: a history of AIDS through its images*. Oakland: University of California Press.

Freud, S. (2001) 'Psycho-analytic notes on an autobiographical account of a case of paranoia (dementia paranoides)'. In *The standard edition of the complete psychological works of Sigmund Freud*, ed. J. Strachey; trans. J. Strachey and A. Freud, with A. Strachey and A. Tyson, London: The Hogarth Press and the Institute of Psychoanalysis, 24 vols., vol. XII.

Gagnon, M. (1992) 'A convergence of stakes: photography, feminism and AIDS', in *Fluid exchanges: artists and critics in the AIDS crisis*, ed. J. Miller. Toronto: University of Toronto Press, pp. 53–64.

Grover, J. (1992) 'Visible lesions: images of the PWA in America', *Fluid exchanges: artists and critics in the AIDS crisis*, ed. J. Miller. Toronto: University of Toronto Press, pp. 23–51.

Hallas, R. (2010) *Reframing bodies: AIDS, bearing witness and the queer moving image*. Durham: Duke University Press.

Hofstadter, R. (1964/2008) *The Paranoid Style in American Politics: And Other Essays*. New York: Vintage.

Iversen, M. (2017) *Photography, trace, and trauma*. Chicago and London: University of Chicago Press.

Katz, J. and R. Hushka (2015) *Art AIDS America*. Washington: Tacoma Art Museum.

Kerr, T. (2014) 'Within our rooms of nostalgia: AIDS, communication and each other', *In The Flesh*, 28 February. http://www.inthefleshmag.com/internalpolitix/within-our-rooms-of-nostalgiaaidscommunication-and-each-other/ Last accessed 4/9/2018.

Kerr, T. (2016) 'Erasing black AIDS histories', *The New Inquiry*, 1 January.https://thenewinquiry.com/erasing-black-aids-histories/ Last accessed 4/9/2018.

Klein, M. (1975a) 'A contribution to the psychogenesis of manic-depressive states'. In *The writings of Melanie Klein, volume I*, ed. Roger Money Kyrle *et al.* New York: Free Press, pp. 262–289.

Klein, M. (1975b) 'The Oedipus complex in the light of early anxieties'. In *The writings of Melanie Klein, volume I*, ed. Roger Money Kyrle *et al.* New York: Free Press. pp. 370–419.

Klein, M. (1975c) 'Notes on some schizoid mechanisms', in *The writings of Melanie Klein, volume III*, ed. Roger Money-Kyrle *et al.* New York: Free Press. pp. 1–24.

Klein, M. (1998) *Narrative of a child analysis*. London: Vintage.

Kristeva, J. (1982) *Powers of horror*, trans. Leon S. Roudiez. New York: Columbia University Press.

Laing, O. (2015) *The lonely city*. London: Canongate.

Leonard, Z. (2010) 'Interview #106'. *The ACT UP oral history project*, 13 January. http://www.actuporalhistory.org/interviews/images/leonard.pdf Last accessed 4/9/2018.

Meyer, R. (1992) 'Rock Hudson's body', in D. Fuss (ed.), *Inside/out: lesbian theories, gay theories*. London and New York: Routledge, pp. 258–288.

Nixon, M. (2005) *Fantastic reality: Louise Bourgeois and a story of modern art*. Cambridge, Massachusetts: MIT Press.

Pearl, M. B. (2015) *AIDS literature and gay identity: the literature of loss*. New York and London: Routledge.

Rose, J. (1986) *Sexuality in the field of vision*. London: Verso.

Santner, E. L. (1994) *My own private Germany*. Princeton: Princeton University Press.

Schulman, S. (1994) *My American history: lesbian and gay life in the Reagan/Bush years*. New York: Routledge.

Sedgwick, E. K. (1990) *Epistemology of the closet*. Berkeley: University of California Press.

Sedgwick, E. K. (2003) 'Paranoid reading and reparative reading, or, you're so paranoid, you probably think this essay is about you', in *Touching feeling: affect, pedagogy, performativity*. Durham: Duke University Press. pp. 123–151.

Stonebridge, L. (1999) *The destructive element: British psychoanalysis and modernism*. London and New York: Routledge.

Visual AIDS (2013) 'As we canonise certain producers of culture we are closing space for a complication of narratives', *The Visual AIDS Blog*, 10 December.https://www.visualaids.org/blog/detail/as-we-canonize-certain-producers-of-culture-we-are closing-space-for-a-comp. Last accessed 3/9/2018.

Watney, S. (1987) *Policing desire: AIDS, pornography and the media*. London: Methuen & Co.

Part 4

The suppressed madness of sane men

Chapter 10

Nazism's inner demons
Psychoanalysis and the Columbus Centre (1962–1981)

Danae Karydaki

In his seminal and controversial essay 'Components of the National Culture', the British historian Perry Anderson (1968) argued that although psychoanalysis had found its way to post-war British clinical practice and Britain had 'one of the most flourishing [psychoanalytic] schools in the world', the impact of psychoanalysis on British culture had been 'virtually nil'. 'There is no Western country' he continued 'where the presence of psychoanalysis in general culture is so vestigial' as it is in Britain and, unlike diverse thinkers from the Continent, such as Theodor Adorno or Louis Althusser, '(t)here is no comparable English thinker who has been remotely touched' (Anderson, 1968, p. 42). More recently, historians including Daniel Pick (2003) and Mathew Thomson (2006) have been inclined to agree, albeit not categorically, on the relative absence of psychoanalysis in the wider intellectual and cultural life of post-war Britain.

However, an investigation into largely neglected archives shows that Freud did not only influence thinkers in post-war Paris and Frankfurt, but at least two important figures in the cultural life of London too: David Astor, editor of *The Observer* (1948–1975), and Norman Cohn, historian and author of *The Pursuit of the Millennium* (1957). These two people were the main funder and the academic director, respectively, of the Columbus Centre, a remarkable, if now largely forgotten, research institute that was established at the University of Sussex between 1966 and 1980, aiming to employ psychoanalysis as an interpretative tool for the history of persecution, discrimination, and mass violence (Karydaki, 2016). The scope of the Columbus Centre, according to Astor (1962b), was to 'study the fate of the Jews as one example, albeit by far the worst, of a widespread human phenomenon, namely, man's capacity to destroy his fellow beings without rational motives'. In the context of the Columbus Centre, psychoanalysis became a crucial theoretical tool for understanding this human capacity to destroy fellow humans without rational motives or what I call 'Nazism's Inner Demons', echoing the title of Cohn's book on the European witch-hunt (Cohn, 1975). 'Nazism's Inner Demons' denotes here the unconscious psychological mechanisms at work in Nazism, but I also use this case study to think more widely about how psychoanalytic

DOI: 10.4324/9781003200765-14

work can be used to explore the psychological mechanisms that might be at work when an individual or a group perform other types of atrocity; when they behave, in other words, in what is largely believed to be an 'inhuman' manner.

This essay will map the role of psychoanalysis in the framework of the Columbus Centre through the views of its protagonists, in order to shed light both on the largely neglected influence of psychoanalysis on post-war British culture and on the broader significance of psychoanalysis in investigating 'man's inhumanity to man'.

The Columbus Centre

The Columbus Centre was founded in response to claims of a lamentable dearth of British academic research about Nazism and the Holocaust. Astor and Cohn brought together researchers with specialisms in history and the social sciences, such as the historian of antisemitism Léon Poliakov, social and gender historian Christina Larner, and social psychologists Nevitt Sanford and Rae Sherwood, along with various psychoanalytically informed psychiatrists, such as Henry Dicks and Anthony Storr, and political activists, such as anti-apartheid fighter Albie Sachs and Roma rights advocate Grattan Puxon, in order to involve them in the Centre's research and to publish their books in the Columbus series.

The diverse backgrounds and research topics of the Columbus Centre's participants indicate the original founders' intention to approach what Astor (1962b) called 'man's capacity to destroy his fellow beings without rational motives' in an interdisciplinary manner. Their intention was also attuned to a new ethos of interdisciplinary learning that emerged at the University of Sussex at the time. After being granted a royal charter which raised it to full university status in August 1961, the University of Sussex admitted its first 51 students in October 1961 (Cragoe, 2015, pp. 225–230). The aim of the founding team was to model the university in a different way from traditional British universities and to redraw, in second vice chancellor of Sussex and historian Asa Briggs's words, 'the map of learning' (Briggs, 1964). Hence, instead of conventional departments, three new multidisciplinary 'Schools' in the humanities and the social sciences (European Studies, English and American Studies, and Social Studies) quickly emerged at Sussex (Cragoe, 2015, p. 231). During the time that the Columbus Centre was functioning, Astor was in correspondence with two of the University's vice chancellors, John Fulton (1961–1967), who, incidentally, had been Astor's tutor before the war at Oxford and Asa Briggs (1967–1976), who was also based at Oxford from 1945 to 1955. The university's emphasis on cross-disciplinarity as well as new intakes made it perfectly suited for a research project aiming at bringing together history and psychology. However, the Columbus Centre members rarely met at Sussex, opting instead for London, where Cohn also had his office around Bloomsbury. 'They [at Sussex]' said Cohn at an interview with

Daniel Pick in 2006, 'sponsored the whole thing but I operated from London largely because the sources I needed for [the] work were there' (Pick, 2006).

What most obviously distinguished the Columbus Centre from other British institutions of the time with similar scopes (such as the Wiener Library in London or the Parkes Library at the University of Southampton) was its emphasis on psychoanalysis. Although these institutions also sought to investigate the history of prejudice and especially antisemitism, David Astor, Norman Cohn, and their associates at the Columbus Centre stood out because of their particular insistence on the relevance of Freudian thought to the study of persecution, racial discrimination, mass violence, and genocide.

The Columbus Centre was born as an idea in Astor's mind. He first made a plea for a psychoanalytically informed academic study of Nazism in the *Observer* article 'The Meaning of Eichmann' in 1961 and then, one year later, in a speech at the Warsaw Ghetto Uprising commemoration in London, published afterwards in the *Encounter* (Astor, 1961, 1962b). In this speech, Astor noted that what was missing from Anglophone historiography was not just a full historical study of the Third Reich or the Holocaust; on the contrary, he explicitly stated that he did not question the value of the work of scholars such as Gerald Reitlinger (1953, 1956) or Raul Hilberg (1961), who had published meticulous historical accounts of the facts of the Nazi regime on both sides of the Atlantic by that time. What was missing instead was, in Astor's words, an inquiry into 'the full reality and meaning of these facts', an effort to mobilise the insights of psychoanalysis to understand the multiple horrors of collective 'inhumanity' and 'atrocity' in the course of modern history and politics (Astor, 1962b).

Astor's project is thus significant because it represents a theoretical attempt to understand the psychological mechanisms at work in Nazism and other historical instances of discrimination, persecution, and mass violence. He urgently emphasised the need for 'an attempt to understand what happened, an attempt to insure that the underlying psychological processes will become better known'. He argued that to do so would provide some opportunity 'to reduce the chances of further mass destruction in the future'. The endeavour to revisit this past through psychoanalysis, and to learn lessons from it, would be, in Astor's view, 'a worthy monument to the memory of the six millions' (Astor, 1962b). 'Ever since the end of the war' responded Norman Cohn to his plea in a letter on 23 July 1962, 'I have been trying to further just such an enquiry ... I have on various occasions tried to launch such an undertaking – usually with the help of some American foundation – but I never succeeded' (Cohn, 1962a). Hence, their mutual interest in psychoanalysis as a tool of understanding history and politics led them, among other things, to decide, a few weeks later, to launch the Columbus Centre.

From very early on, the Columbus Centre members, and Astor in particular, resolved to treat psychoanalysis as their principal interpretative tool. 'I feel', wrote Astor to Cohn on 24 March 1965, we should take the [psychoanalytic] side of our endeavour particularly seriously as it is the side on which we hope to make an advance. After all, everything else about Auschwitz is already known except the psychological processes going on in the minds of the perpetrators and the relationship of these processes to the rest of life.

(Astor, 1965)

Indeed, what bound together a wide spectrum of research topics and scholarly interests at the Columbus Centre was the 'ordinariness' and 'human origin' of the Nazi crimes and their 'repeatability' under different historical conditions, such as apartheid in modern-day South Africa in Sachs's work or the witch-hunts of sixteenth- and seventeenth-century Europe in Cohn's and Larner's books.

The 'ordinariness', 'human origin', and 'repeatability' of the Nazi crimes resonates with what the philosopher Hannah Arendt called 'the banality of evil' in her 1963 book *Eichmann in Jerusalem* (1994), which Norman Cohn characterised as a source of 'valuable and varied insight into the Nazi mentality' (Cohn, 1967, p. 290). After attending the Adolf Eichmann trial in Jerusalem, which was also the trigger for the founding of the Columbus Centre, Arendt challenged mainstream representations of the Nazis' demonisation, which implied that they found some sort of delight in the crimes they performed. Unlike most previous accounts which painted the Nazis as the incarnation of sadistic, savage, and mentally ill individuals or, at the very least, as pure ideologues who would employ any means to further their ends, Arendt saw Eichmann as a thoughtless bureaucrat, an ordinary person who was simply following orders; he was, like so many others, in Arendt's words, 'terribly and terrifyingly normal'. Especially with regard to the frequently repeated argument that the Nazis were psychotic or sadistic personalities, Arendt reported in her book that '(h)alf a dozen psychiatrists had certified him as "normal"—"More normal, at any rate, than I am after having examined him", one of them was said to have exclaimed' (Arendt, 1994, pp. 25–26).

Hence, in order to address these 'ordinary' and 'banal' crimes, the Columbus Centre's participants adopted a psychoanalytical understanding of history, culture, and society precisely because psychoanalysis locates sadism, murderous fantasies, and, at times, even evil itself, within the human psyche.

David Astor and psychoanalysis

Astor was born in London in 1912 into an upper-class English family with American origins; his father was Viscount Waldorf Astor, owner of *The Observer* from 1915 onwards, and his mother, with whom David was at odds almost all of his life, was Nancy Astor, the first woman ever to take a seat in the British House of Commons as a Tory MP (Cockett, 1991; Lewis, 2016). Despite his upper-class upbringing, wealth, Oxford education, and the conservative background of his family, Astor was fundamentally a liberal; he devoted his life to fighting injustice and advocating for human rights and decolonisation. For example, in 1948, the year when Astor became chief editor of *The Observer* and the National Party won the elections in South Africa, the newspaper published an article entitled 'The Meaning of Malan' in which the correspondent alerted the readers to the Nazi sympathies and white-supremacist discourse of the new regime (The Observer, 1948b). 'I am so glad' Astor's friend George Orwell wrote to him at the time '[that] the *Obs.* is taking up Africa so to speak' (Orwell, 2010, p. 422). In addition to promoting social justice causes, Astor was also interested in exploring—or rather finding the people suitable for exploring—discrimination and violence as aspects of the human psyche. *The Observer* under his editorship was a revealing indication of this attitude; his proposal for an academic inquiry into persecution and genocide was another such indication. 'With all his tolerance', wrote the former *Observer* journalist and writer Anthony Sampson, 'David was stubborn about pursuing policies he really believed in, and defied anyone who crossed him on questions like nuclear disarmament, African independence or Freudian interpretations' (Sampson, 2001).

Anna Freud and Astor: psychoanalysis as a private matter

From his early Oxford years, during which he suffered a nervous breakdown, David Astor had become a fervent advocate of psychoanalysis. In fact, Astor's attachment to psychoanalysis was apparent enough to anyone who knew him well and was publicly revealed on various occasions. To start with, he was an analysand of Sigmund Freud's daughter, Anna. He regarded his psychoanalytic treatment with Anna Freud as very successful although, as he confessed to Sampson, he sometimes went to sleep during sessions (Sampson, 2001). According to Anna Freud's biographer Elisabeth Young-Bruehl, Astor became Anna's 'friend'. My own research into Anna Freud's papers, held at the Freud Museum in London, reveals that Astor's second wife, Bridget, had developed a more personal relationship with Anna Freud, sending her a birthday card in 1955 and giving her a terracotta figurine of a child's head as a gift (Young-Bruehl, 2008, p. 357; Astor, 1955).

It is thus not surprising that on 28 February 1964 Astor contacted Anna Freud to ask her to read Cohn's preliminary report of the Columbus Centre and act as a referee for possible sponsors (Astor, 1964). 'Although I should be very interested to read it' she wrote back a few days later 'I cannot help feeling that I am not qualified to pronounce any kind of judgment on it since neither relevant studies nor experience have equiped (sic) me for such a task' (Freud, 1964). Though she kindly refused Astor's proposal, she did suggest two other people who could offer what she called 'an opinion from the psycho-analytic side', Robert Waelder and Heinz Hartmann, both of whom were Viennese psychoanalysts and émigrés to the United States (Guttman, 1969; Loewenstein, 1970). It should be noted, however, that Anna Freud had in the past been involved with similar research projects, such as a UNESCO initiative in 1948 for a proposal about educational and psychological techniques for changing the mental attitudes that shape international understanding. This suggests that the therapeutic relationship she once had with Astor might have been another reason for her refusal, in addition to her 'limited experience' in these issues (Freud, 1948).

Psychoanalysis arrives at the university

Astor's involvement with psychoanalysis is also described in the book *Dimensions of Psychoanalysis* (1989), edited by Joseph Sandler, a major figure in the Anna Freud circle. Sandler described at length how Astor contributed to the development of British psychoanalysis. Astor endowed the Freud Memorial Chair of Psychoanalysis, a new visiting professorial post at University College London (UCL), in 1974. It was the first Chair of psychoanalysis in Britain and its occupant became known as the Freud Memorial Professor (Lighthill, 1989, pp. ix–xv; Sandler, 1989, p. vii). James Lighthill, Provost of UCL at the time, argued that Astor's aim in establishing a Chair of Psychoanalysis was that 'students in general should have a chance to hear the discipline of psychoanalysis expounded by its most authentic exponents, psychoanalysts' and should have 'actual views of Freud presented together with their ever-changing contemporary application' (Lighthill, 1989, p. x).

The well-known American psychoanalyst Erik Erikson was supposed to be the first Freud Memorial Professor in 1974–1975, but his ill health prevented him from moving to Britain, so many distinguished psychoanalysts such as John Sutherland, Charles Rycroft, Anne-Marie Sandler, and Enid Balint gave lectures during that academic year. The first Freud Memorial Professor was eventually the analyst Roy Schafer in 1975–1976. His successors included the psychoanalysts Hanna Segal, André Green, John Bowlby, Janine Chasseguet-Smirgel, and the historian Christofer Lasch. In 1984, David Astor, as the benefactor, along with UCL's Board of Management, decided to extend the tenure of the Chair holder. Joseph Sandler became the first long-term holder of the Freud Memorial Chair and the UCL Psychoanalysis Unit—still active today—was established under his direction (Ibid., p. xi–xv).

In 1965, Astor had hoped that the Columbus Centre would be 'the first unit in a British university that explicitly includes [psychoanalysis] in its set-up' revealing once again the emphasis he placed on the role of psychoanalysis as an interpretative tool outside the clinic (Astor, 1965). Given the scarcity of existing information about the Columbus Centre compared to the plethora of sources about the Psychoanalytic Unit at UCL, perhaps what Astor did not accomplish with the former, which anyway was more focused on the specific topic of exploring the psychology of Nazi atrocity, he did manage to accomplish with the latter.

The Observer

Astor's fascination with psychoanalysis was perhaps most evident at *The Observer*, which, under his editorship, gradually transformed into a newspaper that emphasised psychological understanding and, especially, psychoanalysis (Cockett, 1991, p. 169). To start with, in 1956, a year that marked the centennial of Freud's birth, *The Observer* hosted a series of 'Centenary' articles on Freud on its first pages. Later reprinted as a pamphlet under the title 'The meaning of Freud', the series comprised biographical sketches by Freud's translator Nancy Procter-Gregg and articles that discussed the influence of Freud on medicine (by the editor of the *International Journal of Psycho-analysis* at the time, W. Hoffer), literature (by *Observer* journalist Philip Toynbee), and religion (by psychiatrist David Stafford-Clark) (Hoffer, 1956; Procter-Gregg, 1956b, 1956a; Stafford-Clark, 1956; Toynbee, 1956). Indeed the title 'the meaning of...' which appears in 1956 in reference to Freud and bears certain psychoanalytic resonances, seems to be particularly appealing to Astor judging by its similarity to other *Observer* titles, such as the aforementioned articles 'The Meaning of Malan' (The Observer, 1948b) and 'The Meaning of Eichmann' (Astor, 1961) as well as others such as 'The Meaning of Maoism' (Green, 1952), 'The Meaning of the Witch-Hunt' (Bloodworth, 1955), 'The Real Meaning of Masada' (Kenyon, 1965), and 'The Meaning of Watergate' (Sampson, 1973).

Moreover, from 1964 on, *The Observer* featured a psychology correspondent whose role was to offer specialised commentary on issues directly related to psychology and particularly psychoanalysis. It should be noted that in other British Sunday newspapers of the time, such as *The Times*, there was no psychology correspondent; on the rare occasions when a psychological issue was raised, it was done so by a medical or science correspondent. Psychoanalysis in particular was, more often than not, mentioned in *The Times* only in the context of the obituaries of famous psychoanalysts such as John Rickman, Karen Horney or Melanie Klein (Money-Kyrle, 1951; The Times, 1952, 1960).

During the years that Astor edited the paper, opinion articles that stressed the importance of the application of social sciences such as psychology or the introduction of psychoanalysis in British universities, appeared frequently (Taylor, 1950; Our Psychology Correspondent, 1965). The paper also featured full-page articles that profiled psychoanalysts such as Carl Jung (The Observer, 1948a), Ernest Jones (The Observer, 1953), Melanie Klein (Rycroft, 1961b), and Lou Andreas Salome (Toynbee, 1963). Moreover, contributors to the paper included psychoanalysts like Charles Rycroft (1961a) and Donald Winnicott (1964), as well as psychoanalytically informed scholars such as the anthropologists Margaret Mead (1948) and Geoffrey Gorer (1960, 1971). Under Astor's editorship, psychoanalysis was also often employed as a tool to interpret culture in *The Observer*. For example, the theatre critic Kenneth Tynan (1958) and the poetry critic Al Alvarez (1970) often used psychoanalytic vocabulary in their writings from the late 1950s until the early 1970s. The language of psychoanalysis also permeated articles discussing a range of other subjects, such as the 1970s women's movement in the United States (Egginton, 1971).

Finally, Astor's insistence on the importance of psychoanalysis as a methodological approach to history was demonstrated, for instance, in publishing a psychoanalytically inflected article in 1969 about Churchill by the Jungian psychoanalyst Anthony Storr, a regular contributor to the paper and Columbus Centre participant, who argued that it was 'the inner drives that made Sir Winston a great wartime leader' (Storr, 1969).

Norman Cohn and psychoanalysis

Norman Cohn was born in London in 1915 into a British middle-class family and, like Astor, went to study at Oxford. During the Second World War he served as an army official charged with the task of editing the decoded German signals of the Enigma code (Pick, 2006; Lamont, 2007; Lay, 2007) and as soon as the war was over he returned to academia and began working as a historian. His first breakthrough, triggered by his wartime experience in combination with scrupulous research, came in 1957 with the publication of the *Pursuit of the Millennium* (Cohn, 1957).

In defence of Freud

Like Astor, Cohn had an interest in psychology and the study of persecution, possibly cultivated during his service in the Intelligence Corps during the Second World War (Lamont, 2007). Cohn said in an interview with Daniel Pick in 2006 that he underwent psychoanalytic treatment with various analysts, the longest of which was with a Jungian therapist named Carl Oppenheimer, who knew all about Freud but was at the same time critical of him 'in a very rational way'. He added that he also had therapy with Dr Goldblatt, a Freudian who worked at the Tavistock Clinic (Pick, 2006).

Although less a 'pilgrim' of psychoanalysis than Astor, Norman Cohn was nonetheless intrigued by a study of history and culture through psychoanalysis, especially in the early stages of planning the creation of the Columbus Centre. In 1962, Cohn responded to Astor's plea for an academic investigation into Nazi crimes by highlighting his own psychological understanding of history and culture. He portrayed, in this respect, his own book on the traces of Nazi and Communist fanaticism in medieval Europe, *The Pursuit of the Millennium* (1957), as 'a modest excursion into the almost unexplored territory of what [Astor] called "political psycho-pathology"'. What should be sought, Cohn added, was a massive exploration of political psycho-pathology by historians and psychologists, but also perhaps by anthropologists and sociologists. 'This exploration should not be limited to Nazism or antisemitism', he argued, but rather range over 'the vast field of fanatical beliefs and behaviour' (Cohn, 1962a). In other words, Cohn picked up the threads of Astor's proposal to study the Nazi crimes and other 'atrocities' through a psychoanalytic lens and suggested a broader theoretical intervention for the study of history and politics, which consisted treating these historical examples also as a consequence of inner conflicts and unconscious psychological fixations. What Cohn thought at the time that could be a possible model for their initiative was the Institut für politische Psychologie, founded in 1956 at the University of Vienna by the Austrian psychoanalyst Wilfried Daim.

A short while after Astor and Cohn's first encounter in 1962, Cohn got upset with the Psychoanalytical Society analyst and *Observer* contributor Willie Hoffer, who challenged *The Pursuit of the Millennium*'s bibliography as being not sufficiently psychoanalytically grounded. Astor tried to mitigate its consequences by stressing that Hoffer, while being 'a wise and able man' was 'too elderly and [...] too specialised as merely an analyst rather than being a social thinker' (Astor, 1962a). Cohn, apparently enraged with the accusation, responded with two consecutive letters in which he attempted to defend his psychoanalytic background. 'I wonder why Hoffer assumes I don't know such a very stock work as Freud's *Group Psychology and the Analysis of the Ego?*', he wrote somewhat bitterly,

> I know it as *Massenpsychologie und Ich-Analyse* and regard it as a basic work as far as it goes—or could go when it was written, forty years ago. But presumably Hoffer had not read Chapter III of my book.
> (Cohn, 1962b)

Without waiting for Astor's reply, he added in a second letter, two days later, that

> Hoffer may like to know that I have frequently lectured to gatherings of psychoanalysts both here and in the United States. He will find the text of one of my talks, given at Columbia University, in the Spring issue of *Psychoanalysis and the Psychoanalytical Review*.
> (Cohn, 1962c)

The Institute for Social Research and the Columbus Centre

Another instance of Cohn's involvement with psychoanalysis occurs in 1963, when he visited Germany and, especially, the Institute for Social Research, home of the Frankfurt School. In a report of his visit to the Columbus Centre's members, Cohn recognised the Institute for Social Research under the leadership of Theodor Adorno and Max Horkheimer as the only full-time centre for research in the field of political psychology in Germany (Cohn, 1963b). However, while the Frankfurt School aimed at revisiting and bringing together Marx and Freud, Cohn gave more weight to the psychological rather than the political or social aspect of the Institute for Social Research. Indeed, of all the Institute's participants, Cohn distinguished the work of Frau Dr Wanda von Baeyer-Katte, who carried out a psychoanalytical study of the Nazi regime. 'The relevance of psychoanalysis' he wrote in his report, in which Marx was strikingly never mentioned, 'is taken for granted; not only are psychoanalytical findings on the basis of the empirical research, but close relations are maintained with the Frankfurt Institut für Psychiatrie und Psychoanalyse, under Mitscherlich' (Cohn, 1963a). The fact that Cohn refers here to Alexander Mitscherlich, a psychoanalyst intensely interested in the psychoanalytical interpretation of prejudice and subsequent co-author of the seminal account *The Inability to Mourn* (Mitscherlich and Mitscherlich, 1975), reveals how much Cohn was determined, at that stage, to employ psychoanalysis as a historiographical approach to persecution, discrimination, fanaticism, and mass violence.

A couple of years later, in 1965, Cohn contacted the American psychologist Nevitt Sanford to ask him to participate in the Columbus Centre. In this letter, in which he invited Sanford to contribute his American experience of the applications of psychoanalysis, he stressed the methodological importance of the talking cure for the study of history and politics: 'We are primarily interested' wrote Cohn, 'in the genesis and institutionalisation of unconscious negative projections; i.e. finding out how a society or social unit comes to regard a certain category (real or imaginary) of human beings as less than humans, —as demons, animals or things' (Cohn, 1965).

It is apparent from this passage that Cohn regarded psychoanalysis as necessary for understanding the psychological mechanisms through which, under certain historical and social circumstances, a group of people is dehumanised and demonised, allowing for its discrimination, targeting, persecution, and, sometimes, murder and systematic annihilation. According to Cohn, psychoanalysis would help comprehend dark moments in the history of humanity such as the Nazi camps, where the Jews, a group of people distinguished and targeted for their 'sub-human' race, were sentenced to death; the sixteenth- and seventeenth-century witch-hunt, in which a certain type of women—old, 'ugly', infertile, financially independent—were also dehumanised, persecuted and, ultimately, burnt as 'witches'; the apartheid regime in South Africa, where black people were not considered sufficiently 'human' to enjoy the human rights that their white fellow countrymen did; and the neglect, persistent discrimination and persecution of the Roma people as 'non-human' pariahs in Europe. All these dark moments were taken up by the Columbus Centre members and were turned into the Columbus series books *Licenced Mass Murder: A Socio-psychological Study of some SS Killers* by Henry Dicks (1972), *Enemies of God: The Witch-hunt in Scotland* by Christina Larner (1981), *Justice in South Africa* by Albie Sachs (1973), and *The Destiny of Europe's Gypsies* by Donald Kenrick and Grattan Puxon (1972), respectively.

Psychoanalysis, in other words, was deemed necessary in the context of the Columbus Centre for understanding the unconscious process of dehumanisation that has so often affected the course of human history.

Strikingly, in the same letter to Sanford, Cohn emphasised the need for the researchers of the Columbus Centre to have undergone psychoanalytic therapy:

> The object of the investigation should be to find out why and how such differences came about ... it should be carried out by historians, sociologists and (one hopes) field-workers who have been psychoanalysed and would be able to apply the insights of psychoanalysis to their findings; and it should also make use of professional psychoanalysts.
>
> (Cohn, 1965)

Europe's Inner Demons

In 1975, in what Cohn himself called a postscript of 'psycho-historical speculations' to his first edition of his Columbus series book about the sixteenth- and seventeenth-century European witch-hunt, *Europe's Inner Demons*, Cohn emphasised fantasy as a core psychoanalytic category for the analysis of the witch-hunt. 'For what we have been examining', he argued, 'is above all fantasy at work in history (and incidentally, in the writing of history). It is fantasy and nothing else that provides the continuity in this story' (Cohn, 1975, p. 258). Especially with regard to the accusation of cannibalistic infanticide as a similar mechanism to that of the witches, Cohn further elaborated on the role of psychoanalysis in his account:

> It seems plain that both stereotypes draw on one and the same archaic fantasy. Psycho-analysts would maintain that the unconscious roots of this fantasy lie in infancy or early childhood. Psycho-analysts of the Kleinian school would argue, more specifically, that infants in the first two years of life experience cannibalistic impulses which they project on to their parents; and that the source of the fantasy lies there [...] It is, that the theme of cannibalistic infanticide, which has bulked so large in this book, owes part of its appeal to wishes and anxieties experienced in infancy or early childhood, but deeply repressed and, in their original form, wholly unconscious
>
> (Ibid., pp. 260–261).

Cohn seems to have drawn his concept of 'fantasy', and especially cannibalistic fantasy, from Melanie Klein. We can make this assumption not only because he mentions it here but also because his account resonates with the Tavistock psychiatrist Henry Dicks's Kleinian interpretation of the behaviour of the former SS officials in *Licenced Mass Murder: A Socio-psychological Study of some SS Killers* (Dicks, 1972), a book that Cohn meticulously edited for the Columbus Series before writing *Europe's Inner Demons*, as revealed in the Henry Dicks papers held at the Welcome Archive in London.

According to Kleinian theory, during the very first months of a baby's life, s/he is in a psychic state which Klein called the 'paranoid-schizoid position'. At this time, strong feelings of love and hate co-exist and are pre-eminently directed towards the primary object, i.e. the mother in most cases. However, during these first few months, the object is not perceived as a whole, but as fragmentary, in terms both of its function and the degree to which it satisfies the baby's needs and desires. Hence, because of the intimate relationship that is developed during breastfeeding, the baby's feelings are mainly directed to the mother's breast instead of the mother as a whole. At the same time, this breast is perceived as split: 'good' when it satisfies its feeding purpose and 'bad' when it frustrates the baby's real or fantasised hunger. During this period, the dominant mental capacities of the baby are introjection, i.e. a process through which external objects are taken in/devoured as if by oral means, and projection, a term that in Klein's writings broadly denotes that an internal feeling/conflict is experienced as if coming from the outside and is, more specifically, caused by the object. Hence, when the object fulfils or fails the baby's needs, powerful feelings of love or hatred are respectively projected onto the object. Subsequently, the object that is perceived once as 'good' and another time as 'bad' is introjected as two separate split objects. Therefore, the baby's own sadistic impulses towards the frustrating mother are experienced, through the mechanism of projection, as if the 'bad' object is persecuting the baby in order to destroy him/her. This source of persecutory anxiety results in the mobilisation of defence mechanisms that guarantee the denial of this unbearable reality. The process of splitting, for example, preserves the goodness of the loved object, whereas early obsessional thinking magically constrains paranoia (Klein, 1923, 1935, 1946). In his Columbus series book edited by Cohn, Dicks applied this Kleinian concept of persecutory anxiety in his analysis of the SS officials he interviewed; he argued that the killers were terrified of their victims because they projected parts of themselves on them (Dicks, 1972, p. 265). For Dicks, given that all German people had to abide by Nazi laws, the greatest difference between those who eventually also became the 'willing executioners' of Nazi atrocities and those who managed to avoid them 'seems to be inside the man's own mind—the degree of hate and paranoid-projection between self as pitiless authority and self as a victim of a pitiless authority outside' (Ibid., p. 229).

While in Klein's theorisation the fantasy of good and bad objects is staged in the mind of the infant, the Columbus Centre members, and Cohn in particular, sought to investigate this fantasy in the context of collective action, arguing that it is crucial in understanding the process of dehumanisation and demonisation that led to the persecution, discrimination, and murder of millions of people in the course of human history. Cohn's observation in his letter to Sanford that often society 'comes to regard a certain category (real or imaginary) of human beings as less than humans' (Cohn, 1965) reinforces the argument that fantasy unconsciously intervenes both in the selection of the targeted group, such as in the case of the persecution of the imaginary or fantasised category of 'witches', and in their demonisation and dehumanisation, i.e. the process of their transformation into absolute 'bad' objects, when the frustration of the individual is experienced as if coming from the outside, from the members of the targeted group.

The last sentence of Cohn's postscript in *Europe's Inner Demons* is an encouragement to 'others, better equipped, to venture further—downwards, into the abyss of the unconscious', indicating how central psychoanalysis as an interpretative tool was to Cohn's thinking (Cohn, 1975, p. 263). Indeed, more recently, scholars such as Jacqueline Rose and Lyndsey Stonebridge have 'venture[d]' into this 'abyss': while Jacqueline Rose (1998) stressed the importance of psychoanalysis in understanding politics and history in *States of Fantasy*, Lyndsey Stonebridge (2009, p. 103) observed that 'the true scandal about war for Freud in 1915 was not its barbarism, which hardly surprised him, but the way it turns our unconscious fantasies about death into history'. Both, following Cohn, have further and more convincingly elaborated on the role of unconscious fantasy in human history.

However, this psychoanalytically informed postscript was removed in the second edition of the book in 1993. This omission seems to have been anything but random. In his interview with Daniel Pick, Cohn said that this postscript was the least satisfactory thing he had ever written and that he regretted 'not using psychoanalysis sensibly' without providing, however, a definition of what a 'sensible' use of psychoanalysis would be. 'Human beings just behave like this', said Cohn dismissively, 'we don't need psychoanalysts to tell us so' (Pick, 2006). In other words, as time went by, Cohn's views shifted from rather favourable to critical of psychoanalysis as a methodological approach to history.

Conclusion

Psychoanalysis was promoted by Astor and Cohn as one of the basic lenses through which historical issues would be addressed at the Columbus Centre. Their initial ambition to make the Columbus Centre a research institute exclusively specialised in the use of psychoanalysis for the study of 'man's inhumanity to man' was, for various reasons (personal, institutional, and cultural), not fulfilled (Karydaki, 2016). However, Astor's enduring interest and commitment to psychoanalysis as a tool for interpreting history and culture, evident in the establishment of a Chair in Psychoanalysis at UCL and the transformation of *The Observer* into a newspaper sympathetic to psychoanalysis, and, especially, his and Cohn's initial pursuit of a psychoanalytical investigation of 'Nazism's inner demons' in the Columbus Centre, indicates that, contrary to the historical consensus, psychoanalysis did have a marginal impact on post-war British culture.

It comes as no surprise that this marginal impact of psychoanalysis on British culture was demonstrated in a research centre for the study of discrimination and mass violence that originally aimed at understanding the Nazi atrocities and exploring, more broadly, the meaning of irrational inhumane behaviour. Psychohistory—the largely controversial branch of history that focuses on, and often speculates about, psychological motivations behind historical events, and thus offers an analysis of history from the point of view of psychology or psychoanalysis—was quite popular during the post-war period in the United States, where, unlike Britain, there was a cultural elevation of Freud in the 1950s by writers such as Lionel Trilling (1955) and Philip Rieff (1959). Indeed, the historian William L. Langer famously called for the employment of psychoanalysis in the study of history in his 1957 annual presidential address to the American Historical Association (Langer, 1958). American psycho-historical accounts on Nazism written in the time of the Columbus Centre include Peter Loewenberg's *The Psychohistorical Origins of the Nazi Youth Cohort* (1971), while infamous cases—in that they were frequently derided by professional historians—include *The Mind of Adolf Hitler* (1972) by Walter Langer, brother of William Langer.

However, what the Columbus Centre members, and especially Astor and Cohn, contributed to 1960s and 1970s British historiography of mass violence was not a speculative sort of psychohistory, but rather the historiographical familiarity with abnormality that psychoanalysis can offer. 'If the Third Reich could not be explained away by psychology', wrote Daniel Pick in *The Pursuit of the Nazi Mind*, 'the charismatic allure of the Nazi leader and the subterranean attractions of his cause continued nonetheless to be examined and interpreted by many post-war writers' (2012, p. 217). And this largely happens because psychoanalysis suggests that destructiveness, even sadism, is universal. Hence, although problematic in various ways, a critically engaged employment of psychoanalysis in the study of history can break a well-established stereotype that the Nazis were mad, exceptionally sadistic and a unique type of perpetrator, presenting them, instead, as 'ordinary' and 'banal' human beings. As we know well, Hannah Arendt was by no means a Freud enthusiast. Yet, the Columbus Centre project was inspired both by Arendt's concept of the 'banality of evil' and the psychoanalytic notion of normal and ubiquitous unconscious murderous fantasies. This indicates, as Lyndsey Stonebridge (2011b, 2011a) has also aptly pointed out, that the Arendtian and Freudian readings of history are not mutually exclusive and can benefit from each other. Or as Arendt herself put it '(t)he need of reason is not inspired by the quest for truth but by the quest for meaning' (Arendt, 1978, p. 15).

Still, the resistance to employing psychoanalysis in the study of the long history of so-called 'inhumanity', as chronicled by many scholars and, in the end, by Norman Cohn himself, seems to lie in the fact that it risks normalising and trivialising evil. Nonetheless, perhaps this resistance does not only lie in the ethical implications of normalising evil but in the threatening prospect of seeing evil as a potential aspect of the normal self. In 'The Meaning of Eichmann', Astor argued accordingly that 'people's difficulty in reacting [to the Nazi crimes] is connected, as some psychologists have suggested, with a numbing inner awareness of the possibilities of violence that exist in mankind' (Astor, 1961, p. 10). And Freud might have agreed with this statement. We all are, in other words, in a constant battle with 'Nazism's inner demons'. The role of psychoanalysis lies in providing a language for understanding these demons, re-imagining our political and historical lives, and tracing the ever-evasive meaning of what it is to be human.

Acknowledgements

I am particularly indebted to Mr Richard Astor who very kindly gave me permission to study David Astor's private collection of papers, held at Boodle and Hatfield law firm in London, as well as solicitor Mr Geoffrey Todd and Ms Paula Corbett for their eagerness to help in this process. My gratitude also goes to Daniel Pick, Lyndsey Stonebridge, Dan Stone, Shaul Bar-Haim, Helen Tyson, Elizabeth Coles, Jacqueline Rose, and Michalis Sialaros who read and commented on this paper at various stages of my writing.

Bibliography

Primary sources

Alvarez, A. (1970) 'From Keystone to Kafka', *The Observer*, 15 November, p. 30.
Astor, B. (1955) '60th birthday letter to Anna Freud'. Anna Freud Papers (1880–1998), AF/03/07/02/041, Freud Museum, London.
Astor, D. (1961) 'The meaning of Eichmann', *The Observer*, 26 March, p. 10.
Astor, D. (1962a) 'Letter to Norman Cohn'. Astor Papers, Box 10 BH, Folder: Project General 1958–1962, Boodle Hatfield, London.
Astor, D. (1962b) 'Towards a study of the scourge', *Encounter*, August, pp. 60–62.
Astor, D. (1964) 'Letter to Anna Freud'. Astor Papers: Box 10 BH, Folder: Project Sponsors 1962–1964, Boodle Hatfield, London.
Astor, D. (1965) 'Letter to Norman Cohn'. Astor Papers, Box 10 BH, Folder: Columbus Trust General 1964–65, Boodle Hatfield, London.
Bloodworth, D. (1955) 'The meaning of the witch-hunt', *The Observer*, 13 November, p. 2.
Cohn, N. (1962a) 'Letter to David Astor'. Astor Papers, Box 10 BH, Folder: Project General 1958–1962, Boodle Hatfield, London.
Cohn, N. (1962b) 'Letter to David Astor'. Astor Papers, Box 10 BH, Folder: Project General1958–1962, Boodle Hatfield, London.
Cohn, N. (1962c) 'Letter to David Astor'. Astor Papers, Box 10 BH, Folder: Project General1958–1962, Boodle Hatfield, London.
Cohn, N. (1963a) 'Progress report to 1st December 1963'. Astor Papers, Box 10 BH, Folder: 6th, 7th, 8th, 9th Meetings of the Working Party, Boodle Hatfield, London.

Cohn, N. (1963b) 'Work in "political psychology" in Germany'. Astor Papers, Box 10 BH, Folder: 6th, 7th, 8th, 9th Meetings of the Working Party, Boodle Hatfield, London.
Cohn, N. (1965) 'Letter to Nevitt Sanford'. Astor Papers, Box 10, BH, Folder: American Study1965–1966, Boodle Hatfield, London.
Egginton, J. (1971) 'Women's lib', *The Observer*, 31 January, p. 17.
Freud, A. (1948) 'Educational and psychological techniques for changing mental attitudes affecting international understanding'. UNESCO Documentary Database. Available at: http://unesdoc.unesco.org/images/0015/001581/158149eb.pdf (Accessed: 11 April 2016).
Freud, A. (1964) 'Letter to David Astor'. Astor Papers: Box 10 BH, Folder: Project Sponsors1962–1964, Boodle Hatfield, London.
Gorer, G. (1960) 'Putting us in our places', *The Observer*, 3 January, p. 9.
Gorer, G. (1971) 'Freudian interpretations', *The Observer*, 16 May, p. 32.
Green, O. (1952) 'The meaning of Maoism', *The Observer*, 12 October, p. 6.
Hoffer, W. (1956) 'Medicine since Freud', *The Observer*, 20 May, p. 8.
Kenyon, K. (1965) 'The real meaning of Masada', *The Observer*, 11 April, p. 6.
Mead, M. (1948) 'Transatlantic man', *The Observer*, 29 August, p. 3.
Orwell, G. (2010) 'To David Astor', in Davison, P. (ed.) *George Orwell: a life in letters*. London: Harvill Secker, pp. 421–423.
Our Psychology Correspondent (1965) 'Psychoanalysis and the universities', *The Observer*, 14 March, p. 12.
Pick, D. (2006) 'Norman Cohn interview'.
Procter-Gregg, N. (1956a) 'Conflicts & cure', *The Observer*, 6 May, p. 12.
Procter-Gregg, N. (1956b) 'The mind of man', *The Observer*, 29 April, p. 7.
Rycroft, C. (1961a) 'Problem children', *The Observer*, 5 February, p. 27.
Rycroft, C. (1961b) 'The Kleinian viewpoint', *The Observer*, 9 April, p. 3.
Sampson, A. (1973) 'The meaning of Watergate', 4 August, p. 11.
Stafford-Clark, D. (1956) 'Freud and religion', *The Observer*, 27 May, p. 4.
Storr, A. (1969) 'Churchill', *The Observer*, 30 May.
Taylor, G. R. (1950) 'The proper study', *The Observer*, 11 June, p. 4.
The Observer (1948a) 'Profile-C. G. Jung', 11 July, p. 3.
The Observer (1948b) 'The meaning of Malan', 30 May, p. 4.
The Observer (1953) 'Profile-Dr. Ernest Jones', 26 July, p. 3.
The Times (1952) 'Dr. Karen Horney', 6 December, p. 8.
The Times (1960) 'Mrs. Melanie Klein: exploring the child mind', 23 September.
Toynbee, P. (1956) 'Freud and literature', *The Observer*, 3 June, p. 10.
Toynbee, P. (1963) 'Mistress to an age', *The Observer*, 5 May, p. 26.
Tynan, K. (1958) 'Traumatic values', *The Observer*, 27 July, p. 13.

Books

Cohn, N. (1957) *The pursuit of the millennium*. London: Secker & Warburg.
Cohn, N. (1967) *Warrant for genocide: the myth of the Jewish world-conspiracy and the protocols of the elders of Zion*. London: Eyre & Spottiswoode.
Cohn, N. (1975) *Europe's inner demons: an enquiry inspired by the great witch-hunt*. Suffolk: Chatto/Heinemann for Sussex University Press.

Dicks, H. (1972) *Licensed mass murder: a socio-psychological study of some SS killers.* London: Chatto; Heinemann Educational, for Sussex University Press.
Kenrick, D. and Puxon, G. (1972) *The destiny of Europe's gypsies.* London: Chatto-Heinemann Educational for Sussex University Press.
Larner, C. (1981) *Enemies of God: the witch hunt in Scotland.* London: Chatto & Windus.
Sachs, A. (1973) *Justice in South Africa.* Berkeley: University of California Press.

Secondary sources

Anderson, P. (1968) 'Components of the national culture', *New Left Review*, 50, 3–57.
Arendt, H. (1978) *The life of the mind.* San Diego, New York and London: Harcourt, Inc.
Arendt, H. (1994) *Eichmann in Jerusalem: a report on the banality of evil.* London: Penguin.
Briggs, A. (1964) 'Drawing a new map of learning', in Daiches, D. *The idea of a new university: an experiment in Sussex.* Cambridge, Mass.: MIT Press, pp. 60–80.
Cockett, R. (1991) *David Astor and the observer.* London: Andre Deutsch Limited.
Cragoe, M. (2015) 'Asa Briggs and the University of Sussex, 1961–1976', in Taylor, M. (ed.) *The age of Asa: Lord Briggs, public life and history in Britain since 1945.* Basingstoke and New York: Palgrave Macmillan, pp. 225–247.
Guttman, S. A. (1969) 'Robert Waelder—1900–1967', *International Journal of Psycho-Analysis* 50, 269–273.
Hilberg, R. (1961) *The destruction of the European Jews.* London: W. H. Allen.
Karydaki, D. (2016) *Mapping 'man's inhumanity to man': a historical and historiographical investigation into the Columbus Centre for the Study of Persecution and Genocide (University of Sussex, 1962–1981).* London: Birkbeck College.
Klein, M. (1923) 'The development of a child', *International Journal of Psycho-Analysis* 4, 419–474.
Klein, M. (1935) 'A contribution to the psychogenesis of manic-depressive states', *International Journal of Psycho-Analysis* 16, 145–174.
Klein, M. (1946) 'Notes on some schizoid mechanisms', *International Journal of Psycho-Analysis* 27, 99–110.
Lamont, W. (2007) 'Obituary: Professor Norman Cohn', *The Independent*, 29 September.
Langer, W. (1972) *The mind of Adolf Hitler: the secret wartime report.* New York: Basic Books.
Langer, W. L. (1958) 'The next assignment', *The American Historical Review* 63 (2), 283–304.
Lay, P. (2007) 'Obituary: Norman Cohn', *The Guardian*, 9 August.
Lewis, J. (2016) *David Astor: a life in print.* London: Jonathan Cape.
Lighthill, J. (1989) 'Foreword: the Freud memorial professorship at University College London', in Sandler, J. (ed.) *Dimensions of Psychoanalysis.* London: Karnac Books.
Loewenberg, P. (1971) 'The psychohistorical origins of the Nazi youth cohort', *The American Historical Review* 76 (5).
Loewenstein, R. M. (1970) 'Heinz Hartmann—1894–1970', *The International Journal of Psychoanalysis* 51, 417–419.

Mitscherlich, A. and Mitscherlich, M. (1975) *The inability to mourn: principles of collective behavior.* New York: Grove Press.
Money-Kyrle, R. (1951) 'Dr. John Rickman', *The Times,* 9 July, p. 8.
Pick, D. (2003) 'The id comes to Bloomsbury', *The Guardian,* 16 August.
Pick, D. (2012) *The pursuit of the Nazi mind: Hitler, Hess, and the analysts.* Oxford: Oxford University Press.
Reitlinger, G. R. (1953) *The final solution: the attempt to exterminate the Jews of Europe, 1939–1945.* London: Vallentine, Mitchell.
Reitlinger, G. R. (1956) *The SS: alibi of a nation, 1922–1945.* London: Heinemann.
Rieff, P. (1959) *Freud: the mind of the moralist.* New York: Viking Press.
Rose, J. (1998) *States of fantasy.* Oxford: Oxford University Press.
Sampson, A. (2001) 'Observing David Astor', *The Observer,* 9 December.
Sandler, J. (ed.) (1989) *Dimensions of psychoanalysis.* London: Karnac Books.
Stonebridge, L. (2009) '"What does death represent to the individual?" psychoanalysis and wartime', *differences: a Journal of Feminist Cultural Studies* 20 (1), 102–116.
Stonebridge, L. (2011a) 'Refugee style: Hannah Arendt and the perplexities of rights', *Textual Practice* 25 (1), 71–85.
Stonebridge, L. (2011b) *The judicial imagination: writing after Nuremberg.* Edinburgh: Edinburgh University Press.
Thomson, M. (2006) *Psychological subjects: identity, culture, and health in twentieth-century Britain.* Oxford: Oxford University Press.
Trilling, L. (1955) *Freud and the crisis of our culture.* Boston: Beacon Press.
Winnicott, D. (1964) 'Strength out of misery', *The Observer,* 31 May, p. 33.
Young-Bruehl, E. (2008) *Anna Freud: a biography.* New Haven and London: Yale University Press.

Chapter 11

Reaching into the blind-spot
Rape, trauma and identification in *Blasted*

Leah Sidi

Sarah Kane's first play, *Blasted* (first performed in 1995), begins her lifelong project of creating a formally innovative style of theatre in which painful mental experiences might be simulated for an audience. In attempting to create what she termed 'experiential' theatre, Kane developed dramatic techniques that aimed to disrupt the audience's viewing practice and place them *within* the experience of a mind under mental distress. Whilst she never gave a full definition of the term, Kane set out her understanding of 'experientialism' most directly in an interview, while discussing Jeremy Weller's play, *Mad*, which she had seen at the Edinburgh Festival in 1992 before writing *Blasted*, her first full length play. In this description of a 'totally experiential' play, 'experiential' theatre is directly related to imaginatively and emotionally entering the space of mental illness:

> Instead of sitting, detached, and mildly interested, and 'considering mental illness as an intellectual conceit, [...] *Mad* took me to hell, [...] and the night I saw it I made a decision about the kind of theatre I wanted to make – experiential. [...] It was a bit like being given a vaccine. I was mildly ill for a few days afterwards but that jab of sickness protected me from a far more serious illness'.
>
> (Sierz, 2000, p. 92)

For Kane, Weller's work – the 'only piece of theatre to have ever changed [her] life' – allowed her to enter the space of mental illness in a non-intellectual manner, with the pathology embodied in the drama actually enacted upon her in a kind of mental inoculation (Kane, 1998, p. 12). She described this theatrical encounter spatially, as an experience of moving *through* one mental space and into another, being 'taken to a place of extreme mental discomfort and distress – and popped out the other end' (Sierz, 2000, p. 92). For Kane, then, the 'experiential' ideal to which her theatre apparently aspired was one in which distress is experienced *from within*, and in a genuine manner – a real, smaller dose of pain to ward off 'far more serious illness'.

In *Blasted*, we encounter the mental consequences of violation 'experientially', insofar as Kane invites us to look through a lens which distorts the world according to the logic of a traumatised consciousness. Kane uses a combination of contrasting theatrical styles (naturalism, Brechtian theatre, and expressionism) to replicate a form of mental breakdown within the playtext itself, without 'considering mental illness as an intellectual conceit' (Ibid). Kane's own self-curated account of her development as a writer suggests that seeing Weller's *Mad* represented a turning point in her artistic aims and methods. *Mad* 'was a piece of devised and confessional theatre in which a group of performers, predominantly female, talked about their personal relationships, their experiences of clinical depression and the treatment they had received' (Iball, 2008, p. 28). In its focus on the experiences of mental illness and personal relationships of women, *Mad* resonates with the themes of the Kane's first experiments with dramatic writing: a trio of monologues entitled *Sick*, which she wrote whilst an undergraduate at Bristol University. These monologues written for women include *Starved*, which details the experience of a teenage girl suffering from bulimia and sectioned under the Mental Health Act; *What She Said*, which tells the speaker's story of her first experience in a same-sex relationship; and *Comic Monologue* in which an unnamed woman recounts her oral rape at the hands of her boyfriend Kevin, and concludes that the trauma of rape is one from which the victim can never recover. Kane's move from writing monologues to writing *Blasted* (via seeing Weller's play) marked a shift in the way in which these themes of mental pain, pathology and sexuality were to appear in her works. *Blasted* picks up the theme of domestic rape that was the central concern of *Comic Monologue*, but does not have any character voice the mental consequences of rape onstage. Unlike the speakers in *Sick*, the characters onstage in *Blasted* are extremely reticent when it comes to actually voicing any aspect of their interior life. This lack of verbalisation of the effects of rape and violence in *Blasted* have led some critics to view it as an amoral, judgement-free play.[1] Nevertheless neither authorial judgement nor the mental consequences of violence are removed from the concerns of *Blasted*. Rather they are *relocated*, relegated or elevated, from the play's narrative into the play's form and structure. The characters of *Blasted* do not disclose their inner lives in a confessional manner, unlike the speakers of Weller's *Mad* or of Kane's *Sick* monologues, because the play itself is an attempt to enact the inner life of a person who has been violated.

Approaching *Blasted*'s affective structure from a psychoanalytic perspective enables us to uncover and articulate the way in which Kane uses that which is *unseen* in order to manipulate her audiences' encounters with representations of sexual violence. André Green argues in his book on psychoanalytic theatre criticism that:

> The aim of a psycho-analytic reading is the search for the emotional springs that make the spectacle an affective matrix in which the spectator

sees himself involved and feels himself not only solicited but welcomed, as if the spectacle was intended for him.

(Green, 1979, p. 18)

For Green, this 'affective matrix' is located in the 'architecture' of the play itself, encompassing the writing style and narrative as well as the matrix of objects, sounds, rhythms and temporalities taking place on stage (Ibid., p. 62). Kane's first play is unusual insofar as this architecture is constructed through a contrast between forms of violence which are either completely obscured or hyper-visual. In Ancient Greek tragedy, violence was narrated but invisible. It was relegated into the 'obskene', or offstage – the term from which we get the modern word 'obscenity' – a process Kane seemingly had no truck with, claiming 'I've always hated those plays – everything happens offstage' (Sierz, 2001, p. 109). Nevertheless, *Blasted*'s architecture exploits the invisibility of 'obskene' violence alongside excessive onstage violence (obscenity in the modern sense) in order to 'experientially' represent the mental consequences of traumatic sexual assault, in which an originary moment of violence is both repressed and inescapable.

From a psychoanalytic perspective, *Blasted* represses the rape of its female protagonist, Cate, into the structure of the play itself, temporally eliding it in a scene break. *Blasted* stages the narrative of Ian, 45, and Cate, 21, arriving at a hotel room in Leeds. Throughout the first scene Ian, a racist and homophobic tabloid journalist, physically and psychologically abuses Cate. Cate has a series of fits which appear to be both psychosomatic and epileptic. Scene two takes place the following morning in which it emerges that Ian has raped Cate during the night (during the scene break). From this moment the naturalist style of the play begins to fall apart. Cate disappears through the bathroom window, and an unnamed, generically foreign soldier appears at the hotel room door. An explosion blasts a hole in the back of the set. The soldier rapes Ian and sucks out his eyes whilst narrating the atrocities he has committed in an unspecified war. Following this, the soldier takes his own life. Cate returns from the war zone carrying a baby which has died, buries it in the floor and leaves in search of food. The final scene contains eight tableaux of Ian performing abject acts (defecating, masturbating, attempting to eat the baby) separated by blackouts, after which he buries himself in the floor and '*dies with relief*', only to wake up again and find it is raining (Kane, 2001a, p. 60). Cate returns with blood seeping down her legs having found food and feeds him, and he thanks her.

Twice in the play does Cate emerge from the 'obskene' as a bloodied messenger of the invisible violence enacted against the play's only female body. The play caused a now-famous media storm when it opened, with tabloids and broadsheets alike condemning its explicit content and experimental style. Since Kane's suicide in 1999, both newspaper critics and academic criticism have re-assessed her first work. Like the original newspaper reviews, however, much subsequent academic criticism is devoted to onstage obscenity in the play, reading it variously as typical 1990s 'in-yer-face' shock tactics,[2] Jacobean metaphysical concerns,[3] or an attempt to ethically re-focus the audience's attention on contemporary war, and violence in the media.[4] Yet in many of these academic works, Cate's off-stage rapes tend to be relegated to a background context and coda to the more 'real' violence that takes place onstage. In 2007 Kim Solga's feminist re-reading of *Blasted* noted '[a] curious blind spot remains in the critical response to Sarah Kane's *Blasted*: the rape of Cate by Ian' (Solga, 2007, p. 347). Solga's essay represents a departure from previous Kane criticism insofar as she attempts to correct 'Cate's marginalisation in criticism of the play, and especially by the near-total lack of scholarly engagement with the unique representational circumstances of her rape' (Ibid). These 'unique circumstances' are the consistent invisibility of acts of violence against Cate's body in a play in which explicit violence is frequently staged. The rape of Cate is not only a 'blind spot' in critical approaches to the work; it is a blind spot in the play itself which thematically mirrors the gaping hole left in the wall by the mortar bomb. With the exception of a notable chapter by Elaine Aston (2003), there remains little literature on the representation of the female body in Kane's play following Solga's article, and none on the specific mechanisms by which Kane represents female subjectivity in *Blasted*. Ian Ward (2013) has contributed an interesting analysis of Kane's representations of rape from a legal humanities perspective. Ward emphasises the specificity of the rapes in *Blasted* and *Phaedra's Love*, and the possibility of reading these plays as a critique of rape myths. In what follows, my own focus on Cate is intended to shift criticism away from a preoccupation with violence per se towards a psychoanalytic consideration of the dramatic mechanisms by which Kane enacts a particular version of psychic life for her audience. This is not to deny the significance of the play as a commentary on war, especially in the context of the Bosnian conflict.[5] Rather it is to suggest that Kane thematises the shocking, frequently mediatised male violence of warfare through the perspective of a mind that has already been shattered and remade by an unseen and socially unrepresentable act of rape.

Traumatic 'architecture'

The rape of Cate and her subsequent absence is itself a cornerstone of *Blasted*'s architecture, without which the two halves of the play – naturalistic and non-naturalistic; domestic and military – struggle to hold together. As Kane explained:

> [T]he soldier is the way he is because of the situation, *but the situation exists because of what Ian has created in that room, of what he has done to Cate* [...] If you skip the connection between all this, if you skip the emotional reason, the play does appear to be completely broken backed, just split into two halves which means it fails totally.
>
> (Saunders, 2002, pp. 45–46, my emphasis)

Kane's representations of rape in both domestic and military spaces in this play suggest a kind of equivalence between forms of sexual violence. Describing the process by which she arrived at writing *Blasted*, Kane suggests that the combination of settings in the play is based in a belief that there is something inherent to all sexual violence that links domestic and military rape. What's more, she suggests that the kernel of rampant military sexual violence and atrocity is present in the act of domestic rape:

> I asked myself: 'What could possibly be the connection between a common rape in a Leeds hotel room and what's happening in Bosnia?' And then this penny dropped and I thought: 'Of course, it's obvious. One is the seed and the other is the tree'.
> (Sierz, 2000, p. 101)

Kane's treatment of sexual trauma in *Blasted* is historically situated in a moment in which trauma, and specifically PTSD, was emerging as the dominant category for theorising the mental consequence of violence. Whilst we do not have a record of her reading on the subject, Kane almost certainly had an understanding of the version of trauma presented in the PTSD diagnosis, given its rising cultural prevalence in mental health discourses, the women's movement, and feminist theatre in the 1980s and 1990s in the UK. Kane's own summary of this version of trauma can be found in her fourth play, *Crave* (1998), in which C's experience of sexual abuse is described as a temporal gap: 'And though she cannot remember she cannot forget/ And has been hurtling away from that moment ever since' (Kane, 2001b, p. 158). In her important book on the history of rape, Joanna Bourke warns of essentialising or universalising sexual violence. For Bourke, such an attitude risks eliminating the specific social and political circumstances in which rapists commit violence (Bourke, 2007). On the other hand, Roger Luckhurst suggests that studies of trauma and the campaign for PTSD diagnosis have taken the opposite view, insisting on a measure of equivalence across all potentially trauma-inducing events. Luckhurst argues that the increasing popularity of the 'trauma paradigm' is rooted in a deliberate comparing of different contexts of violence, similar to Kane's comments on the similarities between different forms of rape:

> Advocates [of trauma theory are] self-consciously comparative, seeking out links to studies of the psychological reactions of those who survived the Hiroshima bombing, the victims of Nazi persecution, the consequences of slavery and segregation on African-American identity, and women who [have] suffered incest or rape trauma.
> (Luckhurst, 2008, pp. 61–62)

Similarly, Didier Fassin and Richard Rechtman suggest that a 'new condition of victimhood [is] established through the concept of trauma', whereby violent acts with various political and social significances are understood as causing equivalent psychological symptoms, and enter a metaphorical framework in which they are comparable. Kane's representation of sexual violence in *Blasted* seems to take place somewhere between these two poles, and there is certainly some ambiguity in her perspectives on the universality (or not) or traumatic violence.[6] Following Cate's rape in *Blasted*, violence is repeated, magnified and distorted, but always in reference to the initial hidden act of abuse. The specificity of Cate's rape is the fact of its invisibility, as Kane uses Cate's literal absence from the stage to suggest that the consequences of domestic rape and child abuse include the obliteration of the victimised subject from her own psychic experience. This invisibility is compounded by the references to it in the sexual violence perpetrated against Ian by the soldier, which both signifies for itself *and* emerges from the invisible moment of Cate's trauma. The resonances and articulations between the violent acts staged between men in *Blasted* and those which remain invisible come together to present a potential audience with a dramatic architecture which is only coherent when the onstage acts are considered in light of what is left out.

Kane's specific vision of the mental consequences of sexual violence can be best understood through Sándor Ferenczi's 'mimetic' model of trauma, which theorises the victim's 'identification or [...] introjection of the aggressor' (Ferenczi, 1949, p. 228).[7] Ferenczi famously disagreed with Freud over the latter's rejection of the validity of patient's testimonies of childhood sexual abuse. According to Ferenczi's mimetic model, the survivor's ability to perceive is shattered by the traumatic event to the extent that they are no longer able to experience themselves as an autonomous subject.[8] It alters the way the survivor actually sees the outside world, enacting 'a pervasive change in someone's perceptual world' (Frankel, 2002, p. 102). As a consequence, the survivor 'mimetically incorporate[s] the thoughts and feelings of the aggressor', and their own subject-position becomes occupied by the traumatising 'other' (Leys, 2000, p. 173). The survivor is 'shocked out of consciousness into a condition of trance-like incorporation or imitation of the violent other' (Ibid., p. 175). Kane enacts this process both on Cate and on the structure of *Blasted* itself, in an attempt to signal and simulate the decimation of identity that follows sexual abuse. On the one hand, following her rape, Cate's interior world is slowly invaded by Ian's 'perceptual world' as she internalises his misogyny and paranoia and reappears in scene five having abandoned what little signs of subjectivity she had betrayed to the audience in scene one. On the other, the play itself has Cate and her narrative 'shocked out' of it by the soldier and the mortar bomb (Ibid.). The reader and potential audience member is left with nobody but Ian and the Soldier to identify with, as Ian's worldview is totalised and his paranoid and racist fantasies seem to be confirmed. In terms of the play's 'architecture', the consequence of Cate's rape is the absolute dominance of Ian in the potential audience's field of vision.

In *Blasted*, instead of showing us the rape of Cate, Kane shows us its effects – its traumatic invisibility and the overwhelming repetitions of violence that follow. In so doing, she demonstrates her familiarity with the major cultural assumptions surrounding trauma in the 1990s. Ruth Leys summarises these assumptions as follows:

> The idea that, owing to the emotions of terror and surprise caused by certain events, the mind is split or dissociated: it is unable to register the wound to the psyche because the ordinary mechanisms of awareness and cognition are destroyed. As a result, the victim is unable to recollect and integrate the hurtful experience into normal consciousness: instead she is haunted or possessed by intrusive traumatic memories. The experience of trauma, fixed or frozen in time, refuses to be represented as past, but is perpetually re-experienced as a painful, dissociated, traumatic present.
> (Leys, 2000, p. 20)

By the time of Kane's writing, the dissociation, loss, and symptomatic repetition of traumatic memory according to PTSD had become the cultural prism *par excellence* for understanding the effects of violence on mental life.[9] Returning to Ferenczi's much earlier understanding of trauma adds a third effect to this model – one which is outside of mainstream PTSD diagnosis. As well as affectively losing and then re-experiencing a traumatic moment, Ferenczi argues that the victim of sexual assault experiences a powerful identification with the perpetrator (Ferenczi, 1949). In *Blasted* Kane adapts the loss-repetition prism to include precisely this form of identification. By examining the architecture of *Blasted* in light of this dissociation-repetition-identification model, it is possible to see that despite her actual absence on stage, Cate remains at the core of the play's 'affective matrix' (Green, 1979, p. 18).

Dissociation and loss

Blasted manipulates the viewing experience of a potential spectator in an attempt to place them *within* the experience of traumatic dissociation, repetition and identification. The play begins with a situation that would be at home in naturalist theatre: two people enter a hotel room, previous connections between them are revealed through dialogue, and conflict occurs. The opening scene follows the rules of naturalism, as everything that occurs can be explained by the internal logic of the plot – either suggested (Cate's fits are caused by abuse) or explicit (Cate is here because Ian asked her to be). At the beginning of scene one for example, there is a bunch of flowers in the hotel room. Their presence is consistent with the expensiveness of the room and with Ian's romantic intentions. The audience may assume that Ian has requested for them to be there before arriving. At the end of the scene Ian picks them up and gives them to Cate.

In the beginning of scene two the flowers have begun to function in terms of a new signifying logic for which the audience has not been prepared: *'The bouquet of flowers is now ripped apart and scattered around the room'* (Kane, 2001a, p. 24). Whilst it is possible that either Ian or Cate themselves ripped apart and distributed the flowers, the event is neither discussed, nor does it fit with the events of the night as they emerge from Ian and Cate as the scene progresses. The destruction of the flowers does not feature in the narrative the audience pieces together regarding the events of the night in which Cate and Ian go to bed together and hold hands, following which Ian rapes Cate and performs violent oral sex on her causing her to bleed through the night. The bouquet, in other words, no longer responds to the 'ordinary mechanisms of awareness and cognition' of naturalism that were established in scene one (Leys, 2000, p. 20). Instead they belong to a new form of reference and signification, in which their destruction obliquely points to the unseen violence that occurred in the scene break and is now emerging outside of realism's representative channels. The blasting of a hole into the back wall of the stage at the end of scene two is an escalation of the blasting of the bouquet, as the violence of and towards the set escalates alongside the violence perpetrated by and towards the characters. These physical forms of blasting, reflected in the play's title, point to an increasingly ubiquitous form of destruction emerging from an 'obskene' source. Violence begins to erupt into the visible theatre space without a specific theatrical genre or narrative to contain it, potentially disorientating the audience.

This disruption of the logic of naturalism is also detectable on the level of narrative. As several of *Blasted*'s initial reviewers noted, even before the entrance of the soldier, Cate and Ian's characters emerge with inconsistencies.[10] Ian was a journalist in scene one, but scene two reveals him as a slightly unbelievable Pinteresque secret agent (or a journalist with paranoid fantasies in which he is in MI6). Cate on the other hand goes from being so averse to sexual contact that she has a psychosomatic fit in response to being kissed, to being willing to perform oral sex and bite her aggressor's penis in an act of revenge. Whilst neither of these inconsistencies is totally unbelievable, they nevertheless destabilise the kind of narrative logic that scene one has established for the audience. Where aggression and violence were contained within the logic of a domestic narrative, now they emerge unexpectedly from sources outside of the premised plot. The disorienting experience of viewing these scenes might undergo a split, as the audience observe the unfolding of the plot and experience an emotional response to it on the one hand, and simultaneously attempt to assimilate the illogical additions to it on the other. The soldier's entrance from an unnamed warzone escalates the disorientation that has been playing itself out since Cate's un-staged rape. The rape marks a gap in the potential audience's narrative experience, subsequent to which the play's means of signification are irrevocably altered.

Repetition

The events and images that unfold in *Blasted* follow the logic of traumatic repetition, constantly referring the audience back to a moment of unrepresented violence. Psychic repetition of a painful event has been a key aspect of all theories of trauma, going back to Freud's *Beyond the Pleasure Principle*. This repetition disrupts the survivor's internal chronology, holding them in a traumatic present rather than allowing memory to be consigned to the past. To return to Leys' summary: 'the victim [...] is *haunted or possessed by intrusive traumatic memories*. The experience of trauma [...] is *perpetually re-experienced as painful, dissociated, traumatic present*' (Leys, 2000, p. 3). The architecture of *Blasted* itself becomes possessed by distorted repetitions of Cate's rape. Ian's onstage assault and subsequent breakdown in the expressionist tableaux of scene five contain thematic and formal echoes of his unseen aggression towards Cate.

The representation of the rape of Ian especially parallels the simulation of the rape of Cate in scene two. After Cate faints following a 'fit' in scene two, Ian '*puts the gun to* [Cate's] *head, lies between her legs, and simulates sex*'. As he orgasms she begins another 'fit', in which she laughs hysterically '*until she isn't laughing anymore, she's crying her heart out*' (Kane, 2001a, p. 27). When the soldier later rapes Ian, he does so in the same position, and he too is '*crying his heart out*' (Ibid., p. 39). This connection between the simulated rape of Cate and the actual rape of Ian is one that Kane herself was emphatic about, deploring her reviewers for 'ignoring [...] the fact that [the soldier] does it with a gun to his head which Ian has done to Cate earlier – and he's crying his eyes out as he does it' (Saunders, 2002, p. 46). But the violence of scene three is not simply a reiteration of the simulation of scene two. They are both repetitions, references to an assault that is not staged but eclipsed by the chronological structuring of the play which elides the rape of Cate in the scene break. Each act of violence builds on the last in a reiterative rather than narrative logic. By the time we get to the final tableaux the narrative logic of the play has broken down completely. Ian's abject acts nevertheless escalate the thematic concerns of the first scene. Masturbation connects with the first (forced) sex act, cannibalism with Cate's disgust at Ian's meat-eating, defecating with the constant trips to the bathroom, burying himself in the floor with the hole in the back wall – the first violation of the stage itself. Rather than a simple litany of degradation, the play follows a careful pattern of distortion, repetition and escalation, giving its audience visual and thematic connections between the scenes without a traditionally unfolding narrative that provides a logic of 'before' and 'after'. The potential audience is therefore *put through* the effects of traumatic repetition, experiencing narrative dissociation, confusion, and repeated reference to an invisible source.

Identification

The third mechanism by which Kane simulates a traumatic perspective in *Blasted* is through the absence of Cate herself, and the audience's implicit identification with Ian. According to Ferenczi, the traumatised subject literally leaves themselves in order to avoid feeling the pain of abuse, and takes up the subject position of their own aggressor instead: 'I do not feel the pain inflicted upon me at all, because I do not exist. On the other hand, I do feel the pleasure gratification of the attacker, which I am able to perceive' (Ferenczi, 1988, p. 104). Jay Frankel has noted the extent to which this identification is understood as a survival mechanism in Ferenczi's work: 'Knowing the aggressor "from the inside" in such a closely observed way allows the child to gauge at each moment precisely how to appease, seduce, flatter, placate, or otherwise disarm the aggressor' (Frankel, 2002, p. 104). This is not done consciously. Rather '[i]dentifying with the aggressor involves *feeling* what one is expected to feel, whether this means feeling what the aggressor wants his particular victim to feel or feeling what the aggressor himself feels' (Ibid.). In *Blasted* the audience learns of Cate's rape and yet is invited to identify with the play's original perpetrator through his continuing presence and demise onstage. Cate herself is absent from the overwhelming scenes of violence in the second half. The potential spectator is taken out of a pseudo-naturalistic situation in which it was possible to empathise with the female protagonist, into one in which the images of male violence are so explicit they seem to render the first half of the play irrelevant. By creating a situation in which it is very difficult to see anything but the immediate images of Cate's perpetrator onstage, Kane simulates the kind of traumatic identification found in Ferenczi's theory of identification in trauma.

Following Cate's rape, the dramatic universe and her interior world become overrun by Ian's 'perceptual world' (Frankel, 2002, p. 102). Ian's paranoia and rampant racism construct a fantasy that the outside world is violent and threatening. Afraid that the 'Wogs and Pakis' are taking over the city outside the window and that the woman he is attempting to possess is a 'nigger-lover', Ian perceives himself as under attack from a myriad of others (Kane, 2001a, p. 4, p. 5). In the first scene Cate resists both the racism and the sense of external threat. Whilst Ian needs to answer the door with a loaded gun, Cate knows the name of the waiter bringing up the room service. Ian is outraged that Cate attends football matches, assuming that she would 'get stabbed' by 'fucking football fans' (Ibid., p. 19). The world that Ian reads as teeming with violence is one that Cate is initially happy to interact with.

After the scene break in which Ian rapes Cate, the violent and threatening fantasy through which Ian sees the world begins to seep into Cate's perceptual frame, and then takes over the dramatic universe itself. Throughout the scene, Cate absorbs Ian's fear of the outside world. She colludes with his earlier assessment of the view from the window commenting that it 'looks like there's a war on' (Ibid., p. 33). And whilst she was incredulous at Ian's fear of opening the door in scene one, in scene two she responds to knocks at the door with terror. Following Cate's coming around to the perspective that the world is filled with violence and threat, the world of the play actually changes and she herself leaves the stage, only to return briefly after the onstage violence has occurred. Cate's narrative is 'shocked out' of the play itself, and the potential audience are left only with Ian's narrative to identify with, although this narrative is constantly destabilised by the dissociations and repetitions outlined above (Leys, 2000, p. 175).

Conclusion

From an 'experiential' perspective, an unseen and temporally elided violation acts as a catalyst for the entrance of male violence into *Blasted* and for Cate's own disappearance, leaving the audience only Ian and the soldier to identify with. Following the rape of Cate, which is invisible, all subsequent violence is presented with startling explicitness and the dramatic universe of the play becomes a site of extreme aggression. For Ferenczi, traumatic confusion 'arises mainly because the attack and the response to it are denied by the guilt-ridden adults, indeed, are treated as deserving punishment' (Leys, 2000, p. 154). The attack itself causes a voiding of subjectivity, but it is the guilt and ambivalence of the attacker that fills the void, as Kane herself knew: 'when people are intensely violent they manage to make the victim feel guilty' (Saunders, 2002, p. 46). In *Blasted*, however, Kane alters this introjection. Ian's violent misogyny and entitlement are so strong that he feels no guilt with regard to his abuse of Cate, and therefore no guilt is introjected by Cate, or into the form of the play. Instead, the world of the play becomes soaked in the violence of Ian and the soldier which seem to block out and overwhelm everything else. Ian as the victim and perpetrator of this violence (against himself and the baby) becomes the play's epicentre, and it is difficult to look past his dominance onstage to see Cate at all. If the play's dominant features and aesthetic identity are its onstage violence, as newspaper reviews and academic criticism seem to suggest, then this violence is engendered by the rape of Cate. In other words, the representational challenges of her rape shape the dramatic universe itself, forming a novel dramaturgy out of the obliteration of the first act of violence.

The extent to which this dominance is successful is demonstrated in the newspaper reviews of the three major London productions that have taken place of *Blasted* since its opening. The now infamous reviews of the play's 1995 premiere largely follow the same pattern: a summary of scenes one and two followed by an extensive list of the abject and violent acts committed onstage, and some gleeful condemnation of them and of the Royal Court's decision to stage the play. Reviewers of the Royal Court's 2001 revival of the production were largely preoccupied with retracting some of the negative sentiment of their previous reviews following Kane's suicide. Nevertheless, one feature that remains from the original reviews is the focus on onstage violence and the degradation of Ian's body.[11] The 2001 reviews largely attempt to justify the onstage violence in the face of Kane's death, either with the argument that scenes just as violent can be seen on news channels (De Jongh, 2001), in Beckett plays, or in Jacobean drama (Bassett, 2001; Nightingale, 2001; Logan, 2001; Spencer, 2001), or with speculation that Kane was making 'a point' about Bosnian violence (Billington, 2001; Nightingale, 2001; Brown, 2001; Spencer, 2001; De Jongh, 2001), or about the personal horrors of depression (Gross, 2001; Smith, 2001; Billington, 2001; Logan, 2001). Reviews of Sean Holmes' 2010 production at the Lyric Hammersmith are more nuanced, the event being at a greater distance from Kane's suicide. Nevertheless, the reviews emphasise the image of Ian's body as the most impactful of the play, and Danny Webb's portrayal of Ian as its stand-out performance. Several reviewers viewed Ian as a modern-day Lear (Clapp, 2010; Spenser, 2010; Murphy, 2010), while others made a comparison between Ian's body at the end of the play and the religious paintings of Francis Bacon (Murphy, 2010; Taylor, 2010; Hitchins, 2010; Billington 2010). The directing, design, and performances of the 2010 production established Ian as the anti-hero of the play, who 'rapes his epileptic former girlfriend and thereby unleashes a surreal storm of retributive horrors that blast the play into a different shape' (Taylor, 2010, p. 1241). These productions, none of which diverged too far from Kane's text, presented their reviewers with a dramatic world which revolved around Ian, in which Cate's narrative was seen as a stepping stone and coda to the savagery suffered and perpetrated by the male characters.

These reviews point to the inevitable problem of attempting to enact a process of forgetting, or disappearing, on an audience. Solga argues that although the unique status of Cate's rape in Kane's oeuvre – as a dramatically and temporally hidden act – might make it stand out from an intellectual perspective, nonetheless its being a non-event onstage does not make it noticeable. If we are to notice it, we can only do so after the fact, when the subsequent sexual assaults refer us back to an original victim, and then only if directorial, design, and performance decisions choose to point an audience in this direction. The rape of Cate is not something we are made to notice so much as something we have to make an effort to see, a blind spot in the visual field of the play. Nevertheless, the violence of the play's second half appears broken-backed without the pattern that links it back to the invisible source. Readings that make use of trauma theory only in relation to the play's male characters cannot therefore account fully for its unusual structure. Reading *Blasted* as the tragic fall of the traumatised anti-hero, for example, Patrick Duggan (2012) concludes that the play is possessed by a violence that is 'chaotic' rather than reiterative and structured. By creating an anti-heroic narrative arc for Ian, and making him the centre of the onstage violence,

Kane invites her reader or potential spectator into an identification with him. She also thwarts this identification by making Ian a repulsive character and by making the formal logic of the play hang on an assault that is invisible and a character who is absent. It is in this way that the experience enacted by *Blasted* most resembles the 'mimetic model' of trauma. Following an invisible act, the audience is only able to see the perpetrator, and only able to identify with him (or with nobody), and yet this identification is rendered senseless because of the breakdowns in form and logic that ensue. Ian's narrative, as a stand-alone story, makes no sense. The sense of the play takes place outside of narrative, as a demonstration and enactment of the consequences of violence that emerges from the 'obskene' and from a woman whom it renders barely visible.

Notes

1. See for example Lublin (2010), Urban (2001) and Rebellato (2010).
2. See for example, Sierz (2000) Rabey (2003).
3. Saunders (2004), Saunders (2002), Pankratz (2010).
4. Urban (2001), Singer (2004).
5. For an excellent article on the Bosnian context and afterlife of *Blasted* see Radosavljević (2012).
6. Whilst Kane's staging of violence in *Blasted, Phaedra's Love* (1996) and *Cleansed*, would seem to represent a certain universalism, in interviews Kane moves from making sweeping connections with different forms of violence (above) to discussing the cultural specificity of rape in certain fields of war (Saunders, 2002, p. 48).
7. Ruth Leys (2000) terms Ferenczi's model of trauma 'mimetic' in her overview of his work in *Trauma: A Genealogy*, in which she distinguishes it from a Freudian 'originary' model of trauma. This should be distinguished from René Girard's famous understanding of 'mimetic violence' which refers to the contagious nature of violence within communities, rather than identification.
8. Mikkel Borch-Jacobsen (1988) has taken ideas about mimetic subjectivity further in *The Freudian Subject*. Here he argues that not only traumatic subjects, but all subjectivity is constituted through identification and mimesis. Whereas Ferenczi argued that the traumatic event destroys a previously whole subject, Borch-Jacobsen maintains that any original sense of subjectivity is illusory. For a comparison between Borch-Jacobsen and Ferenczi, see Leys (2000). For the political implications of such a mimetic approach to subjectivity see Chow (2006).
9. Leading trauma theorist Cathy Caruth noted in 1995, 'this classification and its attendant official acknowledgement of a pathology has provided a category of diagnosis so powerful that it has seemed to engulf everything around it' (Caruth 1995, p. 3).
10. See for example Billington (1995).
11. Aston (2010) argues that the original reviews of *Blasted* 'affect stripped' the play, by focussing only on the body of Ian.

Bibliography

Appignanesi, L. (2008) *Mad, bad and sad: a history of women and the mind doctors from 1800 to the present*. London: Virago.

Aston, E. (2003) *Feminist views on the English stage*. Cambridge University Press: Cambridge.

Aston, E. (2010) 'Reviewing the fabric of *Blasted*'. In G. Saunders and L. De Vos (eds). *Sarah Kane in context*. Manchester: Manchester University Press, pp. 13–27.
Bassett, K. (2001) Independent on Sunday, 8 April. *Theatre Record* 21 (7), 420.
Billington, M. (1995) Guardian, 20 January. *Theatre Record*, 15 (1–2), 39.
Billington, M. (2001) Guardian, 4 April. *Theatre Record* 21 (7), 421.
Billington, M. (2010) Guardian, 29 October. *Theatre Record* 30 (22), 1240.
Borch-Jacobsen, M. (1988) *The Freudian subject*, trans. C. Porter. Stanford University Press: Stanford.
Bourke, J. (2007) *Rape: a history from 1860 to the present*. London: Virago.
Brown, G. (2001) Mail on Sunday, 8 April. *Theatre Record* 21 (7), 422.
Buse, P. (2001) *Drama + theory: critical approaches to modern British drama*. Manchester: Manchester University Press.
Caruth, C. (1995) *Trauma, explorations in memory*. Baltimore: John Hopkins University Press.
Chow, R. (2006) 'Sacrifice, mimesis and the theorizing of victimhood (a speculative essay)', *Representations* 94, 131–149.
Clapp, S. (2010) Observer, 31 October. *Theatre Record* 30 (22), 1240.
De Jongh, N. (2001) Evening Standard, 4 April. *Theatre Record* 21 (7), 418.
Duggan, P. (2012) *Trauma-tragedy: symptoms of contemporary performance*. Manchester: Manchester University Press.
Fassin, D. and R. Rechtman (2009) *The empire of trauma*. Princeton: Princeton University Press.
Ferenczi, S. (1949) 'Confusion of tongues between the adults and the child – the language of tenderness and of passion', *International Journal of Psychoanalysis* 30, 225–230.
Ferenczi, S. (1988) *The clinical diary of Sandor Ferenczi*, trans. by J. Dupont. Cambridge MA: Harvard University Press.
Frankel, J. (2002) 'Exploring Ferenczi's concept of identification with the aggressor: its role in trauma, everyday life and the therapeutic relationship', *Psychoanalytic Dialogues* 12 (1), 101–139.
Green, A. (1979) *The tragic effect: the Oedipus complex in tragedy*, trans. A. Sheridan. Cambridge: Cambridge University Press.
Gross, J. (2001) Sunday Telegraph, 8 April. *Theatre Record* 21 (7), 420.
Hitchins, H. (2010) Evening Standard, 29 October. *Theatre Record* 30 (22), 1240.
Iball, H. (2008) *Sarah Kane's Blasted*. London: Continuum International Publishing Group.
Kane, S. (1998) 'The only thing I remember is …', *The Guardian*, 13 August, A12.
Kane, S. (2001a) Blasted. In *Sarah Kane: complete plays*. London: Methuen Drama, pp. 1–62.
Kane, S. (2001b) Crave. In *Sarah Kane: complete plays*. London: Methuen Drama, pp. 153–202.
Leys, R. (2000) *Trauma: a genealogy*. Chicago: University of Chicago Press.
Logan, B. (2001) Time Out, 11 April. *Theatre Record* 21 (7), 422.
Lublin, Robert I. (2010) '"I love you now": time and desire in the plays of Sarah Kane'. In G. Saunders and L. De Vos (eds.) *Sarah Kane in context*. Manchester: Manchester University Press, pp. 115–125.
Luckhurst, R. (2008) *The trauma question*. Abingdon: Routledge.
Murphy, S. (2010) Metro (London), 3 November. *Theatre Record* 30 (22), 1241.

Nightingale, B. (2001) The Times, 5 April. *Theatre Record* 21 (7), 421.
Pankratz, A. (2010) 'Neither here nor there: theatrical space in Kane's work'. In G. Saunders and L. De Vos (eds.) *Sarah Kane in context*. Manchester: Manchester University Press, pp. 149–160.
Rabey, D. I. (2003) *English drama since 1940*. London: Pearson Education Limited.
Radosavljević, D. (2012) 'Sarah Kane's Illyria as the land of violent love: a Balkan reading of Blasted', *Contemporary Theatre Review* 22 (4), 499–511.
Rebellato, D. (2010) 'Sarah Kane before Blasted, the monologues'. In G. Saunders and L. De Vos (eds.) *Sarah Kane in context*. Manchester: Manchester University Press, pp. 28–44.
Saunders, G. (2002) *Love me or kill me: Sarah Kane and the theatre of extremes*. Manchester: Manchester University Press.
Saunders, G. (2004) '"Out vile jelly": Sarah Kane's Blasted and Shakespeare's King Lear', *New Theatre Quarterly* 20, 69–77.
Shepherd, B. (2000) *A war of nerves*. London: Jonathan Cape.
Sierz, A. (2001) *In-yer-face theatre: British drama today*. London: Faber and Faber.
Singer, A. (2004) 'Don't want to be this: the elusive Sarah Kane', *TDR: The Drama Review* 48, 139–171.
Smith, A. (2001) Observer, 8 April. *Theatre Record* 21 (7), 421.
Solga, K. (2007) 'Blasted's hysteria: rape, realism, and the thresholds of the visible', *Modern Drama* 50 (3), 346–374.
Spencer, C. (2001) Daily Telegraph, 5 April. *Theatre Record* 21 (7), 419.
Spenser, C. (2010) Daily Telegraph, 1 November. *Theatre Record* 30 (22), 1240.
Taylor, P. (2010) Independent, 2 November. *Theatre Record* 30 (22), 1241.
Tinker, J. (1994) Daily Mail, 19 January.*Theatre Record*1995, 42.
Urban, K. (2001) 'An ethics of catastrophe: the theatre of Sarah Kane', *PAJ: A Journal of Performance and Art* 33 (3), 36–46.
Ward, I., (2013) 'Rape and rape mythology in the plays of Sarah Kane', *Comparative Drama* 47, 225–248.

Chapter 12

Freud, the Enlightenment and the Public Sphere[1]

D'Maris Coffman

Over 230 years after the question '*Was ist Aufklärung?*' was posed by Johann Friedrich Zöllner in a sly fashion in a footnote to his piece in the *Berlinische Montasscrhift* on the merits of civil marriage ceremonies, historians, cultural critics, and sociologists are still arguing about the meaning of the Enlightenment (Schmidt, 1996, p. 2). In early 2018, cognitive psychologist's Steven Pinker's polemical treatise, *Enlightenment Now: The Case for Reason, Science, Humanism, and Progress*, crowned the non-fiction bestseller lists with its impassioned defence of progress, its rehabilitation of what the author understands as 'Enlightenment values' and its denouncement of both Donald Trump's demagoguery and the Left's 'identity politics' as illiberal and a threat to the public sphere (Pinker, 2018, p. 31, p. 342). Given the praise heaped upon Pinker's intervention as encapsulating the mood of moderate, educated Americans at the present juncture, there is an urgent need to return to the landmark conversation between Immanuel Kant and Moses Mendelssohn about the meaning of the Enlightenment in order to understand how the eighteenth-century Enlightenment came to represent the ideas often ascribed to it. Only then can there be a meaningful discussion of what role, if any, those ideas should play in the logics governing the public sphere as articulated by Jürgen Habermas. Not surprisingly, Freud has more to contribute to this debate than practitioners of twenty-first century cognitive psychology, who tend to see themselves in what they perceive as the Enlightenment's celebration of rationalism, science and civilisation over ignorance, superstition and violence, but who at the same time fundamentally misunderstand the Enlightenment's contribution to hermeneutics.

In a sense, Pinker's contribution has impoverished our appreciation of the legacy of the Enlightenment where he might have instead enriched it. To illustrate why, I return to contemporary debates in the eighteenth century about how to best characterise the Enlightenment. After careful exploration of different manifestations of the Enlightenment across Europe and the Americas, Freud's own troubled relationship to the Enlightenment's legacy becomes clear, and in turn brings into focus what is at stake in as yet ongoing debates about the role that the Enlightenment played in the genesis of the

DOI: 10.4324/9781003200765-16

public sphere. At the same time, and in some sense paradoxically, the psychoanalytic stance, achieved most immediately through psychoanalytic training practices, offers a lens through which to review and possibly resolve some of the difficulties that our society faces in grappling with the modern public sphere.

The question 'What is Enlightenment?' belongs in one sense to a very specific historical moment within the Berlin Enlightenment, one that played out in the pages of the *Berlinische Montasscrhift*. Not long after Zöllner's provocation, the editors published Mendelssohn's response, which might be read as a summary of discussions within the *Mittwochsgesellschaft* (a secret society of 'Friends of the Enlightenment' closely linked to the periodical) to which both Zöllner and Mendelssohn belonged (Schmidt, 1996, p. 3). Kant's '*Beantwortung der Frage: Was ist Aufklärung?*' was the second, and by far the most famous, reply. Afterwards, dozens of authors entered the fray and the debate eventually coalesced around questions of censorship, the relationship between faith and reason, and the role of the Enlightenment in spawning the French Revolution.

Beyond its immediate context, Kant's brief contribution raised questions that have engaged (among others) the likes of Edmund Burke, G. W. F. Hegel, Friedrich Nietzsche, Sigmund Freud, Max Horkheimer and Theodor Adorno, Hans-Georg Gadamer, Jürgen Habermas, and Michel Foucault. Given such a tradition, the danger of Pinker's naïve answer to this question should be obvious. Yet it is equally plain that the 'Enlightenment' cannot be inscribed simply within that debate. The Berlin Enlightenment was one of several national Enlightenments and belonged to a phenomenon that had swept through Western Europe and the Atlantic world. If the *Mittwochsgesellschaft* was paradigmatic of a new form of elite sociability (in which individuals could mingle irrespective of patrons, occupations, class, etc), then that sociability took different forms with different consequences in different places and under different political regimes (Schmidt, 1996, p. 3). Exploring this wider context is critical to understanding why post-war American Freudians could see themselves as bearers of the Enlightenment project and why Pinker and his colleagues can unfurl the Enlightenment banner to celebrate the claims they make for cognitive psychology, even as they denounce Freudian psychoanalysis as a modern unscientific, anti-Enlightenment pseudo-science to be discarded in favour of their own more putatively scientific approaches (Samuels, 2017). Unfortunately, one of the most celebrated historians of eighteenth-century France to use Freudian categories to speculate on the origins of the French Revolution did so in such a reductionist and literal-minded manner as to obscure the very fraught relationship between Freudian hermeneutics and Enlightenment thought (Hunt, 1992).

To arrive at a characterisation of the Enlightenment's fundamental nature, we must, in turn, consider the 'The Enlightenment' as milieu, movement (or project), process, and stance. In the first sense, it was a pan-European cultural and intellectual milieu of the late eighteenth-century. Although many of its adherents might loosely subscribe to Kant's notion of the Enlightenment as 'man's exit from self-incurred immaturity' (Schmidt, 1996, p. 58), the majority had much more concrete and external targets in minds. Their enemies were the vestiges of feudalism, the corruption of venal office-holders, the exemptions and privileges enjoyed by various groups (especially the nobility, the church and the guilds) in the *Ancien Régime*, censorship, religious intolerance and dogma; in short, injustice, inequality and inefficiency. Yet the Enlightenment was not, in its essentials, revolutionary or even always innovatory. In Scotland and England, its adherents were most immediately the intellectual heirs of the seventeenth-century New Science, both in their patterns of sociability and their synthesis of rationalism, scepticism and empiricism (Shapin and Schaffer, 1985; Schofield, 1963), though their politics could range from the secular absolutism of Thomas Hobbes to the Jacobinism of Joseph Priestley and the Lunar Society. In Scotland, the moral philosophies of David Hume and Adam Smith, as well as their writings on political economy, belong to this milieu. In England, the world of Samuel Johnson and his dictionary, Samuel Richardson and the epistolary novel, and even the notorious John Cleland, author of the pornographic *Fanny Hill, or Memoirs of a Woman of Pleasure* (1749), were dominated by these new forms of sociability, what historians now call the 'republic of letters.' While the Atlantic Revolutions took on a political character, extending far beyond norms of polite society and polite learning, they cannot be reduced to the internal logic of Enlightenment principles (Muldoon, 1999; Pocock, 1975). As James Muldoon has argued, in the American context, John Adams and his contemporaries might also be seen as 'defenders of traditional rights as any medieval estate or region,' and that 'the American Revolution may even have been the last medieval political conflict' (Muldoon, 1999, p. 149), whereas John Pocock has famously argued for the importance of Renaissance civic humanism (Pocock, 1975) in understanding their motivations. This ambiguity is so much the case that modern historiography now distinguishes a Radical Enlightenment, in order to refer to those strains which focus on radical equality and the universality of the rights of man (Jacob, 1981; Israel, 2001).

In France, the Philosophes may have been emblematic of the Enlightenment's new forms of sociability, but they were no more interested in political revolution than Kant himself. Betty Behrens neatly summarised the problem in her extended essay on the *Ancien Régime*: 'though their denunciations of arbitrary power were in fact an indictment of it, to have condemned it openly would have been to preach revolution, which [the Philosophes] never contemplated' (Behrens, 1967, p. 131). Rousseau, in his *Contrat Social*, may have been an exception, but he was Swiss and never gained a following before the Revolution. As Behrens very shrewdly and somewhat cynically observed,

> but the famous Philosophes, nearly all of whom were by [the late 1780s] already dead, by continually denouncing the abuses of the régime, yet

providing no programs of reform which could provoke dissension, were able to cater to every kind of discontent, from that of the landless and starving to that of the principal beneficiaries of the régime, whose material advantages increasingly failed to compensate them for the arbitrariness and inefficiencies of absolutism

(Behrens, 1967, p. 131).

In an important sense, Behrens anticipated the current post-revisionist consensus, such that it is, on the relationship between Enlightenment and Revolution in France. Although this is not the place to review that literature at length, what emerged is the sense that the 'high Enlightenment' had run out of steam. The successors to Voltaire and Diderot had 'inherited their social acclaim, [but] had little new to say' (Doyle, 1999, pp. 36–40). Instead they excluded the 'literary rabble' of Paris from their new forms of sociability, provoking resentment amongst the Grub Street press (Darnton, 1982). Two hundred years from now, historians might well have cause to ponder the parallels with the role of new media (particularly social media) and traditional print today during the Brexit campaign and the Trump election. At any rate, Jürgen Habermas furnished the theoretical framework for this interpretation in *The Structural Transformation of the Public Sphere* (Doyle, 1999). Habermas wanted to draw attention to the re-feudalisation of the Kantian public space in post-war Europe; to do so, he had to first investigate the origins of the public sphere, which he found in those new forms of sociability associated with the late eighteenth century. This model has done some important work. It gave us a new interpretation of the French Revolution; Roger Chartier's pithy epigram about the cultural origins that 'made it possible because it was conceivable' nicely encapsulated the accomplishment (Chartier, 1991, p. 2).

But having done that work, it is crucial not to reify the 'public sphere' as an autonomous vehicle for public opinion (Darnton, 2000). The danger can be seen in Lynn Hunt's work on the *Family Romance of the French Revolution* (1992) where the public sphere is deployed as a kind of (psycho-)analytic space in which a new sense of self develops and Oedipal conflicts are mapped onto civil society, thereby collapsing the conceptual distinction between social and the cultural. The problem with her argument, which is, in essence, that revolutionary politics were experienced by their adherents as a kind of family romance, in which participants were freed of their social roles and able to live-out their fantasies of joining the royal family, as evidenced by the emergence of pornographic images of the queen, is that it is by no means obvious that the sexualised images of the monarchy undermined the régime. Although the medium had changed, pornographic treatments of kings and their consorts were nothing new; baroque kingship had a place for it. As it has with Trump's affair with Stormy Daniels, the 'dead cat' of pornography may even have helped trivialise the abuses of rule. Under Charles II in England (in 1674), the earl of Rochester produced raunchy court verse satirising the king: 'Him no ambition moves to get reknown [...] / His scepter and his prick are of a length; And she may sway the one who plays with th' other, And make him little wiser than his brother'.[2] Arguably, the flourishing of this kind of complicit critique rendered the Merry Monarch's regime more (not less) secure; his brother James II may not have been the target of such satires, but his relative sexual probity did not guarantee his crown. The problem in France was not the pornography itself. In part, the growth of print culture (and the shift from scribal to print publication of such material) guaranteed a wider audience; but more significantly, the new forms of elite sociability excluded the authors of these libels. Had the denizens of the *haute*-culture Parisian salons been prepared to laugh with those they deemed scribblers, modern historians might have cause to view the matter very differently. To this question of the Enlightenment as complicit critique we will return presently.

Meanwhile, in Prussia, the Enlightenment took a different course. As Behrens noticed,

> the Enlightenment as [Frederick II understood it], and to the best of his ability translated into practice, produced, by the standards of the times, a high degree of consensus. In Prussia, it was a unifying force while in France a disruptive one.
>
> (Behrens, 1985, p. 185)

In other words, in Prussia it served the neo-Stoic social disciplining function so characteristic of early modern absolutism (Oestreich, 1982). Nowhere is this more evident than in Kant's own definition of Enlightenment. The apparent reversal of commonplace distinctions between public and private, Kant's right of public debate coupled with the duty of private obedience, embraces those Neo-Stoic ideals of *constantia, patientia, firmitas* (steadfastness, patience, firmness): steadfastness in the courage to use that reason, patience with the process of liberation from self-incurred immaturity, and firmness in upholding the distinction between public and private. In a sense, the Kantian stance is the one adopted by post-war American Freudians, who interpreted Freud in this fashion to support their clinical aim of exploring all manner of psycho-sexual urges and fantasies on the couch, with the aim of helping their patients adapt themselves better to their middle class lives (Coffman, 2017). In their account, Freud might have been radical in his ideas about sex, but he was a quite conventional, if frequently penurious, member of the Vienna *bourgeoisie* (Shapiro, 1992).

Just as Kant and Freud are compatible, Kant was not as far from Burke as some historians imagine (Schmidt, 1996, pp. 17–21). The danger comes from reading Burke through the lens of Gadamer's hermeneutics and his rehabilitation of the value of prejudice. But on a critical point they converge. Burke was

> afraid to put men to live and trade each on his own private stock of reason; because we suspect the stock in each man is small, and that the individuals would do better to avail themselves of the general bank and capital of all ages.
>
> (Schmidt, 1996, p. 17)

He advised that man should look for the 'latent wisdom', which prevails in prejudice, uncovering its reason. This 'because prejudice, with its reason, has a motive to give action to that reason, and affection that will give it permanence' (Ibid.). Kant too believed the average stock of reason in each individual was small (though more from lack of exercise than lack of potential),

> hence only a few who have managed to free themselves from immaturity through the exercise of their minds, and yet proceed confidently. But that a public should enlighten itself is more likely; indeed, it is nearly inevitable, if only it is granted freedom.
>
> (Schmidt, 1996, p. 59)

For Kant, the 'private use of reason may be very narrowly restricted without the progress of enlightenment being particularly hindered' (Schmidt, 1996, pp. 59–60). In Burke's view, the Englishman lived under a political regime where prejudice was the only means to disciplining the subversive element within private reason (the state was not going to do it), but where historical forces had evolved an enlightened political constitution. For Kant, the Prussian state served the disciplining function. As long as man patiently and unflinchingly obeyed, he could (and should) get on with improving the 'general bank and capital' on which individuals might draw in their own liberation (Schmidt, 1996, p. 15). Too much attention to the apparent distinction between man's inherent capacity or incapacity to reason well obscures the fact that neither Kant nor Burke had the slightest interest in the use of reason to dissolve the bonds of public order. This 'confusion of tongues' illustrates some of the difficulties of discussing the Enlightenment in a pan-European (much less trans-historical) context. Kant was, especially in his answer, an apologist for an enlightened despot – a revelation which would no doubt come as a surprise to Pinker and his allies, who see in the Enlightenment the genesis of liberal democracy.

The Enlightenment was given its 'project' and stature as a 'movement' after the Revolution, when it became a litmus test for Jacobinism and was tarnished with the totalitarian implications of popular sovereignty embodied in the *Terror*. The point here is not to dispute the linkage of the Revolution with the Enlightenment, but rather to acknowledge that linkage as part of the latter's legacy. The resulting bifurcation of the Enlightenment and its consequent politicisation creates the trap into which Pinker and his followers fell. On the one hand, the Jacobin legacy became the 'Enlightenment project' of classical civic virtue and rational self-improvement of man through the vehicle of the state (Chartier, 1991, p. 17; Koselleck, 1988). In a certain sense, the entire period from 1789–1989 can be taken as a working out of that 'Age of Ideology'. Critics and advocates of the Enlightenment have appropriated and redeployed the idea of Enlightenment for their own instrumental aims (Schmidt, 2000). Advocates call on it for legitimacy; critics, notably Theodor Adorno and Max Horkheimer, in their neo-Hegelian *Dialectic of Enlightenment*, blamed the Enlightenment veneration of rationality for destroying itself and laying waste to Europe in two world wars: 'Enlightenment has always aimed at liberating men from fear and establishing their sovereignty. Yet the fully enlightened earth radiates disaster triumphant' (Horkheimer and Adorno, 1979; Schmidt, 1996, p. 21).

But another, equally important legacy of the Enlightenment, can be found in both German philosophical idealism of the late eighteenth- and early nineteenth-centuries and its most serious critic. That is the notion of Enlightenment as process in the sense identified by Kant as one of long liberation. It might also be framed as a Freudian erotic drive, one that shifts the emphasis from Enlightenment as belief in reason to Enlightenment as liberating self-awareness. This strain of the Berlin Enlightenment was evident from the beginning, when the young Goethe and his circle embraced a cultural revolution that 'liberated' them from the grips of a 'civilizing process' that entailed aping French manners, fashion and courtly society. *Sturm und Drang*, with its emphasis on personal subjectivity, was at least a stepchild of the Enlightenment (and as far as Kant's formulation went might even have a greater claim to legitimacy). This is also the sense of Enlightenment picked up by Friedrich Nietzsche, 'who wants to continue the work of Enlightenment in himself, and to strangle the Revolution at birth' (Schmidt, 1996, p. 25). In a sense, Nietzsche made explicit a tension within the Enlightenment. At the risk of over-schematising these two Enlightenments, I will classify them as the external and internal. A more cynical observer might simply say that the Enlightenment has a way of absorbing its critics. Among those who call themselves intellectuals, almost none want to be associated with promoting ignorance or encouraging man to infantilise himself – even the staunchest critics of unbridled reason speak of it as a new form of enslavement.

In this sense, Freudianism may be the most problematic child of the Enlightenment, or, alternatively, as Berthold Rothschild would have it, partner (Rothschild, 2018). Freud's champions see him as developing a method for systematically exploring his patients' unconscious (mostly sexual) conflicts in order to liberate them; his critics point out that his real aim is to accommodate the individual to the strictures and expectations of bourgeois society and to promote arguably repressive sexual and gender norms. Although declaring the 'death of the Enlightenment' as process would be premature, in the second decade of the twenty-first century committed Jacobins and neo-Freudians are scarce on the ground. At least in the English-speaking world, we have mostly lost our faith in the state as a means to improving man or perfecting human society and in the psychological project (Freudian or otherwise), which is probably why Pinker's attempt to rehabilitate the Enlightenment has found greatest favour among Silicon Valley's tech billionaires, including Bill Gates.

What remains is the question of the Enlightenment hermeneutics or the Enlightenment as a critical and interpretative stance. For the present, perhaps the best entry into this problem can be found in the Gadamer-Habermas debate and the contribution of Gadamerian hermeneutics to the so-called 'linguistic turn'. The problem is one of the ontological status of language and of whether or not there is a reality outside language that is, in any sense, accessible to it. For Gadamer there is no reality outside language, his project is to understand how 'hermeneutics, freed from the ontological obstructions of the scientific concept of objectivity, can do justice to the historicity of understanding' (Gadamer, 2004, p. 265). Gadamer held that 'we can never achieve a "personal or temporal" identity with the author', but rather must content ourselves with being aware of our own biases, fore-meanings, and prejudices, so that 'the text can present itself in all its otherness and thus assert its own truth against one's own fore-meanings' (Gadamer, 2004, p. 266 fn. 187, p. 269). Only then can we obtain his 'fusion of horizons'. In Gadamer's view, prejudices are not only inescapable, but also play a vital role in understanding; Kant's call to outgrow them is thus, as Gadamer would see it, not only impossible but also self-defeating.

While I cannot pretend to offer a solution to the Gadamer-Habermas debate, I am sympathetic to Habermas' position, his insistence on the possibility of rational validity testing of truth claims, his sensitivity to hierarchical relationships, and his demands for an 'institutionally secure' public sphere (Jay, 1982, p. 101). This is a very different version of the Enlightenment from what Pinker (2018, p. 8) presents when he argues that 'reason' and 'reality' are external to discourse, and when he insists that truth claims can be evaluated against 'objective reality' and should be considered without regard for the discursive conventions that generate them, and that doing otherwise fuels the 'contempt for experts' that he laments (Pinker, 2018, p. 29). In defence of my own position, I would like to run the risk of provisionally rehabilitating the analogy between psychoanalysis and social critique (Allen, 2016) drawn from psychoanalytic practice, which Habermas abandoned after *Knowledge and Human Interests* (Habermas, 1986) with one essential modification. This is a problem that cannot, and need not, be resolved from within the 'I-Thou' dyadic relationship (i.e. the patient and the analyst), as many educational theorists have attempted (Gordon, 2002; Josselson, 2004), nor can it be reduced to a question of hermeneutic stances (Blight, 1981), or rather to the endless debate about the correspondence between the patient's fantasies and any realities outside the consulting room.

Another proponent of radical inter-textuality, Dominick LaCapra, inadvertently explained why in *Writing History, Writing Trauma* when he insisted: 'when you study something, at some level you always have a tendency to repeat the problems you are studying' (LaCapra, 2001, p. 142).[3] LaCapra understood this phenomenon as analogous to Freudian transference/countertransference (here the danger is in the fusion of horizon not in the inability to obtain it), where the researcher is implicated in the material and compelled to repeat its dynamics (Ibid.). Having framed it in those terms, he then goes to lengths to 'take his distance from therapeutic conceptions of psychoanalysis', preferring to take it 'in more ethical and political dimensions' (Ibid., p. 143).[4]

LaCapra's concern is with the putative contagiousness of trauma, or 'the way in which it can spread even to the interviewer or commentator' (LaCapra, 2004, p. 81). In his disdain for psychoanalytic practice, he misses a key innovation, one unavailable to Habermas when he first attempted and then abandoned the analogy.

Practitioners of contemporary Freudian psychoanalysis are familiar with the phenomenon LaCapra has described, but the more accurate analogy is not to 'transference' but to 'parallel processing' (Runia, 2004). This is the problem that arises in training when psychoanalytic candidates inadvertently reproduce their problematic interactions with patients in their interactions with their supervisors. In most cases, psychoanalytic practitioners have discovered that the parallelisms 'do not refer to content of the therapeutic process, but to "treatment alliances"—to the tacit rules that form the basis of the therapist-patient relationship' (Ibid., p. 295; Sachs and Shapiro, 1976; Sachs and Shapiro 1974; Sachs and Shapiro 1972). As the Dutch psychoanalyst and historian Eelco Runia (2004) observed, this can also occur in historical work. He cites an example of this phenomenon at work in the Dutch report of the massacres at Srebrenica, where the official Dutch report on the massacre paralleled the events and 'unwittingly replicated key aspects of the events they studied' (Runia, 2004, p. 296).

The solution of practitioners is to establish a form of group supervision where this triadic relationship can be interrogated in a milieu group. This is particularly effective because those tacit rules are common to the group. In historical work, those rules are almost always discursive. The solution for historians and social and cultural critics is to see the scholarly community as that milieu group, an institutionally secure public space, for validity testing, in a manner that also considers the hierarchical positions and power relations between and among interlocutors. Martin Jay objected to Habermas' attempt to find an 'extra-hermeneutic vantage point in Freudian theory' on the grounds that the patient and the analyst have a vested interest in discussing (and if possible 'curing') the patient's neuroses. Jay also highlighted the artificiality of the interaction, with the obvious limitation that the therapist would never tolerate the patient's transference if he were not being paid to do so (Jay, 1982, p. 103). This whole problem can be re-formulated as a triadic relationship of the source, the historian's interrogation of the source, and the historian's historical writing; this re-frames the scholarly community as a kind of group supervision that helps resolve the vagaries of 'parallel processing'.

The scholarly community is, after all, not actually concerned with the relationship between the historian and his source except insofar as it manifests itself in problematic ways in the historical writing. What is true of the historian in this instance is true of the critic more broadly.

Radical sceptics may reply that the group milieu cannot free itself of bias or fore-meanings either. Maybe so, but it can certainly go a great distance towards that aim. The more serious problem, to my mind, is the extent to which our scholarly milieu group is implicated in contemporary social and material realities or in our own mental habits, as has been argued by Stanley Fish (1980) and Pierre Bourdieu (1997). But that is a problem which Pinker and his followers are unwilling even to consider.

I have, in the course of this discussion of Enlightenment as milieu, movement (or project), process, and stance, given my own answer to the question of 'What is Enlightenment?'. Although I have no especially sanguine view of human nature and few illusions about human rationality, I also have no wish to repudiate the Kantian notion of a public space (or more properly public spaces) for the free exercise of reason. What I am arguing for is a commitment to self-reflection on the extent to which the discursive logics of the public sphere reproduce, unwittingly or not, the hierarchical relations of the participants. Yes, of course, privately we all have ethnicities, socio-economic backgrounds, genders, sexualities, and religious beliefs. To varying degrees, most of us experience some oppression because of them and are frequently obligated to act privately in ways we would rather not. But if we cannot agree on the need to preserve the integrity of institutionally protected public spaces in which to debate those completing claims, then we can have very little hope for civil society. We must proceed, but with self-reflection and with caution, as we delineate the boundaries of socio-political institutional legitimacy and authority in a manner not unlike that advocated by both Hannah Arendt and Paul Ricœur (Garduño Comparán, 2014; Ricœur, 1986; Arendt, 1993).[5] But what both Pinker and those applauding him forget in his attempts to reify the topic of his panegyric is that the Enlightenment is best summarised as our collective investment in those spaces.

Notes

1 The author would like to thank the participants and organisers of the 'Psychoanalytic Thought, History and Political Life' forum where this paper was presented under the same title on 13 March 2012 at the Senate House, University of London. Special thanks in particular are due to Daniel Pick, Jacqueline Rose, Matt ffytch, Nemonie Craven, and Shahidha Bari for their very useful comments. The very early drafts of this essay date from the autumn of 2005 when the author was in graduate school at the University of Pennsylvania; Roger Chartier set a question about the many meanings of the Enlightenment as a field exam. The author would also like to acknowledge a long and enduring debt to the late Dr Stanley H. Shapiro (1926–2020), who first introduced her to Freudian hermeneutics through its clinical practice. This essay is dedicated to his memory with warm thanks and fond reminisces.

2   John Wilmot, Earl of Rochester. See [http://jacklynch.net/Texts/charles2.html]. Although Rochester was banished from court over it, this had more to do with the fact that he sprang it on the king as a prank when he had been asked to produce a different poem. His 'Signor Dildo' (which implies that the Spanish Ambassador serves that function for the Duchess of York) [http://www.jacklynch.net/Texts/dildo.html] and 'The Imperfect Enjoyment' (which takes up masturbation) passed without censure.
3   This was LaCapra's solution to the problem of where to position the historian in the process of observing a past which for him 'arrives in the form of texts and textualised remainders-memories, reports, published writings, archives, monuments, and so forth' (LaCapra 1985, p. 128; Hutcheon, 1989).
4   LaCapra (2001, p. 143). This is unfortunately also the position he took in a public debate with David Sachs, a practitioner who has worked with victims of political violence and who has helped to theorise the role of parallel processing in the therapeutic space. Dominick LaCapra, Ph.D. & David Sachs, M.D., 'Trauma: Literary, Historical, and Psychoanalytic Approaches' (16 February 2005) in a scientific program at the Philadelphia Psychoanalytic Center.
5   The author would like to thank Jacqueline Rose for reminding her, albeit too late in the revision process to provoke more than passing mention, of the extent to which Hannah Arendt's work shares many of these same preoccupations. Thanks also to Josef Nothmann for tracking down the reference to Carlos Alfonso Garduño Comparán's essay on the shared preoccupations of Arendt and Ricœur.

Bibliography

Adorno, T. and M. Horkheimer (1979) *Dialectic of Enlightenment*. trans. J. Cumming. London: Verso.

Allen, A. (2016) 'Psychoanalysis and the methodology of critique', *Constellations* 23 (2), 244–254.

Arendt, H. (1993). *Between Past and Future: Eight Exercises in Political Thought*. New York: Penguin Books.

Behrens, C. B. A. (1967) *Ancien régime*. London: Thames and Hudson.

Behrens, C. B. A. (1985) *Society, government and the enlightenment: the experiences of eighteenth-century France and Prussia*. New York: Harper & Row.

Blight, J. G. (1981) 'Must psychoanalysis retreat to hermeneutics?: psychoanalytic theory in the light of Popper's evolutionary epistemology', *Psychoanalysis and Contemporary Thought* 4 (2), 147–205.

Bourdieu, P. (1997) *Pascalian meditations*. Palo Alto: Stanford University Press.

Chartier, R. (1991) *The cultural origins of the French revolution*. Durham: Duke University Press.

Coffman, D. (2017) 'Normal Narcissism in the Age of Trump', *Psychoanalysis and History* 19 (3), 407–413.

Darnton, R. (1982) *The literary underground of the old regime*. Cambridge: Harvard University Press.

Darnton, R. (2000) 'An early information society? News and Media in Eighteenth-Century Paris', *The American Historical Review* 105, 1–35.

Doyle, W. (1999) *Origins of the French revolution*. Oxford: Oxford University Press.

Fish, S. (1980). *Is there a text in this class? The authority of interpretative communities*. Cambridge: Harvard University Press.

Gadamer, H-G (2004 [1980]) *Truth and method*. New York, London: Continuum Books.
Garduño Comparán, C. A. (2014) 'Arendt and Ricœur on Ideology and Authority', *Ricoeur Studies/Etudes Ricoeuriennes*, 5 (2).
Gordon, E. W. (2002) 'Production of knowledge and pursuit of understanding'. In C. Camp-Yeakey (ed.) *Producing knowledge, pursuing understanding*. Bingley: Emerald Group Publishing Limited, pp. 301–318.
Habermas, J. (1986) *Knowledge and human interests*. Cambridge: Polity Press.
Horkheimer, M., T. W. Adorno, and G. Noeri (2002) *Dialectic of enlightenment*. Palo Alto: Stanford University Press.
Hunt, L. (1992) *Family romance of the French revolution*. Berkeley: University of California Press.
Hutcheon, L. (1989) 'Historiographic metafiction parody and the intertextuality of history'. In P. O'Donnell and R. C. Davis (eds.) *Intertextuality and Contemporary American Fiction*. Baltimore: Johns Hopkins University, pp. 3–32.
Israel, J. I. (2001) *Radical enlightenment: philosophy and the making of modernity, 1650–1750*. Oxford: Oxford University Press.
Jacob, M.C. (1981) *The radical enlightenment: pantheists, freemasons, and republicans*. Boston: Allen & Unwin.
Jay, M. (1982) 'Should intellectual history take a linguistic turn?'. In *Modern European Intellectual history*. Ithaca: Cornell University Press.
Josselson, R. (2004) 'The hermeneutics of faith and the hermeneutics of suspicion', *Narrative Inquiry* 14 (1), 1–28.
Koselleck, R. (1988) *Critique and crisis: enlightenment and the pathogenesis of modern society*. Cambridge: MIT Press.
LaCapra, D. (1985) *History and criticism*. Ithaca, NY: Cornell University Press.
LaCapra, D. (2001) *Writing history, writing trauma*. Baltimore: Johns Hopkins University Press.
LaCapra, D. (2004) *History in transit: experience, identity, critical theory*. Ithaca, NY: Cornell University Press.
Muldoon, J. (1999) *Empire and order: the concept of empire, 800–1800*. New York: St Martin's Press.
Oestreich, G. (1982) *Neostoicism and the early modern state*. Cambridge: Cambridge University Press.
Pinker, S. (2018) *Enlightenment now: the case for reason, science, humanism, and progress*. London: Penguin.
Pocock, J. G. A. (1975) *The Machiavellian moment: Florentine political thought and the Atlantic republican tradition*. Princeton: Princeton University Press.
Ricœur, P. (1986). *Lectures on ideology and utopia*. New York, NY: Columbia University Press.
Rothschild, B. (2018) 'The betrayed lover: psychoanalysis and the enlightenment: who broke up with whom?', *Psychoanalysis and History* 20 (1), 5–21.
Runia, E. (2004) 'Forget about it: "parallel processing" in the Srebrenica report', *History and Theory* 43, 295–320.
Sachs, D. M. and S. H. Shapiro (1972) 'Comments on teaching the psychoanalytic psychology of adolescence to residents', *Journal of the American Academy of Child Psychiatry* 11, 201–211.

Sachs, D. M. and S. H. Shapiro (1974) 'Comments on teaching psychoanalytic psychotherapy in a residency training program', *Psychoanalytic Quarterly* 43, 51–76.

Sachs, D. M. and S. H. Shapiro (1976) 'On parallel processes in therapy and teaching', *Psychoanalytic Quarterly* 45, 319–415.

Samuels R. (2017) 'The backlash politics of evolutionary psychology: Steven Pinker's blank slate'. In *Psychoanalyzing the politics of the new brain sciences*. London: Palgrave Pivot.

Schmidt, J. (1996) 'What is enlightenment? A question, its context, and some consequences'. In *What is enlightenment? Eighteenth-century answers and twentieth-century questions*. Berkeley, CA: University of California Press.

Schmidt, J. (2000) 'What enlightenment project?', *Political Theory* 28 (6), 734–757.

Schofield, R. E. (1963) *The lunar society of Birmingham: a social history of provincial science and industry in eighteenth-century England*. Oxford: Clarendon Press.

Shapin, S. and S. Schaffer (1985) *Leviathan and the air-pump: Hobbes, Boyle, and the experimental life*. Princeton: Princeton University Press.

Shapiro, S. H. (1992) 'Freud, Dora, and Vienna 1900: by Hannah S. Decker', *International Review of Psycho-Analysis* 19, 512–514.

Index

References to figures are indicated in *italics*. References to endnotes consist of the page number followed by the letter 'n' followed by the number of the note.

9/11 terrorist attacks xv, xvi, xxiii

Abel, Elizabeth 96
Abraham, Karl 73, 75
ACT UP (AIDS Coalition to Unleash Power) 126; New York chapter 126, 136, 138
Adams, John 182
Adler, Alfred xxv
Adorno, Theodor W. xxiv, xxxiii, xxxiv, 147, 155, 181, 186
African National Congress (ANC) 40
African refugees 'left-to-die boat' case (March 2011) *see* Bergvall's *Drift* (Catherine Humble)
Afrikaners 44–45, 47
Ahmed, Sara 43–44
Aichhorn, August 27
AIDS *see* ACT UP (AIDS Coalition to Unleash Power); *Art AIDS America* (exhibition); Klein and the representation of people with AIDS (Theo Gordon)
AIDS ACTION NOW! 125
Alexander, J. 19
Alexander, Sally xxviii
Al-Qaeda xvi
Althusser, Louis 147
Alvarez, Al 153–154
American Revolution 182
Anderson, Perry 147
Andersson, Ola 22
Andreas-Salomé, Lou 87
anthropology: and cannibalism 67, 69; and colonialism 67, 68–70; and psychoanalysis 68

Antigone xxix
anti-Semitism: and Columbus Centre 148, 149, 154–155; and Freud xxxiv, 70, 76, 77–78, 79; and Horkheimer/Flowerman's Studies in Prejudice Series xliiin9; and Jung 71
apartheid 39–40, 148, 150, 156; *see also* psychoanalysis and South African Satanism scare (Nicky Falkof); segregation
Arendt, Hannah 189; *Eichmann in Jerusalem* and the 'banality of evil' 150, 160; on the 'need of reason' 160; *The Origins of Totalitarianism* 101
Aristotle, on proton pseudos 21–22
Armstrong, Isobel 5
Art AIDS America (exhibition) 137, 142
Assoun, Paul-Laurent 19
Aston, Elaine 168, 177n11
Astor, David: Columbus Centre, foundation of 147, 148, 149–150; family background and liberal views 150–151; Freud Memorial Chair of Psychoanalysis (UCL), endowment of 152, 159; Hoffer-Cohn dispute 155; 'The Meaning of Eichmann' (*The Observer*) 149, 153, 161; *The Observer* editorship (1948–75) 147, 151; *The Observer* editorship and emphasis on psychology/psychoanalysis 153–154, 159; psychoanalysis and relationship with Anna Freud 151–152; 'Towards a study of the scourge' (*Encounter*) 149; *see also* Columbus Centre, University of Sussex (Danae Karydaki)

Astor, Nancy, Viscountess Astor 150
Astor, Waldorf, 2nd Viscount Astor 150
Attridge, Derek 13n2
Augustine, Saint 6
'authoritarian personality' concept xxxiii

Bacon, Francis 176
Baeyer-Katte, Wanda von 156
Baldwin, James 55–56, 57
Balint, Enid 152
Bar-Haim, Shaul 88; *see also* wild analysis (S. Bar-Haim, E. S. Coles and H. Tyson)
Bari, Shahidha *see* Freud, Ferrante and feet in Jensen's *Gradiva* (S. Bari)
Batsch, Manuel *see* Freud's 'Project for a Scientific Psychology' (Manuel Batsch)
Beacon Hill School 85, 88–89, 94, 95, 100; *see also* Russell, Bertrand; Russell, Dora
Becker, Howard S. 39
Bedales School 94
Behrens, Betty 182–183, 184
Belloc, Hillaire 90
Benetton *see* United Colours of Benetton
Bennington, Geoffrey 13n9
Ben-Yehuda, Nachman 43
Bergvall's *Drift* (Catherine Humble): chapter overview xxxviii; African refugees 'left-to-die boat' case (March 2011) 105; Bergvall's *Drift* book, content and structure of 105; Bergvall's performance of *Drift* as visual-sound poem 105; drawings opening book 105–106, 108–109, 110–111, 113–114, 118–120; 'Lines 6' drawing *117*; 'Lines 11' drawing *106*; 'Lines 12' drawing 111–113, *111*; 'Log' section 109; 'Report' chapter based on Goldsmiths report 105, 107–108, 109, 113; trauma 110–111, 112–113, 118–120, 121n5, 121n8; viewing refugees 108–111; Winnicott's squiggle game and work with WWII evacuees 106–107, 114–117; Winnicott's squiggle game, Bergvall's drawings and bearing witness 106, 117–120
Berlin Enlightenment 181, 186
Berlin Psycho-Analytical Society 86
Berlinische Montasscrhift, 'Enlightenment' debate 180, 181
Bernard A. Zuckerman Museum of Art (Kennesaw, Georgia), *Art AIDS America* (exhibition) 142

Bernardi, Daniel 58
Bersani, Leo xxiii, xxxix, 11, 135, 140–141, 142
Bion, Wilfred R. xv, 13n4
The Birth of a Nation (D. W. Griffith) 54, 57, 62
Blasing, M. K. 13n3, 14n17
Blease, Cole 62
Blumenberg, Hans xxx
Bodichon, Barbara Leigh Smith 94
Bogle, Donald 58
Bollas, Christopher xxiii, xliiin5
Bonaparte, Marie 28
Borch-Jacobsen, Mikkel 177n8
Bordowitz, Gregg 134
Botha, P. W. 40
Bourdieu, Pierre 189
Bourgeois, Louise xxiv
Bourke, Joanna 169
Bowlby, John 152
Bowlby, Rachel xxx
Bradley-Perrin, Ian, *Your Nostalgia is Killing Me!* (Bradley-Perrin and Chevalier) 125–126, *125*
Bradshaw, David 94
Breuer, Josef 132
Brexit xix, xxxiii, 183
Brickman, Celia 70
Briggs, Asa 148
Brill, A. A. xxvi
British Psycho-Analytical Society 91, 96, 100; Controversial Discussions (1940s) 4, 91
Buckley, William F. 134
Burke, Edmund 181, 184–185
Bush, George W. xvi, xixn1
Butler, Judith xxiv, xxviii, 60
Butler, Samuel 91

Cameron, Laura 87, 102n3
cannibalism *see* Freud and the cannibal (Marita Vyrgioti)
cannibalistic infanticide 157
Carson, Anne 11
Caruth, Cathy 112–113, 119, 177n9
Caselli, Daniela 92, 93
Charles II, King of England 183–184
Chartier, Roger 183
Chasseguet-Smirgel, Janine 152
Chevalier, Vincent, *Your Nostalgia is Killing Me* (Bradley-Perrin and Chevalier) 125–126, *125*

childhood, modernism and progressive education (Helen Tyson): chapter overview xxxviii; Beacon Hill School (Dora and Bertrand Russell) 85, 88–89, 94, 95, 100; Bertrand Russell's 'Free Speech in Childhood' and critical responses 85–86, 88, 89–94, 95; democracy and modernist fantasy of the child 86, 93–94, 101; democracy and self-governance by children 88–89, 92; Klein-Anna Freud debate on education and child analysis and Alix Strachey 86–87, 88; Klein's and Winnicott's vs. Russell's theories 93–94; language and modernist fantasy of the child 92–93; Malting House Garden School (Geoffrey Pyke and Susan Isaacs) 87–88, 91, 94; psychoanalysis and education 86–94; Virginia Woolf, psychoanalysis, and Melanie Klein 95–96, 100, 101; Virginia Woolf's *The Waves* and progressive education 86, 94–95; Virginia Woolf's *The Waves*, childhood and fascism 96, 100–101

Christ *see* Jesus Christ

Christianity and Freud *see* Freud and the cannibal (Marita Vyrgioti)

Churchill, Winston, Anthony Storr's *Observer* article (1969) 154

Clancier, Anne 7

Cleland, John 182

climate catastrophe xviii, xix

Coffman, D'Maris *see* Freud, Enlightenment and Public Sphere (D'Maris Coffman)

Cohen, Stanley 42, 43

Cohn, Norman: Columbus Centre, foundation of 147, 148–149, 150; Columbus Centre, preliminary report 151; *Europe's Inner Demons* 147, 150, 157–159; family background, war years, and academia 154; fantasy, dehumanisation and Klein's paranoid-schizoid position 157–159; Institute for Social Research (Frankfurt School), report of visit to 155–156; Nevitt Sanford, letter to 156, 157, 158–159; psychoanalysis and study of history and politics 154–155, 159, 160; psychoanalysis recommended for Columbus Centre researchers 157; psychoanalysis to understand dehumanisation process 156–157; psychoanalysis with various analysts 154; *The Pursuit of the Millennium* 147, 154, 155; Willie Hoffer, dispute with 155; *see also* Columbus Centre, University of Sussex (Danae Karydaki)

Coles, Elizabeth Sarah xxiv, xxxvii; *see also* wild analysis (S. Bar-Haim, E. S. Coles and H. Tyson); Winnicott and the finding of literature (E. S. Coles)

colonialism: and anthropology 67, 68–70; and psychoses 39–40, 48

Columbus Centre, University of Sussex (Danae Karydaki): chapter overview xl–xli; British culture and Freud/psychoanalysis 147, 159–160; Centre's interdisciplinary research group 148–149; Columbus series books 156–158; David Astor and creation of Centre 147, 148, 149–150; David Astor and psychoanalysis 150–154; Norman Cohn and creation of Centre 147, 148–149, 150; Norman Cohn and psychoanalysis 154–159; psychoanalysis, Nazi crimes and 'banality of evil' 150, 160; psychoanalysis as tool to explore man's inhumanity to man xxvii, 147–148, 149–150, 159, 160–161; psychohistory and Arendtian/Freudian readings of history 160–161; summary and concluding remarks 159–161; *see also* Astor, David; Cohn, Norman

Controversial Discussions (British Psycho-Analytical Society, 1940s) 4, 91

Copjec, Joan 29–30

Corbin, Henri 13n11

Courtney, Susan 60, 61

Crimp, Douglas 135, 136

Critcher, Chas 43

'critique' (in literary criticism) *see* Winnicott and the finding of literature (E. S. Coles)

crowd psychology xvi, xxxi–xxxii; *see also* mass psychology

Crowther, Bosley 55

cultural experience, location of xxxvi–xxxix

Daim, Wilfried 155

Davies, Erica 29

De la Mare, Walter 90
democracy, and progressive education 86, 88–89, 92, 93–94, 101
Derrida, Jacques xxix, xxxi, 7, 13n9, 20–21, 24, 31
Dicks, Henry 148; *Licenced Mass Murder: A Socio-psychological Study of some SS Killers* 156, 157–158
Diderot, Denis 183
Dighton, Ralph 55
disavowal (psychoanalytic concept) 45–46, 94
Dixon, Thomas, *The Clansman* 54
Doyle, W. 183
Du Bois-Reymond, E. 18
Duggan, Patrick 176
Dunne, Philip 53
Dutoit, Ulysse 11

education: and psychoanalysis 86–94; *see also* childhood, modernism and progressive education (Helen Tyson)
Eichmann, Adolf 149, 150, 153, 161
Einstein, Albert xvii
Eliot, T.S. 31
Ellison, Ralph 55, 57
Ellmann, Maud xliiin6
Encounter, 'Towards a study of the scourge' (David Astor) 149
Engelman, Edmund 27
English Enlightenment 182
Enlightenment *see* Freud, Enlightenment and Public Sphere (D'Maris Coffman)
Erikson, Erik xxvii, 152

Falkof, Nicky *see* psychoanalysis and South African Satanism scare (Nicky Falkof)
Fanon, Frantz xxiv, xxxv, 39, 54–55, 58, 60, 62–63
Farley, Lisa 116–117, 118
fascism xxxiii, 92, 93, 94, 100–101; *see also* Nazism
Fassin, Didier 169–170
Felman, Shoshana: 'chain of witnesses' 119; interpretation as 'gift of language' 13n13; 'To open the question' xxix; 'unthought' of psychoanalysis xxiii; 'vulgar application' of psychoanalysis to literature xxiv, xxvii, xxxvii, xliiin6
Felski, Rita xxxvii, 5

Ferenczi, Sándor: Controversial Discussions (1940s) 4; Freud's letter to re. psychoanalysis and race 71; Freud's letter to re. 'wild psycho-analysis' xliiin1; mimetic model of trauma 170, 171, 174, 175; seduction 5; transference 6
Ferrante, Elena xxv; *see also* Freud, Ferrante and feet in Jensen's *Gradiva* (S. Bari)
fetishism 31, 45–46
ffytche, Matt xxviii
Fiddian-Qasmiyeh, Elena 110, 111
Finklestein, Avram 126
Fish, Stanley 189
Fliess, Wilhelm 17, 22, 25
Flowerman, Samuel xliiin9
Forrester, John 87, 102n3
Foucault, Michel 181
Frankel, Jay 170, 174
Frankfurt Institut für Psychiatrie und Psychoanalyse 156
Frankfurt School 155–156
Frazer, James 73
Frederick II, King of Prussia 184
French Enlightenment 182–183
French Revolution 181, 182, 183, 185–186
Freud, Anna: analysed by her father xviii; David Astor's psychoanalyst 151–152; debate with Klein on child psychoanalysis and education 86, 87, 91; narration of film of Freud at home (1937) 28
Freud, Sigmund: analysis of own daughter xviii; and anti-Semitism xxxiv, 70, 76, 77–78, 79; *Beyond the Pleasure Principle* 91, 121n8, 173; and British culture, influence on 147, 159–160; *Civilisation and its Discontents* xxxiii–xxxiv, 29, 77; Columbus Centre's interest in 147, 149; cultural elevation of in United States (1950s) 160; disavowal 45; Dora, case of 29–30; ego and 'trend towards unification' xxx; 'Femininity' 35; fetishism 31, 45; film of Freud at home (1937) 28; and Frankfurt School 156; *The Future of an Illusion* 77; 'The History of the Psychoanalytic Movement' xxv; individual psychology and collective life xvii; infantile sexuality 22, 24, 45;

interpretation in psychoanalysis 4; Jung, split with xxv, 70–72, 73, 79; mass mind, pathologies of xv–xvi; *Massenpsychologie und Ich-Analyse* (*Group Psychology and the Analysis of the Ego*) xv, xxxi–xxxii, xxxvi, 155; memory xxix–xxx; metapsychology 16, 17, 19, 25; *Moses and Monotheism* 77–78; 'Mourning and Melancholia' 74–75; narcissism xxxiii–xxxiv, 74–75; 'Negation' 13n4; 'A Note Upon the Mystic Writing Pad' xxix–xxx; *The Observer* 'Centenary' articles ('The meaning of Freud') 153; Oedipus xxx, xxxvii; paranoia as repressed homosexuality (Judge Schreber) 142; pre-Oedipal relationship to mother 100; psychoanalysis as meta-discipline xxiii–xxiv; *The Question of Lay Analysis* xvii; 'Rat Man' xxv; repression concept 44; *Studies on Hysteria* (with Breuer) 132; sublimation xxxvi; 'thing-presentations' and 'word-presentations' 113; *Three Essays on the Theory of Sexuality* 73–74; *Totem and Taboo* 34, 69–73, 77; transference 6; trauma 112, 113, 121n8, 173, 177; the uncanny, essay on xviii; unconscious murderous fantasies and history 160, 161; Virginia Woolf's attitude towards 95–96; war and unconscious fantasies about death 159; 'wild analysis' concept xviii; '"Wild" Psycho-Analysis' xxi–xxii; Woodrow Wilson, psychobiography of xvii; *see also* Freud and the cannibal (Marita Vyrgioti); Freud, Enlightenment and Public Sphere (D'Maris Coffman); Freud, Ferrante and feet in Jensen's *Gradiva* (S. Bari); Freud's 'Project for a Scientific Psychology' (Manuel Batsch); wild analysis (S. Bar-Haim, E. S. Coles and H. Tyson)

Freud and the cannibal (Marita Vyrgioti): chapter overview xxxv–xxxvi; anthropology and cannibalism 67, 69; cannibalism, colonialism and racial representation 68–70; Freud's 'cannibal' joke 67; Freud's dispute with Jung over race and Christianity 70–72, 73, 79; Freud's 'Get rid of Jesus Christ' joke 67; Freud's psychoanalytic account of cannibalism, totemism and Christianity 72–73; Freud's theory on cannibalism and Holy Communion 68, 75–76, 78; Freud's use of cannibal trope as postcolonial method of critique 68, 78–79; *Moses and Monotheism*, cannibalism and hypocrisy of Christian anti-Semitism 77–78; 'Mourning and Melancholia' and cannibalisation of the object 74–75; racialising logic of identification in psychoanalysis 73–76; *Three Essays on the Theory of Sexuality* and oral cannibalism 73–74; *Totem and Taboo* and anthropology 69–70; *Totem and Taboo* and cannibalism as critique of Christianity 70–73

Freud, Enlightenment and Public Sphere (D'Maris Coffman): chapter overview xli–xlii; Berlin Enlightenment 181, 186; *Berlinische Montasscrhift* debate 180, 181; Burke on Enlightenment 181, 184–185; Enlightenment and American Revolution 182; Enlightenment and French Revolution 181, 182, 185–186; Enlightenment as milieu/movement/process/stance 181–182, 189; Enlightenment in England 182; Enlightenment in France 182–183; Enlightenment in Prussia 184; Enlightenment in Scotland 182; Freud and Enlightenment 180, 181, 186–187; Gadamer-Habermas debate and linguistic turn 187; Goethe and *Sturm und Drang* 186; Habermas and Freudian theory 188; Habermas on public sphere 180, 183, 187; Horkheimer and Adorno on Enlightenment 181, 186; Kant on Enlightenment/public space 180, 181–182, 184, 185, 186, 187, 189; Kantian stance and post-war American Freudians 184; Mendelssohn's reply to Zöllner 180, 181; Nietzsche and Enlightenment 181, 186; Pinker's *Enlightenment Now* 180, 181, 185, 187, 189; psychoanalysis, parallel processing, and historical work 188–189; psychoanalysis and social critique 187–189; public sphere and French Revolution 183–184; public sphere and psychoanalysis 181, 188–189; Radical Enlightenment 182; Zöllner's 'What is Enlightenment?' 180, 181

Freud, Ferrante and feet in Jensen's *Gradiva* (S. Bari): chapter overview xxxi; Ferrante's Neapolitan novels and female volition 27–28, 33–34, 35; Ferrante's views on psychoanalysis 34–35; Freud's consulting rooms and Gradiva image 27, 28; Freud's essays on Jensen's *Gradiva* 27; Freud's view of Jensen's fiction as psychoanalytical enterprise 28–29, 35; Freud's view of Jensen's Gradiva as author's forgotten memory of dead sister 29–30; Freud's view on young women's 'psychical rigidity' ('Femininity') 35; Gradiva, man's desire and deletion of women 30–31, 35; Gravida's feet and female emancipation 32–33; Jensen's novella, summary of 28; Jensen's story as staging psychoanalytic method 29–30

Freud Memorial Chair of Psychoanalysis (University College London) 152, 159

Freud's 'Project for a Scientific Psychology' (Manuel Batsch): chapter overview xxx–xxxi; Freud's Project and neuro-psychoanalysis 16–17, 18; Freud's renunciation of the Project 17–20; hysteria, memory and Derrida's reading of the Project 20–21, 24; hysterical memories, sexuality and transcendental lies 21–24; theory of proton pseudos 21–23, 24; universal character of hysteria 24; Witch Metapsychology 25

Friedman, J. 19
Frosh, Stephen xxiii, xxviii, xliiin9, 70
Fulton, John 148
Fuss, Diana 75

Gadamer, Hans-Georg 181, 184, 187
Garnett, David 'Bunny' 95
Gates, Bill 187
Gay, P. 73
Gebre, Daniel Haile 108, 121n2
gender: and mass psychology xxxiv; *see also* Freud, Ferrante and feet in Jensen's *Gradiva* (S. Bari); *Pinky* (Ian Magor)
Gever, Martha 132–133
Gherovici, Patricia xxviii
Giliomee, Herman 45
Gilman, Sander L. 70–71
Girard, René 67, 177n7

Goethe, Johann Wolfgang von: *Faust* 25; *Sturm und Drang* 186
Goldblatt, Dr (Tavistock Clinic) 154
Goldsmiths, University of London, 'Report on the "*Left-To-Die Boat*"' 107
Goode, Erich 43
Gordon, Peter E. xxxiii
Gordon, Theo *see* Klein and the representation of people with AIDS (Theo Gordon)
Gorer, Geoffrey 153
Gorham, Deborah 89
Gradiva *see* Freud, Ferrante and feet in Jensen's *Gradiva* (S. Bari)
Graham, Jorie 3, 12
Gran Fury 126
Green, André xxiii, 118, 152, 166–167
Griffith, D. W., *The Birth of a Nation* 54, 57, 62
group/mass mind xv–xvi; *see also* crowd psychology; mass psychology
Grover, J. 131
Guantanamo Bay detention camp xvi

Habermas, Jürgen 180, 181, 187, 188; *Knowledge and Human Interests* 187; *The Structural Transformation of the Public Sphere* 183
Hall, Stuart 46
Hallas, Roger 131
Haring, Keith 125
Hartmann, Heinz 151
Hegel, G. W. F. 181
Heidegger, Martin 3
Helmholtz school 18
Herz, Max 22
Herzog, Dagmar xxviii
Hier, Sean 42
Hilberg, Raul 149
history: psychohistory xxvii–xxviii, 160; *see also* Columbus Centre, University of Sussex (Danae Karydaki)
Hitler, Adolf xxvi, xxvii, 160
HIV/AIDS *see* ACT UP (AIDS Coalition to Unleash Power); *Art AIDS America* (exhibition); Klein and the representation of people with AIDS (Theo Gordon)
Hobbes, Thomas 182
Hocquenhem, Guy 142
Hoffer, Willie 153, 155

Hofstadter, Richard 134
Holmes, Sean 176
Holocaust 148, 149–150
Hook, Derek 40, 48
hooks, bell 57
Horkheimer, Max xliiin9, 155, 181, 186
Horney, Karen 153
Howe, Susan 11
Hudson, Rock 129, *130*, 131, 134, 135, *138*
Hug-Hellmuth, Hermine 87
Humble, Catherine *see* Bergvall's *Drift* (Catherine Humble)
Hume, David 182
Hunt, Lynn 183
hysteria: and South African Satanism scare 46–47; *Studies on Hysteria* (Freud and Breuer) 132; *see also* Freud's 'Project for a Scientific Psychology' (Manuel Batsch)

Iball, H. 166
identity politics 180
infantile sexuality, Freud's theories 22, 24, 45
Institut für politische Psychologie, University of Vienna 155
Institute for Social Research (Frankfurt School) 155–156
International Psychoanalytical Association xxi, xxvi, 71
interpretation (in psychoanalysis) 4, 6–8
Intruder in the Dust (film) 55
Isaacs, Susan 87, 88, 102n1, 102n3
Iversen, Margaret 139

Jacobus, Mary 30
James, D. 13n2
James II, King of England 184
Jay, Martin 188
Jenkins, Philip 42
Jensen, Wilhelm *see* Freud, Ferrante and feet in Jensen's *Gradiva* (S. Bari)
Jesus Christ 67, 71, 72
Jewishness: Jung's quote on 'Aryan' vs. Jewish unconscious 71; and psychoanalysis 70–71; *see also* anti-Semitism
Johnson, Samuel 182
Jones, Ernest 28, 153
Judt, Tony 121n12
Jung, Carl: and anti-Semitism 71; archetypes xxxvii; 'Aryan' vs. Jewish unconscious 71; Freud, split with xxv, 70–72, 73, 79; Jesus Christ as 'typical manifestation of the self' 71; *The Observer* profile (1948) 153; *Symbols of Transformation* and Freud's response 71–72

Kalmanovitch, Jeanine 7
Kane, Sarah xxv; *see also* Kane's *Blasted* (Leah Sidi)
Kane's *Blasted* (Leah Sidi): chapter overview xxxli; domestic and military rape theme 166, 167, 168, 169; 'experiential' theatre and mental illness 165–166; Kane's views on Weller's *Mad* 165, 166; newspaper reviews and academic criticism 167–168, 175–176; outline of plot 167; play's architecture and offstage/onstage violence 167–168; psychoanalytic perspective on play 166–167, 168; reference to *Cleansed* 177n6; reference to *Crave* 169; reference to *Sick* monologues 166; references to *Phaedra's Love* 168, 177n6; Sándor Ferenczi's model of trauma 170, 171, 174, 175; trauma theory and PTSD 169–170, 171; traumatic 'architecture' 168–171; traumatic dissociation and loss 171–172; traumatic identification 174–175, 176–177; traumatic repetition 173
Kant, Immanuel 180, 181–182, 184, 185, 186, 187, 189; 'Beantwortung der Frage: Was ist Aufklärung?' 181
Karydaki, Danae *see* Columbus Centre, University of Sussex (Danae Karydaki)
Katz, Jonathan 137–138
Kazan, Elia, *Pinky* 52
Kenrick, Donald 156
Kerr, Ted 126
Khanna, R. 70
Kirby, David 126
Klein, Melanie: Anna Freud-Klein debate on child psychoanalysis and education 86–87, 88; cannibalistic impulses and paranoid-schizoid position 79n1, 157–158; hatred and child psychoanalysis 93–94; 'Hitler inside Mummy' fantasies xxvi; *Narrative of a Child Analysis* 127, 128; *The Observer* profile (1961) 153; 'The Oedipus

Complex in the Light of Early Anxieties' 127, *127, 128; The Psycho-Analysis of Children* 95–96; *The Times* obituary 153; and Virginia Woolf's *The Waves* 95–96, 100, 101; *see also* Klein and the representation of people with AIDS (Theo Gordon)

Klein and the representation of people with AIDS (Theo Gordon): chapter overview xxxviii–xxxix; Chevalier/Bradley-Perrin's *Your Nostalgia is Killing Me!* 125–126, *125*; Klein's paranoid-schizoid position and violence of media coverage 126, 127–129, 131, 133; Klein's 'Richard case' with Richard's drawings 127–128, *127, 128*, 131; Klein's theory of reparation (depressive position) and Leonard's *Strange Fruit* 126, 140, 141; Klein's theory of reparation (depressive position) and paranoia during AIDS crisis 140–142; *Los Angeles Times'* coverage of Rock Hudson's death 129, *130*, 131, *138*; paranoia and AIDS crisis in United States 133–135; paranoia and (homo)phobia 135–137, 142; photographs of Meeks and Reagan, contrast between 135, *136, 137*; Stuart Marshall's *Bright Eyes* video *129*, 131–133, *132, 133;* Sunday People's 'What the Gay Plague did to Handsome Kenny' 129, *129*, 131–132, 133; Zoe Leonard's *Strange Fruit* 126, 138–141, *139, 141*

Knight, Isabel F. 17–18, 19
Kofman, Sarah 30
Koppel, Thomas 120n1
Kris, Ernst 17
Kristeva, Julia 9, 140
Kurdi, Aylan 109, 110
Kybartas, Stashu, *Danny* (video) 135

Lacan, Jacques xxvi, xxix, 13n9, 31
LaCapra, Dominick xxviii; *Writing History, Writing Trauma* 187–188
Lacoue-Labarthe, Philippe 72, 74
Laing, Olivia 139–140
Lane, Homer 88
Langer, Walter C., *The Mind of Adolf Hitler* xxvii, 160
Langer, William L. 160
Laplanche, Jean: 'anti-hermeneutics' of psychoanalysis xxvii; 'enigmatic signifiers' xxx; on Freud's 'Project for a Scientific Psychology' 17; on hysteria 46; interpretation in psychoanalysis 4; on proton pseudos 23; psychoanalysis under scrutiny xxiii; on repression 44; *Vocabulaire de la psychanalyse* (with Pontalis) xxv, xliiin1

Larner, Christina 148, 150, 156
Larsen, Nella, *Passing* 59–60
Lasch, Christofer 152
Latour, Bruno xxiv–xxv
Lawrence, D. H. 91
Le Bon, Gustave xvi, xxxi
'left-to-die boat' case (March 2011) *see* Bergvall's *Drift* (Catherine Humble)
Leonard, Zoe, *Strange Fruit* 126, 138–141, *139, 141*
Levin Becker, D. 13n14
Lévinas, Emmanuel 110, 111
Levine, H. 110, 121n8
Leys, Ruth 109, 113, 121n10, 170, 171, 173, 177n7
Life, on Rock Hudson and AIDS 135
Light, Alison 100
Lighthill, James 152
literary criticism *see* Winnicott and the finding of literature (E. S. Coles)
literature: and psychoanalysis xxiv–xv, xxix–xxxi; *see also* Freud, Ferrante and feet in Jensen's *Gradiva* (S. Bari); Winnicott and the finding of literature (E. S. Coles)
Loewenberg, Peter, *The Psychohistorical Origins of the Nazi Youth Cohort* 160
Los Angeles Times, coverage of Rock Hudson's death 129, *130*, 131, *138*
Lost Boundaries (film) 53, 64n8
Low, Barbara 85, 90–92, 93, 94, 95, 100
Lubbock, John 69
Luckhurst, Roger 169
Lunar Society 182
Luther, Martin xxvii

McBride, J. 53
Macé, Marielle 13n6
McGowan, Pat 40, 44
McMillan, Rachel 88
madness, suppressed madness of sane men xxxi–xliii
Maeder, Alfonse 70
Magor, Ian *see* Pinky (Ian Magor)
Mahler, Gustav xviii

Makari, George 70
Malan, Daniël François 151, 153
Malcolm, Janet 18–19
'male gaze' concept 54, 56
Malting House Garden School 87–88, 91, 94
Manners, Marilyn 30–31
Mannoni, Octave 45
Manzo, Kate 40, 44
Mapplethorpe, Robert 137–138
Marcuse, Herbert xxiv
Marsden, Dora 91
Marshall, Stuart, *Bright Eyes* (video) *129*, 131–133, *132, 133*
Marx, Karl xxviii, 156
mass psychology xxviii, xxxi–xxxviii; mass/group mind xv–xvi; *see also* crowd psychology
Mbembe, Achille xxxv, 40
Mead, Margaret 153
Meeks, Ken 135, *136*
memory: Freud's theory xxvii–xxviii; *see also* Freud's 'Project for a Scientific Psychology' (Manuel Batsch)
Mendelssohn, Moses 180, 181
metaphors xxx
metapsychology 16, 17, 19, 25
Meyer, Richard 134
Milner, Marion xxix–xl
miscegenation 53–54, 55, 62, 63
Mitchell, Juliet xxiv, 24, 46–47
Mitscherlich, Alexander 156
Mittwochsgesellschaft 181
modernism *see* childhood, modernism and progressive education (Helen Tyson)
Møller, Lis 28
Montessori, Maria 88
Moore, Henrietta L. 68
moral panics 42–43, 46, 47–48
Muldoon, James 182
Mulvey, Laura xxiv, xxxv, 56–57, 62
Museum of Modern Art, *Nicholas Nixon: Pictures of People* 136
'mystic writing pad' xxix–xxx
myth, and psychoanalysis xxx

Nancy, Jean-Luc 72, 74, 112
narcissism xxxiii–xxxiv, 74–75
nationalism xxxiv, 77
Nazism: Columbus Centre's study of 147, 148, 149–150, 154–155, 156, 157–158, 159–161; and Freud's thinking, impact on 77; *see also* fascism
Neill, A. S. 88, 94
neoliberal capitalism xvi
neuro-psychoanalysis 16, 18
The New Statesman and Nation, 'Free Speech in Childhood' (Bertrand Russell) 85–86, 88, 89–94, 95, 100
Nietzsche, Friedrich 181, 186
Nixon, Nicholas 136

The Observer: edited by David Astor (1948–75) 147, 151; emphasis on psychology/psychoanalysis under Astor's editorship 153–154, 159; Freud 'Centenary' articles ('The meaning of Freud') 153; 'The Meaning of Eichmann' (David Astor) 149, 153, 161; 'The Meaning of Malan' (on National Party, South Africa) 151, 153; Storr's article on Churchill (1969) 154; Viscount Waldorf Astor's ownership of paper 150
Oedipus xxx, xxxvii, 127, *127, 128*
'one-drop' rule 54, 59, 63
Opperheimer, Carl 154
Orbach, Susie xxviii–xxix
Orwell, George 151

'parallel processing' concept 188–189
paranoia: Freud on ('Judge Schreber' case) 142; *see also* Klein, Melanie; Klein and the representation of people with AIDS (Theo Gordon)
Parkes Library (University of Southampton) 149
'passing' (racial 'passing') 53, 54, 58, 59–60
Phillips, Adam 10, 115
Philosophes (France, 18th century) 182–183
Pick, Daniel: Norman Cohn interview 149, 154, 159; psychoanalysis and imaginaries of violence xxviii; psychoanalysis in post-war Britain 147; 'Psychoanalytic Thought, History and Political Life' forum xxii–xxiii; *The Pursuit of the Nazi Mind* 160; Strachey's translation of Freud's *Massenpsychologie und Ich-Analyse* xxxi–xxxii; *see also* psychoanalysis and politics (D. Pick and J. Rose)

Pinker, Steven, *Enlightenment Now* 180, 181, 185, 187, 189
Pinky (Ian Magor): chapter overview xxxv; book (*Quality*) and film (*Pinky*) 52, 63; casting of white actress in role of Pinky 53, 55, 57–59; cycle of five films on race 53, 55; denigration of Pinky 61–63; female vs. male gaze 54, 56; film plot 53; film targeted at white audience 57–58; general acclaim and box-office success 53; miscegenation and actors' skin colour 53–54, 55; miscegenation and end of film 63; miscegenation and slavery 62; perception of black and white actors by black audiences 55–56; popularity of film among black audiences 58; racial 'passing' 53, 54, 58, 59–60; representation of black men in American cinema 54–55; science, racism, and unconscious prejudice 56; sexualisation of black body 54, 61–62; womanhood in cinema and black female spectatorship 56–57
Plessy, Homer Adolph 59
Plessy v. Ferguson (1896) 59
Pocock, John G. A. 182
Poliakov, Léon 148
politics: and psychoanalysis xxviii–xxix; *see also* Columbus Centre, University of Sussex (Danae Karydaki); psychoanalysis and politics (D. Pick and J. Rose)
Pontalis, Jean-Bertrand xxv, xliiin1, 44, 46
populism xix, xxviii, xxxiii
Portman Hall School 94
Post-traumatic stress disorder (PTSD) 169, 171
post-truth era xxxiii
Powell, Adam Clayton 58
Priel, Beatrice 45
Priestley, Joseph 182
Procter-Gregg, Nancy 153
progressive education *see* Beacon Hill School; childhood, modernism and progressive education (Helen Tyson); Malting House Garden School; Summerhill School
proton pseudos 21–23, 24
Proust, Marcel 140
Prussian Enlightenment 184
psychoanalysis: and anthropology 68; 'disavowal' concept 45–46, 94; and education 86–94; 'interpretation' issue 4, 6–8; and Jewishness 70–71; and literature xxiv–xxv, xxix–xxxi; and myth xxx; neuro-psychoanalysis 16, 18; Oedipus xxx, xxxvii, 127, *127, 128*; parallel processing 188–189; and politics xxviii–xxix; and race 70–71; representation and trauma 110–111; 'repression' concept 44; sublimation xxxvii, 87; transference 6, 188; Virginia Woolf's ambivalence towards 95–96; and women's movement 154; *see also* Columbus Centre, University of Sussex (Danae Karydaki); psychoanalysis and politics (D. Pick and J. Rose); psychoanalysis and South African Satanism scare (Nicky Falkof); wild analysis (S. Bar-Haim, E. S. Coles and H. Tyson)
psychoanalysis and politics (D. Pick and J. Rose): 9/11 and war on terror xv, xvi–xvii; group/mass mind and Western governments' actions xv–xvi; psychoanalysis and political questioning xvii, xix; 'wilding' and 'rewilding' xviii
psychoanalysis and South African Satanism scare (Nicky Falkof): chapter overview xxxiv–xxxv; apartheid and white South Africans' psychoses 39–40; charged political climate and white Satanism 40–41; media coverage and manifestations of Satanism scare 41–42, 47; moral panics, affect, and psychoanalysis 42–44, 46, 47–48; Satanism scare and fetishism/disavowal 45–46; Satanism scare and hysteria 46–47; Satanism scare and repression 44–45
'Psychoanalytic Thought, History and Political Life' forum xv, xvi, xix, xxii–xxiii, xxviii, xxix
psychobiographies xvii, xxvii
psychohistory xxvii–xxviii, 160
PTSD (Post-traumatic stress disorder) 169, 171
public sphere *see* Freud, Enlightenment and Public Sphere (D'Maris Coffman)
Puxon, Grattan 148, 156
Pyke, Geoffrey 87

Qasmiyeh, Yousif M. 105–106

race: miscegenation 53–54, 55, 62, 63; 'one-drop' rule 54, 59, 63; 'passing' 53, 54, 58, 59–60; and psychoanalysis 70–71
racism: and mass psychology xxxiii, xxxiv, xxxv; and psychoses 39–40, 48; *see also* apartheid; Freud and the cannibal (Marita Vyrgioti); *Pinky* (Ian Magor); segregation; slavery
Radical Enlightenment 182
rape *see* Kane's *Blasted* (Leah Sidi)
Raworth, Tom 11
Reagan, Ronald 135, *137*
Rechtman, Richard 169–170
Reed, G. 110, 121n8
refugees *see* Bergvall's *Drift* (Catherine Humble)
Reik, T. 67
Reininger, Alon 135
Reinisch, Jessica 116
Reitlinger, Gerald R. 149
representation (in psychoanalysis) 110
'repression' concept 44
'rewilding' term xviii
Richardson, Dorothy 91
Richardson, Samuel 182
Ricketts Sumner, Cid *see* Sumner, Cid Ricketts
Rickman, John 87, 153
Ricoeur, Paul 4, 5, 19, 189
Rieff, Philip 160
Rochester *see* Wilmot, John, 2nd Earl of Rochester
Rogin, Michael P. 61
Roma people 148, 156
Roper, Lyndal xxvii–xxviii
Rose, Jacqueline: on Arendt and anti-totalitarianism 101; on child, adult fantasy of 92–93; on Freud-Jung dispute 70; on Freud's *Massenpsychologie und Ich-Analyse* xxxii; on *Hamlet* 31; psychoanalysis and imaginaries of violence xxviii; 'Psychoanalytic Thought, History and Political Life' forum xxii–xxiii; and Said, public conversation with on Israel-Palestine conflict xliiin5; *States of fantasy* 159; *see also* psychoanalysis and politics (D. Pick and J. Rose)
Rosset, Clément 25n3
Rothschild, Berthold 186
Roudinesco, Élisabeth xxviii

Rousseau, Jean-Jacques, *Contrat Social* 182–183
Rowland, Antony 121n9
Ruddick, Lisa 5
Ruefle, Mary 11
Runia, Eelco 188
Russell, Bertrand: *On Education, Especially in Early Childhood* 102n3; 'Free Speech in Childhood' 85–86, 88, 89–94, 95, 100
Russell, Dora 85, 88–89, 91, 95
Rycroft, Charles 152, 153

Sachs, Albie 148, 150, 156
Sachs, David 190n4
Said, Edward xxiv, xxxv, xliiin5, 77, 78
Salome, Lou Andreas 153
Sampson, Anthony 151
Sandler, Anne-Marie 152
Sandler, Joseph 152
Sanford, Nevitt 148, 156, 157, 158–159
Santayana, George xl
Santner, Eric 134
Satanism *see* psychoanalysis and South African Satanism scare (Nicky Falkof)
Scarfone, D. 110, 121n8
Schafer, Roy xxvi, 152
Schmidt, J. 182, 185, 186
Schulman, Sarah 134
scientific psychology *see* Freud's 'Project for a Scientific Psychology' (Manuel Batsch)
Scott, Joan xxiv, xxvii
Scottish Enlightenment 182
Sedgwick, Eve Kosofsky 4, 5, 134–135, 142
Segal, Hanna 152
segregation 52, 53–54, 55, 58, 59, 60, 63; *see also* apartheid; slavery
Sendak, Maurice, *Where the Wild Things Are* xviii
Serrano, Andreas 137–138
sexual violence *see* Kane's *Blasted* (Leah Sidi)
Shakespeare, William, *Hamlet* xxix, 31
Shapira, Michal 86
Sheffer, Jolie A. 62
Sherwood, Rae 148
Sidi, Leah *see* Kane's *Blasted* (Leah Sidi)
Silence = Death Collective 126
slavery 54, 60, 61, 62
Smith, Adam 182

Smith, Valerie 58
Snead, James A. 64n6
Snell, Reginald, *Progressive Schools: Their Principles and Practice* 94
Solga, Kim 168, 176
Solms, Mark 18
Sontag, Susan 110, 121n6
South Africa: apartheid 39–40, 148, 150, 156; D. F. Malan's (National Party's) victory at 1948 elections 151, 153; *see also* psychoanalysis and South African Satanism scare (Nicky Falkof)
Spivak, Gayatri Chakravorty xxxv, 119
squiggle game *see* Winnicott, D. W.
Srebrenica massacre, Dutch report on 188
Stafford-Clark, David 153
Steiner, J. xxxiv
Stephen, Adrian 96
Stocking, George W. 68–69
Stokes, Adrian 13n5
Stoler, Ann L. 69
Stonebridge, Lyndsey xxviii, 112, 133, 159, 160
Storr, Anthony 148, 154
Strachey, Alix 86–87, 88, 91, 94, 95–96
Strachey, James: Freud's *Massenpsychologie und Ich-Analyse*, translation of xv, xxxi–xxxii; Freud's 'Project for a Scientific Psychology' 17, 19; in Klein's preface to her *Psycho-Analysis of Children*, reference to 95; on proton pseudos 21–22; psychoanalysis and education 86, 87, 91
Sturm und Drang 186
sublimation xxxvii, 87
Summerhill School 94
Sumner, Cid Ricketts, *Quality* 52, 63
The Sun, representation of refugees by 109
Sunday People, 'What the Gay Plague did to Handsome Kenny' 129, *129*, 131–132, 133
Sutherland, John 152

Tabensky, Pedro Alexis 40
Tacoma Action Collective 142
Tacoma Art Museum, Washington, *Art AIDS America* (exhibition) 137, 142
Tagore, Rabindranath xxxvi–xxxvii
Tarde, Gabriel xxxi
Taylor, Barbara xxviii

Taylor, Clyde 61–62
Taylor, P. 176
terrorism: 9/11 terrorist attacks xv, xvi, xxiii; 'war on terror' policy xvi
Thaggert, Miriam 57
Thomson, Mathew 147
Time, on Rock Hudson and AIDS 135
The Times, coverage of psychology/psychoanalysis (1950s-60s) 153
Toynbee, Philip 153
transference 6, 188
trauma: Ferenczi's mimetic model of trauma 170, 171, 174, 175; Freud's theory 112, 113, 121n8, 173, 177; PTSD (Post-traumatic stress disorder) 169, 171; *Writing History, Writing Trauma* (Dominick LaCapra) 187–188; *see also* Bergvall's *Drift* (Catherine Humble); Kane's *Blasted* (Leah Sidi)
Trilling, Daniel 109, 110
Trilling, Lionel 160
Trump, Donald xix, xxix, xxxiii, 180, 183
Tylor, Edward B. 69
Tynan, Kenneth 153–154
Tyson, Helen xxiv; *see also* childhood, modernism and progressive education (Helen Tyson); wild analysis (S. Bar-Haim, E. S. Coles and H. Tyson)

UCL *see* University College London (UCL)
Underwood, J. A. xxxii
United Colours of Benetton, advert with David Kirby dying from AIDS 126
United States: 9/11 terrorist attacks xv, xvi, xxiii; segregation 52, 53–54, 55, 58, 59, 60, 63; violent intervention overseas xvi; 'war on terror' policy xvi; *see also* Klein and the representation of people with AIDS (Theo Gordon); *Pinky* (Ian Magor)
University College London (UCL): Freud Memorial Chair of Psychoanalysis 152, 159; Psychoanalytic Unit 152
University of London *see* Goldsmiths, University of London
University of South Africa, 'The Bible, The Church and Demonic Powers' (conference, 1986) 41
University of Southampton, Parkes Library 149

University of Sussex *see* Columbus Centre, University of Sussex (Danae Karydaki)
University of Vienna, Institut für politische Psychologie 155

van der Westhuizen, Christi 40, 44
van Zyl, James 41
Voltaire 183
Vyrgioti, Marita *see* Freud and the cannibal (Marita Vyrgioti)

Waelder, Robert 151
Waldeyer-Hartz, Heinrich von 18
'war on terror' policy xvi
Ward, Ian 168
Watkins, Mel 56
Weller, Jeremy, *Mad* 165, 166
Wenders, Wim xv
White, Walter 58
Wiener Library (London) 149
Wier, John 126
'wild', use of term in book xvii–xviii
wild analysis (S. Bar-Haim, E. S. Coles and H. Tyson): Freud's claim to sole right to define psychoanalysis xxv; Freud's *Massenpsychologie und Ich-Analyse* xxxi–xxxii; Freud's 'Note Upon the Mystic Writing Pad' xxix–xxx; Freud's vision of psychoanalysis as 'meta-discipline' xxiii–xxiv; Freud's '"Wild" Psycho-Analysis' essay xxi–xxii; location of cultural experience xxxvi–xxxix; mass psychology xxviii, xxxi–xxxviii; psychoanalysis and literature xxiv–xxv, xxix–xxxi; psychoanalysis and other disciplines xxiii–xxiv, xxviii; psychoanalysis and politics xxviii–xxix; 'Psychoanalytic Thought, History and Political Life' forum xxii–xxiii, xxviii, xxix; psycho-history/psychobiography as examples of wild analysis xxvii–xxviii; suppressed madness of sane men xxxix–xliii; wild analysis and disagreements between different schools xxvi; wild analysis and psychoanalysis as science of its own resistance xxiii; wild analysis and psychoanalytic ideas at their limits xxii; wild analysis and uncomfortable truths xlii–xliii; wild analysis in clinical setting and abusive practices xxvi; wild analysis, re-appropriation of in this book xxvi–xxvii, xxviii; wild psycho-analysis as defined by Laplanche/Pontalis xxv; wild vs. unorthodox psychoanalysis xxv–xxvi; Winnicott's 'The Location of Cultural Experience' xxxvi–xxxviii
Williams, W. E. 85, 90, 92
Wilmot, John, 2nd Earl of Rochester 184
Wilson, Woodrow xvii
Winnicott, Clare 115
Winnicott, D. W.: *Deprivation and Delinquency* 115; 'The Evacuated Child' 115–116; 'Evacuation of a Small Child' (letter to *British Medical Journal*) 115; 'Fear of Breakdown' 110–111; 'Hate in the Counter-transference' 122n14; hatred and child psychoanalysis 93–94; 'I' ('me') and 'not-I' ('not-me') xl, 3–4; 'The Location of Cultural Experience' xxxvi–xxxviii, 7; *The Observer* contributions 153; Oxfordshire hostel notebook (1945) 117, 122n14; 'The Problem of Homeless Children' 122n14; squiggle game and Caroline Bergvall's *Drift* drawings 106, 117–120; squiggle game and work with WWII evacuees 106–107, 114–117; *Therapeutic Consultations in Child Psychiatry* 114, 118; 'Transitional Objects and Transitional Phenomena' 116; *see also* Winnicott and the finding of literature (E. S. Coles)
Winnicott and the finding of literature (E. S. Coles): chapter overview xxx; creation of 'we' and literature 3; 'critique', problem of and Winnicott's theories 4–5; critique and creative imagination 5–7; found objects, language and literary criticism 7–9; love, destruction and the case of literature 9–12; psychoanalysis and interpretation issue 4, 6–7; Winnicott on: art and poetry 10–11; bond between 'we' and 'I' 3; 'creating' and 'finding' 4, 7–9; creative imagination 6–7; interpretation in psychoanalysis 6, 7–8; mirror-role of mother 8; transitional object/phenomena and object-relating 4; 'true self' and object-relating theory 9–10; words 'us[ing] us' 12; Winnicott's creative written style 7

Witz, Leslie 47
Wojnarowicz, David 138
women *see* Freud, Ferrante and feet in Jensen's *Gradiva* (S. Bari); *Pinky* (Ian Magor)
women's movement, and psychoanalysis 154
Woolf, Leonard 95
Woolf, Virginia xxv; *Between the Acts* 94; engagement diaries *97–99*; psychoanalysis, ambivalence towards 95–96; *Three Guineas* 94; *The Waves* 85, 86, 94–95, 96, 100–101; *The Years* 94

Woolley, Agnes 119
World War II evacuees 115–116

Young-Bruehl, Elisabeth 151

Zach, Ingar 120n1
Zanuck, Darryl, *Pinky* 52, 53, 63n2, 64n7
Zaretsky, Eli xxviii–xxix, xxxiii
Zöllner, Johann Friedrich 180, 181
Zuckerman Museum of Art *see* Bernard A. Zuckerman Museum of Art (Kenneshaw, Georgia)

Printed in the United States
by Baker & Taylor Publisher Services